FORENSIC PATHOLOGY REVIEW

Questions and Answers

Forensic Pathology Review

Questions and Answers

John M. Wayne, MD
Forensic Pathologist
Forensic Medical Management Services of Texas, P.A., Beaumont, Texas

Cynthia A. Schandl, MD, PhD
Associate Professor, Department of Pathology and Laboratory Medicine
Medical University of South Carolina (MUSC)

S. Erin Presnell, MD
Professor, Department of Pathology and Laboratory Medicine
Medical University of South Carolina (MUSC)

CRC Press
Taylor & Francis Group
Boca Raton London New York

CRC Press is an imprint of the
Taylor & Francis Group, an **informa** business

CRC Press
Taylor & Francis Group
6000 Broken Sound Parkway NW, Suite 300
Boca Raton, FL 33487-2742

Printed on acid-free paper

International Standard Book Number-13: 978-1-4987-5638-9 (Paperback); 978-1-138-08845-0 (Hardback)

Library of Congress Cataloging-in-Publication Data

Names: Wayne, John M., author. | Schandl, Cynthia A., author. | Presnell, S. Erin, author.
Title: Forensic pathology review / Dr. John M. Wayne, Dr. Cynthia A. Schandl, Dr. S. Erin Presnell.
Description: Boca Raton, FL : CRC Press/Taylor & Francis Group, [2018] |
Includes bibliographical references and index.
Identifiers: LCCN 2017015922| ISBN 9781498756389 (pbk. : alk. paper) |
ISBN 9781315152936 (ebook) | ISBN 9781138088450 (hardback : alk. paper)
Subjects: | MESH: Forensic Pathology--methods | Autopsy--methods | Examination Questions
Classification: LCC RA1057.5 | NLM W 618.2 | DDC 614/.1--dc23
LC record available at https://lccn.loc.gov/2017015922

Visit the Taylor & Francis Web site at
http://www.taylorandfrancis.com

and the CRC Press Web site at
http://www.crcpress.com

CONTENTS

AUTHORS

John M. Wayne, MD, is a Forensic Pathologist in private practice with Forensic Medical Management Services of Texas. Prior to medical school, Dr. Wayne served in the United States Air Force as a medical laboratory technician. It was during this time that he developed an interest in forensic pathology after attending an autopsy. He is board certified by the American Board of Pathology in anatomic, clinical, forensic, and hematology pathology.

Cynthia A. Schandl, MD, PhD, is a tenured Associate Professor in the Department of Pathology and Laboratory Medicine at the Medical University of South Carolina (MUSC). She is board certified by the American Board of Pathology in anatomic, clinical, and forensic pathology and acts as Co-Director of the MUSC Medical and Forensic Autopsy Section and the Medical Director of the MUSC Clinical Cytogenetics and Genomics Laboratory. She is the immediate past Director of the ACGME-accredited MUSC Forensic Pathology Fellowship program for which she designed the curriculum.

S. Erin Presnell, MD, is a tenured Professor in the Department of Pathology and Laboratory Medicine at the Medical University of South Carolina (MUSC). She is board certified in anatomic, clinical, and forensic pathology and acts as Medical Director of the Medical and Forensic Autopsy Section at MUSC. Dr. Presnell has been director of the MUSC College of Medicine (COM)'s pathology curriculum for over 15 years and has been extensively involved in medical school curricular development. She has a strong interest in constructing and evaluating knowledge assessment tools.

CHAPTER 1

NATURAL DEATHS

QUESTIONS

Q1.1 The photograph below is most likely associated with which of the following disease processes?

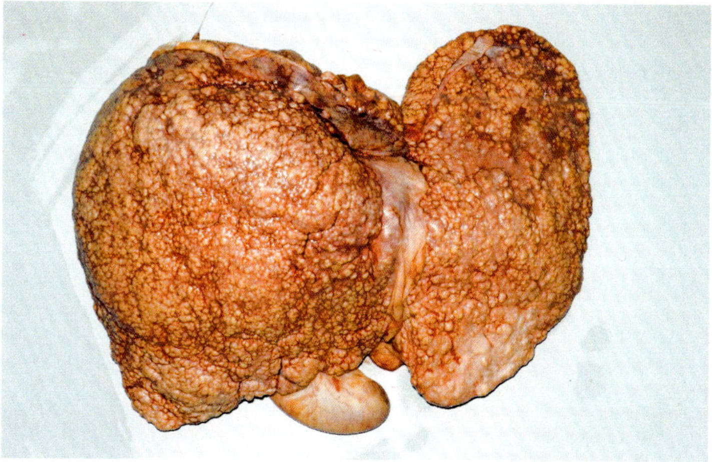

Figure 1.1

A. Chronic ethanolism
B. Diabetes mellitus
C. Hepatitis C infection
D. Iron overload
E. Metastatic cancer

Q1.2 A 50-year-old man with liver failure and a history of oxycodone abuse is found dead in bed. Autopsy reveals severe jaundice, a dark brown, cirrhotic liver, massive ascites, and esophageal varices. Liver histology demonstrates abundant dark brown intracytoplasmic hepatocyte pigment that stains positive for iron. Which of the following mutations is likely present?

A. *BCR-ABL1*
B. *CYP2D6*
C. *EWSR1*
D. *HFE*
E. *KRAS*

Q1.3 What structure does this Bielschowsky stain highlight?

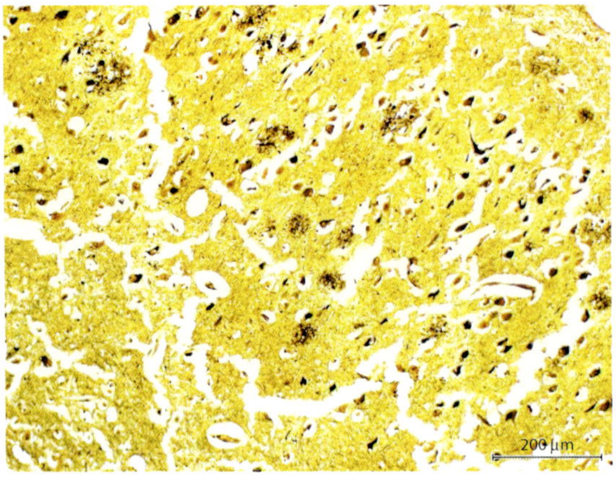

Figure 1.2

A. Amyloidosis
B. Formalin artifact
C. Lewy body
D. Neuronal plaque
E. Nocardia infection

Q1.4 What is depicted in the retroperitoneum of this 56-year-old man?

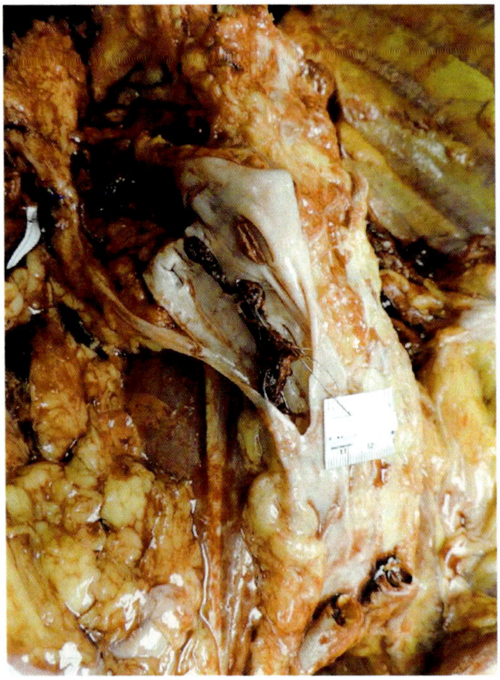

Figure 1.3

A. Embolized vascular stent
B. Greenfield filter with thromboemboli
C. Flechette projectile with associated hemorrhage and thrombosis
D. Shrapnel from an explosive device
E. Surgical vascular ligation hardware

Q1.5 The histological findings in the myocardium featured below are suggestive of what disease process?

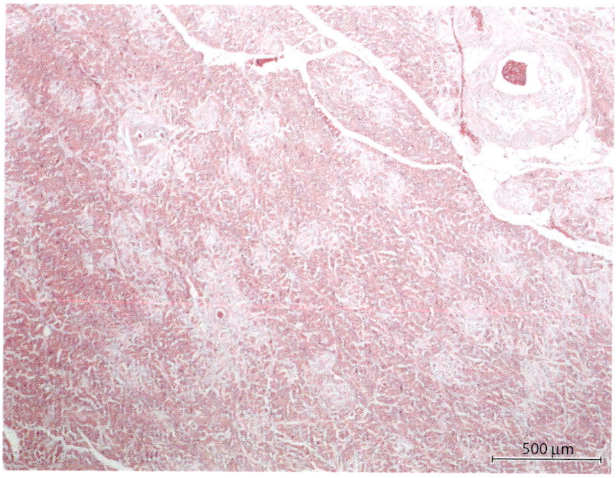

Figure 1.4

A. Amyloidosis
B. Ischemic interstitial fibrosis
C. Myocardial fungal infection
D. Neurofibromatosis
E. Sarcoidosis

Q1.6 What is the most likely malignancy related to this (Figure 1.4) cardiac finding?

A. Diffuse large B-cell lymphoma
B. Liposarcoma
C. Non-small cell lung cancer
D. Plasma cell myeloma
E. Small cell lung cancer

Q1.7 What lesion is depicted in this brainstem?

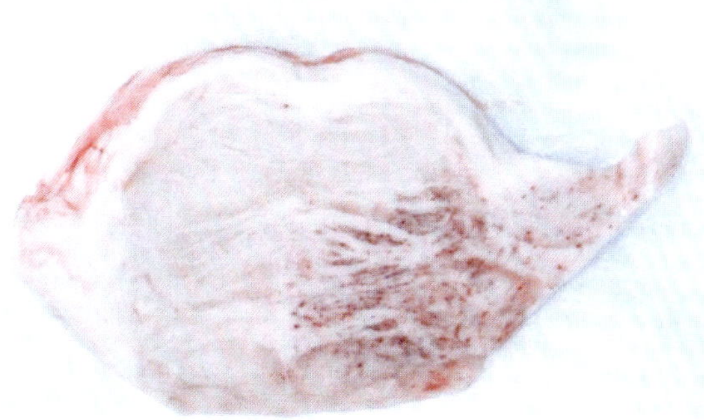

Figure 1.5

A. Arteriovenous malformation
B. Infectious process
C. Petechial hemorrhages due to fat embolism
D. Thrombotic stroke
E. Telangiectasia

Q1.8 What is the most likely diagnosis?

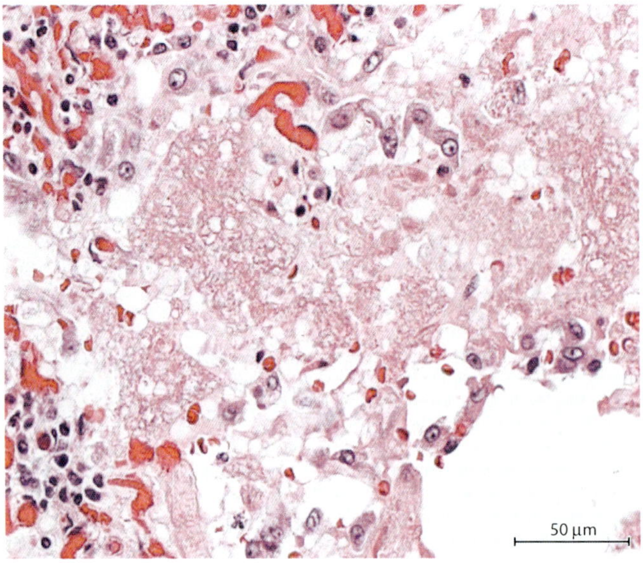

Figure 1.6

A. Alveolar proteinosis
B. *Cryptococcus* infection
C. Diffuse alveolar damage
D. *Pneumocystis jiroveci* infection
E. Tuberculosis

Q1.9 A 63-year-old male collapsed after experiencing acute chest pain. During autopsy the left anterior descending coronary artery was sampled and a representative cross section is pictured in Figure 1.7. What is the most likely underlying cause of death?

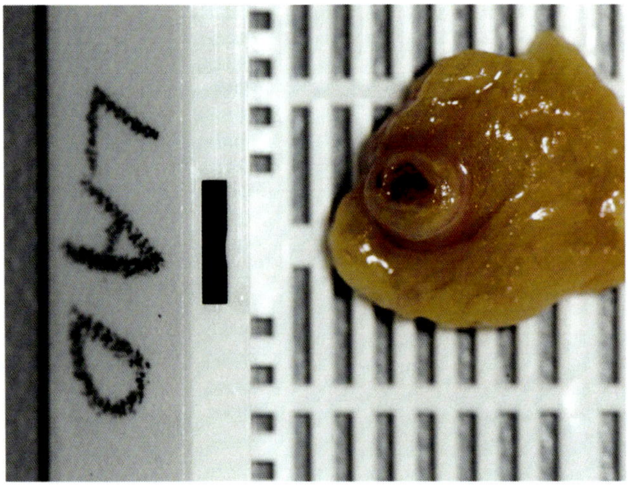

Figure 1.7

A. Atherosclerotic cardiovascular disease
B. Myocardial infarction
C. Platelet adhesion
D. Pulmonary embolism
E. Ventricular arrhythmia

Q1.10 What is the manner of death associated with the previous question?

A. Accident
B. Homicide
C. Natural
D. Suicide
E. Undetermined

Q1.11 Characterize the age of the depicted myocardial infarction.

Figure 1.8

A. Acute, 6 hours
B. Acute, 24 hours
C. Remote, 6 months
D. Subacute, 3 days
E. Subacute, 10 days

Q1.12 The following finding was documented at autopsy. Which of the following sites is most common for this anomaly?

Figure 1.9

A. Anterior communicating artery
B. Aortic iliac bifurcation
C. Basilar artery
D. Internal carotid artery
E. Posterior communicating artery

Q1.13 What is the most likely source of hemorrhage in Figure 1.10?

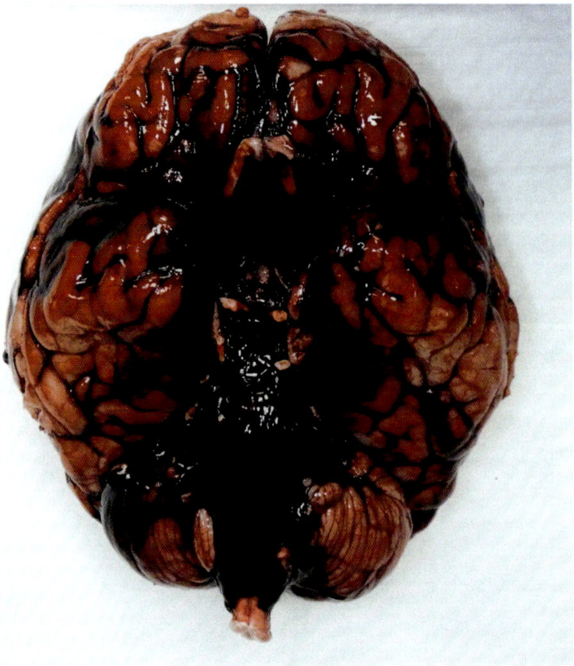

Figure 1.10

A. Anterior communicating cerebral artery
B. Basilar artery
C. Internal carotid artery
D. Middle cerebral artery
E. Middle meningeal artery
F. Vertebral artery

Q1.14 What clinical finding is most likely associated with the finding in Figure 1.11?

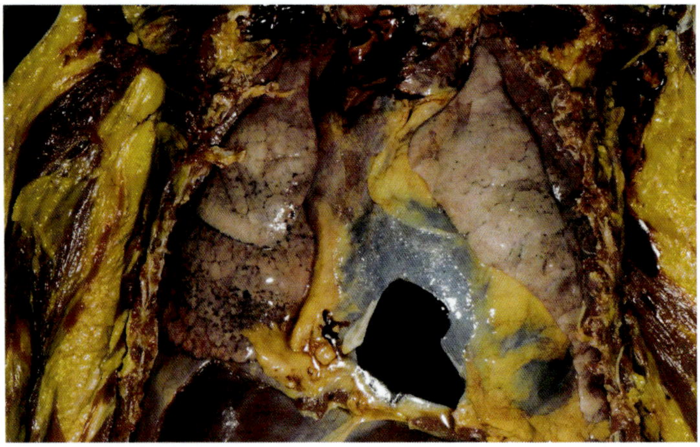

Figure 1.11

A. Bradycardia
B. Diaphoresis
C. Elevated D-dimer
D. Hypertension
E. Pulseless electrical activity

Q1.15 A 40-year-old woman with a history of hypertension complains of the worst headache in her entire life. She is found deceased on the couch the following morning. Autopsy reveals dense basilar subarachnoid hemorrhage obscuring the circle of Willis. What additional finding might be expected at autopsy?

A. Hepatic adenoma
B. Nodular glomerulosclerosis
C. Polycystic kidneys
D. Pheochromocytoma
E. Temporal arteritis

Q1.16 A 32-year-old man complained of shortness of breath and collapsed. He could not be revived. Based on histopathology, what is the most likely cause of death?

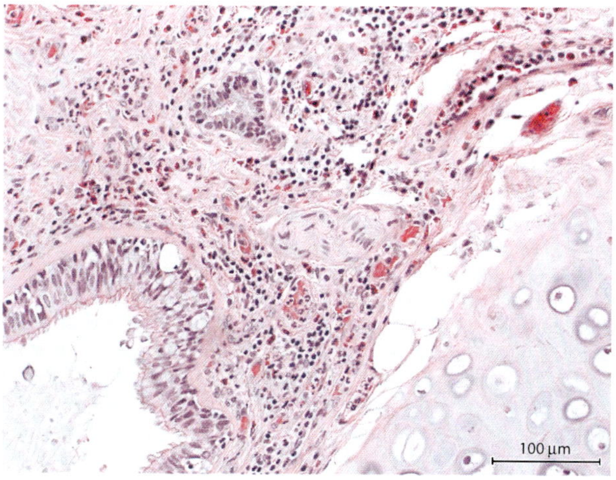

Figure 1.12

A. Anaphylaxis
B. Bronchopneumonia
C. Chronic bronchitis
D. Parasitic bronchiolitis
E. Status asthmaticus

Q1.17 With what disease is cerebellar vermal atrophy associated?

A. Acquired immunodeficiency syndrome
B. Autoimmune deficiency
C. Chronic alcoholism
D. Congenital anomaly
E. Remote trauma

Q1.18 A 12-year-old boy is punched in the chest during an initiation rite into a gang. He immediately collapses and cannot be resuscitated. The autopsy is negative. What is the most likely underlying mechanism of death in this case?

A. Abnormal electrical reentrant pathway between the atria and ventricles
B. Asymmetric left ventricular hypertrophy with myofibril disarray
C. Electrical disruption of the cardiac cycle during the ascending phase of the T wave
D. Electrolyte imbalance
E. Prolonged QT interval

Q1.19 A 54-year-old man developed altered mental status while in the hospital for a pulmonary infection from which he later died. Sections of brain were sampled because of the history. What special stain may help with the diagnosis?

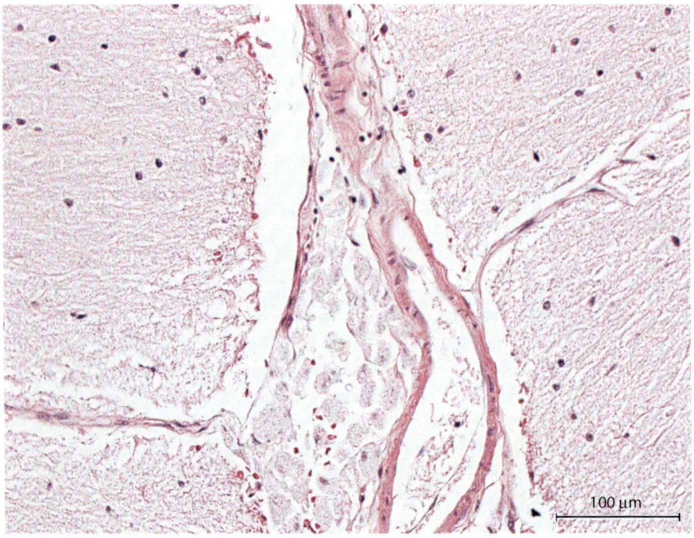

Figure 1.13

A. Bielschowsky
B. Brown–Brenn
C. Mucicarmine
D. Nissl
E. Ziehl–Neelsen

Q1.20 Which of the following is the most likely diagnosis based on Figure 1.14?

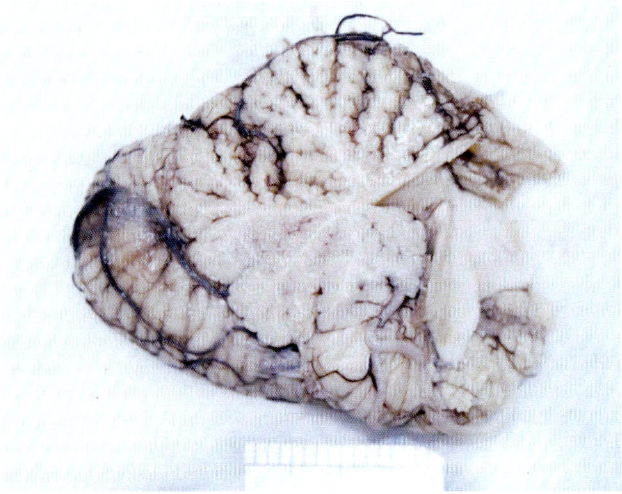

Figure 1.14

A. Arnold–Chiari malformation
B. Carbon monoxide exposure
C. Chronic ethanol use
D. Hypertension
E. Vitamin B_{12} deficiency

Q1.21 This is a liver removed from a 55-year-old male. It shows no trauma. What is the mechanism of death associated with the finding observed in Figure 1.15?

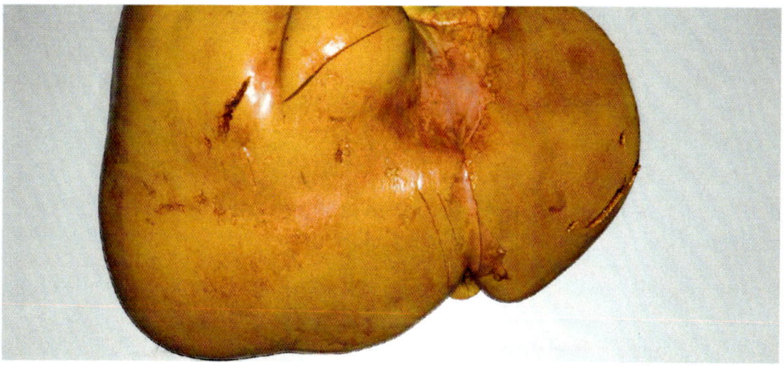

Figure 1.15

A. Atrial fibrillation
B. Coronary artery thrombosis
C. Diabetic ketoacidosis
D. Disseminated intravascular coagulation
E. Ventricular arrhythmia

Q1.22 Based upon the findings in these photographs, what is the best interpretation of the lesion?

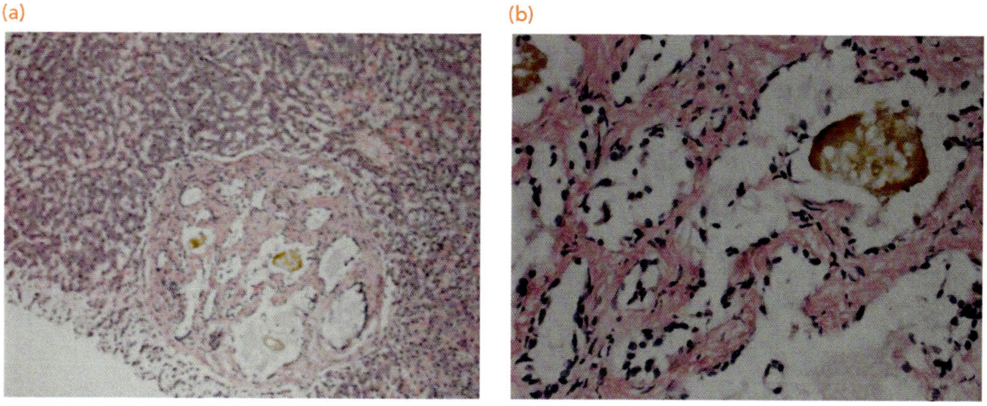

Figure 1.16

A. Bile duct hamartoma
B. Cholangiocarcinoma
C. Hepatocellular carcinoma
D. Metastatic cancer
E. Steatohepatitis

Q1.23 What is the most likely positive serum marker associated with these microscopic photographs of liver from a 45-year-old male?

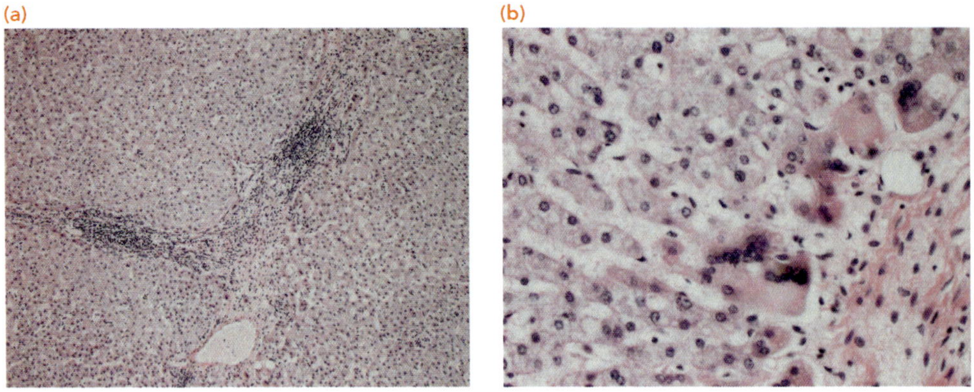

Figure 1.17

A. HAV IgM
B. HBcAb
C. HBsAb
D. HBsAg
E. Anti-HCV

Q1.24 What does the center of the photograph of this heart from a 55-year-old female represent?

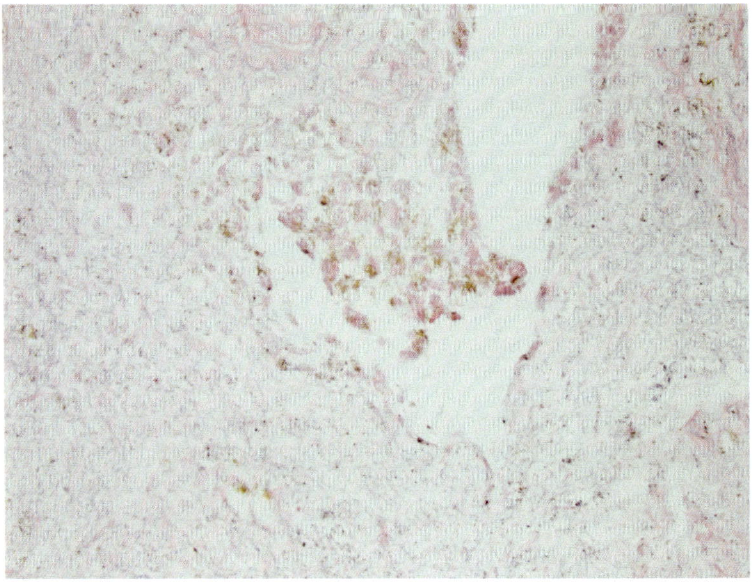

Figure 1.18

A. Artifact
B. Bile staining
C. Iron deposition
D. Fungal elements
E. Viral inclusion

Q1.25 What is the most likely diagnosis based on Figure 1.19?

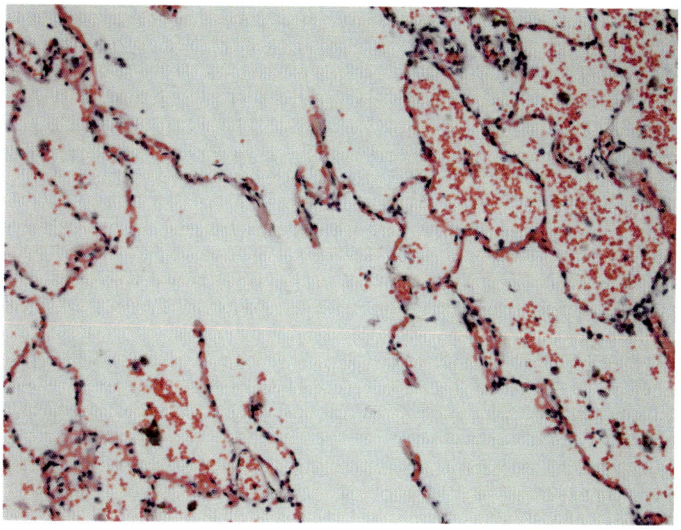

Figure 1.19

A. Asthma
B. Diffuse alveolar damage
C. Emphysema
D. Hypersensitivity pneumonitis
E. Usual interstitial pneumonia

Q1.26 What is the most likely diagnosis?

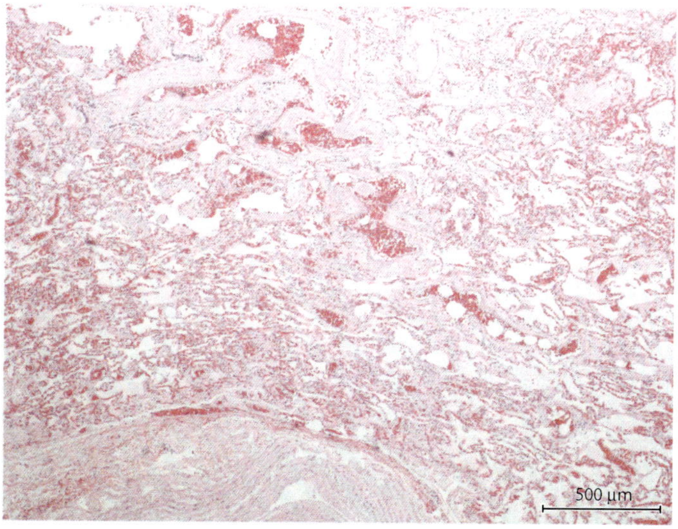

Figure 1.20

A. Postmortem artifact
B. Air embolus
C. Bone marrow embolus
D. Fat embolus
E. Normal lung

Q1.27 A 61-year-old man dies in a motor vehicle crash. A 0.5 cm nodule is found at the base of the brain and sampled for histology. What is the diagnosis?

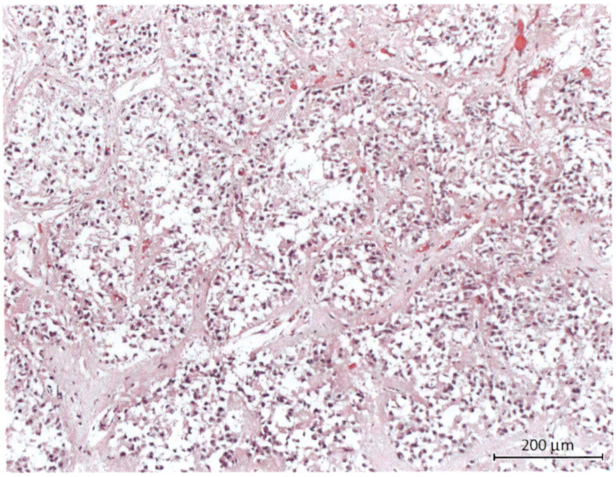

Figure 1.21

A. Astrocytoma
B. Metastatic adenocarcinoma
C. Neuroendocrine tumor
D. Normal pineal gland
E. Pituitary adenoma

Q1.28 Which of the following scenarios best characterizes the following finding?

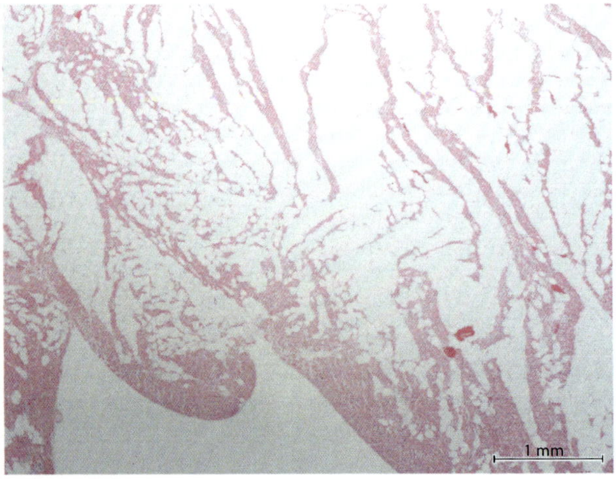

Figure 1.22

A. 22-year-old woman with congenital aortic coarctation who was found deceased in bed
B. 32-year-old woman with no medical history who collapsed while jogging
C. 42-year-old man with a chronic obstructive pulmonary disease who died in a car crash
D. 60-year-old man with severe coronary atherosclerosis who died while mowing the lawn
E. 71-year-old chronic alcoholic who was found deceased in bed

Q1.29 What is the most likely diagnosis?

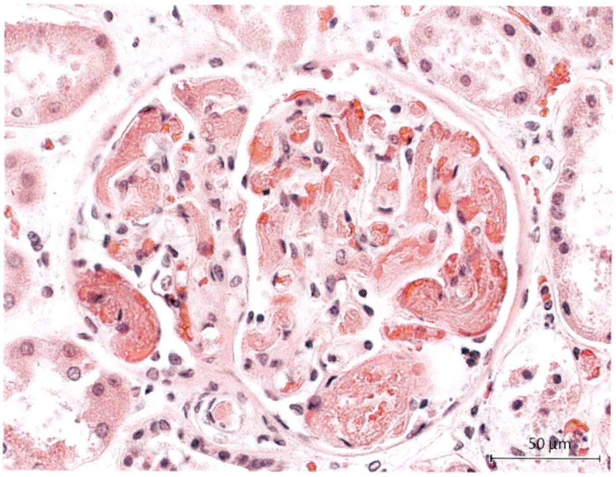

Figure 1.23

A. Atherosclerotic cardiovascular disease
B. Crescentic glomerulonephritis
C. Disseminated intravascular coagulation
D. Ethylene glycol toxicity
E. Nodular glomerulosclerosis

Q1.30 A 22-year-old marine recruit dies with signs of disseminated intravascular coagulation. Autopsy shows multiple skin and organ petechiae and purpura. The adrenal glands are hemorrhagic. What underlying cause of death should be suspected?

A. Dehydration
B. Electrocution
C. Folate deficiency
D. Inherited platelet disorder
E. Sepsis

Q1.31 This finding is seen in the right chest cavity at the autopsy of a 60-year-old man. What underlying disease process is most likely present?

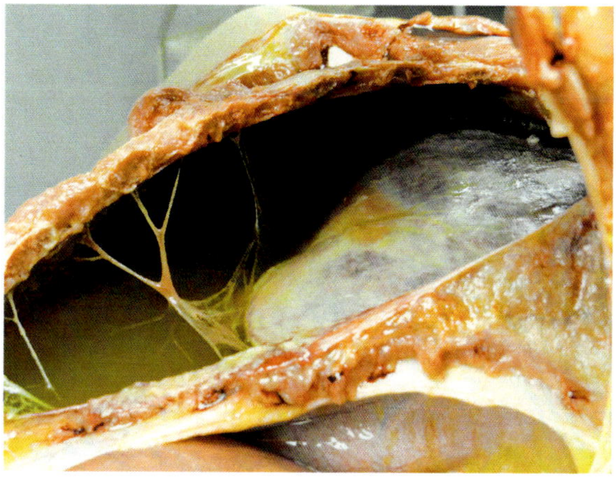

Figure 1.24

A. Abscess
B. Vasculitis
C. Hepatic cirrhosis
D. Iatrogenic fluid overload
E. Hyperchylomicronemia

Q1.32 What is the most likely cause of the findings featured in this lung section?

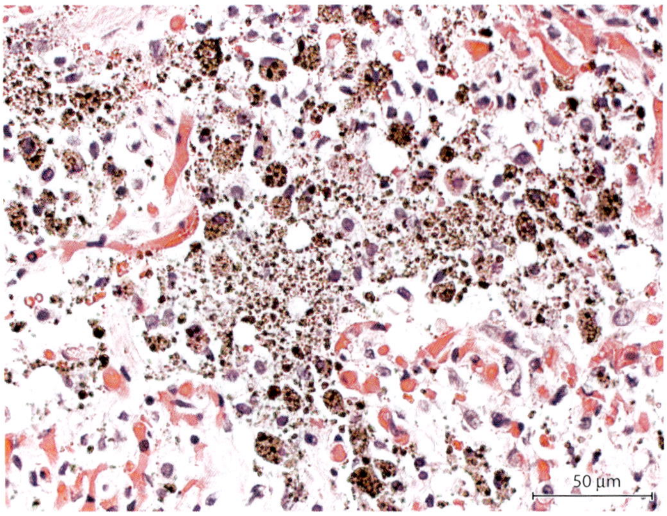

Figure 1.25

A. Cigarette smoking
B. Heart failure
C. Asbestos exposure
D. Histoplasmosis
E. Wilson disease

Q1.33 What disease process should be considered high in the differential in the autopsy of this 62-year-old man found deceased in bed?

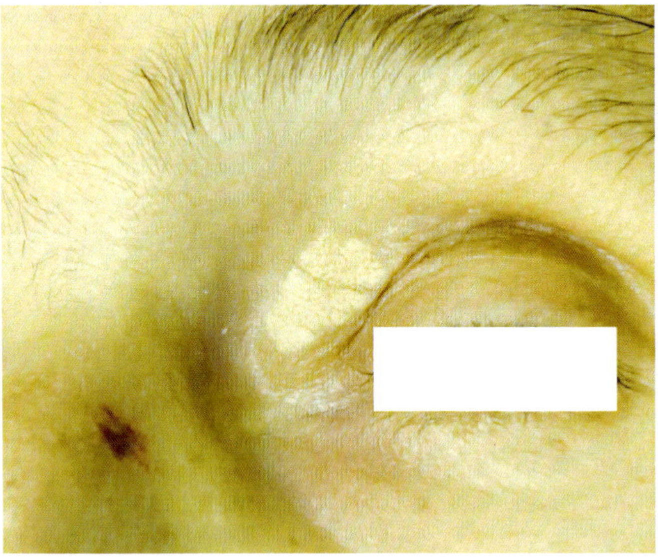

Figure 1.26

A. Atherosclerotic cardiovascular disease
B. Pulmonary thromboembolism
C. Pneumonia
D. Granulomatous vasculitis
E. Intravenous drug abuse

Q1.34 A 14-year-old girl suddenly collapsed during a dance class. Despite resuscitative efforts, she was pronounced dead. A microscopic section of her heart taken at autopsy is featured below. Which of the following was most likely present at the time of autopsy?

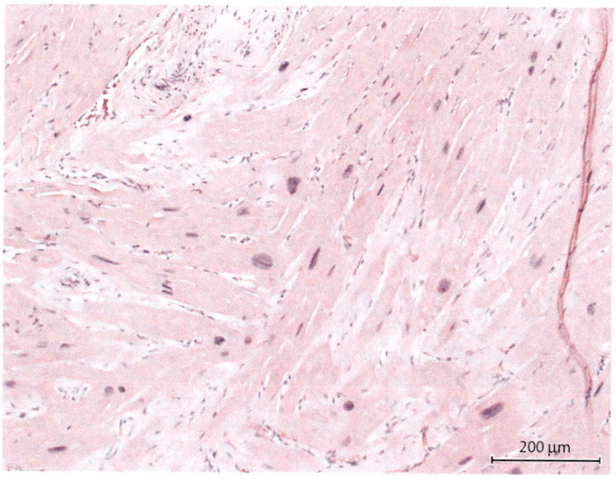

Figure 1.27

A. Coronary artery aneurysm
B. Heart weight 700 grams
C. Mediastinal and pulmonary hilar lymphadenopathy
D. Mitral valve endocarditis
E. Patent foramen ovale

Q1.35 A 22-year-old woman with sickle cell disease presents with acute pain syndrome and complaints of shortness of breath. Despite medical intervention, she rapidly deteriorates and is pronounced dead. Autopsy shows the lung findings featured below. Postmortem toxicology reveals a blood morphine concentration of 50 ng/mL. The remainder of the autopsy is negative. What is the most likely cause of death?

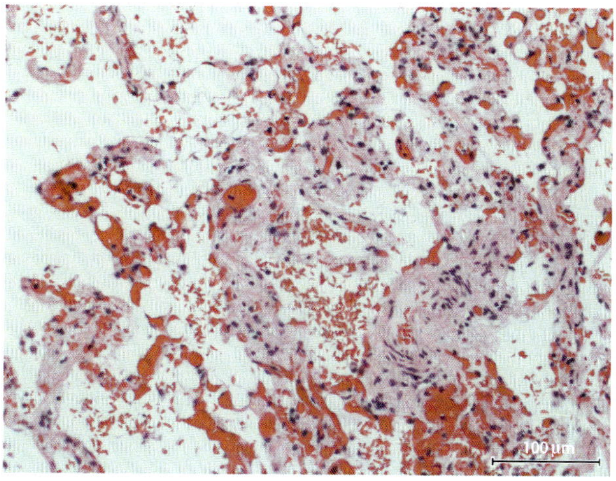

Figure 1.28

A. Acute chest syndrome
B. Morphine toxicity
C. Systemic air emboli
D. Viral pneumonia

Q1.36 The finding below is found in a 24-year-old woman. Which of the following is the most likely scenario surrounding her death?

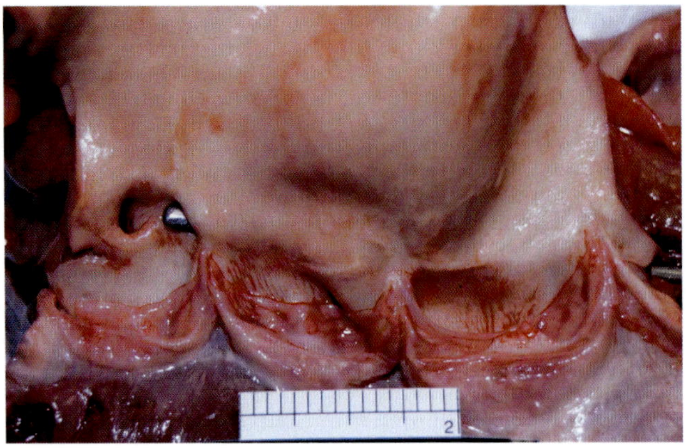

Figure 1.29

A. Altered mental status with hemiparesis
B. Congestive heart failure years after an untreated streptococcal infection
C. Discrepant blood pressure between the upper and lower extremities
D. Sudden collapse while playing soccer
E. Complaints of severe upper back pain in a tall patient with hyper-extensible joints

Q1.37 A 28-year-old man who was meeting with a contractor at a convenience store was witnessed to collapse and experience a seizure. The seizure was intractable, and resuscitative efforts failed. The decedent had no medical history except for previous headaches. Autopsy revealed the basal ganglia lesion featured below. The remainder of the autopsy was negative. What is the most likely diagnosis?

(a) (b)

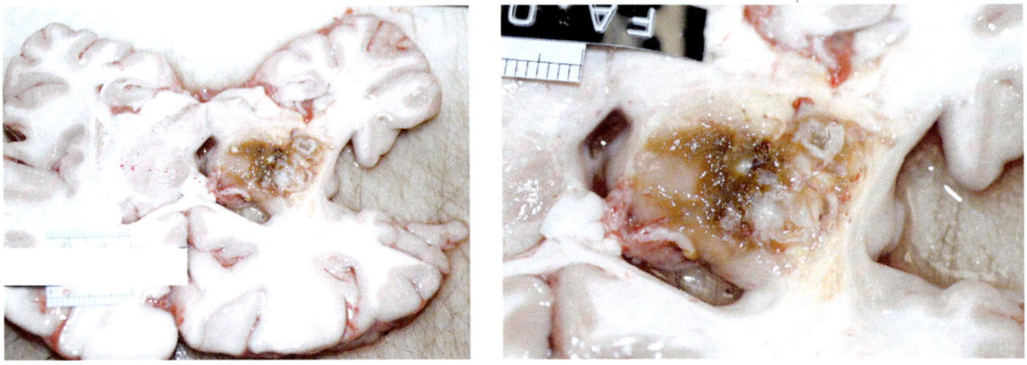

Figure 1.30

A. Arteriovenous malformation
B. Glioblastoma
C. Ischemic stroke
D. Metastatic tumor

Q1.38 A 55-year-old man is found deceased in his hotel room with voluminous amounts of blood on the bathroom floor and in the toilet. Autopsy revealed the following finding (inverted esophagus). What is the most likely diagnosis?

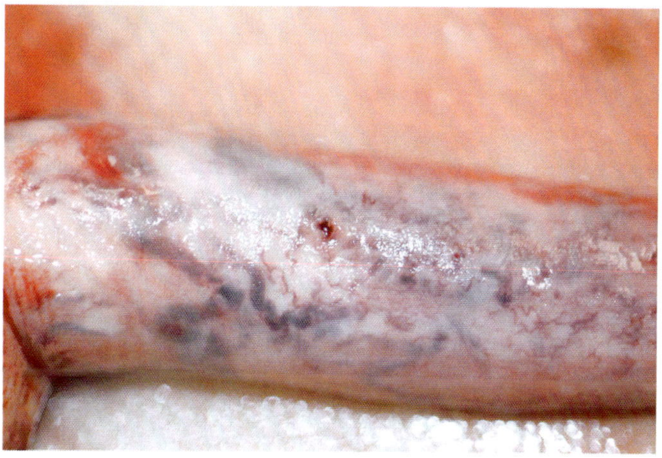

Figure 1.31

A. Boerhaave syndrome
B. Esophageal squamous cell carcinoma
C. Gastroesophageal reflux with Barrett esophagitis
D. Mallory–Weiss tear
E. Ruptured esophageal varices

Q1.39 A 58-year-old man dies in the hospital a week after being admitted for pneumonia. During his hospital course, he developed diarrhea. His colonic mucosa at autopsy is depicted below. What is the most likely diagnosis?

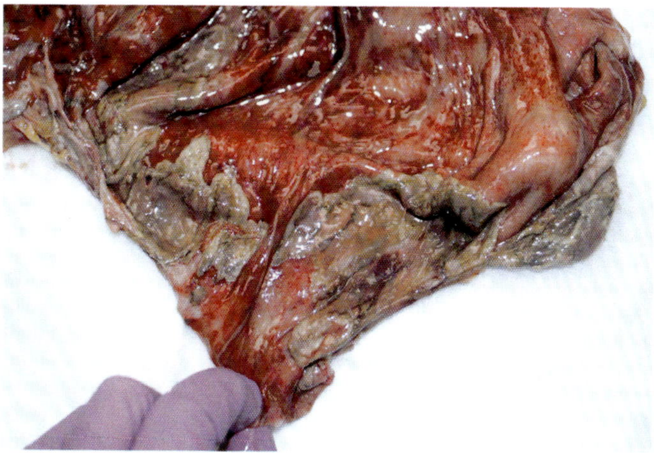

Figure 1.32

A. Crohn's disease
B. Ischemic colitis
C. Pseudomembranous colitis
D. Sepsis with colonic involvement
E. Ulcerative colitis

Q1.40 A 70-year-old man with a history of hypertension dies after a sudden collapse at home. He had no recent complaints or illnesses. At autopsy, the heart weighed 400 grams, and mild coronary artery atherosclerosis was present. A cross section of the right and left cardiac ventricles is featured below. What would be the expected histologic appearance of the myocardium?

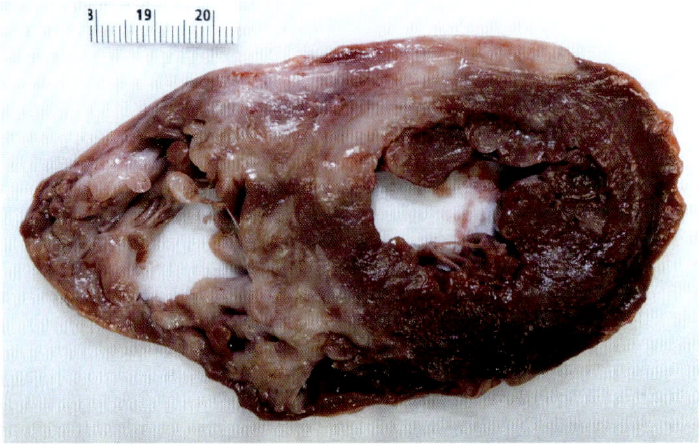

Figure 1.33

A. Diffuse lymphohistiocytic infiltrates
B. Myocyte replacement by fatty ingrowth
C. Noncaseating granulomatous inflammation
D. Patchy amorphous eosinophilic infiltrate
E. Regional areas of interstitial fibrosis

Q1.41 An incidental finding in the interatrial septum of an individual who died from a gunshot wound is featured below (lesion is bisected). What is the diagnosis?

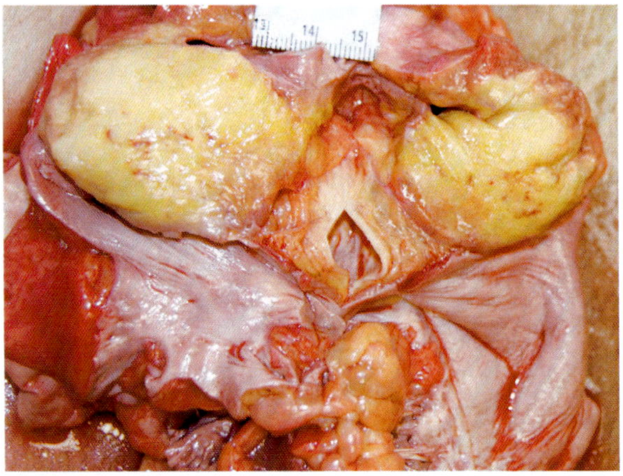

Figure 1.34

A. Fat necrosis
B. Lipomatous hypertrophy
C. Lipoma
D. Liposarcoma
E. Sarcoidosis

Q1.42 A 56-year-old man described intense neck pain followed by vomiting and diarrhea. He was admitted to the hospital with hypotension and presumed volume depletion. His neck pain increased persistently without responding to narcotic analgesia, and he developed swelling of the neck with ecchymosis and edema over the right lateral neck, shoulder, and chest area (see photograph at autopsy). A computed tomography (CT) scan showed significant swelling and induration of the retropharyngeal space. Despite medical intervention, he acutely decompensated and died the following day. What organism most likely grew from an antemortem nasopharyngeal culture?

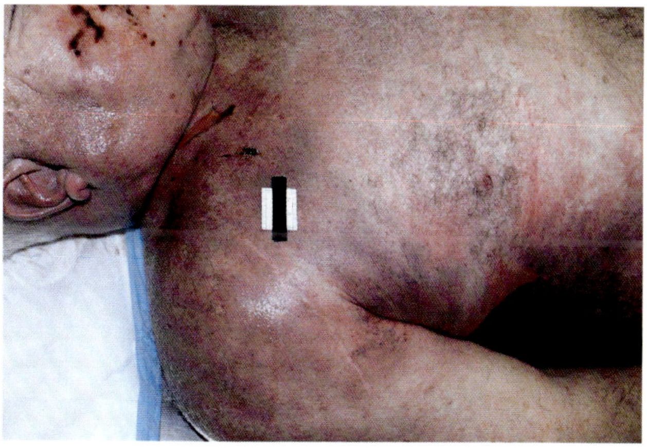

Figure 1.35

A. *Haemophilus influenzae*
B. *Neisseria meningitidis*
C. *Rhizopus* species
D. *Staphylococcus aureus*
E. *Streptococcus pyogenes*

Q1.43 The internal aspect of the frontal calvarium of a 58-year-old woman struck by a car is pictured. What is the diagnosis?

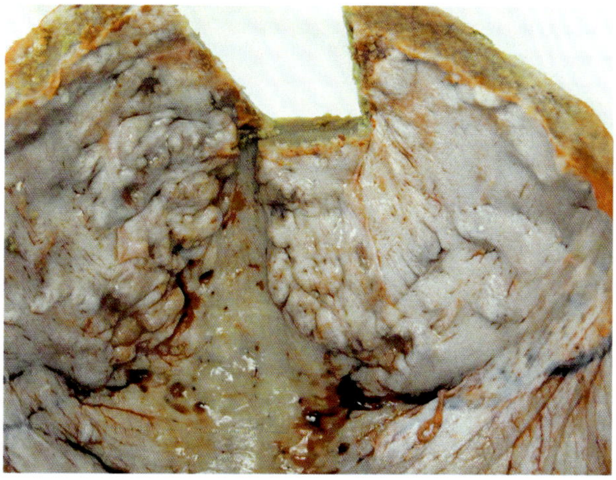

Figure 1.36

A. Hyperostosis frontalis interna
B. Meningioma
C. Osteosarcoma
D. Paget disease
E. Remote bony injury

Q1.44 This kidney and associated mass are removed from an obese man with hypertensive cardiovascular disease. What is the most likely diagnosis?

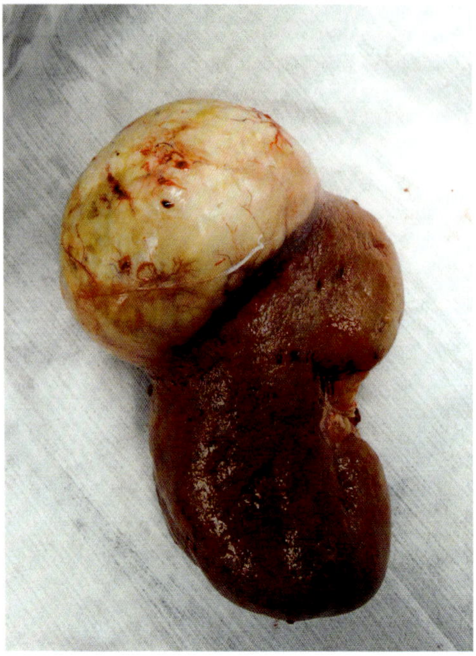

Figure 1.37

A. Adrenal adenoma
B. Adrenal hyperplasia
C. Lipoma
D. Pheochromocytoma
E. Renal cell carcinoma

Q1.45 What is the most likely diagnosis?

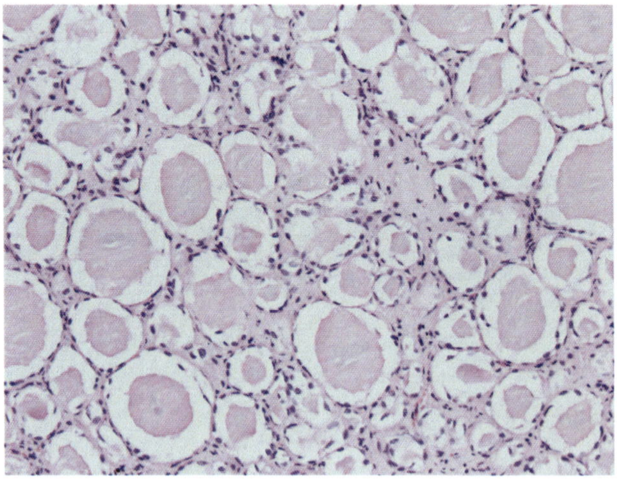

Figure 1.38

A. Alveolar proteinosis
B. End-stage renal disease
C. Graves disease
D. Hashimoto thyroiditis
E. Ovarian teratoma

Q1.46 A 60-year-old man with a history of hypertension and cirrhosis is found at the bottom of a flight of stairs. Autopsy reveals scalp contusions, right-sided space-occupying subdural hematoma, patchy subarachnoid hemorrhage, contusions of the inferior frontal and temporal lobes, and a 2 cm cavitation of the right internal capsule with surrounding orange discoloration of the parenchyma. What is the most likely manner of death?

A. Accident
B. Homicide
C. Natural
D. Suicide
E. Undetermined

Q1.47 A 60-year-old man is found deceased on the floor in his bathroom at home. The bedroom and bathroom are in disarray. The following intracranial hemorrhage is present at autopsy. What is the most likely underlying cause of the hemorrhage?

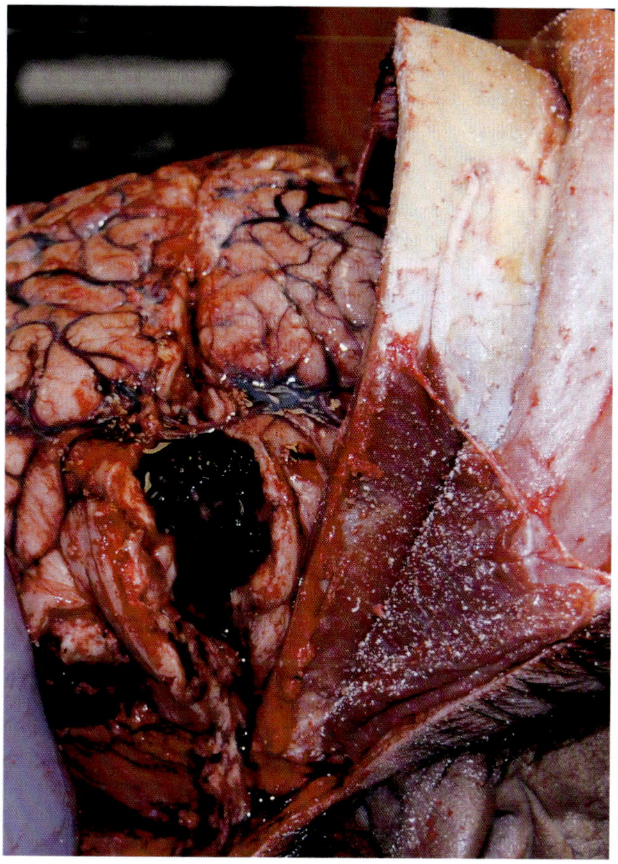

Figure 1.39

A. Blunt trauma
B. Congenital anomaly
C. Hypertension
D. Infection
E. Opiate intoxication

Q1.48 A 42-year-old woman is found dead in bed. Autopsy reveals the following cardiac finding. Which of the following is the most likely diagnosis?

Figure 1.40

A. Arrhythmogenic right ventricular dysplasia
B. Cardiac amyloidosis
C. Concentric left ventricular hypertrophy
D. Idiopathic hypertrophic cardiomyopathy
E. Pulmonary hypertension

Q1.49 The following histological finding was present in the lung sections of a 42-year-old woman. What is the diagnosis?

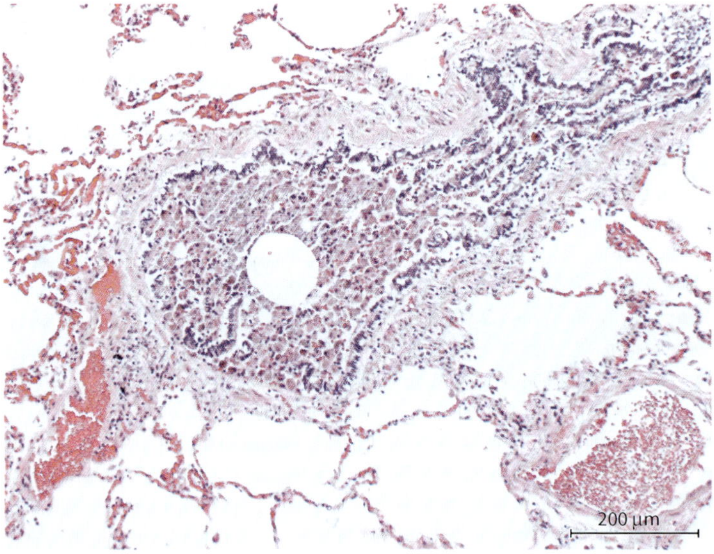

Figure 1.41

A. Aspiration pneumonia
B. Bacterial bronchopneumonia
C. Heart failure
D. Intravenous drug use
E. Respiratory bronchiolitis

Q1.50 The following histological findings were present in the thyroid section of a 40-year-old woman. What is the diagnosis?

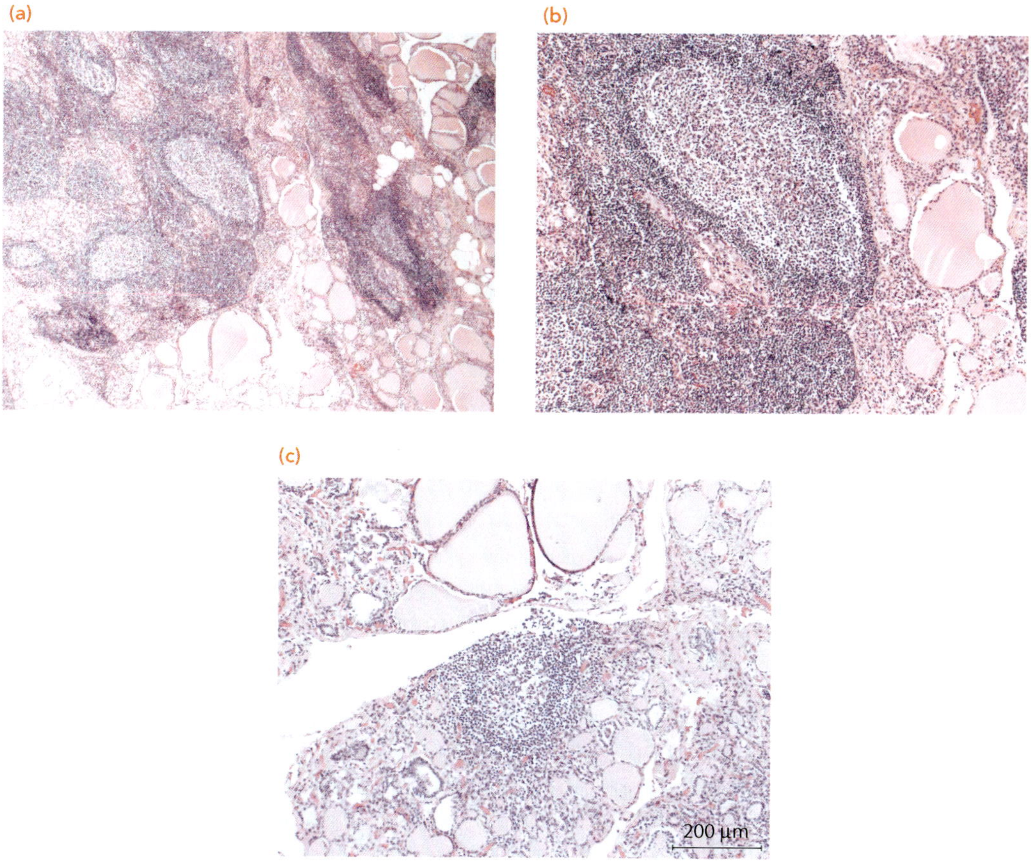

Figure 1.42

A. Goiter
B. Hashimoto thyroiditis
C. Infectious thyroiditis
D. Metastatic papillary thyroid carcinoma
E. Sarcoidosis

Q1.51 A 42-year-old obese man complains of difficulty breathing. His wife reported him patting his chest then reaching for his inhaler prior to collapsing. Resuscitative efforts are unsuccessful, and emergency medical services (EMS) personnel report difficulty during intubation attempts. Medical history included an upper respiratory tract infection over the preceding week. There were no known allergies, and he was in good health prior to this incident. At autopsy, the epiglottis has the following appearance (trachea opened posteriorly). What is the most likely diagnosis?

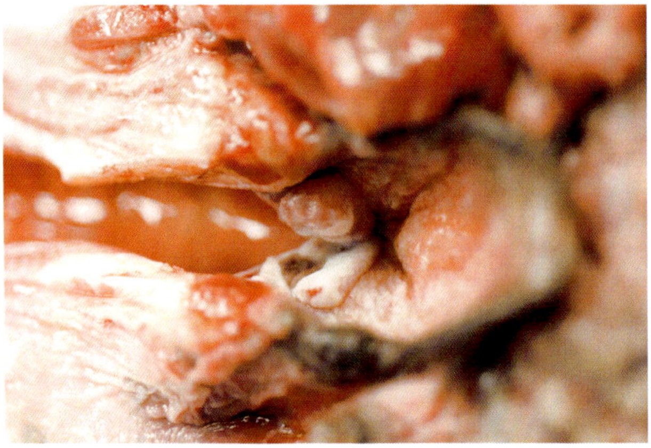

Figure 1.43

A. Amyloidosis
B. Anaphylaxis
C. Café coronary
D. Laryngotracheitis
E. Laryngeal papillomatosis

Q1.52 A 35-year-old man was found deceased in a hotel. Past medical history was not known. Autopsy revealed a 450 gram heart with moderate coronary atherosclerosis and granular kidneys. A section of kidney is featured below. Which of the following ancillary studies should be considered in the postmortem workup of this death?

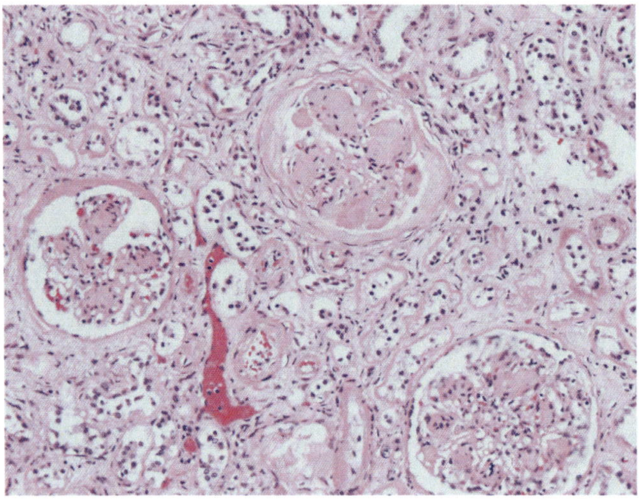

Figure 1.44

A. Antistreptolysin O titer
B. Antinuclear antibodies
C. Ethylene glycol
D. Fibrinogen
E. Glucose

Q1.53 A 35-year-old woman with a history of episodic hypertension is found deceased on her kitchen floor. Histopathology of an adrenal mass is featured below. What is the likely diagnosis?

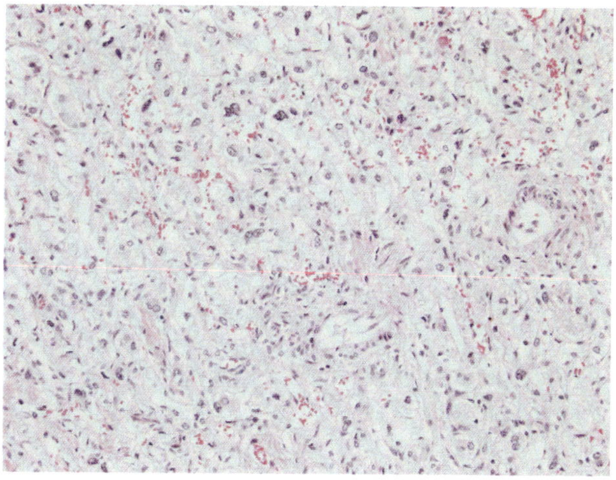

Figure 1.45

A. Adrenal adenoma
B. Adrenal carcinoma
C. Adrenal hyperplasia
D. Pheochromocytoma
E. Waterhouse–Friderichsen syndrome

Q1.54 A 55-year-old man collapses after mowing the lawn. Resuscitation is attempted but unsuccessful, and he is pronounced dead 30 minutes later. Autopsy documents a 450 g heart and significant coronary artery atherosclerosis. Histopathology of the heart is featured below. What is the best interpretation of the depicted finding?

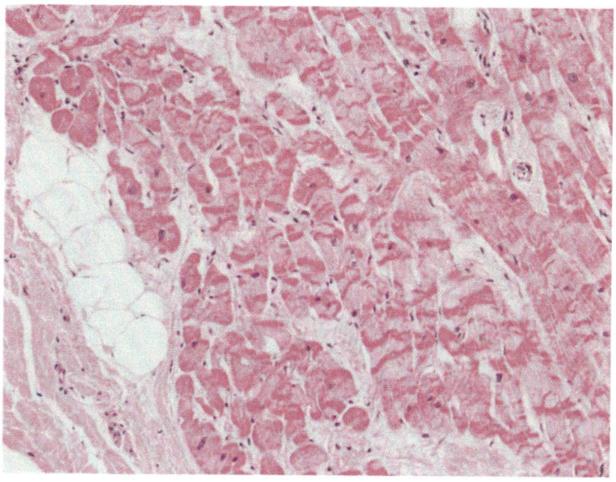

Figure 1.46

A. Contraction bands
B. Intercalated discs
C. Myocarditis
D. Processing artifact
E. Resuscitation artifact

Q1.55 A 42-year-old woman with asthma has the following finding on lung histopathology at autopsy. No gross masses were reported. The abnormality is limited to this field. What is the diagnosis?

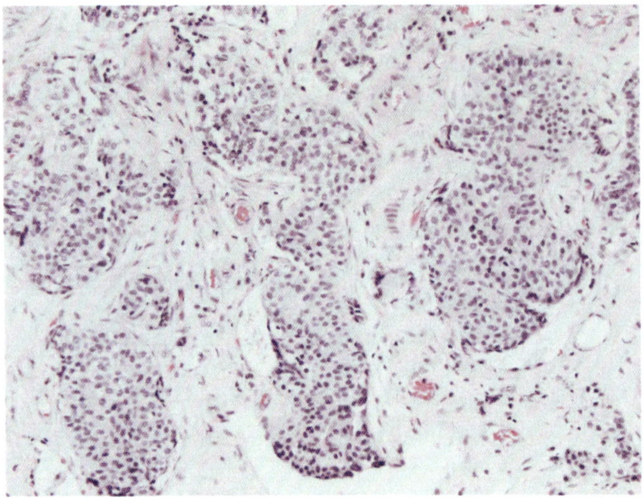

Figure 1.47

A. Adenocarcinoma in situ
B. Pulmonary carcinoid tumorlet
C. Microscopic metastatic lesion
D. Pulmonary sarcoidosis
E. Squamous metaplasia

Q1.56 A section of cerebrum taken from a patient who died with liver failure and encephalopathy is featured below. What is the best interpretation?

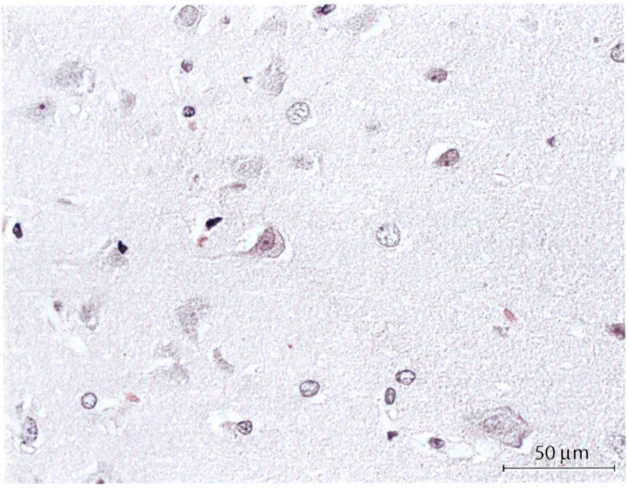

Figure 1.48

A. Acute metabolic disorder
B. Degenerative brain disease
C. Normal histology
D. Viral infection

Q1.57 A 50-year-old man complains of chest pain and then subsequently collapses. Resuscitation is unsuccessful. Autopsy shows the following aortic abnormality. What is the underlying cause of death?

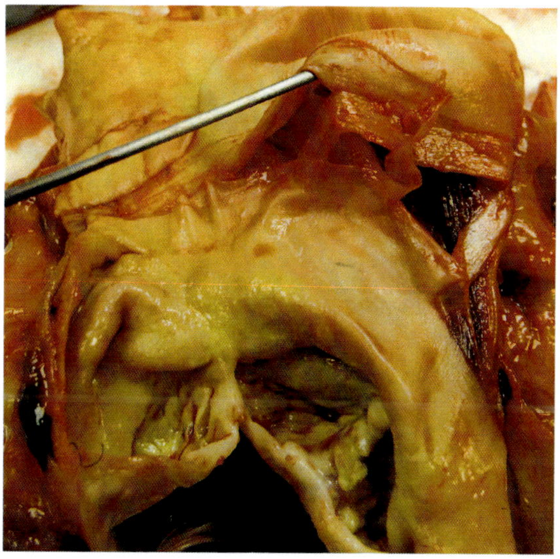

Figure 1.49

A. Aortic atherosclerosis
B. Bacterial endocarditis
C. Cardiac tamponade
D. Congenital bicuspid aortic valve
E. Coronary artery atherosclerosis

Q1.58 A 42-year-old man was found unresponsive in his wheelchair at home. Autopsy documented atrophic skeletal musculature of the lower extremities. A section of brain is featured below. What is the most likely diagnosis?

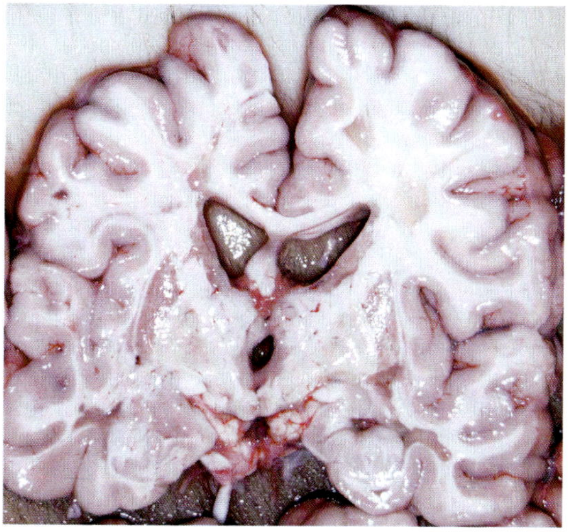

Figure 1.50

A. Astrocytoma
B. Ex vacuo hydrocephalus
C. Leukodystrophy
D. Multiple sclerosis
E. Parkinson disease

Q1.59 What is the most likely diagnosis from the findings in the photograph below?

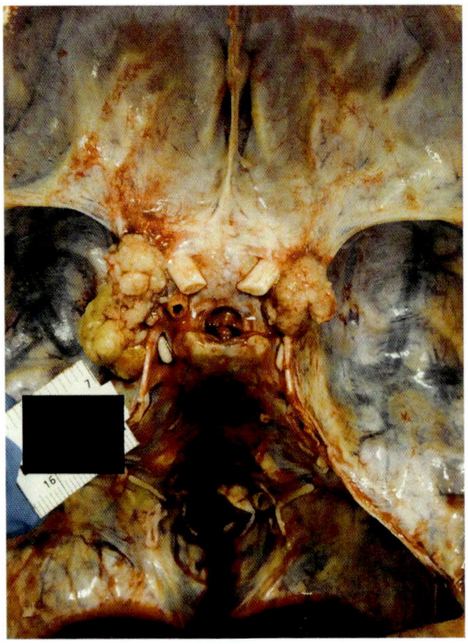

Figure 1.51

A. Craniopharyngioma
B. Hyperostosis frontalis interna
C. Meningioma
D. Paget disease
E. Pituitary adenoma

Q1.60 What is the underlying infection associated with the following lesions depicted in this photograph?

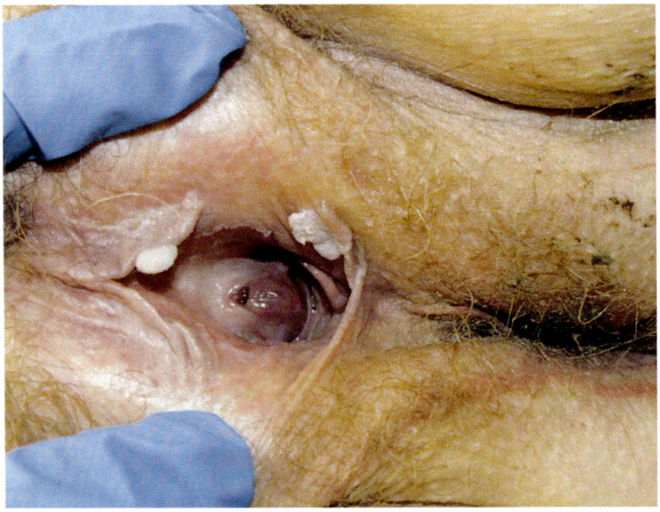

Figure 1.52

A. Chlamydia
B. Herpes simplex virus II
C. Human papilloma virus
D. Gonorrhea
E. Syphilis

Q1.61 What is the most likely diagnosis based on the findings depicted in this bisected kidney?

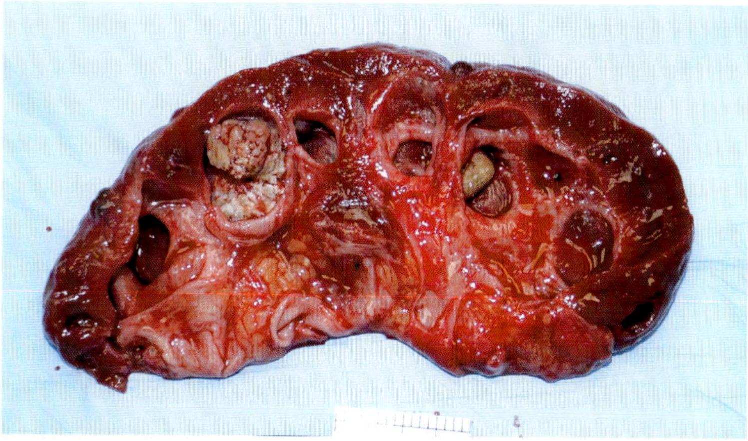

Figure 1.53

A. Nephrolithiasis
B. Nephrosclerosis
C. Polycystic kidney disease
D. Pyelonephritis
E. Systemic lupus erythematosus

Q1.62 Which of the following is the proper diagnosis in this formalin-fixed brain?

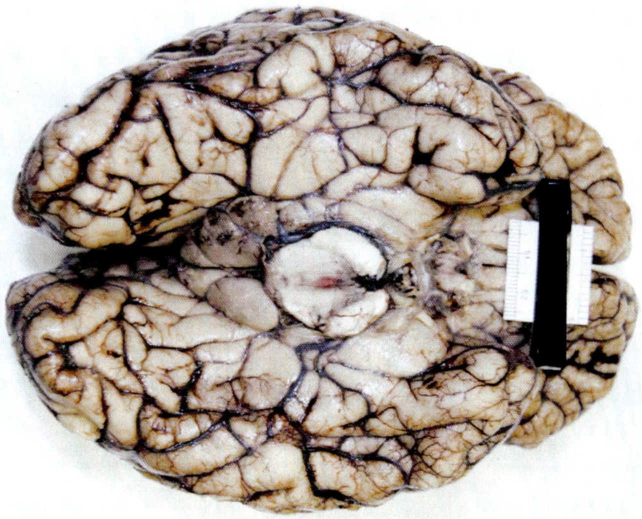

Figure 1.54

A. Bacterial meningitis
B. Hydrocephalus
C. Hydrogen sulfide toxicity
D. Meningioma
E. Uncal herniation

Q1.63 A 41-year-old man is working in the garage when he suddenly collapses. At autopsy, the left atrium is opened, as below. No other significant organ pathology is present. What is the most likely cause of death?

Figure 1.55

A. Congenital valvular stenosis
B. Endocarditis
C. Hypertrophic cardiomyopathy
D. Mitral valve prolapse
E. Rheumatic heart disease

Q1.64 What is the most likely diagnosis based on the findings depicted below?

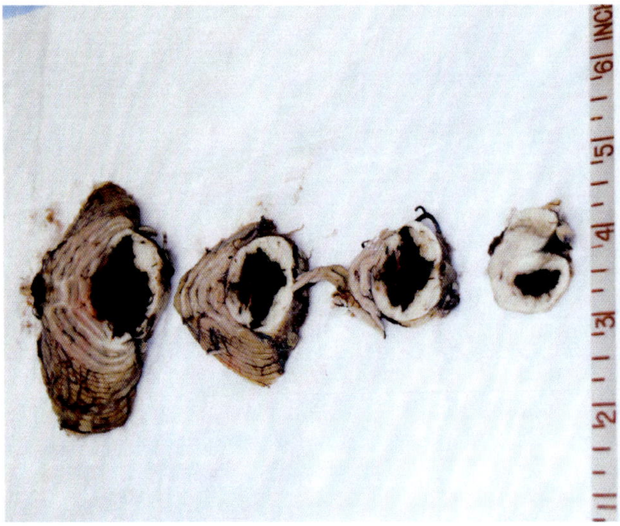

Figure 1.56

A. Arteriovenous malformation
B. Acute carbon monoxide exposure
C. Duret hemorrhages
D. Hypertensive stroke
E. Infectious vasculitis

Q1.65 The following section is of the AV nodal area in the interventricular septum in a 30-year-old man who suddenly collapsed while exercising. He had no past medical history. What is the most likely diagnosis?

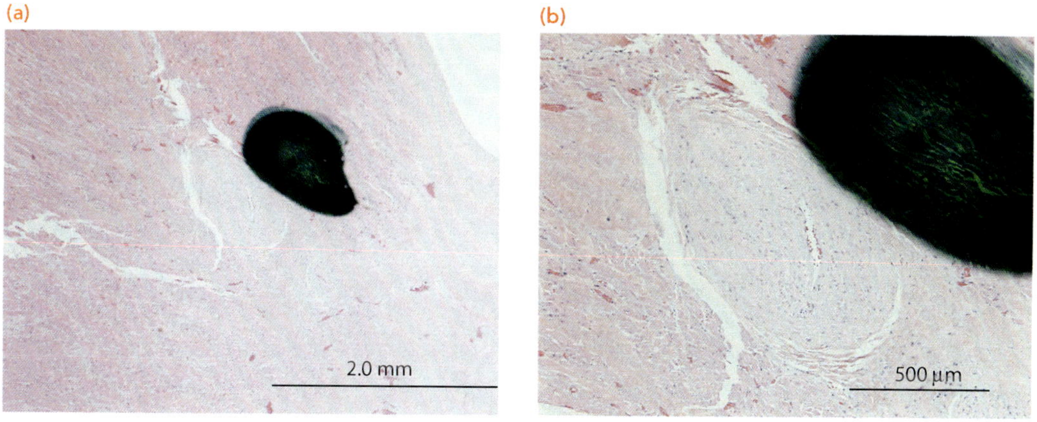

Figure 1.57

A. Atherosclerotic intimal thickening
B. Fibromuscular dysplasia
C. Hypertensive arterial changes
D. Immune vasculitis
E. Long QT syndrome

Q1.66 A 55-year-old man was autopsied, and the cause of death was ascribed to the finding depicted in the gastric-duodenal specimen below. Which of the following did the decedent most likely report?

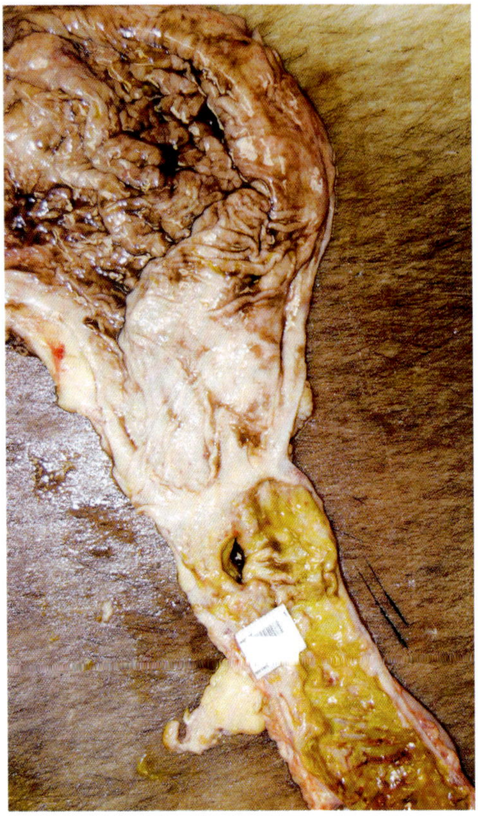

Figure 1.58

A. Melena
B. Pica
C. Polyuria and polydipsia
D. Right shoulder pain
E. Voluminous steatotic stools

ANSWERS: CHAPTER 1

A1.1 The correct answer is C. Hepatitis C infection

- Answer A is incorrect. The photograph depicts a liver that is cirrhotic. Of the choices listed, the one most often associated with hepatic cirrhosis is hepatitis C infection. Chronic alcoholism or chronic ethanolism (alcoholism) was the leading cause of cirrhosis but is now the second leading cause in the United States, causing approximately 21% of the cases of cirrhosis (see Wolf, David C. *Cirrhosis*. Located at http://emedicine.medscape.com/article/185856-overview last updated January 8, 2017. Last accessed May 30, 2017.).
- Answer B is incorrect. Diabetes mellitus would more likely manifest as fatty liver, although it can cause cirrhosis. Nonalcoholic fatty liver disease is a frequent but not the most common cause of cirrhosis.
- Answer C is correct. Hepatitis C infection is the most common cause of cirrhosis in the United States, accounting for approximately 26% of the cases although hepatitis B infection is more common worldwide.
- Answer D is incorrect. Iron overload is classically seen in hereditary hemochromatosis, which is an autosomal recessive condition that causes excess deposition of iron in hepatocytes and can cause cirrhosis. Due to the relative rarity of the condition, it is not the most common cause of cirrhosis.
- Answer E is incorrect. Metastatic cancer would likely present as more discrete nodules with some normal appearing liver tissue.

A1.2 The correct answer is D. *HFE*

- Answer A is incorrect. *BCR-ABL1* is a translocation associated with the Philadelphia chromosome and is primarily associated with chronic myelogenous leukemia (CML). Detection of the *BCR-ABL1* translocation is the defining diagnostic feature of CML. It is also found less commonly in acute lymphoblastic leukemia (ALL). It is not found in hereditary hemochromatosis.
- Answer B is incorrect. *CYP2D6* is the gene that encodes for the cytochrome p450 system in the liver that is responsible for metabolism of many drugs. Polymorphism in this gene can cause people to metabolize drugs more quickly (ultra-rapid metabolizers) or more slowly (poor metabolizers). Currently, there are no known gross or microscopic findings associated with *CYP2D6* variations. The variations can only be confirmed by molecular methods.
- Answer C is incorrect. *EWSR1* is the gene associated with Ewing sarcoma.
- Answer D is correct. *HFE* is the gene associated with hereditary hemochromatosis, which is what the findings in the question describe. Hereditary hemochromatosis is an autosomal recessive inherited condition that causes cirrhosis of the liver. The two most common mutations of the *HFE* gene are C282Y and H63D. These missense mutations are responsible for the majority of hereditary hemochromatosis cases. European descent is the most common ethnicity associated with this disease.
- Answer E is incorrect. *KRAS* is a gene associated with colorectal cancer.

A1.3 The correct answer is D. Neuronal plaque

- Answer A is incorrect. To identify amyloid, a Congo Red stain may be used with polarization or as viewed under a fluorescent microscope (rhodamine channel).
- Answer B is incorrect. Formalin pigment artifact, which may be especially prominent in decomposing or bloody specimens, usually has a yellow-brown to black-brown appearance microscopically and is seen without special stains.
- Answer C is incorrect. Lewy bodies are generally identified by routine hematoxylin and eosin (H&E) staining.
- Answer D is correct. Bielschowsky is a silver stain commonly used in the brain to assist in identification of nerve fibers and axons, and it also stains neurofibrillary tangles and neuronal ("senile") plaque. The background color is an amber-yellow, and the positive, silver staining regions are brown-black. Neuronal plaques are difficult to identify by H&E routine staining and appear as a vague pink blush, while once stained, the pathologist may count them with ease in the workup of dementia. The photomicrograph (Figure 1.2) demonstrates a significant increase in neuronal plaques, and clinical and pathological criteria were met for Alzheimer disease.
- Answer E is incorrect. Nocardial organisms may be best identified using an acid-fast stain, such as Ziehl–Neelsen.

A1.4 The correct answer is B. Greenfield filter with thromboemboli

- Answer A is incorrect. Vascular stents are generally tubular or cylindrical in shape and not multi-tined.
- Answer B is correct. The gross photograph shows in situ dissection of the inferior vena cava adjacent to the pelvic bowl. Where the lumen of the vein is exposed, a metal, several-pronged filter is present, and entangled in its tines is a red-brown thromboembolism or several thromboemboli. Inferior vena cava filters are placed in order to capture thrombi that become dislodged from more peripheral veins, most commonly popliteal or femoral (deep venous thrombosis). A vena caval filter is also known as a Greenfield filter, which is a trademarked name for a specific device of this type.
- Answer C is incorrect. Flechette projectiles come in many varieties, but in the photograph, there is no evidence of hemorrhage or of trauma.
- Answer D is incorrect. Shrapnel would be associated with hemorrhage, trauma, or evidence of healing, such as a scar or encapsulation.
- Answer E is incorrect. Vascular ligation hardware is built to mimic the structure and function of the vessel and would be tubular in appearance.

A1.5 The correct answer is A. Amyloidosis

- Answer A is correct. Multiple regions of amorphic pink material appear to be in the myocardial interstitium. In addition, the same pink material (see arrow in Figure 1.59) is seen in the artery in the photograph. These findings should raise suspicion of amyloidosis. Gross changes to the heart with a firm, tan-gray appearance may be seen but may also be subtle. Ischemic interstitial fibrosis likely has a different, more serpiginous pattern. However, if uncertain, the pathologist could perform special stains (Congo Red for amyloid or Masson trichrome stain for fibrosis) to more confidently differentiate the two processes. Histopathology of other organs may also be supportive of a diagnosis of amyloidosis, and history may assist in the evaluation as well. The photograph in Figure 1.59b is from the same general area of the H&E stained section depicted in 1.59a and shows the apple-green birefringence that can be seen upon polarization of Congo Red stained tissues in regions of amyloid deposition.
- Answer B is incorrect. Ischemic interstitial fibrosis likely has a different, more serpiginous pattern. However, if uncertain, the pathologist could perform special stains (Congo Red for amyloid or Masson trichrome stain for fibrosis) to more confidently differentiate the two processes.
- Answer C is incorrect. A myocardial fungal infection would likely demonstrate a mixed inflammatory infiltrate in response to the fungal elements, and Langerhans giant cells might be seen. Inflammation is not apparent in the provided photograph.
- Answer D is incorrect. Although neurofibromatosis may have areas of amorphous pink material, spindle cellular elements are also associated with this process and are not observed in the photomicrograph.
- Answer E is incorrect. Cardiac sarcoidosis would have the typical composition of noncaseating granulomas.

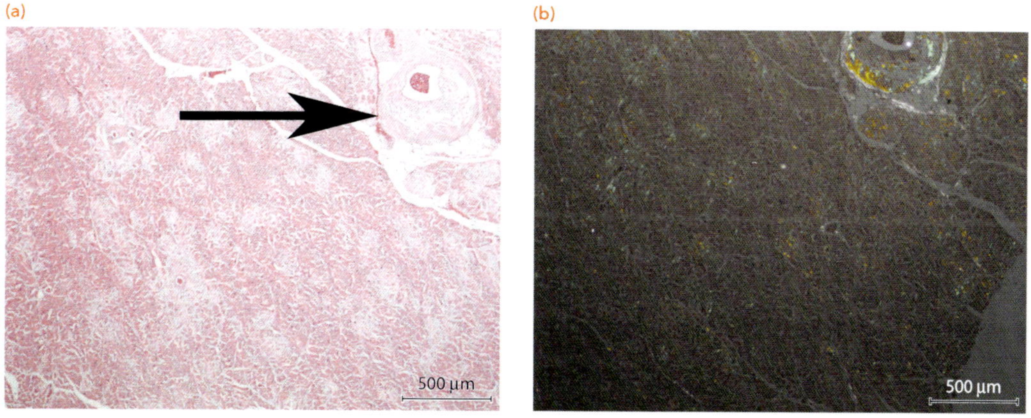

Figure 1.59

A1.6 The correct answer is D. Plasma cell myeloma

- Answer A is incorrect. Diffuse large B-cell lymphoma rarely involves the heart. When it does, one may expect to see irregular large mononuclear cells that demonstrate clonality by flow cytometry or immunohistochemistry.
- Answer B is incorrect. Liposarcoma may present as a paucicellular process if well-differentiated or a highly cellular process with extensive atypia if dedifferentiated or undifferentiated. The patchy myocardium shown here does not appear to demonstrate any cells besides myocytes.
- Answer C is incorrect. Metastasis of non-small cell lung cancer (e.g., adenocarcinoma, squamous cell carcinoma) to the heart is uncommon. However, if present, histopathology would be expected to demonstrate the cellular atypia of the original tumor. Cellular atypia is not apparent in the photomicrograph. Lung adenocarcinoma is the most common malignancy to metastasize to the heart. Other tumors that may metastasize to the heart include breast and melanoma.
- Answer D is correct. Plasma cell myeloma is a proliferation of clonal plasma cells, and although amyloidosis may result from plasma cell dyscrasia, there are other possible causes. When amyloidosis is identified, however, it may be important to obtain additional medical history or even sample bone marrow in order to exclude this etiology. If important to the investigation, the sample may be sent for liquid chromatography-mass spectrometric (LC-MS) analysis in order to differentiate the amyloid type.
- Answer E is incorrect. Small cell lung cancer may metastasize to the heart and would appear histologically similar to the tumor at its site of origin. Small cell lung cancer does not metastasize to the heart as often as does non-small cell carcinoma.

A1.7 The correct answer is E. Telangiectasia

- Answer A is incorrect. An arteriovenous malformation (AVM) is also a vascular malformation that can occur in the central nervous system (CNS); however, the AVM is composed of larger vasculature and has a greater tendency to bleed. This is secondary to the malformation itself, which couples the higher-pressure arterial circulation directly with the venous circulation without an intervening capillary bed.
- Answer B is incorrect. An infectious process may lead to diffuse intravascular coagulopathy and formation of small hemorrhage, which may have a similar appearance. However, the lesion pictured is unilateral, which would not fit with sepsis or hematogenous spread of a pathogen.
- Answer C is incorrect. Significant fat emboli may be associated with petechial hemorrhages in the brain in what is known as the fat embolism syndrome (FES). Histologic sectioning would reveal these to be hemorrhagic lesions instead of vascular malformation. History should also indicate significant trauma, probably with long bone fractures.
- Answer D is incorrect. An acute thrombotic stroke would likely appear normal grossly; additionally, this would be an unusual distribution for thrombosis. With reperfusion, the ischemic area may demonstrate hemorrhage, which would be confluent in the area of injury.
- Answer E is correct. The photograph demonstrates a capillary telangiectasia in the pons. The pons is the most common CNS site for this lesion, which is usually asymptomatic but may hemorrhage. Thus, if a pontine hemorrhage is observed, it may be useful to sample the region histologically in order to discern the etiology of the bleed.

A1.8 The correct answer is D. *Pneumocystis jiroveci* infection

- Answer A is incorrect. In alveolar proteinosis, the alveolar space is filled with homogeneous eosinophilic material.
- Answer B is incorrect. *Cryptococcus* infection is likely to elicit a granulomatous response if the individual is immunocompetent. The organisms may be viewed by hematoxylin and eosin (H&E) staining as round with slightly basophilic cell walls and surrounded by a clear zone. These organisms may be stained with mucicarmine, Periodic Acid Schiff, silver staining, and India ink staining.
- Answer C is incorrect. Diffuse alveolar damage (DAD; also termed hyaline membrane disease) is evidenced microscopically by eosinophilic material adherently lining the alveolar walls, although the early phase is exudative and may not show the hyaline membranes. The material essentially eliminates the alveolar-capillary interaction where present and leads to significant gas exchange deficits when extensive. DAD is most frequently encountered during long-term intubation.
- Answer D is correct. The photomicrograph shows an alveolar space filled with a granular or frothy-appearing eosinophilic substance that is characteristic of infection by *Pneumocystis jiroveci*. Reactive pneumocytes are also present. To better visualize the infectious agent, a Grocott-Gomori methylamine-silver stain may be utilized as imaged in Figure 1.60. This organism frequents the lungs of the healthy as well, but only in immunocompromised states does it tend to lead to opportunistic infection. It is an indicator that the CD4 lymphocyte count is low when present and suggests a level less than 200 cells per milliliter in one diagnosed with HIV (human immunodeficiency) infection.
- Answer E is incorrect. Tuberculosis is likely to cause a granulomatous reaction with caseous necrosis in the immunocompetent as well as immunocompromised individual. Immunocompromised individuals are more likely to have disseminated disease. *Mycobacterium avium* complex is another acid-fast organism common in immunocompromised hosts.

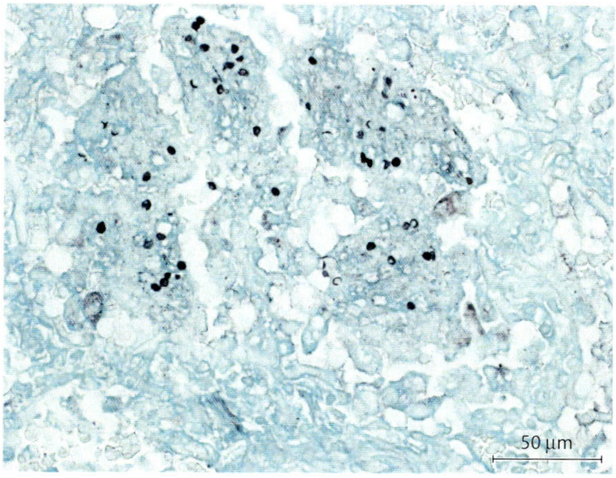

Figure 1.60

A1.9 The correct answer is A. Atherosclerotic cardiovascular disease

- Answer A is correct. The underlying or proximate cause of death is the event that initiated an unbroken chain of events that caused death. In this case the underlying cause that started the chain of events is the atherosclerosis that caused critical blockage of the vessel that resulted in ischemia to the heart that resulted in arrhythmia that caused death.
- Answer B is incorrect. Myocardial infarction is a result of the atherosclerosis. It is part of the unbroken chain of events but did not initiate the cascade of events leading to death. Thus, it is not the proximate or underlying cause of death. It would be better classified as an intervening or immediate cause of death.
- Answer C is incorrect. Platelet adhesion does contribute to the blockage of the vessel but is not part of the mechanism associated with the underlying atherosclerosis.
- Answer D is incorrect. Pulmonary embolism is a cause of death that is related to venous thromboembolism and is not related to the arterial blood system except in cases of cardiac septal defect, which is not described in the given case.
- Answer E is incorrect. Ventricular arrhythmia is the final step in the unbroken chain of events and would be the immediate cause of death.

A1.10 The correct answer is E. Undetermined

- Answer A is incorrect. There is no mention of any toxicological data in the question. You must account for the possibility of a stimulant drug such as methamphetamine or cocaine that may have contributed to death. If that was the case then the manner would be classified as accident.
- Answer B is incorrect. The circumstances indicate there is no reason to believe this was a homicide. If the decedent had collapsed at gunpoint during a robbery, a case for homicide as the manner of death could be made on the grounds that the sudden catecholamine release exacerbated the underlying heart disease, and the person would not have died without the added stress. However, it should be noted that this is a very controversial subject.
- Answer C is incorrect. Although this appears to be a natural death on the surface, no mention is made of any toxicology data that if positive for drugs such as cocaine or methamphetamine could possibly change the manner from natural to accident.
- Answer D is incorrect. Nothing in the scenario suggests the person took his or her own life; thus, suicide is excluded.
- Answer E is correct. Since there is no toxicology data, the possibility of two different manners of death exist, natural or accident. Since neither of these can be established without relevant toxicological data, the manner should be classified as undetermined.

A1.11 The correct answer is C. Remote, 6 months

- Answer A is incorrect. No grossly visible changes are observed the first 4 hours after an infarct. Mottling can appear as early as 4 hours and up to 24 hours after the infarct.
- Answer B is incorrect. The myocardium has white scarring. Mottling, which is indicative of an acute infarct, is seen between 4 and 24 hours.
- Answer C is correct. About 2 months after a myocardial infarction, white fibrous scar tissue appears and would be expected to be seen at 6 months as well.
- Answer D is incorrect. After 1–3 days, the infarct becomes tan-yellow. This is followed by softening of the center with hyperemia at the border of the normal myocardium and infarcted tissue at around days 3–7.
- Answer E is incorrect. A subacute infarct at 10 days would be expected to exhibit yellow-tan myocardium with red-tan margins. Days 7–10 show a transition of the infarct to yellow-tan with red-tan margins. The infarct is at its softest at this point, and the myocardium is most susceptible to rupture in this window. Around 1 month the infarcted area becomes red-gray and has depressed borders. There is also some overlap as gray-white granulation tissue is seen at this stage and may be seen as early as 2 weeks and as late as 2 months.

A1.12 The correct answer is A. Anterior communicating artery

- Answer A is correct. The most frequent site of saccular (berry) aneurysms is the anterior circulation of the circle of Willis at the brain base. The probe demonstrates the most common site: anterior communicating artery. The incidence of intracranial aneurysm is approximately 2% on average and up to 6% in those with risk factors (also see Rinkel GJE et al. Prevalence and risk of rupture of intracranial aneurysms—A systematic review. *Stroke* 1998, 29: 251–6.); although only a minority rupture.
- Answer B is incorrect. The photograph illustrates the circle of Willis, not the aorta. However, aortic aneurysms, which are typically atherosclerotic in etiology, commonly form in the region proximal to the iliac bifurcation due to the increased blood flow turbulence at that site.
- Answer C is incorrect. Basilar artery saccular aneurysms are less common than those of the anterior communicating artery.
- Answer D is incorrect. Internal carotid artery saccular aneurysms are less common than those of the anterior communicating artery.
- Answer E is incorrect. Saccular aneurysms of the posterior communicating artery are encountered with less frequency than are those at the anterior communicating artery, but this may be considered the second most common site.

A1.13 The correct answer is A. Anterior communicating cerebral artery

- Answer A is correct. Although any surface artery may form an aneurysm with consequent rupture, the most common is the anterior communicating cerebral artery. The arteries of the circle of Willis are frequently implicated in basilar subarachnoid hemorrhage such as that shown. However, in a case such as that illustrated, the pathologist may perform a directed dissection of the circle of Willis and vessels originating from it in order to define the causative lesion.
- Answer B is incorrect. The basilar artery is not the most common artery involved in berry aneurysm formation and rupture with resultant basilar subarachnoid hemorrhage.
- Answer C is incorrect. The internal carotid artery is not the most common artery involved in berry aneurysm formation and rupture with resultant basilar subarachnoid hemorrhage.
- Answer D is incorrect. The middle cerebral artery traverses the brain parenchyma, and its disruption would be less likely to demonstrate this brain base pattern, although if an aneurysmal rupture occurred at the vessel origin from the internal carotid, it could.
- Answer E is incorrect. The middle meningeal artery is the most common site associated with epidural hemorrhage as it supplies the dura mater and calvarium. The distribution of the hemorrhage is not epidural in nature in this case; thus, choice E can be excluded.
- Answer F is incorrect. The vertebral arteries are not the most common arteries involved in berry aneurysm formation and rupture with resultant basilar subarachnoid hemorrhage.

A1.14 The correct answer is E. Pulseless electrical activity

- Answer A is incorrect. The finding in the photograph is hemopericardium. Hemopericardium can present clinically as cardiac tamponade. Bradycardia is not associated with tamponade. However, tachycardia and tachypnea are common signs.
- Answer B is incorrect. In contrast, cardiac tamponade may result in cold clammy extremities.
- Answer C is incorrect. An elevated D-dimer is associated with pulmonary embolism and not cardiac tamponade.
- Answer D is incorrect. Beck triad or acute compression triad describes the classic presentation of cardiac tamponade. It includes increased jugular venous pressure, hypotension, and diminished heart sounds.
- Answer E is correct. Pulseless electrical activity is associated with cardiac tamponade.

A1.15 The correct answer is C. Polycystic kidneys

- Answer A is incorrect. The scenario described the presentation of a cerebral berry aneurysm. Berry aneurysms have been associated with autosomal dominant polycystic kidney disease, which may be associated with hepatic cysts, but not hepatic adenomas.
- Answer B is incorrect. The scenario described the presentation of a ruptured cerebral berry aneurysm. Berry aneurysms have been associated with autosomal dominant polycystic kidney disease.
- Answer C is correct. Autosomal dominant polycystic kidney disease can be associated with berry aneurysms, liver cysts, and cardiac valvular disease. In the described scenario, a berry aneurysm of the circle of Willis ruptured producing abundant basilar subarachnoid hemorrhage, obscuring the remnant aneurysm.
- Answer D is incorrect. Pheochromocytomas are associated with episodic hypertension, which may lead to cerebral vascular stroke. However, the scenario described was that of a ruptured berry aneurysm.
- Answer E is incorrect. Temporal arteritis is associated with headaches, although not usually described as the worst in life, but is a granulomatous vasculitis.

A1.16 The correct answer is E. Status asthmaticus

- Answer A is incorrect. Mast cell degranulation would be expected in anaphylaxis. Careful review of the photomicrograph does not reveal any significant population of mast cells.
- Answer B is incorrect. The main cellular response to bacterial bronchopneumonia would be neutrophils, and they would congregate within alveolar spaces rather than around large airways.
- Answer C is incorrect. Chronic bronchitis would not likely demonstrate the number of eosinophils seen here, although mucus inspissation and thickening of the basement membrane may be present.
- Answer D is incorrect. Parasitic infections lead to hypereosinophilia, but there is no evidence in the photomicrograph of a parasite. Additionally, parasitic infections are not as likely to demonstrate significant airway mucus.
- Answer E is correct. The photograph shows an influx of eosinophils and apparent loose eosinophilic granules within the subepithelium. In addition, the basement membrane is thickened and inspissated mucus is in the airway. Although not exemplified here, another histological change found in asthma is smooth muscle hypertrophy.

A1.17 The correct answer is C. Chronic alcoholism

- Answer A is incorrect. Cerebral atrophy (not cerebellar atrophy) is more common in HIV dementia associated with AIDS. It often involves the caudate region.
- Answer B is incorrect. Generally, autoimmune deficiency is not related to central nervous system (CNS) atrophy. However, autoimmune diseases may be. For example, in a small study, it was shown that Hashimoto thyroiditis may result in acquired cerebellar ataxia with cerebellar vermal atrophy (thought to be reversible with treatment of the hypothyroidism) or olivopontocerebellar atrophy. (Selim M and Drachman D. Ataxia associated with Hashimoto disease: Progressive non-familial adult onset cerebellar degeneration with autoimmune thyroiditis. *J Neurol Neurosurg Psychiatry* 2001, 71[1]: 81–7.)
- Answer C is correct. Chronic alcoholism or ethanolism affects the brain in many ways, including causing cerebral atrophy and cerebellar vermal atrophy. Note that a degree of cerebellar vermal atrophy appears to occur with aging and is unrelated to symptomatology (primary cerebellar degeneration).
- Answer D is incorrect. Multiple CNS malformations may occur during development. These have been divided into generalized and focal as well as hypoplastic or dysplastic. (See Patel S and Barkovich AJ. Analysis and classification of cerebellar malformations. *Am J Neuroradiol* 2002, 23: 1074–87.) Although very rare, there are at least 10 types of pontocerebellar hypoplasia, but these are not atrophic conditions since they are present at birth.
- Answer E is incorrect. Significant trauma to the brain, including the cerebellum, leads to cavitation in the long term. Chronic head trauma (such as experienced by professional contact sports players) may lead to generalized brain atrophy but is more commonly associated with cerebral atrophy (chronic traumatic encephalopathy). (Also see McKee et al. Chronic traumatic encephalopathy in athletes: Progressive tauopathy after repetitive head injury. *J Neuropathol and Experimental Neurol* 2009, 68[7]: 709–35.)

A1.18 The correct answer is C. Electrical disruption of the cardiac cycle during the ascending phase of the T wave

- Answer A is incorrect. Wolff–Parkinson–White syndrome is characterized by an abnormal electrical reentrant pathway between the atria and ventricles. The normally conducted signal from the atrioventricular (AV) node to the ventricles is redirected back to the atria with resultant atrial contraction and re-stimulation of the AV node. Tachycardia is a common finding (also termed *atrioventricular reentrant tachycardia* or AVRT).
- Answer B is incorrect. Asymmetric left ventricular hypertrophy with myofibril disarray characterizes hypertrophic cardiomyopathy. Although sudden death may be associated with this disease, it is generally associated with physical exertion.
- Answer C is correct. The scenario is most compatible with cardiac stunning or concussion, termed *commotio cordis*. If a blow occurs at a specific time in the cardiac cycle, during the ascending phase of the T wave, arrhythmia may occur. Classically, autopsy will not identify any gross or microscopic evidence of trauma.
- Answer D is incorrect. Although an electrolyte imbalance may lead to arrhythmia, the scenario is more consistent with blunt trauma as the cause of collapse.
- Answer E is incorrect. A prolonged QT interval is commonly associated with medications such as the tricyclic class of antidepressants (classically amitriptyline), which are not cited in the current scenario.

A1.19 The correct answer is C. Mucicarmine

- Answer A is incorrect. Bielschowsky Silver stain is commonly used to identify plaques and tangles in Alzheimer disease as it highlights nerve fibers.
- Answer B is incorrect. Brown–Brenn is a form of Gram stain useful for finding bacteria, not fungal organisms.
- Answer C is correct. Fungal organisms are present within the meninges of this patient and have the size and configuration of *Cryptococcus* species. Mucicarmine aids in identification of polysaccharide components in the prominent capsule. Alcian Blue Periodic Acid Schiff stain will also highlight the capsule. A Gomori methenamine silver (GMS) stain would also assist in identification of fungus and also will stain other organisms. A good knowledge of fungal morphology is most important, but special stains can be used to find rare organisms and assist in morphological analysis.
- Answer D is incorrect. Nissl is a cresyl violet stain that will stain neurons pink-violet.
- Answer E is incorrect. Ziehl–Neelsen, an acid-fast stain most commonly used to identify mycobacterium, may stain *Blastomyces* or *Histoplasma*, but is less specific and does not stain *Cryptococcus*.

A1.20 The correct answer is C. Chronic ethanol use

- Answer A is incorrect. The cerebellum in Arnold–Chiari malformation is small with an extension of cerebellar tissue through the foramen magnum.
- Answer B is incorrect. Acute carbon monoxide (CO) exposure typically shows no gross cerebrovascular manifestations, although chronic CO exposure may result in basal ganglia necrosis.
- Answer C is correct. The featured gross lesion is termed *cerebellar vermal atrophy*, as evidenced by the space between the cerebellar folia. This usually involves the superior vermis and is consistent with chronic ethanol use (alcoholism).
- Answer D is incorrect. The cerebellum is a common location for a hypertensive stroke, but there is no evidence (e.g., gross hemorrhage) of that here.
- Answer E is incorrect. Vitamin B_{12} deficiency may result in neurological abnormalities, but the gross lesions typically involve the spinal cord, not the cerebellum.

A1.21 The correct answer is E. Ventricular arrhythmia

- Answer A is incorrect. The most common abnormal heart rhythm is atrial fibrillation. However, it is not associated with fatty liver. It is commonly associated with hypertension and valvular heart disease.
- Answer B is incorrect. Coronary artery thrombosis is not directly attributable to fatty liver. It is a common result of prolonged atherosclerotic cardiovascular disease, of which hyperlipidemia is a risk factor.
- Answer C is incorrect. Fatty liver can be seen in diabetics, but the fatty liver does not directly contribute to the ketoacidosis. Diabetic ketoacidosis can occur in the setting of fatty or nonfatty livers.
- Answer D is incorrect. Although a coagulopathy can be associated with end-stage liver disease, it is usually not seen in the setting of fatty liver.
- Answer E is correct. The photograph depicts a fatty liver. Ventricular arrhythmia in the case of fatty liver is due to prolonged QT_c interval, which initiates the arrhythmia and would show a torsades de pointes finding on electrocardiogram (ECG). (Targher G. et al. Association of nonalcoholic fatty liver disease with QTc interval in patients with type 2 diabetes. *Nutr Metab Cardiovasc Diseases* 2014, 24(6):663–9; Hung, Chi-Sheng et al. Nonalcoholic fatty liver disease is associated with QT prolongation in the general population. *J Am Heart Assoc* 2015;4:e001820 doi: 10.1161/JAHA.115.001820; Campbell RWF, Day CP, James OFW, Butler TJ. QT prolongation and sudden cardiac death in patients with alcoholic liver disease. *Lancet* 1994, 341(8858):1423–28.)

A1.22 The correct answer is A. Bile duct hamartoma

- Answer A is correct. The low-power view shows a well-circumscribed lesion in the liver. Higher power reveals ductules that are not as crisp as typical bile ducts. One of the ductules has a bile crystal within it. Bile duct hamartomas are benign lesions found in the liver of patients of all ages.
- Answer B is incorrect. Cholangiocarcinoma is a malignancy of the bile ducts. The cytologic and architectural features are benign in the case. Malignant features such as enlarged bizarre nuclei with increased nuclear/cytoplasmic ratios are not observed as would be expected in cholangiocarcinoma.
- Answer C is incorrect. Hepatocellular carcinoma is a primary malignancy of the liver. As in choice B, the features are not suggestive of a malignant process.
- Answer D is incorrect. Metastatic cancer would most likely present as multiple nodules within the liver, although a single metastatic focus can occur. Microscopically, you would expect features such as large bizarre nuclei, architectural disarray, and increased nuclear/cytoplasmic ratios.
- Answer E is incorrect. Steatohepatitis is characterized by steatosis with inflammation. There is no steatosis or fatty change seen in the photographs, and there is no significant inflammatory change.

A1.23 The correct answer is E. Anti-HCV

- Answer A is incorrect. The photomicrographs show chronic viral hepatitis in a hepatitis C patient. HAV IgM is the antibody that is associated with hepatitis A infection. Microscopic sections of liver may show abundant plasma cells in the portal tracts or extensive microvesicular steatosis, which is not observed in this case.
- Answer B is incorrect. HBcAb stands for hepatitis B core antibody. It typically forms about 6 weeks after exposure to the hepatitis B virus. Please do not confuse the "c" in the designation with an association with hepatitis C. Specific features associated with hepatitis B infection are ground glass hepatocytes, which are not seen in this case.
- Answer C is incorrect. HBsAb stands for hepatitis B surface antibody. This marker is seen about 8 months after exposure and signifies recovery. Ground glass hepatocytes are associated with hepatitis B, which is not observed in this case.
- Answer D is incorrect. HBsAg stands for hepatitis B surface antigen. This is seen about 4 weeks after exposure and usually diminishes after about 6 months. If both HBsAb and HBsAg are seen together, this represents a chronic carrier state. As mentioned previously, microscopic findings associated with hepatitis B are ground glass hepatocytes, which represent abundant HBsAg in the cytoplasm.
- Answer E is correct. The microscopic photos represent hepatitis C virus infection. Hepatitis C has more abundant lymphoid inflammation in a portal distribution, and aggregates may occasionally have follicles that can be observed. The higher-power image shows bizarre multinucleated hepatocytes, and the other image shows the lymphoid aggregates. Although not absolutely specific, this is very good evidence for hepatitis C virus infection. Antibodies develop to hepatitis C (anti-HCV) but do not confer immunity.

A1.24 The correct answer is A. Artifact

- Answer A is correct. The microscopic photograph represents decomposed heart tissue. There are no readily identifiable myocytes, only faint outlines of cells. If you were not told this was heart tissue, it would be hard to tell that it was cardiac in origin. The brown pigment is most likely due to formalin artifact.
- Answer B is incorrect. Bile staining would be expected in the liver or in an entity such as a bile duct hamartoma in which bile is actively made. The "pigment" is not really within any cellular tissue, it is just artifact.
- Answer C is incorrect. Iron deposition would be expected within actual cellular tissue and would probably need special highlighting by using an iron stain such as Prussian blue.
- Answer D is incorrect. Fungal elements would have hyphae or something suggestive of yeast, and this is not seen. Sometimes decomposed tissue can grow fungus such as *Penicillium* sp., but this would be seen as yeast and hyphae within the tissue, which is not seen here.
- Answer E is incorrect. Many viruses have associated nuclear or cytoplasmic inclusions. Since defined cells are not seen and no apparent lymphocytic infiltrate is present, a diagnosis of viral infection in the tissue cannot be made.

A1.25 The correct answer is C. Emphysema

- Answer A is incorrect. Asthma typically shows mucus plugging of the bronchi more readily appreciated on gross examination, sub-basement membrane fibrosis, and goblet cell metaplasia, none of which is observed in the photograph.
- Answer B is incorrect. Diffuse alveolar damage is the microscopic picture associated with acute respiratory distress syndrome. It is characterized initially by an exudative phase in which inflammatory cells and type I pneumocytes fill the alveoli. The photograph shows enlarged nuclei without any significant filling of the alveolar spaces. Some spaces have red blood cells, but this is an artifact from postmortem congestion.
- Answer C is correct. The photograph shows enlarged alveoli that are permanently hyperexpanded. Classically, as seen here, the club-shaped alveolar walls project into the airspaces. Another clue is that there is no fibrosis of the interstitial space. Emphysema is a manifestation of chronic obstructive pulmonary disease.
- Answer D is incorrect. Hypersensitivity pneumonitis is characterized by small poorly formed noncaseating granulomas adjacent to respiratory or terminal bronchioles. Granulomas are not seen in the photograph.
- Answer E is incorrect. As the name implies, there should be something wrong with the interstitium, namely, foci of fibroblastic proliferation. The interstitial component observed in the photograph is essentially normal.

A1.26 The correct answer is D. Fat embolus

- Answer A is incorrect. Although postmortem gases may be produced by bacterial colonization, the photomicrograph shows no evidence of decomposition in the tissue surrounding the vessel in question. Thus, this finding is likely not due to postmortem artifact in this case.
- Answer B is incorrect. Although air embolization cannot be excluded since the clear round spaces in the vessels are essentially devoid of material due to routine processing, air embolism is thought to be uncommon, while fat embolism is extremely common. Thus, air embolization is not the best answer.
- Answer C is incorrect. In the photomicrograph, only clear round spaces are noted in the vessel and no bone marrow elements are present. Thus, bone marrow embolism is not apparent.
- Answer D is correct. The clear round spaces present in the vessels are most likely due to fat embolism. During routine tissue processing, the fat is expected to be removed. Thus, a special stain to detect fat at this point would most likely be negative. Fat embolism is commonly seen in cases of soft tissue trauma including resuscitation and is a frequent finding in the postmortem examination. If fat embolism is in the differential for a cause of death prior to sample fixation and processing, a frozen section may be obtained and special stains for fat, such as Oil-Red-O, may be used to confirm the composition of the material.
- Answer E is incorrect. Abnormalities shown in the photomicrograph include apparent fat emboli in the vessels and edema in the alveolar spaces. Thus, normal lung is not the best answer.

A1.27 The correct answer is D. Normal pineal gland

- Answer A is incorrect. An astrocytoma is a neoplastic process of glial cells. Histologically, they vary depending on the grade and differentiation of the tumor. Serpentine necrosis and pseudopalisading of the nuclei may be features.
- Answer B is incorrect. The cells shown in the photomicrograph demonstrate bland features with small, regular nuclei and no apparent pleomorphism. Thus, a metastatic tumor is not likely.
- Answer C is incorrect. Well-differentiated neuroendocrine tumors (NETs), also termed *carcinoid tumors*, demonstrate finely granular cytoplasm, which is not apparent in the photomicrograph. However, NETs may demonstrate a similar pattern of growth as seen here. Thus, it is paramount to detail the site of any tissue submitted for histological analysis to avoid possible misdiagnoses.
- Answer D is correct. The photomicrograph demonstrates features of the pineal gland histology including the pinealocytes with clear cytoplasm and monotonous round nuclei, intervening connective tissue, and glial cells. Although rarely sampled during the postmortem examination, it may appear enlarged in cases of neoplasm, and the prosector may submit the gland for histopathological examination. This is an example of a normal pineal gland, the endocrine organ that produces melatonin. Enlargement of the gland in concert with a history of neurological symptoms such as headache, seizures, nausea and vomiting, or visual changes may be due to direct compression of the Sylvian aqueduct by a pineal gland tumor.
- Answer E is incorrect. Pituitary adenoma may demonstrate many different histologic patterns including trabeculae and papillae, and the cells may be acidophilic, basophilic, or chromophobic depending on their cell type. The pituitary adenoma demonstrates lack of an acinar structure upon reticulin staining, and these tumors do not generally demonstrate the connective tissue component seen in the photomicrograph.

A1.28 The correct answer is B. 32-year-old woman with no medical history who collapsed while jogging

- Answer A is incorrect. Aortic coarctation, if not surgically revised, will lead to increased heart work and compensatory left ventricular myocardial hypertrophy, not seen here.
- Answer B is correct. The photomicrograph depicts a section of heart muscle with infiltration of the wall by adipocytes. Focally, the fat comes to within one or two cells of the endocardial surface. In an appropriate clinical scenario, such as that provided in answer B, a diagnosis of arrhythmogenic right ventricular dysplasia may be made. Fibrosis may also be present in this entity.
- Answer C is incorrect. Chronic obstructive pulmonary disease would lead to increased right ventricular work and compensatory right ventricular hypertrophy, not seen here.
- Answer D is incorrect. Severe coronary atherosclerosis may lead to ischemic myocardial damage. By histological examination, one would expect to find no changes if the death was sudden or may find ischemic changes such as wavy fibers, cardiomyocytolysis (contraction band necrosis), interstitial and patchy fibrosis, or other evidence of prior myocardial infarction. None of these changes are evidenced here.
- Answer E is incorrect. Chronic alcoholism or ethanolism frequently has a toxic effect on the myocardium. This may be evidenced by dilated cardiomyopathy or by arrhythmia without gross or microscopic pathology.

A1.29 The correct answer is C. Disseminated intravascular coagulation

- Answer A is incorrect. Atherosclerotic cardiovascular disease would have an effect upon the renal arteries and arterioles and may lead to regional loss of glomeruli by global sclerosis, most commonly in the subcapsular region and in other end arterial locations. Additionally, hypertension often accompanies atherosclerotic disease, and in the kidneys, fibroelastic intimal thickening of the renal arteries would be noted.
- Answer B is incorrect. Crescentic glomerulonephritis is damage to the glomerulus in which there is a collection of cells two or more layers thick within Bowman capsule; these cells include inflammatory cells and parietal epithelial cells most commonly. No increased cellularity is in Bowman's space in the photomicrograph.
- Answer C is correct. The renal glomerulus pictured shows capillary loops that are obstructed by a red-pink fibrillar substance, most compatible with fibrin thrombosis as seen in diffuse intravascular coagulation. A similar finding, but more localized to the afferent/efferent arterioles, would be a thrombotic microangiopathy, such as hemolytic uremic syndrome or thrombotic thrombocytopenic purpura. These entities can be better differentiated by medical course and history.
- Answer D is incorrect. Ethylene glycol toxicity may be missed in a routine examination of the kidney using hematoxylin and eosin (H&E) staining as the calcium oxalate crystals may not be apparent. Polarization would show intratubular laminated oxalate crystals. Thus, it is critical to polarize kidney sections and perform toxicologic analysis to exclude this entity. In addition, calcium oxalate crystals may be demonstrated in the urine if this is available. Microscopically, calcium oxalate monohydrate crystals are dumbbell shaped, and calcium oxalate dihydrate crystals are envelope shaped. Note that not all toxicology laboratories include ethylene glycol in their routine analysis.
- Answer E is incorrect. Nodular glomerulosclerosis is a nodular sclerosis of the glomeruli most commonly seen in diabetic nephropathy. In this entity, glomerular tufts would be replaced by monotonous lightly eosinophilic material (the fibrosis).

A1.30 The correct answer is E. Sepsis

- Answer A is incorrect. In cases of dehydration, the physical examination is likely to show decreased skin turgor, dry mucous membranes, and increased capillary refill times, which are not described in this scenario.
- Answer B is incorrect. Electrocution may show no outward signs in the absence of an entrance site or exit site. Adrenal hemorrhages and widespread petechial hemorrhages are not a feature of electrocution.
- Answer C is incorrect. Folate is a B vitamin, and deficiency leads to megaloblastic anemia. The history and physical examination may reveal skin pallor, tongue smoothness, and sometimes tongue discomfort; these findings are not described in this case.
- Answer D is incorrect. Inherited platelet disorders are one class of bleeding disorder in which the platelets are less in number or defective in function. Physical examination will likely show bruising, and the patient will likely have a history of epistaxis and if female, menorrhagia. Internal bleeding is likely to affect the gastrointestinal tract or oropharynx. Additionally, patients with clinically significant inherited platelet disorders are likely to present in childhood and not in early adulthood (also see Matthews DC. Inherited disorders of platelet function. *Pediatr Clin North Am* 2013, 60[6]: 1475–88).
- Answer E is correct. The compendium of findings makes sepsis the most likely cause of death. Diffuse intravascular coagulation (DIC) may be seen in sepsis, neurotrauma, malignancy, and several other conditions, and of note, is a possible finding in heat stroke, which is another key differential diagnosis in this case. The finding of bilateral adrenal gland hemorrhage can be due to any cause of DIC. When due to sepsis, the finding may be termed *Waterhouse–Friderichsen syndrome*. Any cause of bilateral adrenal hemorrhage may lead to adrenal dysfunction or crisis with up to 50% mortality when due to sepsis. Thus, the finding at autopsy may be of paramount importance in the determination of the cause of death (also see Tormos LT and Schandl CA. The significance of adrenal hemorrhage: Undiagnosed Waterhouse–Friderichsen syndrome, a case series. *J Forensic Sci* 2013, 58[4]: 1071–4).

A1.31 The correct answer is A. Abscess

- Answer A is correct. A right-sided empyema is featured, indicative of a purulent infection, which most likely resulted from a lung abscess. Other causes include communication with an abscess elsewhere (i.e., paravertebral) and penetrating chest trauma with infection.
- Answer B is incorrect. The photograph demonstrates an empyema, which is exudate (pus) in the pleural cavity, reflective of an infectious process.
- Answer C is incorrect. Serous or serosanguineous pleural effusions might be expected in hepatic cirrhosis when intravascular colloidal pressures are diminished. The photograph demonstrates purulent (exudative) material in the chest cavity.
- Answer D is incorrect. Fluid overload would be expected to result in a serous effusion. The photograph demonstrates purulent material in the pleural cavity, reflective of an infectious process.
- Answer E is incorrect. A chylothorax would be expected to appear milky. The photograph demonstrates purulent material in the pleural cavity, reflective of an infectious process.

A1.32 The correct answer is B. Heart failure

- Answer A is incorrect. A respiratory bronchiolitis such as that caused by cigarette smoking is typically manifest by macrophages containing yellow-tan to brown-black, finely granular pigment.
- Answer B is correct. Numerous hemosiderin-laden macrophages are featured in the photomicrograph, consistent with previous episodes of hemorrhage that might be seen with chronic congestive heart failure. The pigment is brown to golden brown and chunky as compared to that seen in a respiratory bronchiolitis where the granularity is finer and the pigments range from golden-tan to black.
- Answer C is incorrect. There is no evidence of asbestos bodies in the photomicrograph, nor a discernible pneumoconiosis.
- Answer D is incorrect. The featured cells are macrophages with chunky brown pigment, characteristic of hemosiderin.
- Answer E is incorrect. Wilson disease is a metabolic disorder with the resultant accumulation of copper, most prominently in the liver, brain, and eye.

A1.33 The correct answer is A. Atherosclerotic cardiovascular disease

- Answer A is correct. The photograph depicts a xanthelasma, a well-demarcated yellow-orange plaque or nodule composed of aggregates of lipid-laden macrophages. They are often found around the eyelids and may be associated with hyperlipidemia and cardiovascular disease.
- Answer B is incorrect. The photograph demonstrates a xanthelasma, associated with lipid disorders. Pulmonary embolism typically has no outward periorbital manifestation.
- Answer C is incorrect. The photograph demonstrates a xanthelasma, a skin lesion, associated with lipid disorders, whereas pneumonia involves the lungs. Watery eyes (epiphora) may be seen in pneumonia, but the lesion depicted is a xanthelasma.
- Answer D is incorrect. Cutaneous granulomatous vasculitis would tend to be larger and have a gray appearance. Here the yellow-orange skin is typical of xanthelasma.
- Answer E is incorrect. It would be unusual for a person to gain intravenous drug access around the eye. More typical locations include the antecubital fossa.

A1.34 The correct answer is B. Heart weight 700 grams

- Answer A is incorrect. The histopathology shows myofibril disarray, a feature of hypertrophic cardiomyopathy.
- Answer B is correct. The scenario and featured histopathology with myofibril disarray and hypertrophy support a diagnosis of hypertropic cardiomyopathy. Heart weights are greatly increased and often demonstrate asymmetrical septal hypertrophy with thicker interventricular septum than left ventricular free wall. This disorder demonstrates autosomal dominant transmission. Numerous genes have been implicated in familial hypertrophic cardiomyopathy with the most common being *MYH7, MYBPC3, TNNT2* and *TNNI3* (https://ghr.nlm.nih.gov/condition/familial-hypertrophic-cardiomyopathy#genes, accessed June 14, 2017).
- Answer C is incorrect. Mediastinal and pulmonary hilar lymphadenopathy are classically associated with sarcoidosis, which microscopically would demonstrate noncaseating granuloma formation, which is not depicted here.
- Answer D is incorrect. Mitral valve endocarditis would be expected to show some inflammation and even colonization by groups or clusters of bacteria, which is not seen here.
- Answer E is incorrect. A patent foramen ovale is better appreciated grossly.

A1.35 The correct answer is A. Acute chest syndrome

- Answer A is correct. The decedent appeared to have a vaso-occlusive crisis with associated pulmonary fat emboli.
- Answer B is incorrect. The concentration of morphine is not elevated, especially in a patient who likely depended on opioids for chronic pain control.
- Answer C is incorrect. Although only fat staining would confirm the features of intravascular clear spaces are fat and not air, the overall appearance in the context of the disease process and presentation support fat emboli as compared to systemic air emboli.
- Answer D is incorrect. Although a viral pneumonia could precipitate an acute chest crisis, the featured histopathology shows no sign of such.

A1.36 The correct answer is D. Sudden collapse while playing soccer

- Answer A is incorrect. Altered mental status with hemiparesis suggests a stroke, which is not featured in the photograph.
- Answer B is incorrect. Congestive heart failure years after an untreated streptococcal infection suggests rheumatic heart disease, which is not featured in the photograph.
- Answer C is incorrect. Discrepant blood pressure between the upper and lower extremities suggests aortic coarctation, which is not featured in the photograph.
- Answer D is correct. The photograph features an anomalous origin of the right coronary artery, which depending on its course and distribution, may predispose individuals to arrhythmia, in particular during periods of physical stress.
- Answer E is incorrect. Complaints of severe upper back pain in a tall patient with hyperextensible joints suggest Marfan syndrome with aortic dissection, not featured in the photograph.

A1.37 The correct answer is A. Arteriovenous malformation

- Answer A is correct. The lesion featured in the photograph is an arteriovenous malformation that was likely the cause of the decedent's terminal seizure. Brown-orange coloration results from previous hemorrhaging with hemosiderin deposition.
- Answer B is incorrect. Glioblastoma can show necrosis and hemorrhage but typically tracks along white matter.
- Answer C is incorrect. The basal ganglia is not a classic location for ischemic (i.e., watershed) stroke.
- Answer D is incorrect. The single brain lesion (and otherwise negative autopsy) argues against metastatic disease.

A1.38 The correct answer is E. Ruptured esophageal varices

- Answer A is incorrect. Boerhaave syndrome is rupture of the esophageal wall that may be due to forceful vomiting. The defect shown does not appear to be transmural, which is characteristic of Boerhaave syndrome.
- Answer B is incorrect. The photograph does not show gross features of a malignant process.
- Answer C is incorrect. The findings of submucosal venous dilation and a mucosal rupture in conjunction with the history are most consistent with ruptured esophageal varices.
- Answer D is incorrect. A Mallory–Weiss tear is a non-transmural tear that is commonly associated with forceful vomiting. It is typified by a longitudinal tear extending from the distal esophagus to the proximal stomach. Dilated vasculature is not a common feature.
- Answer E is correct. The photograph depicts an inverted (turned inside out), distal esophagus with prominent dilated submucosal veins and a punctate rupture site, consistent with ruptured esophageal varices. These findings are not always this prominent, with veins typically collapsing after death and the gastrointestinal tract undergoing notable autolysis and putrefaction.

A1.39 The correct answer is C. Pseudomembranous colitis

- Answer A is incorrect. Crohn's disease typically has areas of intestinal wall thickening, along with "skip" lesions, deep ulcerations, and pseudopolyps.
- Answer B is incorrect. Ischemic colitis would likely appear as large segments of dusky to hemorrhagic intestinal wall.
- Answer C is correct. The colonic mucosa shows multiple pseudomembranous plaques. The decedent's history of likely receiving antibiotics in the hospital makes him susceptible to the development of *Clostridium difficile* colitis.
- Answer D is incorrect. The decedent's history and the appearance of the pseudomembranous colonic plaques are consistent with pseudomembranous colitis.
- Answer E is incorrect. Ulcerative colitis typically shows diffuse colonic involvement and associated superficial ulcerations and pseudopolyps.

A1.40 The correct answer is C. Noncaseating granulomatous inflammation

- Answer A is incorrect. Diffuse lymphohistiocytic infiltrates would be expected in a viral myocarditis. However, the decedent has no symptoms of a viral myocarditis, and the heart is not described as floppy or grossly dilated, which are typical features in a symptomatic myocarditis. Histopathological analysis will assist with the differential diagnosis.
- Answer B is incorrect. This infiltrate in the photograph is not fat.
- Answer C is correct. This is a classic appearance of sarcoidosis, with patchy pale infiltrates within the myocardium. In cardiac amyloidosis, the heart is typically described as rubbery and globoid, although it is not infrequent that the heart appears grossly normal. Ideally, histopathological analysis with Congo Red special staining is performed to confirm the diagnosis.
- Answer D is incorrect. An eosinophilic myocarditis is unlikely to demonstrate specific gross changes, such as the plaques seen here. However, the acute nature of the inflammation may lead to sudden death. Histopathological evaluation will assist with the differential diagnosis.
- Answer E is incorrect. Some of the pale coloration may reflect scarring, but without significant coronary artery disease, the coloration is more likely an infiltrative process such as sarcoidosis.

A1.41 The correct answer is B. Lipomatous hypertrophy

- Answer A is incorrect. Fat necrosis would be expected to show foci of hemorrhage and induration followed later by a yellow-gray-red coloration.
- Answer B is correct. Interatrial lipomatous hypertrophy is characterized by thickening of the interatrial septum by benign fatty tissue and may be mass-like. It is uncommon and usually an incidental finding, although it may be associated with cardiac arrhythmias and superior vena caval obstruction when severe. The area of the foramen ovale is typically spared.
- Answer C is incorrect. Although the fatty material appears mass-like, it is not encapsulated as would be expected in a lipoma.
- Answer D is incorrect. Although the featured lesion is obviously fatty, it is homogenous and well defined, and thus not characteristic of a sarcoma. Cardiac liposarcomas are extremely rare.
- Answer E is incorrect. The featured lesion is fatty. It is not involving the myocardium and does not appear to be a lymph node involved by sarcoid.

A1.42 The correct answer is E. *Streptococcus pyogenes*

- Answer A is incorrect. Although *Haemophilus* can cause necrotizing fasciitis, it is rare.
- Answer B is incorrect. Although *Neisseria* can cause necrotizing fasciitis, it is rare.
- Answer C is incorrect. *Rhizopus* species cause various diseases collectively known as the mucormycoses. Classically, infection occurs in the immunocompromised host and in those with diabetic ketoacidosis. One scenario is a sinus infection that extends into the brain.
- Answer D is incorrect. Although *S. aureus* can cause a necrotizing fasciitis, it is not common.
- Answer E is correct. The rapidity of the disease progression, the severity of the associated pain, and the appearance of the shoulder, neck, and facial area in the photograph are classic for necrotizing fasciitis. Although multiple different bacteria can cause necrotizing fasciitis, it is most commonly caused by group A streptococci (*S. pyogenes*), which is the etiological agent of "strep throat" and impetigo. Necrotizing fasciitis has also been associated with *Clostridium* in those with colonic disease, and may also be polymicrobial. *Vibrio* sp. are implicated with coincident saltwater exposure.

A1.43 The correct answer is A. Hyperostosis frontalis interna

- Answer A is correct. Hyperostosis frontalis interna is the thickening of the internal aspect of the frontal bone. This process is benign and non-neoplastic. It is an incidental finding most commonly seen in postmenopausal women.
- Answer B is incorrect. The bone thickening seen here is not a neoplastic process. In the provided image, the dura has been stripped from the inside of the skull.
- Answer C is incorrect. The bone thickening seen here is not a neoplastic process.
- Answer D is incorrect. The bone thickening seen here is limited to the inner table and does not affect the outer surface, which would be expected in Paget disease of the bone.
- Answer E is incorrect. Bony callus formation seen with healing bone trauma is typically resorbed.

A1.44 The correct answer is E. Renal cell carcinoma

- Answer A is incorrect. The mass featured in the photograph appears to arise from the kidney and is too large to be a benign adrenal adenoma.
- Answer B is incorrect. The mass featured in the photograph appears to arise from the kidney and does not have the nodular appearance of adrenal hyperplasia.
- Answer C is incorrect. Renal lipomas are very rare; this mass would more likely be a renal angiomyolipoma. However, the location, size, and yellow coloration of this mass are most consistent with a renal cell carcinoma. Histologic sampling would confirm the diagnosis.
- Answer D is incorrect. The mass featured in the photograph appears to arise from the kidney and not the adrenal gland.
- Answer E is correct. The location, size, and yellow coloration of this mass is most consistent with a renal cell carcinoma. Histologic sampling would confirm the diagnosis.

A1.45 The correct answer is B. End-stage renal disease

- Answer A is incorrect. The photograph demonstrates renal tubular thyroidization (also termed *tubular atrophy*), not pulmonary tissue.
- Answer B is correct. The photograph demonstrates renal tubular thyroidization with dilated tubules containing pink casts. Tubular thyroidization does not indicate a specific disease entity but is characteristic of end-stage renal disease regardless of cause.
- Answer C is incorrect. Although the featured tissue appears to resemble thyroid tissue, it is actually kidney (tubular thyroidization). In the photograph, there are no C cells (parafollicular cells) present, which would be expected in normal thyroid tissue.
- Answer D is incorrect. The featured tissue appears to resemble thyroid tissue but is actually kidney. Additionally, there are none of the inflammatory processes present that typify Hashimoto thyroiditis.
- Answer E is incorrect. An ovarian teratoma may contain cells from all three germ layers, and rarely thyroid tissue comprises the majority of the mass (struma ovarii). However, the photograph features renal tubular thyroidization (tubular atrophy).

A1.46 The correct answer is A. Accident

- Answer A is correct. The case describes significant traumatic intracranial head injury, which is the likely cause of death. Since the trauma occurred as a result of a fall, the manner is most likely accident.
- Answer B is incorrect. Although without appropriate investigation, homicide cannot be entirely excluded, it is not the most likely manner.
- Answer C is incorrect. Although the decedent had significant natural disease, which may have made him more likely to bleed (i.e., hepatic cirrhosis), the bleed was directly due to trauma. Thus, natural is not the best answer. The pattern depicted correlates with trauma from falling as the antecedent event. An isolated intracerebral hemorrhage with none of the other findings may suggest this was a hemorrhagic stroke due to the underlying hypertension.
- Answer D is incorrect. The scene description is compatible with a fall down stairs. Since an intentional fall is unlikely, a suicide manner is not the best answer.
- Answer E is incorrect. If there was an unresolvable question regarding whether the decedent fell down the stairs or was pushed by someone, an undetermined manner may be correct. In this case, however, there is no evidence for homicide; thus, undetermined is not the best answer.

A1.47 The correct answer is C. Hypertension

- Answer A is incorrect. Blunt trauma would result in cortical contusions, subarachnoid hemorrhage, or subdural blood. The blood mass in the photograph is not a subdural hematoma as it can be seen exuding from the intracerebral parenchyma along the Stryker saw line. No contusions are discernible.
- Answer B is incorrect. A congenital anomaly such as a berry aneurysm would lead to extensive basilar subarachnoid hemorrhage upon rupture.
- Answer C is correct. The hemorrhage most likely resulted from a hypertensive stroke (also known as cerebrovascular accident); this may be surmised from the intracerebral location (hematoma is exuding from the cerebral parenchyma at the site of the Stryker saw line).
- Answer D is incorrect. There is no evidence of bacterial meningitis as the meninges appear thin and translucent. Although an infectious vasculitis could possibly cause cerebral hemorrhages, the size of the hemorrhage (hematoma) coupled with its location and clinical presentation support a hypertensive hemorrhage.
- Answer E is incorrect. Cerebral strokes may be precipitated by sympathomimetic drugs but are not typically associated with opioids.

A1.48 The correct answer is E. Pulmonary hypertension

- Answer A is incorrect. Arrhythmogenic right ventricular dysplasia would show thinning of the right ventricular muscular wall with fibrofatty infiltration.
- Answer B is incorrect. Cardiac amyloidosis may or may not be apparent grossly, with gray waxy-like deposits.
- Answer C is incorrect. The left ventricular myocardium and interventricular septum appear normal.
- Answer D is incorrect. The left ventricular myocardium and interventricular septum appear normal.
- Answer E is correct. Pulmonary hypertension is suggested by the markedly dilated right ventricle, consistent with cor pulmonale. The underlying cause of the pulmonary hypertension may be idiopathic or due to a number of etiologies such as acute or chronic pulmonary thromboemboli, interstitial lung disease, and sarcoidosis.

A1.49 The correct answer is E. Respiratory bronchiolitis

- Answer A is incorrect. Aspiration pneumonia is often typified by a necrotizing pneumonia and associated lipid-laden macrophages. Aspirated oral contents/food particulates may be discernible.
- Answer B is incorrect. There is no sign of an acute neutrophilic inflammatory response, which would be expected in bacterial bronchopneumonia.
- Answer C is incorrect. Heart failure cells are alveolar macrophages containing dark golden brown hemosiderin pigment.
- Answer D is incorrect. There is no evidence of intravascular foreign material (acute use) or foreign body giant cells/granulomas (chronic use) which would be expected with illicit intravenous drug administration.
- Answer E is correct. The photograph shows a classic example of respiratory bronchiolitis as evidenced by abundant macrophage aggregates within the respiratory bronchioles. The macrophages are pigmented, containing dusty tan-brown pigment and black carbon particulates.

A1.50 The correct answer is B. Hashimoto thyroiditis

- Answer A is incorrect. Goiter is a descriptive term indicating an enlarged thyroid, regardless of the underlying etiology.
- Answer B is correct. The finding of lymphoid follicles with germinal centers is characteristic of Hashimoto thyroiditis. At low power, it may be difficult to appreciate Hürthle cells. These findings may indicate functional thyroid disorder.
- Answer C is incorrect. There is no evidence of an acute bacterial or fungal infection or viral agent (i.e., subacute granulomatous thyroiditis).
- Answer D is incorrect. There is no sign of papillary thyroid carcinoma.
- Answer E is incorrect. The pictured "inflammatory" nodule is a lymphoid follicle with a germinal center, not a granuloma.

A1.51 The correct answer is D. Laryngotracheitis

- Answer A is incorrect. Amyloidosis may affect the epiglottis and associated structures, but this is rare and the decedent's history suggests a more acute process.
- Answer B is incorrect. Although extensive edema enlarges the laryngeal structures, there was no history of allergy or possible exposure. In cases of anaphylaxis, degranulating mast cells would be expected on histologic sectioning.
- Answer C is incorrect. There is no food in the laryngopharynx to support airway obstruction by food.
- Answer D is correct. The photograph demonstrates bilateral enlarged supraglottic vestibular folds (false vocal cord) that likely resulted in anatomic laryngeal obstruction and death. Microscopically, massive edema and a mixed inflammatory infiltrate were present, consistent with laryngotracheitis. Laryngotracheitis is often associated with an acute viral illness.
- Answer E is incorrect. Laryngeal papillomatosis is associated with human papilloma virus infection and may cause airway obstruction, but gross pathology would demonstrate warty growth.

A1.52 The correct answer is E. Glucose

- Answer A is incorrect. The histopathology demonstrates nodular glomerulosclerosis (i.e., Kimmelstiel–Wilson disease), which is associated with diabetes mellitus, not streptococcal infection, which may demonstrate a proliferative glomerulonephritis.
- Answer B is incorrect. Antinuclear antibodies may indicate an autoimmune disease such as systemic lupus erythematosus, which may demonstrate normal histology, mesangial proliferation, diffuse or segmental proliferative nephritis, and/or membranous glomerulonephritis. Immune complex deposition may be key to the diagnosis.
- Answer C is incorrect. Ethylene glycol toxicity is typified by acute tubular injury, and calcium oxalate crystals may be present (best viewed under polarized light).
- Answer D is incorrect. Fibrinogen may be deposited in areas of the glomerulus affected by crescent formation in proliferative glomerulonephritides.
- Answer E is correct. Vitreous (not blood) glucose should be measured to document hyperglycemia. If elevated, ketones (e.g. beta hydroxybutyrate) should be quantitated to assess for diabetic ketoacidosis.

A1.53 The correct answer is D. Pheochromocytoma

- Answer A is incorrect. The cells of an adrenal adenoma have the appearance of normal adrenal cortical fasciculata cells.
- Answer B is incorrect. The cells of an adrenal carcinoma typically have the appearance of relatively normal adrenal cortical cells; in addition, hypertension is not likely a side effect.
- Answer C is incorrect. The cells in adrenal hyperplasia have the appearance of normal adrenal cortical cells.
- Answer D is correct. This vascularized mass is an adrenal medullary pheochromocytoma composed of neuroendocrine cells, some of which are large and bizarre appearing. Most pheochromocytomas are benign. These tumors may cause episodic hypertension or hypertensive crises, which can be cured upon removal of the tumor and are secondary to catecholamine excess.
- Answer E is incorrect. The adrenal glands would be hemorrhagic and possibly necrotic in Waterhouse–Friderichsen syndrome.

A1.54 The correct answer is A. Contraction bands

- Answer A is correct. The photograph demonstrates contraction bands or contraction band necrosis (also termed *cardiac myocytolysis*), typified by the deeply eosinophilic wavy bands, traversing the myocytes.
- Answer B is incorrect. Intercalated discs are normal structures that are thinner than contraction bands and connect individual myocytes.
- Answer C is incorrect. There are no inflammatory infiltrates present to indicate an infectious myocarditis.
- Answer D is incorrect. Bands resembling antemortem contraction bands can be seen on mechanically damaged tissues (e.g., at the tissue edges from knife blade crushing, in blunt trauma to the heart, and with thermal damage). In this case, the scenario and the number and location of the bands in the photograph support true antemortem contraction band formation.
- Answer E is incorrect. Occasionally, few small foci of contraction bands can be seen after substantial cardiopulmonary resuscitation efforts, but not to the extent featured here.

A1.55 The correct answer is B. Pulmonary carcinoid tumorlet

- Answer A is incorrect. The small proliferation in the photograph demonstrates cells of neuroendocrine origin and is consistent with a carcinoid tumorlet.
- Answer B is correct. This proliferation of neuroendocrine cells is an incidental pulmonary carcinoid tumorlet, often seen in the setting of chronic lung disease. Carcinoid tumorlets are composed of nests of oval to spindle cells with "salt and pepper" chromatin and are present near bronchioles. Their overall size by definition is less than 0.5 cm. Multiple minute meningothelial-like nodules (MLNs) are also in the differential; these are seen within the interstitium near blood vessels and are composed of oval cells with homogenous chromatin.
- Answer C is incorrect. The small proliferation in the photograph demonstrates cells of neuroendocrine origin and is consistent with a pulmonary carcinoid tumorlet. Cellular and nuclear atypia not appreciated in the provided image but might be expected in metastatic cancer.
- Answer D is incorrect. The proliferations in the photograph are not granulomas, which would demonstrate peripheral giant cells.
- Answer E is incorrect. The cellular proliferations in the photograph show no squamous differentiation.

A1.56 The correct answer is A. Acute metabolic disorder

- Answer A is correct. The photograph demonstrates astrocytes with swollen, vesicular nuclei indicative of Alzheimer type II astrocytes. These cells are generally identified in association with an acute metabolic disorder such as hepatic encephalopathy.
- Answer B is incorrect. Degenerative brain diseases such as Alzheimer may show changes to the neurons such as tangles or plaques, which are not seen here.
- Answer C is incorrect. Alzheimer type II astrocytes are indicative of a pathological process and are not expected in a normal brain.
- Answer D is incorrect. No cellular inclusions typical of viral disease are apparent in the provided photograph.

A1.57 The correct answer is D. Congenital bicuspid aortic valve

- Answer A is incorrect. Some atherosclerotic plaques are noted on the internal aspect of the aortic valvular cusps, but this is not the underlying cause of death.
- Answer B is incorrect. No valvular vegetations are present.
- Answer C is incorrect. The photograph demonstrates a congenital bicuspid aortic valve and an aortic dissection that is visible at the root. In light of the clinical history and the autopsy findings depicted, it is likely a cardiac tamponade developed; however, cardiac tamponade would be the immediate cause of death (versus the underlying cause of death).
- Answer D is correct. The photograph demonstrates a congenital bicuspid aortic valve. This valvular anomaly increases the risk of aortic dissection (also seen in the photograph originating at the aortic root) and is the underlying cause of death in this case. Other risk factors for aortic dissection include hypertension and sympathomimetic drugs.
- Answer E is incorrect. The coronary arteries are not visible in the photograph.

A1.58 The correct answer is D. Multiple sclerosis

- Answer A is incorrect. An astrocytoma is a neoplasm of the astrocytes of the brain and would be expected to form a mass lesion or tumor; no tumor is present in the photograph.
- Answer B is incorrect. Ex vacuo hydrocephalus is characterized by enlargement of the ventricles of the brain. The lateral ventricles in this case appear to be of normal caliber.
- Answer C is incorrect. The leukodystrophies are abnormalities of the central nervous system that result in demyelination and are usually inherited. They are frequently characterized based upon the etiology (e.g., lysosomal such as Krabbe disease or peroxisomal such as adrenoleukodystrophy). Other examples include Canavan disease, Alexander disease, and vanishing white matter disease. The disease presents differently depending on which white matter tracts are affected and which are preserved. These diseases do not classically involve the periventricular white matter as is shown in the photograph.
- Answer D is correct. The photograph shows brown-pink discoloration of the white matter directly adjacent to the lateral ventricles, thus in a periventricular distribution. This distribution of grossly apparent demyelination is classic for multiple sclerosis and may be seen in neuromyelitis optica and termed *periventricular leukomalacia*. Periventricular leukomalacia may also be seen in preterm neonates; this form is thought to be due to ischemia or circulating metabolic toxins.
- Answer E is incorrect. The gross neuroanatomical finding associated with the neurodegenerative disease, Parkinson disease, is a loss of pigment notable grossly in the substantia nigra of the midbrain and corresponding to a loss of these pigmented neurons microscopically. Locus ceruleus neuronal cell death in the pons is also a feature. The midbrain and brainstem are not shown in the provided photograph.

A1.59 The correct answer is C. Meningioma

- Answer A is incorrect. Craniopharyngioma usually arises from the suprasellar region. The adamantinomatous type is a childhood benign tumor and thought to be a Rathke pouch derivative. The papillary type is more common in adults. The tumor pictured is adjacent to but does not arise from the sella turcica.
- Answer B is incorrect. Hyperostosis frontalis interna is a thickening of the frontal bone seen at the internal surface. The lesion shown is in a different location. Note that meningioma of the skull base may demonstrate hyperostosis, which has been shown to represent bony invasion by the tumor (Pieper DR, Al-Mefty O, Hanada Y, and Buechner D. Hyperostosis associated with meningioma of the cranial base: Secondary changes or tumor invasion. *Neurosurgery* 1999, 44[4]: 742–6).
- Answer C is correct. The lesion pictured is a meningioma of the cranial base. These tumors arise from the dura or choroid and are frequently benign and indolent, but may invade the bone and lead to significant space-occupying effects. Histopathological evaluation of the mass may better define its significance in each case; most are incidental at the time of autopsy.
- Answer D is incorrect. Paget disease results in focal thickening of the bone from accelerated remodeling with rare malignant transformation. Long bones and skull bones are commonly affected, but mass formation is not typical.
- Answer E is incorrect. A pituitary adenoma is a benign tumor of the pituitary that is generally localized to the sella turcica, unlike the lesion in the photograph. Functional adenomas present as hormone-excess syndromes depending on the cell type involved (e.g., corticotroph, thyrotroph, lactotroph, etc.). Morbidity may also be due to space-occupying effects.

A1.60 The correct answer is C. Human papilloma virus

- Answer A is incorrect. *Chlamydia trachomatis* infection commonly presents with vaginal or penile discharge rather than warts.
- Answer B is incorrect. Herpes simplex virus type 2 may be evidenced by skin blisters or vesicles in various states of resolution generally in the anogenital or oral region.
- Answer C is correct. Human papilloma virus (HPV) is transmitted via skin contact generally in the context of sexual activity and may result in genital warts such as those pictured. More seriously, high-risk subtype HPV infection (e.g., 16 and 18) is the cause of most cervical carcinoma and may lead to multiple other site malignancy including oropharyngeal, penile, rectal, vaginal, and vulvar. A vaccine is available for low-risk types that commonly cause warts (6 and 11) and the high-risk types most frequently implicated in cancer (16 and 18).
- Answer D is incorrect. Gonorrhea is a sexually transmitted infection (STI) caused by the *Neisseria gonorrhoeae* bacterium. Presentation includes vaginal or penile discharge.
- Answer E is incorrect. Physical examination of a patient with syphilis may reveal genital or anal ulceration or possibly a rash involving the palms and soles, but not warts. *Treponema pallidum* is the spirochete bacterium that causes syphilis, which is most commonly transmitted during sexual activity and may complicate pregnancy.

A1.61 The correct answer is A. Nephrolithiasis

- Answer A is correct. The photograph depicts a kidney with significant calyceal dilation and with solid tan material within the calyces. The material appears compatible with kidney stones (nephrolithiasis).
- Answer B is incorrect. Nephrosclerosis is a description of a kidney with chronic changes and is generally associated with hypertension. Grossly, one may see granularity of the renal cortex with pitting or scarring, which is not highlighted in the photograph.
- Answer C is incorrect. Polycystic kidney disease (PKD) is a genetic disorder in which both kidneys demonstrate numerous cysts. The autosomal dominant form is the most common and is due to an abnormality of the PKD1 (chromosome 16) or PKD2 (chromosome 4) genes. PKHD1 on chromosome 6 is the gene implicated in the autosomal recessive form of the disease. Cystic disease is not shown in the photograph. Of note, nephrolithiasis is common in PKD (also see Igarashi P, Somlo S, and Feature Editor. Genetics and pathogenesis of polycystic kidney disease. *J Am Soc Nephrol* 2002, 13[9]: 2384–98; or Wilson PD. Molecular mechanisms of polycystic kidney disease. *Biochim Biophys Acta* 2011, 1812[10]: 1201 for review).
- Answer D is incorrect. One may see gross pus or tan discoloration of the renal parenchyma in cases of pyelonephritis. Neither are present in the photograph.
- Answer E is incorrect. The kidneys may appear "flea-bitten," pale, and enlarged grossly in cases of systemic lupus erythematosus due to glomerulonephritis.

A1.62 The correct answer is E. Uncal herniation

- Answer A is incorrect. Although diffuse cerebral edema is present, there is no clouding of the meninges, which might suggest an exudative inflammatory process typically associated with bacterial infection.
- Answer B is incorrect. Hydrocephalus occurs when there is an increased amount of cerebrospinal fluid in the central nervous system. This process can result in enlarged ventricles, depending on the underlying etiology of the hydrocephalus. In this brain, only the aqueduct is visible, and it does not appear enlarged.
- Answer C is incorrect. Although cerebral edema may be present in cases of hydrogen sulfide toxicity, this brain is lacking a green coloration that would raise the possibility of exposure to hydrogen sulfide.
- Answer D is incorrect. There is no evidence of a tumor growth.
- Answer E is correct. Diffuse cerebral edema is present, as evidenced by flattening of the gyri. Additionally, the medial portions of the temporal lobes appear enlarged and notched, consistent with transtentorial/uncal herniation.

A1.63 The correct answer is D. Mitral valve prolapse

- Answer A is incorrect. This mitral valve does not appear stenotic and most likely has a component of regurgitation.
- Answer B is incorrect. Vegetations are not present in the photograph, although the valvular leaflet edges are not visible.
- Answer C is incorrect. The defect featured in the photograph is mitral valve prolapse, which has no association with hypertrophic cardiomyopathy.
- Answer D is correct. This is an extreme example of mitral valve prolapse demonstrating profound ballooning of the valvular leaflets. Mitral valve prolapse is most commonly a benign, incidental finding. However, in the absence of other organ pathology and coupled with the presentation (sudden collapse) and the severity of prolapse, it is most likely this decedent's cause of death.
- Answer E is incorrect. This mitral valve does not appear stenotic, the most likely complication affecting the mitral valve in rheumatic heart disease.

A1.64 The correct answer is D. Hypertensive stroke

- Answer A is incorrect. Arteriovenous malformations may be located in the brainstem and may rupture; however, they are composed of a tangle of arterial and venous vessels, which are not evident in the photograph. Histological sampling would confirm the composition of this hemorrhage.
- Answer B is incorrect. Acute carbon monoxide (CO) exposure typically shows no gross cerebrovascular manifestations, although chronic CO exposure may culminate in basal ganglia necrosis.
- Answer C is incorrect. Duret hemorrhages are midline hemorrhages in the brainstem resulting from stretching or kinking of the penetrating arteries caused by uncal herniation.
- Answer D is correct. The pons and midbrain are effaced by a massive acute hemorrhage, consistent with a hypertensive stroke. The pons is one of the three most common areas affected by hypertensive hemorrhages, the other two being the basal ganglia and the cerebellum.
- Answer E is incorrect. Although vasculitides may be prone to bleed, this massive hemorrhage effacing the pontine structures is classic for a hypertensive hemorrhage.

A1.65 The correct answer is B. Fibromuscular dysplasia (of the AV nodal artery)

- Answer A is incorrect. The atrioventricular (AV) nodal artery wall thickening is not due to atherosclerotic deposits.
- Answer B is correct. The AV nodal artery shows thickening, most prominently in the media, with marked narrowing of the lumen. The underlying pathophysiology is not known.
- Answer C is incorrect. The decedent had no history of hypertension.
- Answer D is incorrect. There is no evidence of inflammation of the AV nodal artery.
- Answer E is incorrect. Long QT syndrome is a conduction abnormality with no specific histological findings.

A1.66 The correct answer is A. Melena

- Answer A is correct. The featured pathology is a duodenal ulcer. Bleeding from such an ulcer in the upper gastrointestinal tract would have resulted in melena (black tarry stool).
- Answer B is incorrect. Duodenal ulcers do not stimulate consumption of non-nutritive materials.
- Answer C is incorrect. Polyuria and polydipsia are typical of type I diabetes mellitus, not duodenal ulcers.
- Answer D is incorrect. Although pain may be referred, most duodenal ulcers cause pain in the epigastric area. Referred right shoulder pain can be associated with cholecystitis.
- Answer E is incorrect. Pancreatic insufficiency may result in voluminous steatotic stools, but this is not typical of duodenal ulcers.

Chapter 2

MEDICOLEGAL INVESTIGATION OF DEATHS

QUESTIONS

Q2.1 Who is the elected official that has legal authority to order an autopsy?

A. Attending physician
B. Coroner
C. Crime scene investigator
D. Medical examiner
E. State's attorney

Q2.2 In Texas, who is the elected official that has jurisdiction over a death investigation?

A. Coroner
B. Crime scene investigator
C. Justice of the peace
D. Medical examiner
E. Sheriff–coroner

Q2.3 A 3-year-old male presents to the emergency room after coming home with a cold from daycare. He has blue purple petechiae covering his body and a fever of 104.5 F. Subsequent cerebrospinal fluid examination reveals gram-negative cocci. He dies 2 days after admission due to sepsis and meningitis. The attending physician is informed he may not sign the death certificate in this case as this has been deemed a medical examiner case for the following reason:

A. Congenital defect
B. Contagious disease
C. Death in a hospital
D. Suspected physical abuse
E. Suspected neglect

Q2.4 A 42-year-old woman is found deceased in bed after complaints of abdominal pain. Autopsy shows an acute peritonitis and a perforating ulcer at a gastrojejunal anastomosis of a remote Roux-en-Y gastric bypass surgical procedure that was performed for treatment of obesity 10 years earlier. What is the manner of death?

A. Accident
B. Homicide
C. Natural
D. Suicide
E. Undetermined

Q2.5 What is the traditional classification of manner of death in Russian roulette?

A. Accident
B. Homicide
C. Natural
D. Suicide
E. Undetermined

Q2.6 A man fires a gun while hunting deer and strikes and kills a fellow hunter. What is the traditional classification of manner of death?

A. Accident
B. Homicide
C. Natural
D. Suicide
E. Undetermined

Q2.7 A 45-year-old paraplegic man is found dead in bed with extensive stage 4 decubitus ulcers. Postmortem blood cultures are positive for *Escherichia coli*. Caretakers report that the decedent had been despondent and refused assistance from home health-care nurses. How should the manner of death be classified?

A. Accident
B. Homicide
C. Suicide
D. Natural
E. Undetermined

Q2.8 A 72-year-old active woman sustained a hip fracture and was admitted to a hospital, then later discharged to a rehabilitation facility. Medical history included psoriasis for which she was prescribed methotrexate three times each week. Approximately 2 weeks later, the woman developed bone marrow failure with resultant fatal infection, and it was determined the facility staff were administering her methotrexate three times each day. How should the manner of death be classified?

A. Accident
B. Homicide
C. Natural
D. Suicide
E. Undetermined

Q2.9 A commercial bus driver's body is recovered following a collision. Passengers described that the driver appeared to slump over prior to the collision in which the bus left the road and struck a tree. At autopsy, complete transection of the aorta at the level of the ligamentum arteriosum was noted as was 2 L of blood in the pleural spaces. Basilar subarachnoid hemorrhage was present and found to be associated with a cerebral aneurysmal rupture. What is the manner of death?

A. Accident
B. Homicide
C. Natural
D. Suicide
E. Undetermined

Q2.10 A 22-year-old woman is found disarticulated and burned inside a barrel 2 days after she was last seen. At that time she had been arguing with her boyfriend. Autopsy shows extensively charred human remains, with only portions of major internal organs present. Soot is not definitively identified in the remaining airways. Toxicological analysis of remaining liver tissue demonstrates delta-9-tetrahydrocannabinol (THC) at 0.05 mg/kg and oxycodone at 0.1 mg/kg. What is the best characterization of the cause of death?

A. Carbon monoxide toxicity
B. Drug overdose
C. Homicidal violence
D. Thermal injury
E. Undetermined

Q2.11 Where was the first medical examiner system in the United States established?

A. Maine
B. Massachusetts
C. Montana
D. New Hampshire
E. New York

Q2.12 Who was the king that established the office of coroner in England?

A. George III
B. George VI
C. Henry II
D. Louis XIV
E. Richard I

Q2.13 What is cruentation?

A. Opposition to cruel and unusual punishment
B. Careful removal of a body from the ground
C. Belief that a corpse will bleed in the presence of the murderer
D. Study of bones
E. Destruction of a body by heat

Q2.14 What is the most common form of medicolegal death investigation system in the United States?

A. Coroner
B. Justice of the peace
C. Medical examiner
D. Sheriff–coroner

Q2.15 What is the death investigation system in the United States that serves the majority of the population?

A. Coroner
B. Justice of the peace
C. Medical examiner
D. Sheriff–coroner

Q2.16 What is the most common method of legal execution in the United States?

A. Electrocution
B. Firing squad
C. Lethal injection
D. Gas chamber
E. Hanging

Q2.17 What two U.S. states permit execution by firing squad as a form of capital punishment?

A. California and Ohio
B. Delaware and Vermont
C. Nebraska and Louisiana
D. Oklahoma and Utah
E. Tennessee and Texas

Q2.18 What is the legal term that is translated as "the thing speaks for itself?"

A. *Ignorantia juris non excusat*
B. *Res ipsa loquitur*
C. *Respondeat superior*
D. *Rex non potest peccare*
E. *Subpoena duces tecum*

Q2.19 A 30-year-old female is crossing the street and is struck by an automobile. She dies en route to the hospital. The driver flees the scene and turns himself in the next day. He claims that he thought he had killed a deer and did not realize somebody had died until he saw the evening news. The district attorney files negligent homicide charges against the driver. What is the manner of death?

A. Accident
B. Homicide
C. Natural
D. Suicide
E. Undetermined

Q2.20 A husband and wife have a verbal altercation at a local supermarket. The husband slaps the wife, and she exits the store in a rage. Multiple witnesses indicate they heard the lady say, "I'll get you back!" After checkout, the husband exits the store and is struck by the wife's car. Scene investigation reveals no skid marks on the pavement. The cause of death is determined to be blunt force injuries sustained in an automobile–pedestrian collision. What is the manner of death?

A. Accident
B. Homicide
C. Natural
D. Suicide
E. Undetermined

Q2.21 An elderly couple is watching television when a home invasion occurs. The intruders make the couple open their safe that contains diamonds and $20,000 in cash. During the robbery, the elderly man grabs his chest and collapses. The invaders leave and emergency medical services (EMS) is called. The man is pronounced dead and an autopsy is performed, revealing a 600 gram heart and 90% narrowing of the cardiac arteries by atherosclerotic plaque. Toxicology is negative for drugs of abuse and ethanol. What is the manner of death?

A. Accident
B. Homicide
C. Natural
D. Suicide
E. Undetermined

Q2.22 A 55-year-old man with no previously known medical history collapses, and at autopsy the finding depicted in the photograph below is noted. Based on the evidence in the photograph, what is the manner of death?

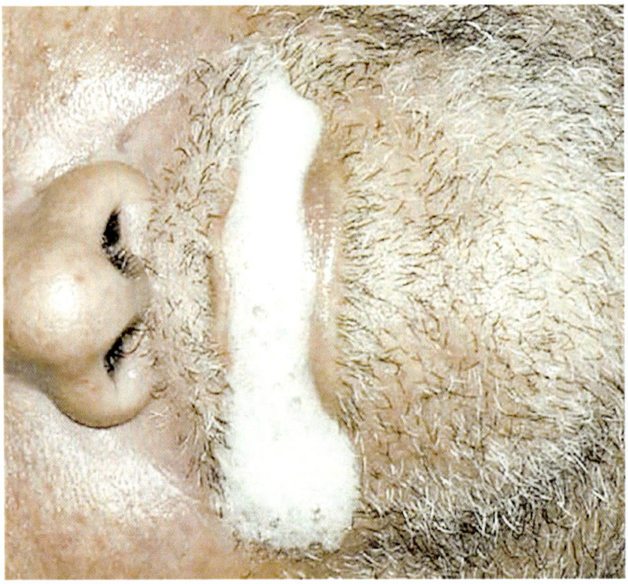

Figure 2.1

A. Accident
B. Homicide
C. Natural
D. Suicide
E. Undetermined

Q2.23 What is the most common manner of death of prison inmates?

A. Accident
B. Homicide
C. Natural
D. Suicide
E. Undetermined

Q2.24 What is the second most common manner of death of prison inmates?

A. Accident
B. Homicide
C. Natural
D. Suicide
E. Undetermined

Q2.25 What is the most common cause of death associated with suicide in prison?

A. Defenestration
B. Drug overdose
C. Gunshot wound
D. Hanging
E. Slitting of wrist with sharp object

Q2.26 What drug is most commonly associated with excited delirium?

A. Amphetamine
B. Cocaine
C. Lysergic acid diethylamide
D. Methamphetamine
E. Phencyclidine

Q2.27 What is the mechanism of excited delirium?

A. Catecholamine toxicity
B. Central nervous system dysfunction
C. Hypokalemia
D. Unknown
E. Ventricular arrhythmia

Q2.28 A person is pulled over in a traffic stop. He swallows an unknown substance and dies about one hour later. Toxicology is positive for cocaine, benzoylecgonine, and ester methyl ecgonine detected in femoral and heart blood. The substance recovered from the stomach is tested and is positive for cocaine. Further investigation reveals the decedent was a known drug dealer. What is the manner of death based on the available information?

A. Accident
B. Homicide
C. Natural
D. Suicide
E. Undetermined

Q2.29 Police respond to a woman wielding a shotgun stating that she does not want to live. Police try to speak with her, and she then points the shotgun at one of the officers who then draws his weapon and shoots, killing the woman. What is the manner of death?

A. Accident
B. Homicide
C. Natural
D. Suicide
E. Undetermined

Q2.30 What type of force employed by law enforcement personnel is the least effective in bringing a person under physical control?

A. Baton
B. Chemical spray
C. Choke hold
D. Complete electromuscular disruption
E. Police dog (K-9)

Q2.31 Which of the following chemical agents when used by law enforcement has not been associated with death?

A. Carfentanil
B. Chloroacetophenone
C. 2-Chlorobenzylidene malononitrile
D. Oleoresin capsicum
E. Sarin

Q2.32 A 32-year-old obese man resists arrest and is subsequently restrained on the ground by five police officers. Within minutes, he becomes unresponsive and cannot be resuscitated. Autopsy shows abundant scleral and conjunctival hemorrhages and mild cardiomegaly. What is the best classification of the manner of death?

A. Accident
B. Homicide
C. Natural
D. Suicide
E. Undetermined

ANSWERS: CHAPTER 2

A2.1 The correct answer is B. Coroner

- Answer A is incorrect. An attending physician may order an autopsy with the permission of the next of kin, but he or she is not an elected official. Most states require the attending physician to certify the natural death of a patient under his or her care, but an autopsy is not required to do so.
- Answer B is correct. Coroners are elected officials who have jurisdiction in medicolegal death investigations.
- Answer C is incorrect. Crime scene investigators may investigate situations that require an autopsy, but they are not elected and they do not have the authority to order an autopsy.
- Answer D is incorrect. Medical examiners have legal authority to order autopsies, but they are appointed to their respective positions and not elected.
- Answer E is incorrect. The state's attorney may be elected, but his or her primary focus is to determine if a crime has been committed.

A2.2 The correct answer is C. Justice of the peace

- Answer A is incorrect. Coroners are elected officials who have authority over death investigations but are not seen in Texas.
- Answer B is incorrect. Crime scene investigators may investigate situations that have medicolegal implications but do not have jurisdiction.
- Answer C is correct. A justice of the peace is an elected official in Texas who has authority over determining cause and manner of death as well as presiding over criminal and civil court cases. He or she also performs marriage ceremonies and issues marriage licenses.
- Answer D is incorrect. Medical examiners are not elected officials as they are appointed. In Texas, large metropolitan areas such as Houston, Austin, and Dallas utilize medical examiners.
- Answer E is incorrect. Sheriff–coroners represent a special type of situation in California where some counties elect a sheriff who also serves as the coroner.

A2.3 The correct answer is B. Contagious disease

- Answer A is incorrect. It is less likely that a congenital disease process would manifest at 3 years of age. A rare form of complement deficiency, specifically C5–C9, may be present that would make one more susceptible to *Neisseria* infections, but the death is still related to bacterial meningitis. Even if the deficiency were present, the contagious disease aspect should not be ignored.
- Answer B is correct. The child has symptoms for bacterial meningitis probably due to *Neisseria meningitides*, a gram-negative diplococcus. Since he probably was exposed at daycare, this should raise concern from an epidemiologic perspective. Most state statutes allow the medical examiner to have jurisdiction over a natural death if it is suspected to come from a contagious disease in order to identify the source and aid in faster, more directed treatment of close contacts.
- Answer C is incorrect. Death in a hospital is not necessarily a qualifier for medical examiner involvement. Many hospitals have policies that require an autopsy be done if the death occurred within 24 hours of admission, but that is a matter of individual hospital policy. If the death surrounded suspicious or violent circumstances, such as death from a gunshot wound, regardless of the time frame, the case would fall under medical examiner jurisdiction.
- Answer D is incorrect. Death from bacterial meningitis is not considered child abuse. Failure to seek timely treatment could be considered abuse or neglect, but there is no reason to suspect this in the given scenario.
- Answer E is incorrect. Death from bacterial meningitis is not considered child neglect.

A2.4 The correct answer is C. Natural

- Answer A is incorrect. Since there is no apparent direct relationship with the remote surgery and the ulceration, the manner of death would not be considered accident. If a perforation occurred at the time of surgery, accident may be considered.
- Answer B is incorrect. Homicide is considered if one person's actions or inactions lead to the death of another person. There is no such relationship in this case.
- Answer C is correct. This individual suffered complications of an ulceration, which is considered a natural manner of death.
- Answer D is incorrect. Suicide is considered when death is the result of a purposeful activity by the individual with apparent intent and reasonable expectation to self-harm. This is not the case in this example.
- Answer E is incorrect. If none of the other named manners of death can be chosen or if two manners are equally possible, a manner of undetermined may be used. This is not the case here.

A2.5 The correct answer is D. Suicide

- Answer A is incorrect. Since the individual purposefully performs the act of firing the weapon at himself or herself, most do not consider the manner accident.
- Answer B is incorrect. Homicide implies death through the actions or inactions of another person. In Russian roulette, the victim knowingly shoots himself or herself.
- Answer C is incorrect. Since death is secondary to a gunshot wound, it would not indicate a natural manner.
- Answer D is correct. Russian roulette is a game whereby the participants partially load a revolver, usually with a single round, spin the chamber so that the live round may be in any position, and then pull the trigger while aiming the weapon at themselves. The weapon is generally aimed at the head, and death is a likely result if the live round is activated. Thus, the individual pulling the trigger is thought to understand the potential consequences of his or her actions, and the manner is thus classified as suicide.
- Answer E is incorrect. In the case of appropriate investigation and scene findings, a manner of death of suicide can be assigned. However, if conflicting information or scene findings are present, a manner of undetermined might be more appropriate.

A2.6 The correct answer is B. Homicide

- Answer A is incorrect. Although the individual firing the weapon may have intended to hit a different target, he or she fired the weapon with volition. Thus, accident is not the best answer.
- Answer B is correct. In this case, one individual died due to the actions (firearm discharge) of another individual. In most jurisdictions, this would be classified as homicide regardless of intent.
- Answer C is incorrect. Since death is due to a gunshot wound, natural is not an appropriate manner.
- Answer D is incorrect. The scenario described is not indicative of the victim intentionally placing himself or herself in the line of fire. Thus, suicide is unlikely.
- Answer E is incorrect. Although the best answer is homicide, if the scene investigation or witness accounts do not lead to a clear interpretation of the events, undetermined may be an appropriate manner of death classification.

A2.7 The correct answer is E. Undetermined

- Answer A is incorrect. The event causing the decedent's paraplegia was not described; therefore, manner of death cannot be determined. For example, if the paraplegia was due to a gunshot received while the decedent was the victim of a robbery, the manner would be homicide. If the paraplegia was secondary to trauma sustained in a motor vehicle collision, the manner would be accident. If paraplegia was sustained when the decedent tried to take his own life, the manner would be suicide. Since there are two or more competing manners of death as the cause of the paraplegia is unknown, the manner is best classified as undetermined.
- Answer B is incorrect. The event causing the decedent's paraplegia was not described; therefore, manner of death cannot be determined.
- Answer C is incorrect. The event causing the decedent's paraplegia was not described; therefore, manner of death cannot be determined.
- Answer D is incorrect. The event causing the decedent's paraplegia was not described; therefore, manner of death cannot be determined. Although sepsis from decubitus ulcers might appear as a natural cause of death, the cause of the underlying condition (paraplegia) that made him bedbound and at risk for the ulcers is unknown, so the manner is undetermined.
- Answer E is correct. The manner of death assignment in cases where an adult who may be dependent on other individuals for care dies from a treatable complication due to neglect is complex. In this scenario, a paraplegic man died from extensive decubitus ulcers complicating his paraplegia. It appears as though the decedent was mentally engaged during life and actively refused care. However, his reported despondency raises the possibility of suicidal intent. Ultimately, it is important not to forget to uncover the incident that initiated the sequence of events leading to the decedent's death—what caused the paraplegia. This was not defined in the scenario; thus, manner of death cannot be reasonably opined.

A2.8 The correct answer is A. Accident

- Answer A is correct. The decedent died from bone marrow failure that resulted from bone marrow suppression caused by methotrexate toxicity. If methotrexate toxicity had occurred despite proper dosing, the death may have been classified as natural (or therapeutic complication). In the described scenario, the decedent's death occurred from a blatant error in medicine dispensation, with massive amounts of methotrexate administered. Therefore, the manner of death is best classified as accident.
- Answer B is incorrect. There was no apparent homicidal intention in the medication mishandling.
- Answer C is incorrect. If methotrexate toxicity had occurred despite proper dosing, the death may have been classified as natural. In some states, "therapeutic complication" is an official manner of death classification, and the described scenario would fit this definition as well.
- Answer D is incorrect. There was no apparent suicidal intention in the medication mishandling.
- Answer E is incorrect. In this case, it is clear that the manner of death is accidental.

A2.9 The correct answer is A. Accident

- Answer A is correct. The pathologist deemed the manner of death "accident" in this case. The justification for that ruling was that the individual was alive at the time of the collision based on the extent of hemorrhage and would have been unable to survive the trauma related to the collision. Other pathologists might rule the manner as "natural" because the history indicates it was likely that rupture of a cerebral artery aneurysm led to unconsciousness, which then led to the collision. However, not all individuals die who suffer such aneurysmal rupture.
- Answer B is incorrect. Based on the scenario, the decedent did not die due to indirect or direct actions of another individual, so homicide may be excluded.
- Answer C is incorrect. The pathologist deemed the manner of death "accident" in this case. The justification for that ruling was that the individual was alive at the time of the collision based on the extent of hemorrhage and would have been unable to survive the trauma related to the collision. Other pathologists might rule the manner as "natural" because the history indicates it likely that rupture of a cerebral artery aneurysm led to unconsciousness, which then led to the collision. However, not all individuals who suffer such aneurysmal rupture die.
- Answer D is incorrect. Since there is no known intent of the decedent to take his own life, suicide can be eliminated as a manner of death.
- Answer E is incorrect. A manner of "undetermined" in this case is not incorrect but may not be the best response.

A2.10 The correct answer is C. Homicidal violence

- Answer A is incorrect. There is no evidence of carbon monoxide exposure (no soot in lungs). Directed analysis for carboxyhemoglobin is recommended; if no blood is present, splenic tissue is suggested.
- Answer B is incorrect. The liver drug concentrations are not associated with toxicity.
- Answer C is correct. The classification of cause and manner of death elicits many discussions among forensic pathologists. In the authors' opinion, based on the circumstances surrounding the death, lack of soot in the airways, and nontoxic drug concentrations in the liver, it is best to classify this death as "homicidal violence," despite "homicide" being a manner of death.
- Answer D is incorrect. There is no evidence of life during the fire, as there was no soot in the larger airways of the lungs. Directed analysis for carboxyhemoglobin is recommended; if no blood is present, splenic tissue is suggested.
- Answer E is incorrect. In the authors' opinion, based on the circumstances surrounding the death, lack of soot in the airways, and nontoxic drug concentrations in the liver, it is best to classify this death as "homicidal violence."

A2.11 The correct answer is B. Massachusetts

The first medical examiner system was established in Massachusetts in 1877.

A2.12 The correct answer is C. Henry II.

Henry II established an office of coroner in England in 1194. All of the other kings proceeded Henry II. Louis XIV was a French king.

A2.13 The correct answer is C. Belief that a corpse will bleed in the presence of the murderer

- Answer A is incorrect. Cruel and unusual punishment is a phrase most notably found in the Eighth Amendment of the United States Constitution and has no relationship to cruentation.
- Answer B is incorrect. Removal of the body from the ground is exhumation.
- Answer C is correct. Cruentation is the belief that a corpse will bleed in the presence of the murderer. This was a widely held belief in Colonial America by coroners and those serving in the coroner's jury.
- Answer D is incorrect. The study of bones is the field of anthropology.
- Answer E is incorrect. The destruction of the body by heat is cremation.

A2.14 The correct answer is A. Coroner

- Answer A is correct. The coroner system is the most common type of medicolegal death investigation system in the United States. This is based on the amount of land mass and not the population.
- Answer B is incorrect. Justice of the peace is a medicolegal death investigation system in counties of Texas too small to have a medical examiner system.
- Answer C is incorrect. Although the medical examiner system is not the most common system in the United States, it does serve the majority of the population.
- Answer D is incorrect. The sheriff–coroner system is seen in California in counties that do not have a medical examiner system.

A2.15 The correct answer is C. Medical examiner

- Answer A is incorrect. The coroner system is the most common type of medicolegal death investigation system in the United States. This is based on the amount of land mass and not the population.
- Answer B is incorrect. Justice of the peace is a medicolegal death investigation system in counties of Texas too small to have a medical examiner system.
- Answer C is correct. Although the medical examiner system is not the most common system in the United States, it does serve the majority of the population.
- Answer D is incorrect. The sheriff–coroner system is seen in California in counties that do not have a medical examiner system.

A2.16 The correct answer is C. Lethal injection

- Answer A is incorrect. Electrocution is the second most common form of legal execution in the United States.
- Answer B is incorrect. Execution by firing squad is the least common method employed in the United States.
- Answer C is correct. Currently, 34 U.S. states allow execution for capital crimes. All 34 states authorize lethal injection making it the most common form of legal execution in the United States.
- Answer D is incorrect. The gas chamber is the third most common form of legal execution in the United States.
- Answer E is incorrect. Hanging is the fourth most common form of legal execution in the United States.

A2.17 The correct answer is D. Oklahoma and Utah

All of the other choices are incorrect because at least one of the states in each choice does not allow execution by firing squad. As of this writing three U.S. states, Mississippi, Oklahoma, and Utah, permit firing squad as a method of execution if other methods are found to be unconstitutional or are unavailable/impractical. (See Death Penalty Information Center, located at https://deathpenaltyinfo.org/methods-execution?scid=8&did=24, last accessed May 29, 2017.)

A2.18 The correct answer is B. *Res ipsa loquitur*

- Answer A is incorrect. *Ignorantia juris non excusat*, "Ignorance of the law does not excuse," is a doctrine that means you can still break the law even if you do not know it.
- Answer B is correct. *Res ipsa loquitur* is translated as "the thing speaks for itself." This is a legal term for what most likely caused an action without any direct proof. For example, a person found dead behind the wheel of a car that has been totaled probably died as a result of the car wreck, even if no one witnessed it.
- Answer C is incorrect. *Respondeat superior,* "let the master answer," is a legal term used to declare that an employer has responsibility for the actions of its employees. An example of this is a technician who is employed by a forensic pathologist and makes a mistake. The pathologist is ultimately responsible for the mistake.
- Answer D is incorrect. *Rex non potest peccare*, "the king can do no wrong," describes the doctrine of sovereign immunity in which the government is legally held harmless for mistakes it makes. This example would be illustrated in medical examiner systems when a medical examiner makes a mistake and cannot be civilly sued as long as he or she was acting in good faith as an agent of the state.
- Answer E is incorrect. *Subpoena duces tecum,* "bring with you under penalty," is a court order compelling a witness or entity to produce or bring forth evidence to a legal proceeding. An example of this is a forensic pathologist who brings the autopsy photographs and autopsy report to the court for a case involving his or her testimony.

A2.19 The correct answer is A. Accident

- Answer A is correct. The women died as a result of the blunt force injuries sustained from trauma caused by the automobile. Since there is no evidence the automobile was used as a weapon, the manner is best classified as accident. Although the district attorney decided to pursue criminal charges, that should in no way motivate you to call the manner of death homicide. Criminal charges can be pursued regardless of the manner of death.
- Answer B is incorrect. Since there is no evidence that the automobile was used as a weapon, the manner should not be classified as homicide.
- Answer C is incorrect. Death from blunt force injuries is not a natural death.
- Answer D is incorrect. Unless there is clear evidence that the decedent deliberately killed herself by throwing herself in front of the automobile, the manner should not be ruled suicide.
- Answer E is incorrect. Since the manner can be determined, choice E is incorrect.

A2.20 The correct answer is B. Homicide

- Answer A is incorrect. Since there was deliberate and intentional use of the motor vehicle as a weapon, the manner of death is not accident.
- Answer B is correct. There is evidence that the automobile was used as a weapon. The eyewitness statements in conjunction with the scene findings that suggest no braking was applied to the vehicle (lack of skid marks) allow this manner to be classified as a homicide.
- Answer C is incorrect. Death from blunt force injuries is not a natural death.
- Answer D is incorrect. Unless there is clear evidence that the decedent deliberately placed himself in front of the oncoming automobile, the manner should not be ruled suicide.
- Answer E is incorrect. Since the manner can be determined, choice E is incorrect.

A2.21 The correct answer is B. Homicide

- Answer A is incorrect. Since the armed invasion of the house was planned and deliberate, the manner would not be classified as accident.
- Answer B is correct. The autopsy showed atherosclerotic cardiovascular disease. Given the symptoms, it appears the decedent had a cardiac event (arrhythmia, ischemia, evolving infarction) brought on, at least in part, due to a catecholamine surge brought on by the stress of the home invasion. Since this was a result of the actions of others, this should be classified as a homicide.
- Answer C is incorrect. Although atherosclerotic cardiovascular disease is a natural cause, the circumstances lend themselves to homicide as the manner of death.
- Answer D is incorrect. There is no evidence that the decedent attempted to end his own life, so the manner should not be ruled suicide.
- Answer E is incorrect. Some forensic pathologists may choose to call this undetermined as there may be some doubt as to how much the stress contributed to death. However, the temporal association with armed invasion makes this more likely to be a homicide.

A2.22 The correct answer is E. Undetermined

- Answer A is incorrect. The photograph depicts white foam characteristic of flash pulmonary edema. Three pieces of information were not included in the question: the toxicology results, the autopsy findings, and the scene findings. If this person had been found in water, these findings in conjunction with other findings would support drowning as a cause of death, and the manner would be classified as accident. Another scenario in which these findings would support accident as a manner of death would be acute drug overdose such as that seen in acute opiate toxicity. Since the scene and toxicology information are not available, the manner cannot be determined.
- Answer B is incorrect. Since the scene and toxicology information are not available, the proper classification should be undetermined.
- Answer C is incorrect. Pulmonary edema can be seen in the agonal phase of a natural death such as seen in a myocardial infarction due to underlying atherosclerotic cardiovascular disease. However, a natural-appearing death should not be signed out until basic toxicology screening is performed to rule out either intentional or accidental drug overdose.
- Answer D is incorrect. If the decedent has taken a deliberate overdose of an opiate, the picture in Figure 2.1 might be seen. Since no toxicology or scene data are reported, the manner should be classified as undetermined.
- Answer E is correct. Without the toxicology and the scene information, the manner of death should be classified as undetermined.

A2.23 The correct answer is C. Natural

- Answer A is incorrect.
- Answer B is incorrect.
- Answer C is correct. The most common manner of death in prison is natural. The second most common is suicide, usually from hanging. All of the other manners happen but are much less common.
- Answer D is incorrect.
- Answer E is incorrect.

A2.24 The correct answer is D. Suicide

- Answer A is incorrect.
- Answer B is incorrect.
- Answer C is incorrect.
- Answer D is correct. The most common manner of death in prison is natural. The second most common is suicide, usually from hanging. All of the other manners happen but are much less common.
- Answer E is incorrect.

A2.25 The correct answer is D. Hanging

- Answer A is incorrect. Defenestration is death as a result of going through a window. If the window has significant height, then death would be death due to blunt force injuries. If the window lacks significant height, then death would most likely be caused by exsanguination due to sharp force injury.
- Answer B is incorrect. Drug overdoses can happen in custody but would more likely be associated with an accidental manner of death.
- Answer C is incorrect. Gunshot wounds happen in prison, but due to the lack of easy access to guns, the manner of death would more likely be homicide.
- Answer D is correct. Hanging is the most common cause of death in prison suicides.
- Answer E is incorrect. Exsanguination from sharp force injury can occur but is less common than hanging.

A2.26 The correct answer is B. Cocaine

- Answer A is incorrect.
- Answer B is correct. All of the other drugs have been reported in excited delirium, but cocaine is the most common.
- Answer C is incorrect.
- Answer D is incorrect.
- Answer E is incorrect.

A2.27 The correct answer is D. Unknown

- Answer A is incorrect.
- Answer B is incorrect.
- Answer C is incorrect.
- Answer D is correct. All of the other mechanisms have been proposed but not proven. Of note, excited delirium is a controversial topic and not all in the forensic community believe in its existence.
- Answer E is incorrect.

A2.28 The correct answer is E. Undetermined (Author note: This is controversial because we do not know what was in the mind of the decedent.)

- Answer A is incorrect. It is clear the decedent died from acute cocaine toxicity as a result of harmful ingestion. What is not clear is the state of mind and hence the controversy. If the decedent did not think he was ingesting a lethal dose and would just "get high" from the cocaine, then this would be best classified as an accident.
- Answer B is incorrect. This manner is incorrect as the decedent was not forced by somebody to ingest the cocaine.
- Answer C is incorrect. Clearly, death from cocaine ingestion is not a natural death.
- Answer D is incorrect. Again the state of mind of the decedent is unclear. Did he have a reasonable understanding that ingestion of the cocaine would cause death and chose to ignore this information in the hopes of avoiding prosecution for illegal possession and/or intent to distribute cocaine? If he had reasonable degree of certainty that the cocaine would kill him and then deliberately ingested it, then the manner would be best classified as suicide.
- Answer E is correct. Since it is not clear what the thinking was of the decedent, the manner in this case should be best classified as undetermined. (Please note that this question is controversial, and many forensic pathologists would choose A, accident, as the manner of death.)

A2.29 The correct answer is B. Homicide

- Answer A is incorrect.
- Answer B is correct. Two lines of thought exist, and this is what causes the controversy. The first is that even though this is a case of "suicide by cop," it is still a homicide as one human being dies as the result of actions of another human being, albeit in self-defense. Another line of thought is that the decedent is using the law enforcement officer as the weapon to end her own life just as surely as if she had pulled the trigger herself; thus, it would be classified as a suicide.
- Answer C is incorrect. Deaths from gunshot wounds are not natural.
- Answer D is incorrect. Some may consider this a suicide as explained above.
- Answer E is incorrect. The manner is able to be determined.

A2.30 The correct answer is D. Complete electromuscular disruption

- Answer A is incorrect. Batons have an effectiveness of around 88% (see Jenkinson E, Neeson C, Bleetman A. The relative risk of police use-of-force options: Evaluating the potential for deployment of electronic weaponry. *J Clin Forensic Med* 2006, 13: 229–241).
- Answer B is incorrect. Chemical spray has an effectiveness of approximately 90%–95%.
- Answer C is incorrect. Choke holds have an effectiveness of around 90% when used properly.
- Answer D is correct. Complete electromuscular disruption (i.e., by use of a conducted energy weapon) has the lowest effectiveness that varies from 52% to 75%.
- Answer E is incorrect. Police dogs have the highest effectiveness rate of around 100%.

A2.31 The correct answer is C. 2-Chlorobenzylidene malononitrile (CS)

- Answer A is incorrect. Carfentanil has no approved human use.
- Answer B is incorrect. This is also known as 1-chloroacetophenone or CN.
- Answer C is correct. 2-Chlorobenzylidene malononitrile, also known as CS gas, is a potent lacrimator. To date, no known deaths have occurred as a result of its use. Of the riot control agents, it has the least systemic effects.
- Answer D is incorrect. OC or pepper spray is a riot control agent that has been associated with death from its use, although this is rare.
- Answer E is incorrect. Sarin is a nerve gas and chemical warfare agent with significant associated morbidity and mortality.

A2.32 The correct answer is B. Homicide

- Answer A is incorrect. The decedent died because of an intentional act; therefore, the manner of death is not accident.
- Answer B is correct. The scenario describes a death due to a positional and/or mechanical asphyxia which was the result of an intentional act on the part of law enforcement. Therefore, the manner of death is best classified as homicide, regardless of the role of other medical disease processes such as obesity and cardiomegaly. Subsequent legal liability is determined by a court of law.
- Answer C is incorrect. The decedent died as a result of an unnatural event; therefore, the manner of death is not natural.
- Answer D is incorrect. The decedent died as a result of an intentional act of other persons; therefore, the manner of death is not suicide.
- Answer E is incorrect. The manner of death is best determined to be homicide.

Chapter 3

MECHANICAL AND PHYSICAL INJURY

QUESTIONS

Q3.1 Upon removal of the skullcap, the pathologist identifies a collection of clotted blood overlying the dura at the left temporoparietal region of the brain. What presentation is most classic for this finding?

A. Hemiplegia and vertigo
B. Immediate loss of consciousness with imminent death
C. Intractable seizure
D. Lucid interval with subsequent loss of consciousness
E. Sudden-onset symptoms with severe headache

Q3.2 What is the best characterization of the external injuries in this man shown in Figure 3.1 below?

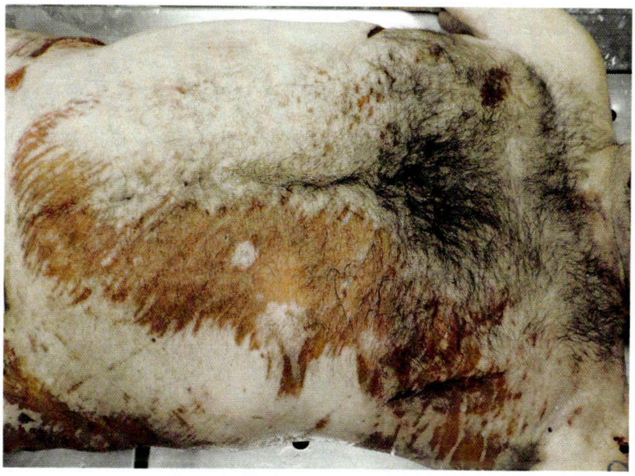

Figure 3.1

A. Hyperextension injuries sustained in a jump from a bridge
B. Motor vehicle crash injuries of an ejected passenger
C. Motor vehicle crash injuries of a restrained driver
D. Postmortem injuries in moving water

Q3.3 What is the location of the most common fatal deceleration injury of the aorta?

A. Abdominal aorta proximal to the iliac bifurcation
B. Aortic arch between the brachiocephalic artery and left common carotid artery
C. Ascending aorta adjacent to the aortic valve
D. Distal descending thoracic aorta immediately proximal to the diaphragm
E. Thoracic aorta just distal to the origin of the left subclavian artery

Q3.4 An individual was involved in a motor vehicle crash in the United States and presents with the injury depicted below to the right side of the face. What was the most likely position of this individual during the crash?

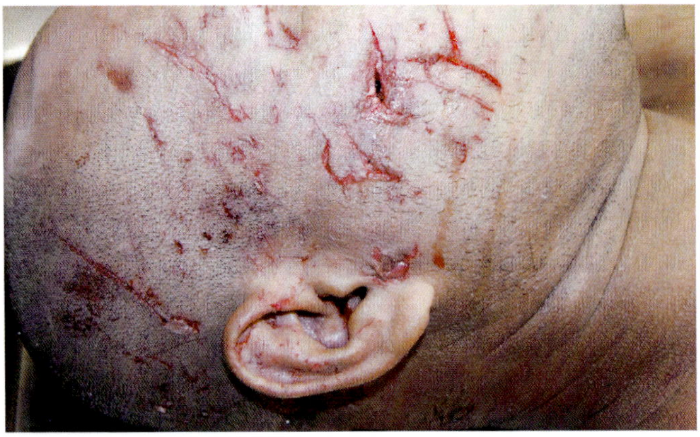

Figure 3.2

A. Captive in the trunk
B. Cyclist, riding a bicycle
C. Driver
D. Passenger, front seat
E. Pedestrian, walking

Q3.5 The finding depicted below is most consistent with which of the following scenarios?

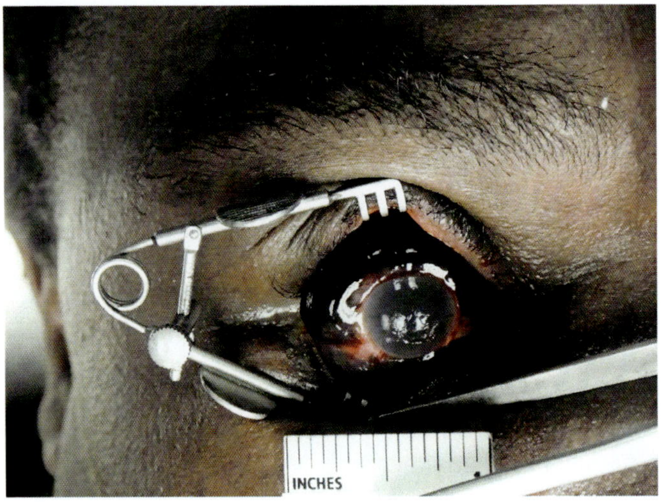

Figure 3.3

A. Drowning of a child
B. Hanging of an adult, suspended by weight of body
C. Manual strangulation of an adult
D. Positional asphyxia in an alcoholic
E. Smothering of an infant

Q3.6 What caused the depicted forehead injury in Figure 3.4?

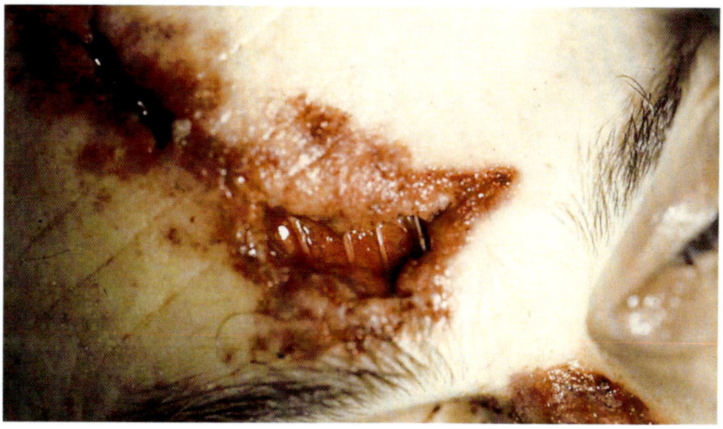

Figure 3.4

A. Animal bite
B. Electrical injury
C. Incised wound
D. Laceration
E. Stab wound

Q3.7 This 48-year-old woman was found deceased on the side of the road. External injuries are depicted below. What is the best conclusion regarding the circumstances surrounding her death?

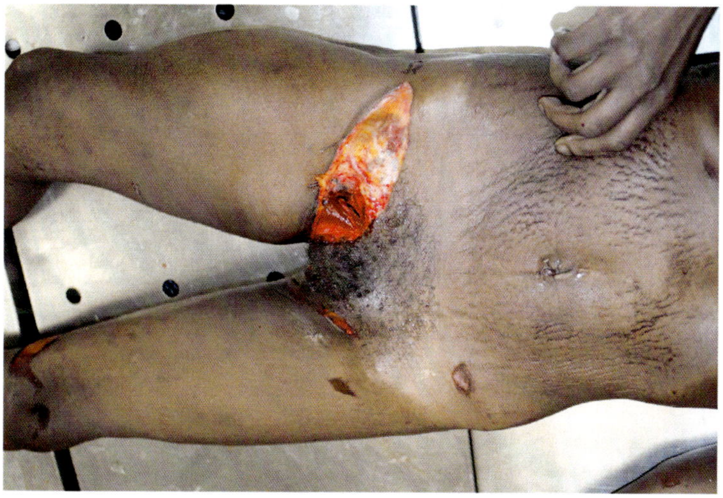

Figure 3.5

A. Dumped on the road after being assaulted with a machete
B. Hit by a vehicle while riding a bicycle
C. Hit by multiple cars
D. Run over by a vehicle while lying on the road
E. Struck from behind by a vehicle while upright

Q3.8 The following was found around the decedent's neck. What is the most likely mechanism of death?

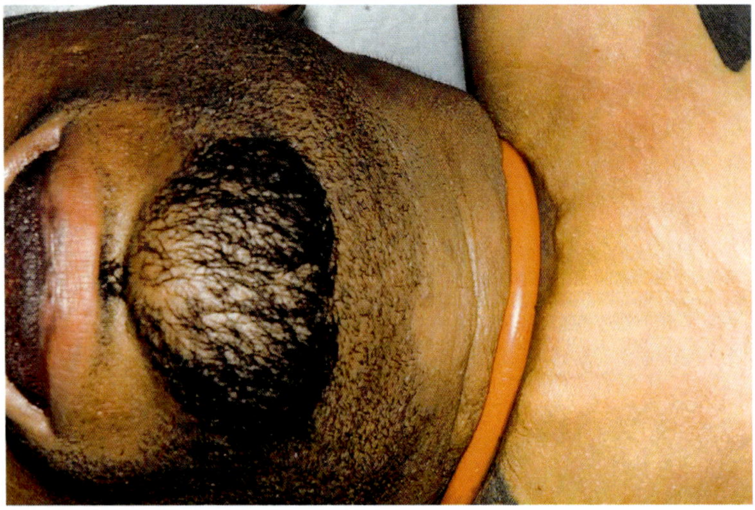

Figure 3.6

A. Asphyxia
B. Catecholamine excess
C. Cervical spine fracture
D. Prolonged QT interval
E. Ventricular arrhythmia

Q3.9 What is the most likely cause of death from the findings in Figure 3.7?

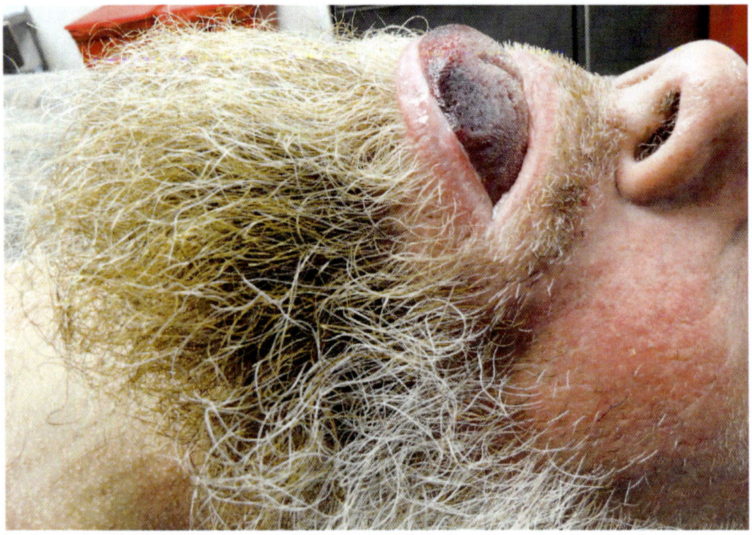

Figure 3.7

A. Drowning
B. Hanging
C. Manual strangulation
D. Smothering
E. Suffocation

Q3.10 From the case above, what is the most likely manner of death?

A. Accident
B. Homicide
C. Natural
D. Suicide
E. Undetermined

Q3.11 In the following scene photograph, what is the most likely cause of the purple coloration of the upper body?

Figure 3.8

A. Bacterial overgrowth and tissue autolysis
B. Blunt trauma
C. Cardiac arrhythmia
D. Hampered venous return to the heart
E. Internal hemorrhage

Q3.12 What is the likely underlying cause of death in the image below?

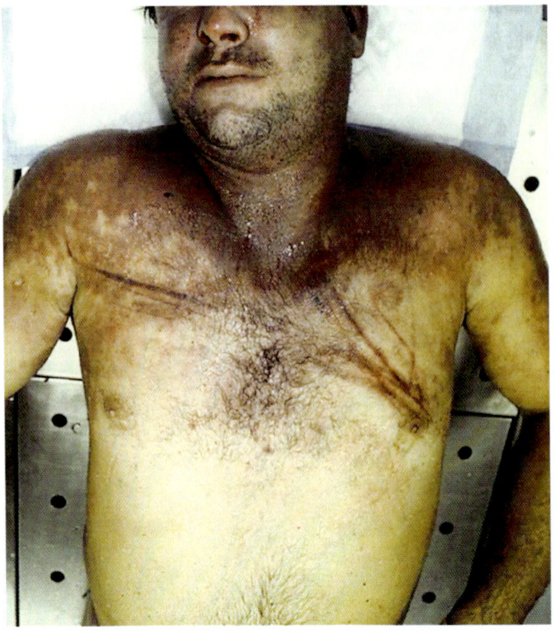

Figure 3.9

A. Choking
B. Hanging
C. Mechanical asphyxia
D. Smothering
E. Strangulation

Q3.13 What is the best description of the pictured wound below?

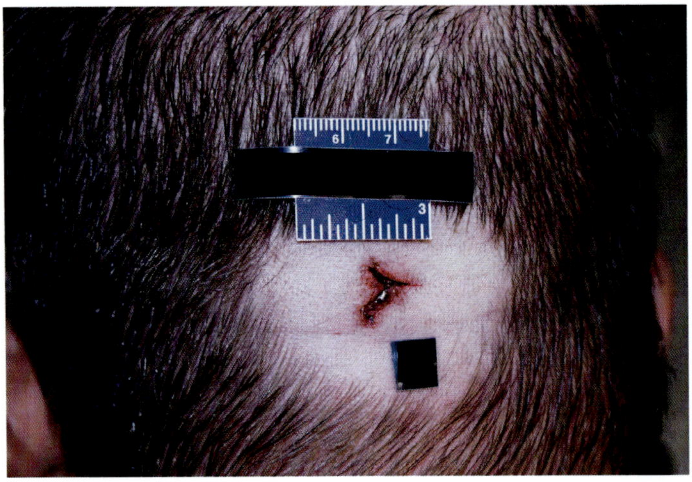

Figure 3.10

A. Close-range gunshot wound
B. Contact gunshot wound
C. Exit gunshot wound
D. Indeterminate range gunshot wound
E. Keyhole gunshot wound

Q3.14 A 42-year-old man was struck by a car and died at the scene. Autopsy shows fatal head trauma, numerous cutaneous abrasions and contusions, and two fractures of the lower legs. The fractures are centered ~8 and 14 inches above the soles of the right and left feet, respectively. What conclusion is suggested regarding the leg fractures?

A. Decedent was struck while the car was braking
B. Decedent was lying on the road
C. Decedent was standing on the road
D. Decedent was thrown over the roof of the car
E. Decedent was walking on the road

Q3.15 What mechanism of death is associated with judicial hanging?

A. Asphyxia
B. Catecholamine excess
C. Cervical spine fracture
D. Prolonged QT interval
E. Ventricular arrhythmia

Q3.16 A 42-year-old man has an entrance gunshot wound in the head. No exit wound is identified. Radiographic images are obtained, and the two projectiles pictured below are recovered. What conclusion can be made?

Figure 3.11 Photograph courtesy of Forensic Medical Management Services, P.A., Beaumont, Texas.

A. Additional entrance wound was subsequently identified
B. Bullet embolus
C. Core separated from jacket
D. One of the projectiles is from a remote gunshot wound
E. Two projectiles entered through single entrance wound

Q3.17 What is the best estimation of range of fire for the pictured entrance gunshot wound?

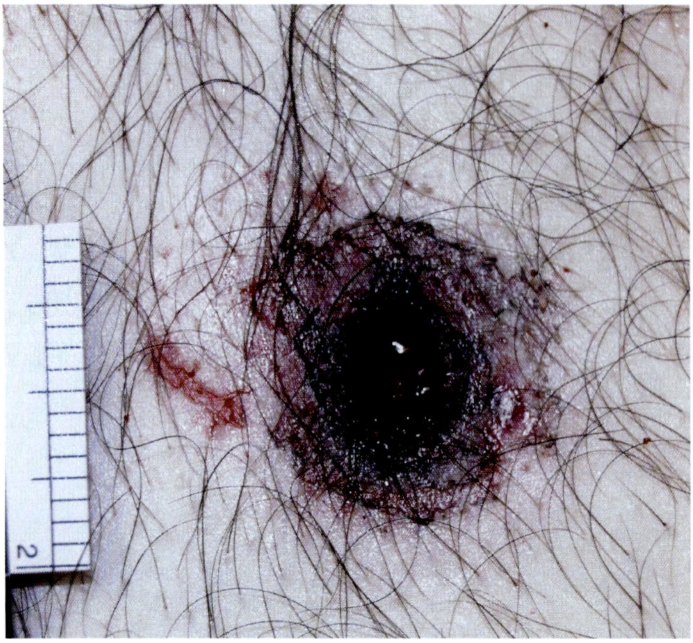

Figure 3.12

A. Contact (at the skin surface)
B. No contact, but less than 12 inches
C. 12–36 inches
D. Greater than 36 inches

Q3.18 What is the range of fire for this gunshot wound?

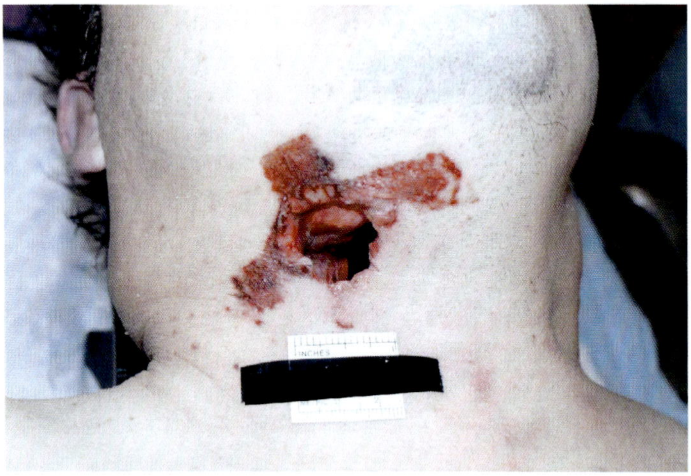

Figure 3.13

A. Contact
B. 2 feet
C. 3 feet
D. 4 feet
E. Over 4 feet

Q3.19 How should recovered bullet fragments and projectiles be handled by the pathologist at the time of autopsy?

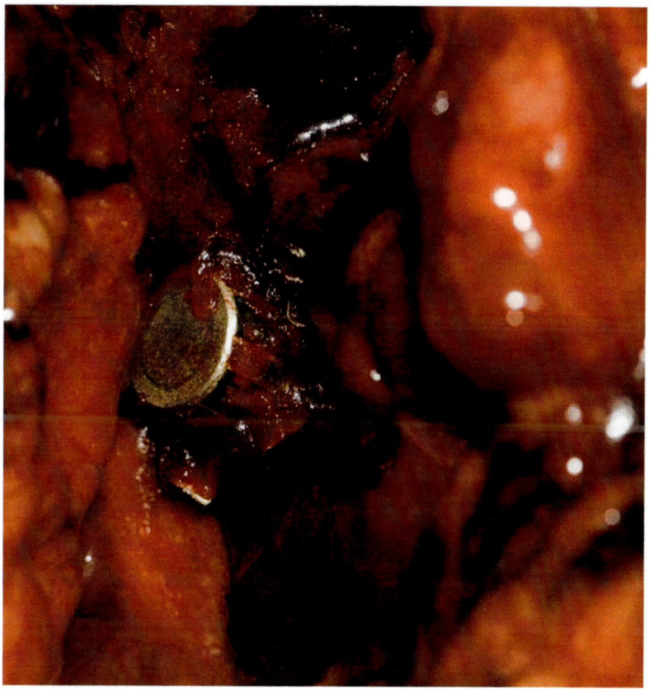

Figure 3.14

A. Placed in bleach for decontamination
B. Removed by metal surgical instruments
C. Removed with nonmetallic instruments
D. Test fire rounds from the suspect weapon for a match
E. Person removing the fragments should carve his or her initials on each of them

Q3.20 What type of ammunition is depicted in this photograph?

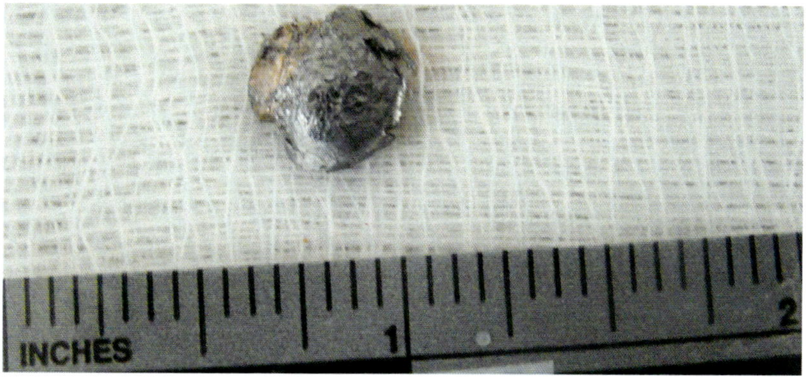

Figure 3.15 Photograph courtesy of Forensic Medical Management Services, P.A., Beaumont, Texas.

A. Birdshot
B. Buckshot
C. Small caliber
D. Large caliber
E. Medium caliber

Q3.21 What is the best estimation of range of fire for the pictured entrance gunshot wound?

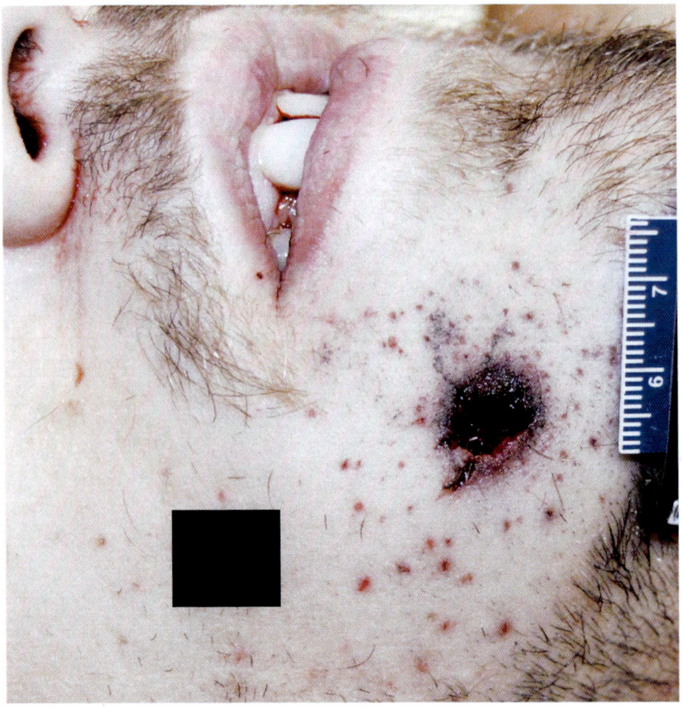

Figure 3.16

A. Contact (at the skin surface)
B. <12 inches
C. 12–36 inches
D. >36 inches

Q3.22 Based on the appearance of this gunshot wound to the nose, what is the best characterization of the direction of the bullet pathway?

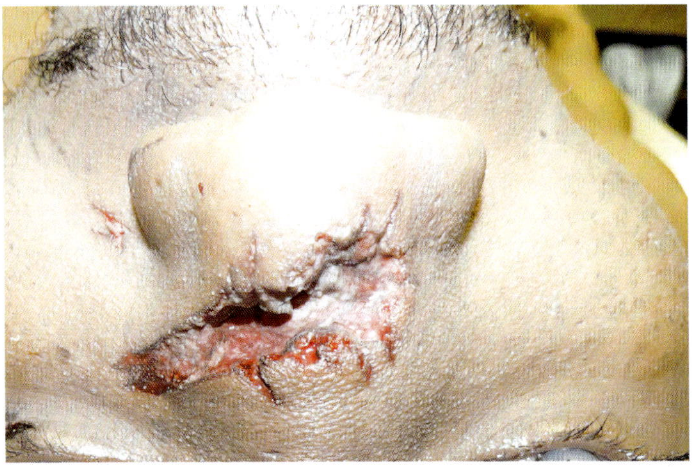

Figure 3.17

A. Bottom to top
B. Not able to be determined
C. Left to right
D. Right to left
E. Top to bottom

Q3.23 What is the most likely source of the radiopaque fragments featured on this x-ray?

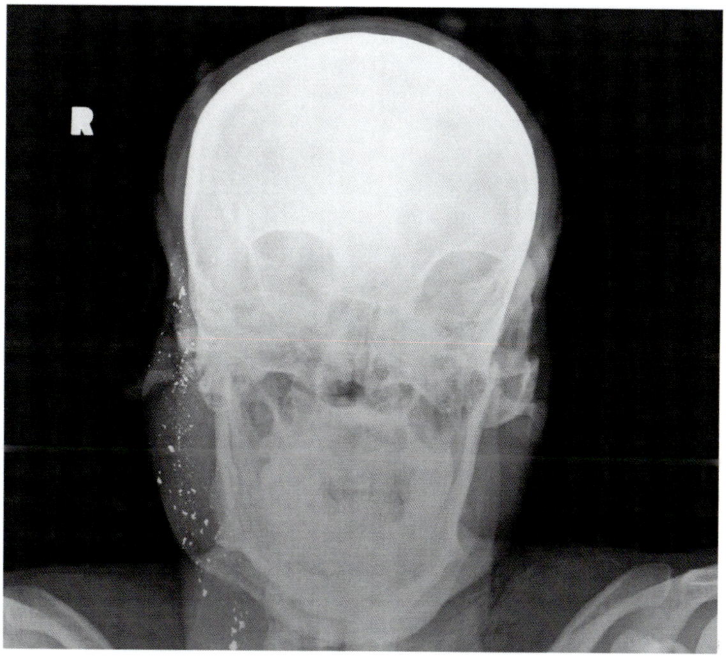

Figure 3.18

A. .22 rimfire rifle
B. High-velocity rifle ammunition
C. Pipe bomb
D. Revolver handguns
E. Semiautomatic handgun

Q3.24 Based on the photograph, how is the projectile best characterized?

Figure 3.19 Photograph courtesy of Forensic Medical Management Services, P.A., Beaumont, Texas.

A. Birdshot
B. Buckshot
C. Small caliber
D. Large caliber
E. Medium caliber

Q3.25 What is the number of equally sized lead balls in one pound defined as?

A. Birdshot
B. Bore
C. Buckshot
D. Caliber
E. Gauge

Q3.26 A man is shot once in the chest while lying in the bathtub on his back. How should this gunshot wound defect on his back be classified?

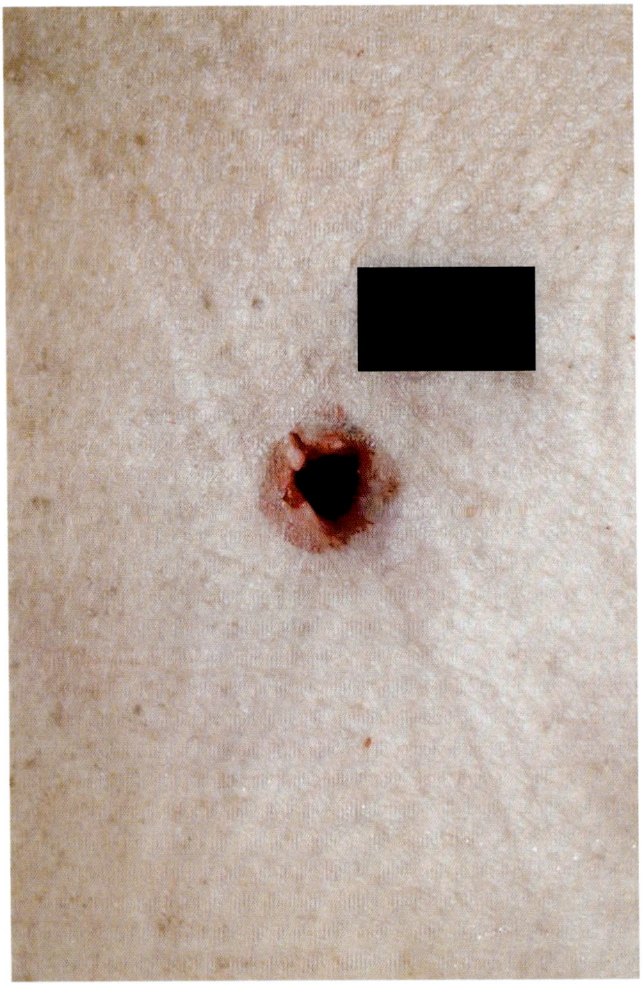

Figure 3.20

A. Distant entrance gunshot wound
B. Intermediate entrance gunshot wound
C. Indeterminate-range entrance gunshot wound
D. Ricochet entrance gunshot wound
E. Shored exit wound

Q3.27 A 28-year-old man is found dead after reports of gunfire. Autopsy radiographs are featured below. What is the likely range of fire?

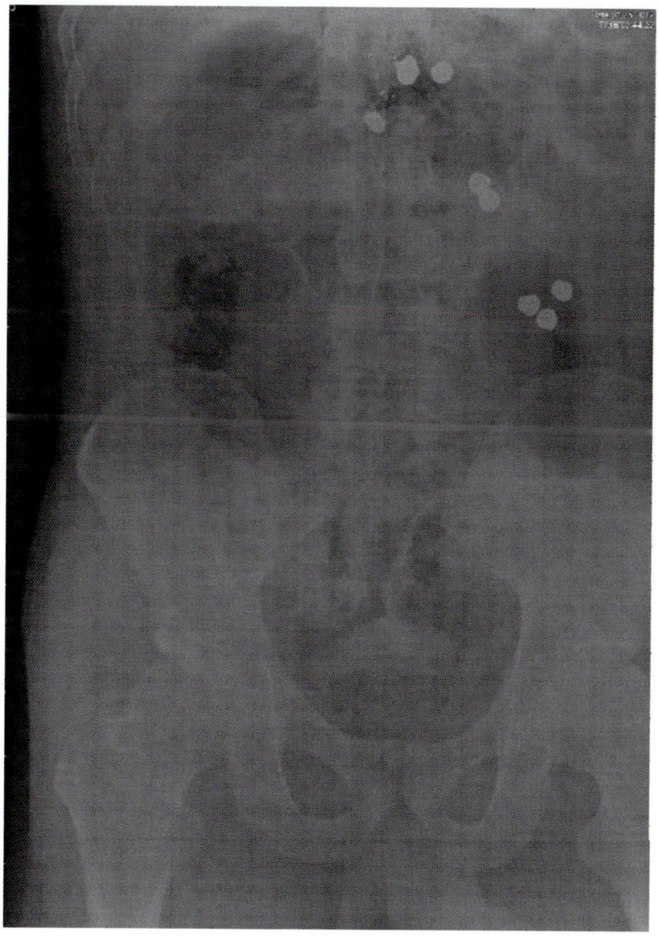

Figure 3.21

A. 0–2 feet
B. 3 feet
C. 4 feet
D. 5–9 feet
E. Cannot be determined by x-ray

Q3.28 What is the most important independent contribution to bullet energy?

A. Caliber
B. Distance
C. Gauge
D. Mass
E. Velocity

Q3.29 Based on the photograph, how is the projectile best classified?

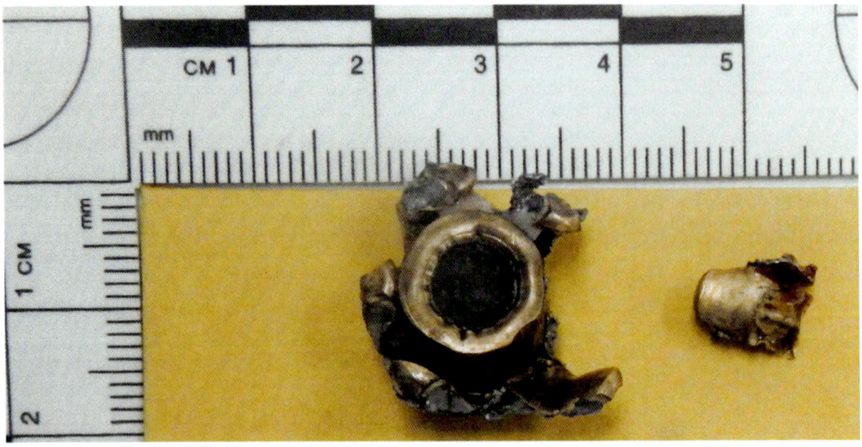

Figure 3.22 Photograph courtesy of Forensic Medical Management Services, P.A., Beaumont, Texas.

A. Birdshot
B. Buckshot
C. Small caliber
D. Large caliber
E. Medium caliber

Q3.30 This image depicts a wound to the head. Further information received from law enforcement indicates the projectile recovered was from a Magnum round. In this case, what does Magnum refer to?

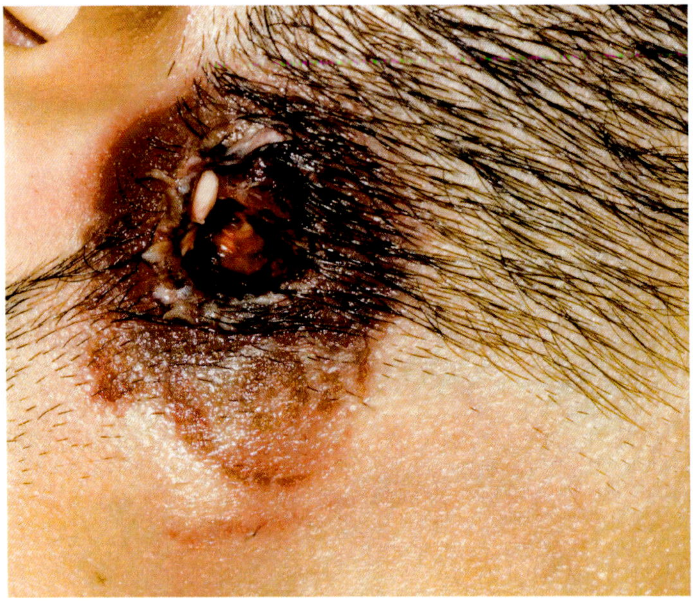

Figure 3.23

A. Caliber
B. Length
C. Load
D. Shape
E. Style

Q3.31 A 22-year-old man sustains a shotgun wound to his chest. The lesion adjacent to the 1 o'clock position of the main defect was most likely caused by which of the following?

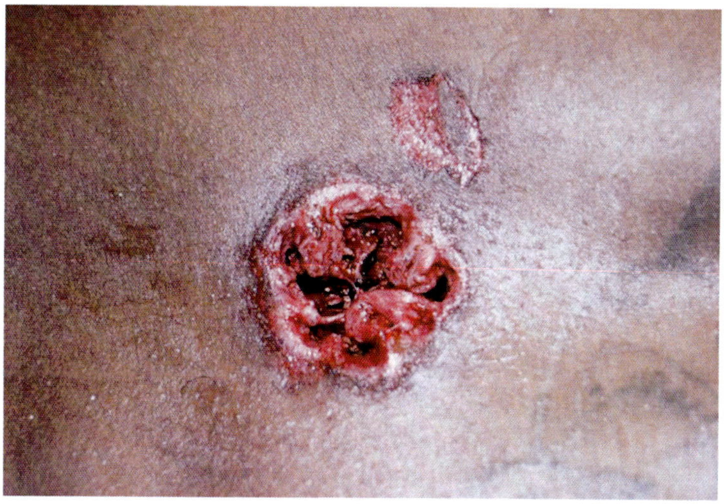

Figure 3.24

A. Butt of the shotgun
B. Intermediate target debris
C. Satellite shot entrance wound
D. Scope
E. Wadding

Q3.32 The blanket pictured below was recovered from the scene of a shooting victim. What type of gun was most likely used?

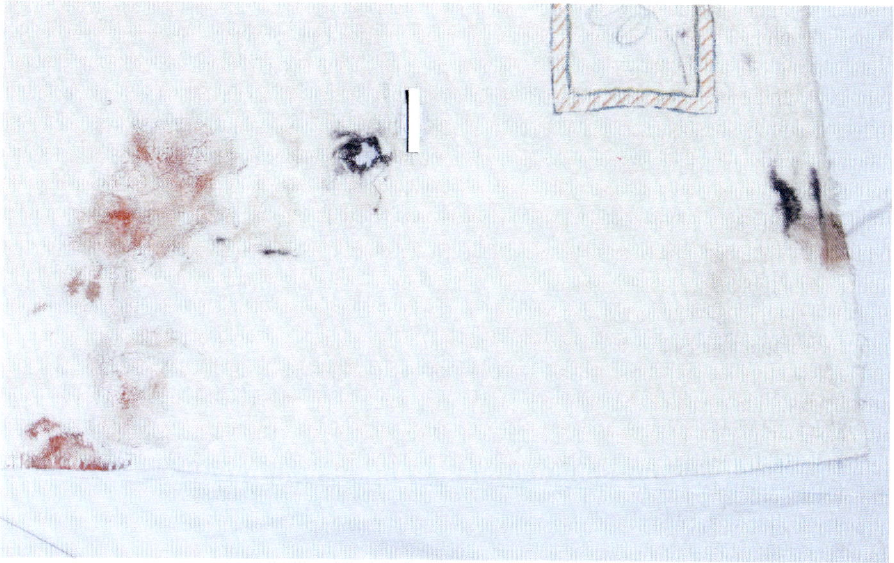

Figure 3.25

A. Revolver
B. .22 Rifle
C. Semiautomatic pistol
D. Shotgun

Q3.33 A 30-year-old man is shot in the chest. No soot or stippling is visible on the skin around the gunshot wound. The decedent's shirt, which was removed by first responders, accompanies the body and shows a defect corresponding to the entrance gunshot wound. What is the most appropriate interpretation regarding range of fire?

Figure 3.26

A. Contact

B. Close range

C. Distant

D. Undetermined

Questions 3.34–3.36 refer to the photograph below.

A skeleton was found in a wet field without any viable tissue.

Figure 3.27 Photograph courtesy of Forensic Medical Management Services, P.A., Beaumont, Texas.

Q3.34 Based on the photograph, what is the most likely injury pattern?

A. Blunt force trauma
B. Entrance gunshot wound
C. Exit gunshot wound
D. Graze gunshot wound
E. Keyhole gunshot wound

Q3.35 Based on the view of the photograph, what is the direction the bullet traveled?

A. Downward
B. Left to right
C. Right to left
D. Toward the viewer
E. Upward

Q3.36 Based on the view of the photograph, what is the range of fire?

A. Cannot be determined
B. Less than 0.1 inch
C. Between 1 and 6 inches
D. Approximately 12 inches
E. Approximately 30 feet

Q3.37 A 25-year-old man is shot once in the chest. No other injuries are present. An anteroposterior (AP) x-ray of the chest is obtained. What should the pathologist do next?

A. Conclude the bullet exited a natural orifice
B. Diagnose sharp force injury from an object such as an ice pick
C. Reposition the x-ray plate to include all the chest soft tissue
D. Report the use of caseless ammunition
E. Report the use of reloaded ammunition

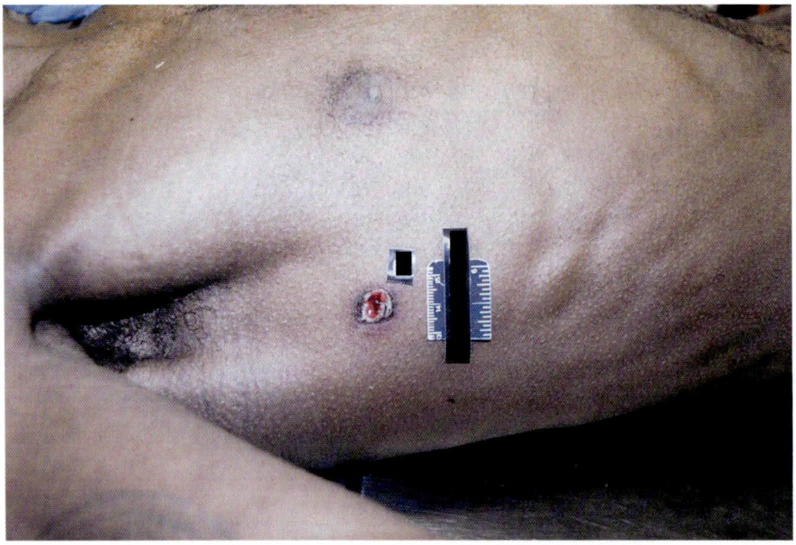

Figure 3.28

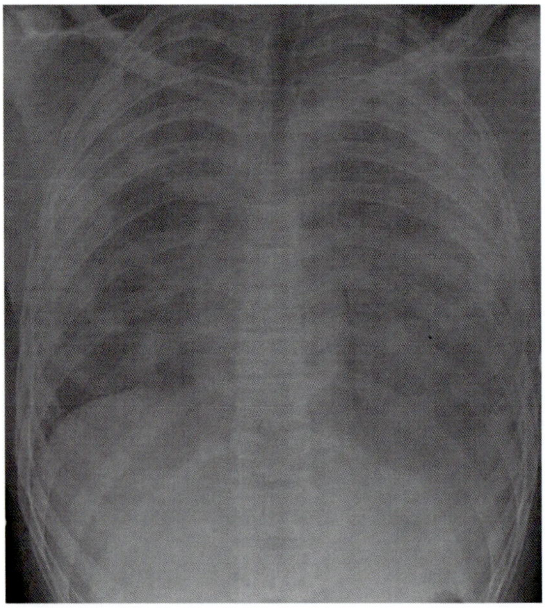

Figure 3.29

Q3.38 High explosives are associated with velocities of at least __________ feet per second.

A. 300

B. 1300

C. 2300

D. 3300

E. 4300

Q3.39 What is the most common cause of death in victims who initially survive an explosion?

A. Cardiac arrhythmia

B. Gastrointestinal hemorrhage

C. Pulmonary barotrauma

D. Spleen rupture

E. Sepsis

Q3.40 A soldier is involved in an explosion caused by an improvised explosive device (IED). She sustained the pictured injury as a result of hitting a vehicle after being propelled by the shock wave of the blast. How should this type of blast injury pattern be classified?

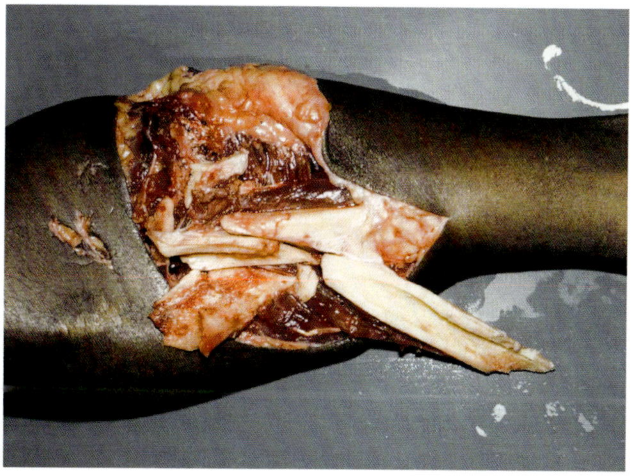

Figure 3.30

A. Primary
B. Secondary
C. Tertiary
D. Quaternary

Q3.41 An airman is involved in an explosion caused by an improvised explosive device (IED). He sustains a penetrating chest injury. How should this type of blast injury pattern be classified?

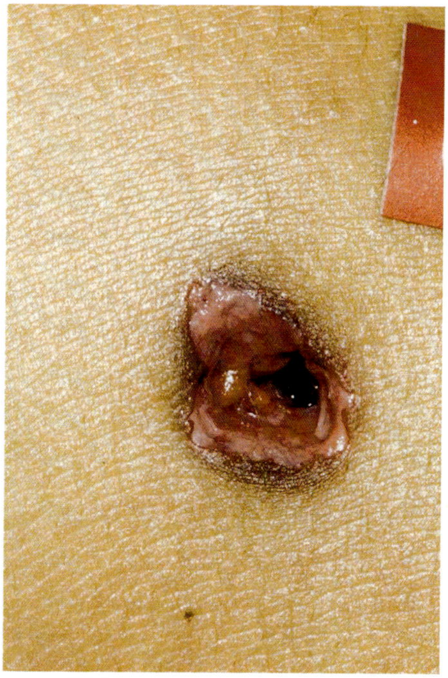

Figure 3.31

A. Primary
B. Secondary
C. Tertiary
D. Quaternary

Q3.42 A person is killed in a gas refinery explosion. He had been standing approximately 20 feet from the center of the blast. The blast injury pattern depicted most likely occurred within what time frame?

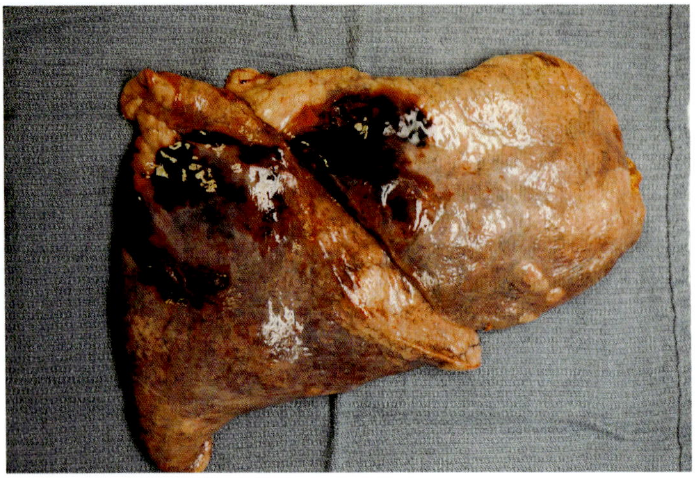

Figure 3.32 Photograph courtesy of Forensic Medical Management Services of Texas, P.A., Beaumont, TX.

A. Milliseconds
B. Seconds
C. Minutes
D. Hours
E. Postmortem

Q3.43 What conclusion can be made regarding the cause of this stab wound?

Figure 3.33

A. Differentiation between a single-edged knife and a double-edged knife cannot definitively be made
B. Made by a double-edged knife
C. Made by a single-edged knife
D. Made by a screwdriver
E. Made by a target arrow

Q3.44 What is the most likely weapon used on this individual's face?

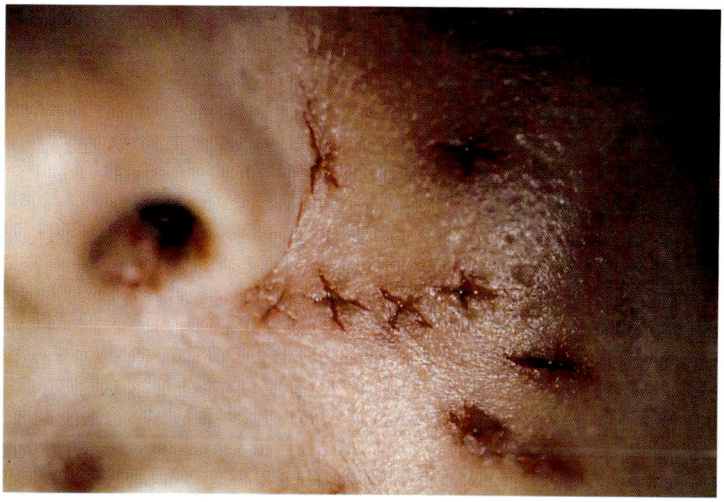

Figure 3.34

A. Arrow
B. Double-edged knife
C. Ice pick
D. Phillips head screwdriver
E. Scissors

Q3.45 How can the following injury on the anterior forearm be characterized?

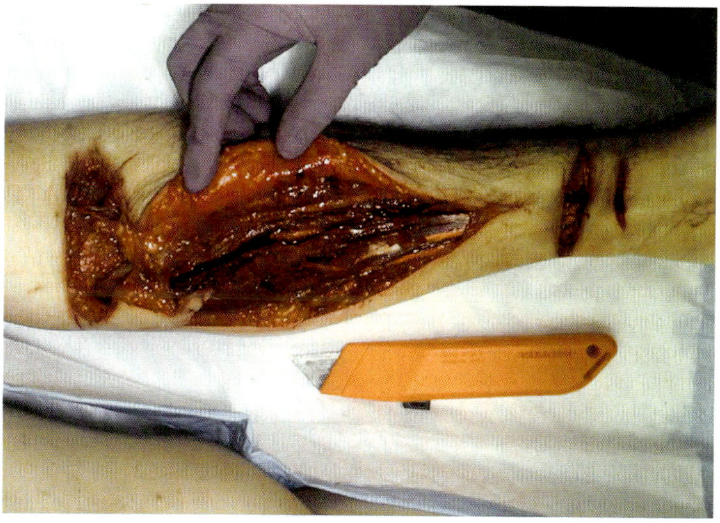

Figure 3.35

A. Accidental injury from broken window
B. Avulsion injury from blunt trauma
C. Defensive injury
D. Homicidal stab wounds
E. Self-inflicted incisions

Q3.46 A man is found deceased after an assault with multiple sharp force injuries to his chest. The injury below is found on the back. What weapon was likely used?

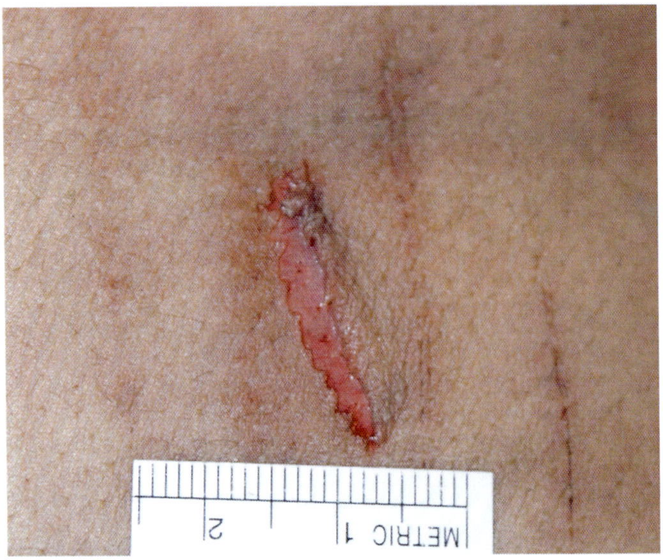

Figure 3.36

A. Broken glass bottle
B. Scissors
C. Serrated knife
D. Single-edged knife
E. Double-edged knife

Q3.47 A 35-year-old woman is found in the yard outside her residence with the injuries depicted below. What is the most likely scenario regarding the circumstances surrounding her death?

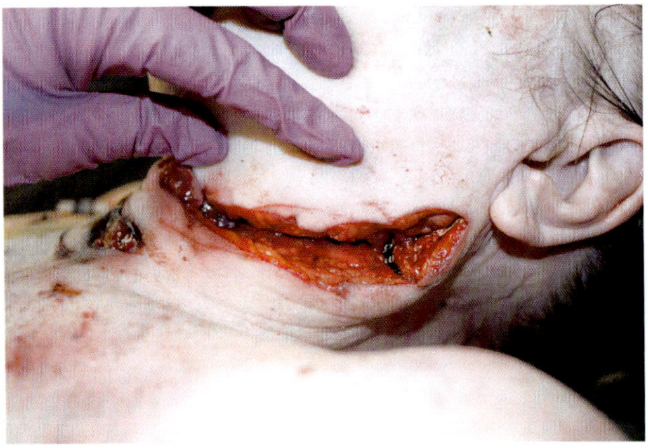

Figure 3.37

A. Assaulted from behind with knife
B. Hanged by rope with large distance drop
C. Involved in face-to-face altercation with axe
D. Struck anteriorly by truck with blunt trauma injury
E. Struck from behind by car with hyperextension injury

Q3.48 A 23-year-old woman has a fatal stab wound to the chest. Several nonfatal incised wounds are on the ulnar surface of her forearms and palms. What is the most likely interpretation of the forearm and palm trauma?

A. Defensive injuries
B. Nonspecific trauma
C. Self-inflicted cuts
D. Sign of sexual assault
E. Terminal fall trauma

Q3.49 Ohm's law is defined as

A. I = VR
B. V = I+R
C. V = I–R
D. V = IR
E. $V = I^2R$

Q3.50 At autopsy, a 58-year-old man who was found dead outdoors demonstrates hemorrhage from the right ear canal. No fractures and no intracranial hemorrhages are present, and no other findings are identified. What cause of death do you suspect?

A. Asphyxia
B. Blunt head trauma
C. Eustachian tube infection
D. Fungal sinusitis
E. Lightning strike

Q3.51 A 65-year-old male was found approximately 5 feet from an electric drill he had been observed using approximately 30 minutes prior to death. A small area was observed on his index finger. Based on the finding in the photograph, what is the most likely mechanism of death?

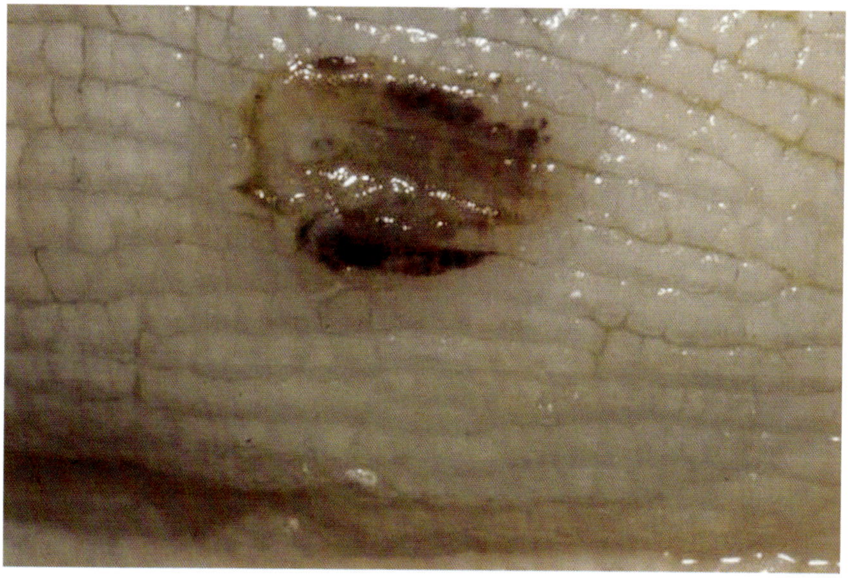

Figure 3.38

A. Central nervous system dysfunction
B. High-voltage electrocution
C. Low-voltage electrocution
D. Thermal injury
E. Ventricular arrhythmia

Q3.52 How would the following axillary injury be characterized?

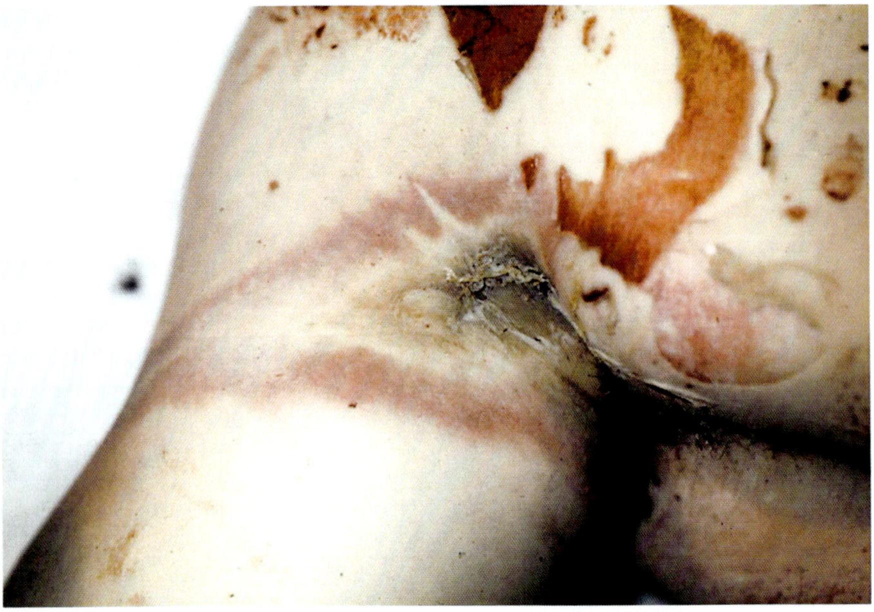

Figure 3.39

A. Erythema chronicum migrans (ECM)
B. Electrical injury
C. Iatrogenic defibrillation injury
D. Necrotizing fasciitis
E. Thermal steam injury

Q3.53 At what voltage is ventricular fibrillation most likely to result?

A. 1 mA
B. 10 mA
C. 100 mA
D. 2000 mA

Q3.54 What is the minimum voltage (expressed in volts) that defines high-voltage electrocution?

A. 0.03
B. 10
C. 100
D. 1000
E. 10000

Q3.55 The following finding is present on the torso of an excavator operator found dead on the ground at a road construction site. Which of the following was likely at the scene?

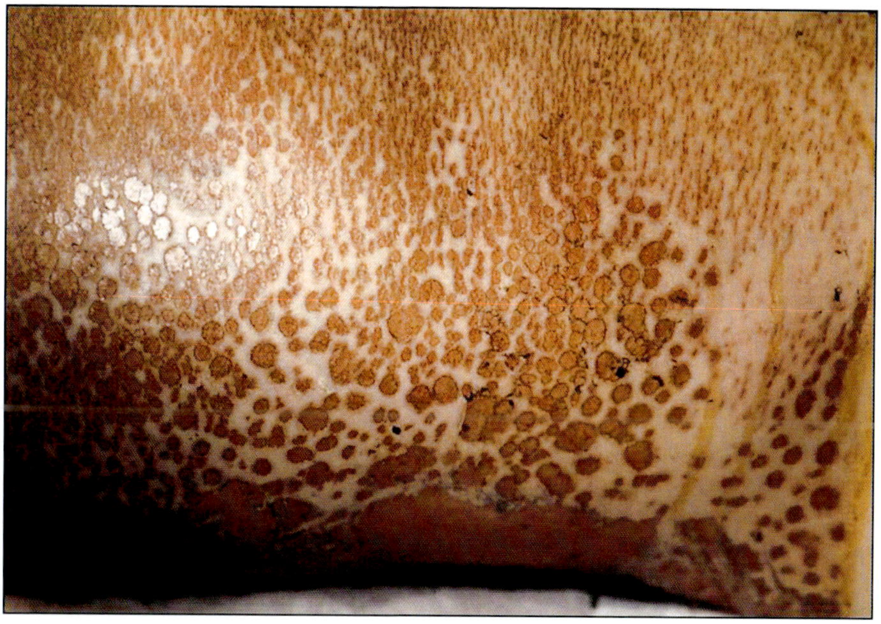

Figure 3.40

A. Ant hills
B. Asphalt surface
C. Electrical power lines
D. Poisonous mushrooms
E. Superheated water

ANSWERS: CHAPTER 3

A3.1 The correct answer is D. Lucid interval with subsequent loss of consciousness

- Answer A is incorrect. Hemiplegia, intractable seizure, and visual field defects are more likely due to parenchymal brain hemorrhage or other abnormality. Vertigo and positional nystagmus are not uncommon with head trauma but are more likely due to direct effects on the inner ear such as by temporal bone fracture or with subarachnoid hemorrhage.
- Answer B is incorrect. Significant head trauma of any sort may present with immediate loss of consciousness with imminent death; however, this is not classic for epidural hemorrhage.
- Answer C is incorrect. Hemiplegia, intractable seizure, and visual field defects are more likely due to parenchymal brain hemorrhage or other abnormality. Seizures may also occur prior to rupture of a berry aneurysm.
- Answer D is correct. The described injury is termed *epidural hemorrhage*. Since the bleed occurs between the dura and the skull, it may be staunched for some time. However, with continued arterial pressure, the dura may detach from the skull and lead to delayed symptomatology, including loss of consciousness and even death, when compression of the cerebrum becomes critical. A classic injury associated with epidural hemorrhage is a tear in the middle meningeal artery due to a temporal bone fracture.
- Answer E is incorrect. The sudden onset of symptoms accompanied by severe headache is more classic for subarachnoid hemorrhage and ruptured berry aneurysm.

A3.2 The correct answer is B. Motor vehicle crash injuries of an ejected passenger

- Answer A is incorrect. Hyperextension injury is characterized by stretching, and frequently laceration of the skin from a force from the opposite side of the injury. For example, hyperextension injury from an auto–pedestrian collision in which the pedestrian is struck from behind would likely be apparent on the anterior body surfaces in areas most prone to hyperextension such as the inguinal regions. Such injuries are frequently bilateral if the impact was straight on.
- Answer B is correct. Pictured is a male torso with numerous roughly parallel, somewhat linear abrasions. This pattern is characteristic of "road rash," which occurs when a body surface is dragged or otherwise propelled across an abrasive surface. Of the choices, the most reasonable scenario would be that in which the individual was ejected from a vehicle and then traversed the road for some distance. The linear aspect of the abrasions is due to the directional inertia, while the extent of the abrasions provides some information regarding the surface area in contact with the abrasive surface (commonly a road).
- Answer C is incorrect. A restrained driver in a motor vehicle collision might show abrasions that approximate the location of the seatbelt—across the left shoulder and chest and then to the right abdomen. Abrasion or contusion may also be present in association with the lap-belt portion of the modern seatbelt.
- Answer D is incorrect. Injuries due to moving water may have a similar appearance if the body of water is shallow and the body is coming into contact with the abrasive surface of the river bed. However, the body would likely change orientation to the abrasive surface as it traversed the moving water, so the injury pattern would be expected to be less regular.

A3.3 The correct answer is E. Thoracic aorta just distal to the origin of the left subclavian artery

- Answer A is incorrect. The abdominal aorta proximal to the iliac bifurcation is a site of increased turbulence and frequent atherosclerotic disease and aneurysm formation, but this is not as vulnerable to deceleration injury as are other sites.
- Answer B is incorrect. The aortic arch is subject to increased turbulence due to the larger take-off arteries; thus, atherosclerotic disease is common at this site. This region of the aorta is relatively mobile in the chest upon deceleration, but the site of tethering at the ligamentum arteriosum is the most likely laceration point.
- Answer C is incorrect. The ascending aorta adjacent to the aortic valve is a common site of aneurysm and of initiation of dissection but is less frequently affected by deceleration injury than other sites.
- Answer D is incorrect. Due to traction at the distal descending thoracic aorta upon deceleration, aortic intimal lacerations are encountered at that site. However, the aorta is fixed in place by surrounding tissue proximally and distally at this site and is not often subject to major life-threatening laceration or transection.
- Answer E is correct. The aorta is vulnerable to intimal laceration, and transmural laceration, and transection at sites where it is focally tethered and otherwise mobile. The most prominent of these sites is at the ligamentum arteriosum, which is of the thoracic aorta just distal to the aortic arch.

A3.4 The correct answer is D. Passenger, front seat

- Answer A is incorrect. The photograph depicts dicing injury from shattered tempered side window glass.
- Answer B is incorrect. A cyclist struck by a car would likely have road rash/brush burn abrasions, but not the typical aggregate of cuts and punctures associated with dicing injury from shattered tempered side window glass.
- Answer C is incorrect. A driver involved in such a crash would likely have dicing injury concentrated on the left side of the body.
- Answer D is correct. The depicted injuries consist of punctate, linear, and angulated cuts, likely due to shattering of the tempered glass side window in the vehicle ("dicing" injury). The location of this injury on the body, especially in seat-belted riders, suggests their sitting location in the vehicle. In this instance, with the injury located on the right side of the face, the decedent was likely the front seat passenger. (This is as it applies to standard vehicles in the United States where traditionally the driver's side is on the left.)
- Answer E is incorrect. A pedestrian struck by a car would likely have road rash/brush burn abrasions, but not the typical aggregate of cuts and punctures associated with dicing injury from shattered tempered side window glass.

A3.5 The correct answer is C. Manual strangulation of an adult

- Answer A is incorrect. Drowning is considered a diagnosis of exclusion as no specific findings may be present. Thus, the apparent scleral hemorrhage is not suggestive of this scenario.
- Answer B is incorrect. When someone dies due to hanging and his or her weight is suspended, the compression of the neck is strong enough to prevent both venous and arterial blood flow. Thus, hemorrhage of the sclera is not typical.
- Answer C is correct. Manual strangulation is the best answer. During the act of strangulation, the victim frequently attempts to defend himself or herself and as the person moves and otherwise resists the assailant, the force to the neck changes. Intermittently, it can be expected that venous flow will be restricted while arterial flow continues, thus leading to bursting of small venules in the skin of the face, conjunctiva, and sclera. Seen here is diffuse and regionally confluent scleral hemorrhage.
- Answer D is incorrect. Positional asphyxia occurs when the airway is obstructed due to the positioning of the body. This may result in someone who is impaired and unable to correct their position, such as a person under the influence of significant concentrations of alcohol. During positional asphyxia, there is no expectation of intermittent arterial impedance; thus, scleral hemorrhage is not a common finding. But, depending on the position, venous impedance may occur and the presence of petechial hemorrhages may be seen both with positional asphyxia as well as strangulation.
- Answer E is incorrect. Similar to drowning, smothering may show no physical signs at autopsy and may only be determined at times by perpetrator confession. Smothering is obstruction of the external airways (i.e., the nose and the mouth) and does not typically involve vascular obstruction unless there is also a component of strangulation. Focal injury may be seen to the oral mucosa in such a case, particularly if the child has erupted teeth.

A3.6 The correct answer is D. Laceration

- Answer A is incorrect. The injury is a laceration. Animal bites vary but often demonstrate both sharp and blunt force injuries in combination.
- Answer B is incorrect. Classically, high-voltage electrical injury will have some evidence of thermal damage, and low-voltage electrocution may show erythema or no finding at all. The tissue bridging is the key feature of this laceration.
- Answer C is incorrect. An incised wound is a sharp force injury pattern in which the wound is longer than it is deep and typically has smooth edges. In this case the edges are abraded and tissue bridging is evident, which is more consistent with a laceration.
- Answer D is correct. The featured injury is an abraded laceration, as evidenced by tissue bridging and marginal abrasions.
- Answer E is incorrect. A stab wound is a sharp force injury pattern in which the wound is deeper than it is long and typically has smooth edges. In this case, the edges are not smooth and tissue bridging is evident, which is the key feature of a laceration.

A3.7 The correct answer is E. Struck from behind by a vehicle while upright

- Answer A is incorrect. Although the cutaneous defects may have resulted from a chop-like injury, the characteristic location and the probable associated pelvic fracture suggest the decedent was a pedestrian struck from behind.
- Answer B is incorrect. The characteristic location and the probable associated pelvic fracture suggest the decedent was a pedestrian struck from behind.
- Answer C is incorrect. Although the decedent may have been struck by multiple vehicles, the characteristic location of the featured injuries and the probable associated pelvic fracture are consistent with the decedent being a pedestrian struck from behind.
- Answer D is incorrect. The characteristic location and the probable associated pelvic fracture suggest the decedent was a pedestrian struck from behind.
- Answer E is correct. The injuries at her groin are consistent with the decedent being upright and being struck from behind. Also notice the averted right thigh which is suggestive of a pelvic or proximal femur fracture.

A3.8 The correct answer is A. Asphyxia

- Answer A is correct. The electrical cord pictured served as the ligature in the hanging that killed the decedent. The mechanism associated with hanging is asphyxia or lack of oxygen. The cause of death is still reported as hanging.
- Answer B is incorrect. Catecholamine excess, as seen in adrenergic storm, is a sudden and dramatic increase in serum levels of the catecholamines epinephrine and norepinephrine with a less significant increase in dopamine. It may cause death because of extreme tachycardia and hypertension. Hanging is not associated with adrenergic storm.
- Answer C is incorrect. Cervical spine fracture in the case of hanging is typically seen in judicial executions. The hangman's fracture occurs classically in the second cervical vertebra. Another clue is the placement of the ligature, which is classically placed directly under the chin, in judicial executions, which is not observed in the photograph.
- Answer D is incorrect. Prolonged QT interval may be caused by genetic factors, can be caused by drugs such as quinidine and amiodarone, and may be associated with fatty liver. Asphyxia is the mechanism of death in hanging.
- Answer E is incorrect. Ventricular arrhythmia would occur as a result of electrocution. This would be a valid choice if the death was by electrocution. Since the electrical cord was used as a ligature to compress the neck the mechanism is asphyxia and not ventricular arrhythmia due to electrocution.

A3.9 The correct answer is B. Hanging

- Answer A is incorrect. Although there are no pathognomonic findings for drowning, which is considered a diagnosis of exclusion, a photograph illustrating a drowning may show evidence of pulmonary edema, such as a foam cap at the oral cavity, which is not seen here.
- Answer B is correct. Hanging is suggested by the protrusion of the tongue with postmortem drying artifact in the photograph. Full suspension of the body results in lifting of the neck organs with consequent tongue protrusion. Of course, to reach this conclusion confidently, adequate scene investigation is imperative.
- Answer C is incorrect. Manual or ligature strangulation does not normally lift the neck organs upward causing pronounced protrusion of the tongue. Also, additional injury to the skin and soft tissues of the neck is expected. A layer-by-layer neck dissection primarily to exclude hemorrhage is a useful tool in this respect.
- Answer D is incorrect. Smothering is the blocking of the external airways (nose and mouth). Smothering may leave only subtle signs such as damage to the oral mucosa or may leave no signs at all. It does not cause lifting of the neck organs upward with protrusion of the tongue.
- Answer E is incorrect. Suffocation refers to a lack of oxygen in the breathing atmosphere. No physical signs may be apparent.

A3.10 The correct answer is D. Suicide

- Answer A is incorrect. Hanging deaths are rarely accidental in manner. However, scene investigation remains key since fatal accidental autoerotic asphyxia may be by hanging.
- Answer B is incorrect. Hanging deaths are rarely homicidal in manner except in the case of judicial hanging, which is less common than in the past. The so-called hangman's fracture is of the second cervical vertebra at the pars interarticularis due to hyperextension and distraction. Such an injury may be sustained in a car collision with the chin striking the dashboard.
- Answer C is incorrect. The finding suggests a non-natural manner of death.
- Answer D is correct. Suicide is the most common manner of death in hanging. The ligature furrow angle should be consistent with the position of the body when suspended and is generally in an inverted Y orientation. Vertebral fractures and strap muscle hemorrhages are uncommon in suicidal hangings unless a significant drop occurred prior to suspension.
- Answer E is incorrect. In the absence of scene investigation, hanging may be considered undetermined in manner as the pathologist must exclude rare circumstances in which other manners are more appropriate.

A3.11 The correct answer is D. Hampered venous return to the heart

- Answer A is incorrect. Although the purple discoloration of the shoulder and arm may mimic decomposition marbling, closer inspection of the scene makes this choice incorrect.
- Answer B is incorrect. The scene neither supports nor refutes significant blunt trauma from the motor vehicle. However, the region of purple coloration is not in direct contact with the vehicle and not likely affected by blunt trauma.
- Answer C is incorrect. The scene photograph with significant discoloration of the shoulder and arm from apparent compression by the motor vehicle tire suggests that the individual's heart was beating at the time of the incident and makes cardiac arrhythmia less likely.
- Answer D is correct. The orientation of the decedent with the tire of the motor vehicle apparently compressing the midsection and with the corresponding vascular changes (congestion versus petechiae) support a scenario in which there was hampered venous return to the heart. As this would lead to impaired respiration, this is considered a form of mechanical asphyxia.
- Answer E is incorrect. Although internal hemorrhage is not excluded by the provided photograph, it is not the best answer.

A3.12 The correct answer is C. Mechanical asphyxia

- Answer A is incorrect. Choking is a description of asphyxia due to blockage of the airway at the level of the larynx, laryngopharynx, or trachea. No illustration of these structures is apparent.
- Answer B is incorrect. Hanging may lead to significant decrease in venous return from the regions above the ligature utilized or may not if there is enough force to also prevent arterial blood flow. However, the purple discoloration in this case extends past the neck and no ligature furrow is seen. These findings make hanging less likely.
- Answer C is correct. The photograph demonstrates a case of mechanical asphyxia. The point of compression can be ascertained to be at the upper chest by the linear abraded or contused areas. In addition, there is apparent vascular congestion superior to the compression point suggestive of impaired venous return. This individual was a motor vehicle driver compressed by the dashboard subsequent to a collision; no significant internal injuries were identified.
- Answer D is incorrect. Smothering entails the blockage of the airways by obstructing airflow at the nose or mouth. This cause of death may not leave any gross findings on the body. However, it is important to inspect the oral mucosa and frenula when smothering is in the differential diagnosis since a struggle during smothering may lead to damage of these structures, particularly in an individual with teeth. The diagnosis of smothering in an infant can be extremely difficult.
- Answer E is incorrect. Strangulation may leave evidence around the neck structures including ligature furrow or abrasion, bruising, defensive fingernail injuries, and so on. Intermittent pressure on the neck from strangulation may lead to various vascular findings including petechial hemorrhages and congestion such as that seen in the photograph (but above the level of the neck structures compressed). The location of the linear abrasions and the extent of vascular congestion do not support a conclusion of strangulation.

A3.13 The correct answer is C. Exit gunshot wound

- Answer A is incorrect. The featured injury has characteristics of an exit gunshot wound. Additionally, no stippling, indicative of a closer range gunshot entrance wound, is present.
- Answer B is incorrect. The featured injury has characteristics of an exit gunshot wound. Additionally, no soot or muzzle imprint, indicative of a contact entrance gunshot wound, is present.
- Answer C is correct. Exit gunshot wound is the best answer as the edges of the wound have a characteristic stellate appearance and the wound edges reapproximate without apparent loss of tissue. Entrance gunshot wounds generally demonstrate tissue loss.
- Answer D is incorrect. The featured injury has characteristics of an exit gunshot wound, not an entrance wound. Range of gunshot wounds is typically based on the entrance wound and not the exit wound. In this case, the term *indeterminate-range gunshot wound* implies assessment of range based on the characteristics of the entrance wound, which this is not.
- Answer E is incorrect. The featured injury has characteristics of an exit gunshot wound. Keyhole gunshot wounds are a combination of entrance and exit wounds, most frequently observed when a gunshot passes tangentially across the curved skull surface. The appearance of a keyhole gunshot wound resembles the appearance of an old-fashioned keyhole.

A3.14 The correct answer is E. Decedent was walking on the road

- Answer A is incorrect. Measuring the height of the vehicle would be required to determine whether braking was occurring at the time the decedent was struck.
- Answer B is incorrect. The described leg fractures are designated "bumper fractures," and suggest an upright position of the decedent.
- Answer C is incorrect. If the decedent had been standing in the road, the height of the bumper fracture would likely be the same on each leg.
- Answer D is incorrect. The bumper fractures provide no information regarding whether the decedent was thrown over the car.
- Answer E is correct. The described leg fractures are most consistent with "bumper fractures" and indicate the upright nature of the decedent as he was struck by a vehicle. The differing heights above the soles of the feet are compatible with one leg being raised in the process of walking.

A3.15 The correct answer is C. Cervical spine fracture

- Answer A is incorrect. The mechanism associated with hanging due to suspension is asphyxia or lack of oxygen. In hanging due to suspension the ligature serves to compress the neck vasculature which in turn results in cerebral hypoxia.
- Answer B is incorrect. Catecholamine excess as seen in adrenergic storm is a sudden and dramatic increase in serum levels of the catecholamines epinephrine and norepinephrine with a less significant increase in dopamine. It may cause death because of extreme tachycardia and hypertension. Hanging is not associated with adrenergic storm.
- Answer C is correct. Cervical spine fracture is seen in judicial executions. The hangman's fracture occurs classically in the second cervical vertebra (axis) and is due to forcible hyperextension of the head.
- Answer D is incorrect. Prolonged QT interval may be caused by genetic factors, can be caused by drugs such as quinidine and amiodarone, and may be associated with fatty liver.
- Answer E is incorrect. Ventricular arrhythmia is not the mechanism associated with judicial hanging.

A3.16 The correct answer is C. Core separated from jacket

- Answer A is incorrect. The photograph shows copper jacketing at the top with a lead core at the bottom. Many ammunition types have a lead core and are surrounded by a copper layer called a jacket. The copper jacket may separate and be recovered in a different or adjacent location from the lead core. Thus, two projectiles may be seen on x-ray for a single bullet. A formula for detecting if you have missed an exit wound or entrance wound during a multiple gunshot wound case is as follows:

  $$(\text{Number of entrance wounds} + \text{number of exit wounds} - \text{number of projectiles})/2 = \text{a whole number}$$

  Example, you have four entrance wounds, three exit wounds, and one projectile (in our example above since the copper jacketing goes with the lead core it is considered one projectile). $(4+3-1)/2 = 3$ which is a whole number so you have accounted for all of your projectiles and wounds. If you had gotten a number like 3.5 or 2.5, start over!
- Answer B is incorrect. An embolus is defined as any solid, liquid, or gaseous substance that migrates from its point of origin to a distant site. Bullet emboli are bullets that travel like other types of emboli. The embolus like other emboli travel within the vascular system. This phenomenon is rare and typically involves .22-caliber ammunition. Although no scale is provided in the photograph, typical .22 rounds consist of only a lead projectile without jacketing.
- Answer C is correct. The top of the photograph depicts a copper jacket and the bottom of the photograph depicts a lead core. As mentioned above, these can become separated once the bullet enters the body as in our case.
- Answer D is incorrect. Occasionally when working up a gunshot case you may come across additional retained projectiles that are the result of past injuries. Usually this is because there is more risk in surgically removing the projectile than letting it stay in the body. For example, bullets located in a portion of the spine where the patient still has function may not be removed because the risk of paralysis outweighs the benefit of bullet removal. Not uncommonly, a fibrous capsule is around the bullet, and there is no associated acute hemorrhage.
- Answer E is incorrect. The photograph shows a bullet that has separated into its jacketing and core. That is consistent with one entrance wound and separation after the bullet entered the body. Sometimes the jacketing separates from the core before entering the body especially if it has struck an intermediate target such as a windshield or door. In such cases you would expect two entrance-type gunshot wounds, one for the jacketing and one for the lead core.

A3.17 The correct answer is A. Contact (at the skin surface)

- Answer A is correct. The wound pictured demonstrates soot around the central defect as well as an apparent muzzle imprint. These features are consistent with the muzzle of the gun held in contact with the skin surface. Note that all distance determinations by this method are estimates and that the best way to determine distance is to test fire with the identical weapon and ammunition used.
- Answer B is incorrect. A wound from less than 12″ but not contact may demonstrate soot deposition but would not show a muzzle imprint; stippling may also be seen.
- Answer C is incorrect. It would be unlikely to find soot at distances greater than 12″ (although stippling may occur up to approximately 36″); however, a muzzle imprint would not be present.
- Answer D is incorrect. Neither soot nor a muzzle imprint would be seen with gunshots greater than 36″ away.

A3.18 The correct answer is C. 3 feet

- Answer A is incorrect. A contact shotgun may or may not have soot or muzzle imprints (absent here), but scalloping of the wound edges would not be expected and the casing/wadding should enter the wound with the shot.
- Answer B is incorrect. At 2 feet, one would expect the casing/wadding to enter the wound with the shot.
- Answer C is correct. Seen here is a close-range shotgun entrance wound as evidenced by the slight scalloping of the wound edges and the angular abrasion on the surrounding skin caused by the shell case (wadding) petals. This combination of findings is most compatible with a distance of 3 feet. It should be noted that this is an estimate of the range of fire. In order to ascertain the distance one must test fire the weapon with the ammunition used.
- Answer D is incorrect. By 4 feet, one would expect to see satellite entrances of the shot.
- Answer E is incorrect. Beyond 4 feet, one would expect to see satellite entrances of the shot or individual pellet entrances.

A3.19 The correct answer is C. Removed with nonmetallic instruments

- Answer A is incorrect. Bullets and other evidence should not be placed in bleach for decontamination. Bleach destroys DNA evidence and can cause corrosion of metallic surfaces.
- Answer B is incorrect. Metal instruments should not be used to recover bullets (projectiles). The metal instruments can cause markings that can deform or crush a bullet limiting its evidentiary value.
- Answer C is correct. Removing a projectile is best accomplished by using plastic forceps. A gloved hand will also preserve evidence, but care must be taken to prevent injury from the sharp metal edges.
- Answer D is incorrect. Forensic pathologists are not firearms examiners, and test firing a weapon should only be done by the firearms examiner and not the pathologist.
- Answer E is incorrect. Initials or other marks should not be carved into the fragments as this can hinder ballistics evaluation. The projectile fragments should be placed in secured packaging such as a paper envelope or plastic container.

A3.20 The correct answer is C. Small caliber

- Answer A is incorrect. Birdshot refers to small round lead pellets in shotgun shells. The photograph designates a shaped projectile much different from birdshot. When recovering projectiles from shotguns, it is good practice to recover the wadding as this may be more useful than the pellets in matching the ammunition, as well as multiple birdshot pellets.
- Answer B is incorrect. Buckshot refers to pellets larger than those seen in birdshot. Since these are used in shotgun ammunition, it is good practice to recover the wadding and a representative sample of the pellets for analysis.
- Answer C is correct. The photograph depicts a copper jacketed lead projectile, in this case from a .25-caliber pistol. You can measure the base of the bullet using the ruler that shows it is approximately 1/4 of an inch, which translates to a caliber of .25 inch. Small-caliber projectiles are those in the range of .170–.29 inch.
- Answer D is incorrect. Large-caliber projectiles are those usually larger than .400 inch. Examples include .44 Magnum, .45 ACP, and .50 caliber.
- Answer E is incorrect. Medium-caliber bullets are those in the range of .30–.399 inch. Of note, some experts consider the .40 caliber a medium-caliber projectile, although it falls outside the "medium-caliber range." Common calibers seen here are 9mm, .38 Special, .357 Magnum, 10mm, and .380 caliber. In general, small-caliber bullets have numbers in the 20s (.22, .25), medium calibers in the 30s (.32, .357), and large calibers in the 40s and above (.44, .45, .50). One of the most common medium-caliber bullets is a 9mm. To convert millimeters to inches, divide by 25.4. In this case a 9mm would be around a .354 caliber.

A3.21 The correct answer is B. <12 inches

- Answer A is incorrect. Contact gunshot wounds are not associated with stippling.
- Answer B is correct. This gunshot wound demonstrates definitive stippling, which is abrasion of the skin caused by gunpowder particulates exiting the gun muzzle. The stippling pattern enlarges in circumference around the central gunshot wound defect with increasing distance from the muzzle to the target. The wound also demonstrates soot at its edges, which increases the likelihood of a closer gunshot wound, although test firing would be definitive.
- Answer C is incorrect. Stippling may be seen at distances less than 36″, but soot is not typically present at distances greater than 12″.
- Answer D is incorrect. At greater than 36″, one would expect neither soot nor stippling although test firing would be definitive.

A3.22 The correct answer is C. Left to right (The photograph depicts a graze gunshot wound. The encircled area shows a skin tag that points to where the bullet originated.)

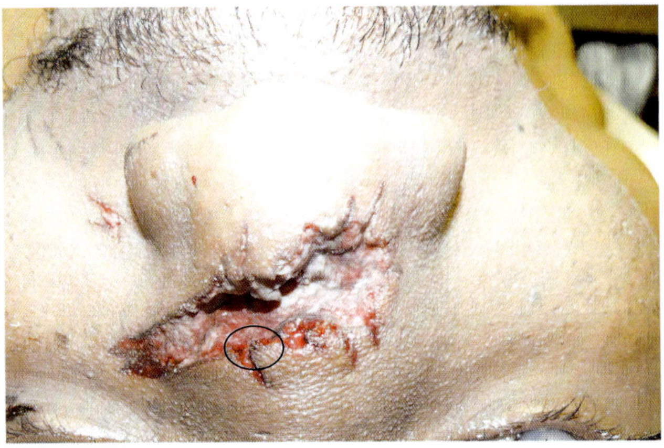

Figure 3.41

- Answer A is incorrect. The direction of fire is from left to right. If the skin tags pointed to the bottom of the photograph then choice A would be correct.
- Answer B is incorrect. The direction of fire can be determined.
- Answer C is correct. The skin tag that is encircled in the photograph points to where the bullet originated, in this case the left of the photograph. Thus, the direction is left to right.
- Answer D is incorrect. If the skin tags pointed to the right then the direction would be right to left.
- Answer E is incorrect. If the skin tags pointed to the top of the photograph then choice E would be correct.

A3.23 The correct answer is B. High-velocity rifle ammunition

- Answer A is incorrect. A .22 rimfire rifle, a revolver, and a semiautomatic handgun are not likely to deliver a projectile with sufficient energy to fragment it to the extent featured in this radiograph.
- Answer B is correct. The radiograph demonstrates multiple small but irregularly sized and shaped radiopaque material along the right side of the face and neck. This is known as a metallic snowstorm and is almost diagnostic by itself for a high-powered rifle round. The fragmentation is more likely due to a weapon able to deliver projectiles with high velocity and thus, more energy: $K = 1/2\ mv^2$ where K is the kinetic energy, m is mass, and v is velocity.
- Answer C is incorrect. A pipe bomb is usually considered a low explosive device and as such would not have enough power to fragment the shrapnel that it delivers to the extent as seen in the photograph.
- Answer D is incorrect. A .22 rimfire rifle, a revolver, and a semiautomatic handgun are not likely to deliver a projectile with sufficient energy to fragment it to the extent featured in this radiograph.
- Answer E is incorrect. A .22 rimfire rifle, a revolver, and a semiautomatic handgun are not likely to deliver a projectile with sufficient energy to fragment it to the extent featured in this radiograph.

A3.24 The correct answer is E. Medium caliber

- Answer A is incorrect. Birdshot refers to small round lead pellets in shotgun shells. The photograph designates a shaped projectile much different from birdshot. When recovering projectiles from shotguns, it is good practice to recover the wadding as this may be more useful than the pellets in matching the ammunition, as well as multiple birdshot pellets.
- Answer B is incorrect. Buckshot refers to lead pellets larger than those seen in birdshot. Since these are used in shotgun ammunition, it is good practice to recover the wadding and a representative sample of the pellets for testing.
- Answer C is incorrect. Small-caliber projectiles are those in the range of .170–.29 inch.
- Answer D is incorrect. Large-caliber projectiles are those usually larger than .400 inch. Examples include .44 Magnum, .45 ACP, and .50 caliber.
- Answer E is correct. The photograph depicts a copper jacketed lead projectile, in this case from a 9mm pistol. You can measure the base of the bullet using the ruler that shows it is between 5/16 and 6/16 of an inch, which translates to a caliber of approximately .313–.375 inches. Medium-caliber bullets are those in the range of .30–.399 inches. Of note, some experts consider the .40 caliber a medium-caliber projectile although it falls outside the "medium-caliber range." Common medium calibers are 9mm, .38 Special, .357 Magnum, 10mm, and .380 caliber. In general, small-caliber bullets have numbers in the 20s (.22, .25), medium calibers in the 30s (.32, .357), and large calibers in the 40s and above (.44, .45, .50). One of the most common medium-caliber bullets is a 9mm. To convert millimeters to inches divide by 25.4. In this case a 9mm would be around a .354 caliber which is between 5/16 and 6/16 of an inch.

A3.25 The correct answer is E. Gauge

- Answer A is incorrect. Birdshot is a designation for small lead pellets used in hunting small game such as birds. The size of birdshot increases as the labeling number decreases. For example, number 7 birdshot pellets each have a diameter of .100 inch and number 9 birdshot pellets each have a diameter of .080 inch.
- Answer B is incorrect. Bore is the term used to identify the internal diameter of the barrel of a firearm usually expressed in inches or millimeters. For example a .270 Winchester rifle has a bore (internal diameter) of approximately .270 inch.
- Answer C is incorrect. Buckshot is a designation for lead pellets that are larger than birdshot and used to hunt larger game such as deer or bear. Similar to birdshot the larger the number, the smaller is the individual pellet. The most common buckshot used is 00 buck, pronounced "double ought buck." Each 00 shell in most cases contains nine equally sized pellets usually made of lead.
- Answer D is incorrect. Caliber is used to designate the diameter of the barrel, expressed in inches or millimeters through which the largest bullet (projectile) can safely pass. It is also the measurement of the diameter of the base of the bullet, not the base of the cartridge or round. A notable exception is the .38 special bullet which has a 0.38 inch diameter base of the cartridge but only 0.357 inch base for the actual bullet.
- Answer E is correct. For firearms, shotguns in particular, gauge is defined as the number of lead balls to make up one pound. For example, 12 gauge means that 12 equal round lead balls are in a pound and that each ball is 1/12 of a pound. The exception to this rule is the .410 shotgun which is based on the caliber of .410 inches. If the gauge definition were used here, a .410 shotgun would be classified as a 67-gauge shotgun.

A3.26 The correct answer is E. Shored exit wound

- Answer A is incorrect. Although at first glance this may appear to be an entrance wound, it is not. The key finding is the description of where the body was found and the relationship of the wound to the body. In this case you are given information that the wound was adjacent to a hard surface, in this case a bathtub. Therefore, based on this scenario, this is not an entrance gunshot wound.
- Answer B is incorrect. Based on this scenario, this is not an entrance gunshot wound.
- Answer C is incorrect. Based on this scenario, this is not an entrance gunshot wound.
- Answer D is incorrect. Based on this scenario, this is not an entrance gunshot wound, including an entrance wound via a ricochet projectile.
- Answer E is correct. According to the history, the victim's back was against the tub when he was shot. The presence of an abrasion border at the location of an exit wound is most consistent with a shored exit wound in which abrasion of the skin is due to the exiting projectile pressing the skin against a hard surface.

A3.27 The correct answer is E. Cannot be determined by x-ray

- Answer A is incorrect. Range of fire cannot be estimated by the pellet distribution internally.
- Answer B is incorrect. Range of fire cannot be estimated by the pellet distribution internally.
- Answer C is incorrect. Range of fire cannot be estimated by the pellet distribution internally.
- Answer D is incorrect. Range of fire cannot be estimated by the pellet distribution internally.
- Answer E is correct. Although most shotguns create classic injury patterns on the skin depending on the distance the victim is from the gun, internally, as seen by x-ray, the distribution of the shotgun pellets cannot be used to estimate range of fire due to the billiard ball effect that occurs when the pellets enter the body and strike each other.

A3.28 Correct answer is E. Velocity

- Answer A is incorrect. Caliber reflects the diameter of the base of the bullet. While it is true that larger calibers tend to have more energy, this is not always the case. For example, a .308 rifle round that is smaller in caliber has more energy than a .45 caliber pistol round.
- Answer B is incorrect. Distance does play some role in bullet energy as bullets cannot travel an infinite amount of distance. Their energy dissipates as the distance from the barrel increases.
- Answer C is incorrect. Gauge is used to indirectly measure the size of shotgun barrel diameter rounds. Although variation in size affects bullet energy, ultimately, the most important contribution is velocity.
- Answer D is incorrect. Mass is an important key player, and if the velocity is the same for two bullets then the one with the larger mass will have more energy.
- Answer E is correct. The most significant variable in the energy of a bullet is velocity. The general formula is $KE = 1/2\ mv^2$, where *KE* stands for kinetic energy, *m* for mass, and *v* for velocity. Since the term for velocity is squared, it will have more significant increase in energy than an increase in mass. For example, the reason a .308 round has more energy than a .45-caliber round even though it is about 30% lighter is because it has 2–2.5 times the velocity of the .45-caliber round. Keeping this in mind, it has four to six times the impact energy based on velocity.

A3.29 The correct answer is D. Large caliber

- Answer A is incorrect. Birdshot refers to small round lead pellets in shotgun shells. The photograph designates a shaped projectile much different from birdshot. When recovering projectiles from shotguns, it is good practice to recover the wadding as this may be more useful than the pellets in matching the ammunition, as well as multiple birdshot pellets.
- Answer B is incorrect. Buckshot refers to lead pellets larger than those seen in birdshot. Since these are used in shotgun ammunition, it is good practice to recover the wadding and a representative sample of the pellets for testing.
- Answer C is incorrect. Small-caliber projectiles are those in the range of .170–.29 inch.
- Answer D is correct. Large-caliber projectiles are those usually larger than .400 inch. Examples include .44 Magnum, .45 ACP, and .50 caliber. The photograph depicts a copper jacketed lead projectile, in this case from a .45-caliber pistol. You can measure the base of the bullet using the ruler that shows it is between 11 and 12 mm in diameter, which translates to a caliber of approximately .433–.472 inches consistent with a large-caliber projectile.
- Answer E is incorrect. Medium-caliber bullets are those in the range of .30–.399 inches. Of note, some experts consider the .40 caliber a medium-caliber projectile although it falls outside the "medium-caliber range." Common medium calibers are 9mm, .38 Special, .357 Magnum, 10mm, and .380 caliber. In general, small-caliber bullets have numbers in the 20s (.22, .25), medium calibers in the 30s (.32, .357), and large calibers in the 40s and above (.44, .45, .50). One of the most common medium-caliber bullets is a 9mm. To convert millimeters to inches, divide by 25.4. In this case, a 9mm would be around a .354 caliber, which is between 5/16 and 6/16 of an inch.

A3.30 Correct answer is C. Load

- Answer A is incorrect. Caliber refers to the diameter of the base of the bullet usually expressed in inches or millimeters.
- Answer B is incorrect. The length of the cartridge varies depending on the type of the round. In general large-caliber rounds have longer cartridges and rifle rounds are longer than pistol rounds. (Note: cartridge is the entire loaded round commonly referred to as a "bullet." The bullet is the portion of the cartridge that is released when the round is detonated. The casing is the remaining portion of the cartridge that is left behind in the gun or ejected after the round is fired. The bullet exits the barrel and hits its target if you are a good shot.
- Answer C is correct. Load as it pertains to firearms is the amount of powder used in a cartridge. One of the most common examples is the .357 Magnum. The cartridge has a .357 inch–diameter bullet just as a .38 Special round has, but the difference is the amount of powder. The .357 round has more powder in it and is a longer round than the .38 Special. It generates about twice as much pressure as the .38 Special round and can have a velocity in excess of 1500 feet per second. For these reasons it is a much more powerful round and is referred to as a "Magnum" round. Some other designators are used to indicated a higher load in a cartridge such as +P and +P+. For example, a .38 +P round is more powerful than a .38 round and even more powerful is the +P+. These designations refer to higher pressures generated when compared to the standard load.
- Answer D is incorrect. Most bullets have a round to ovoid shape and this has nothing to do with the term *Magnum*.
- Answer E is incorrect. Style can refer to many types of bullets. Two common styles seen in autopsy are full metal jacket (FMJ) rounds and hollow point (HP) rounds. FMJ rounds are lead rounds covered by a copper jacket that are designed to pass through tissue and exit the body. HP rounds have a central indentation in the nose, typically exposing the lead core to promote mushrooming and are designed in this way in order to deliver maximum energy to the tissues.

A3.31 The correct answer is E. Wadding

- Answer A is incorrect. The central defect is an entrance shotgun wound; the adjacent abrasion is unlikely to be caused by the butt of the shotgun.
- Answer B is incorrect. The central defect is an entrance shotgun wound demonstrating scalloping (i.e., range of fire is approximately 3 feet). Although intermediate target debris injuries cannot be excluded, the lesion at the 1 o'clock position is most likely a wad mark.
- Answer C is incorrect. The central defect is an entrance shotgun wound with scalloped edges, consistent with the entire shot mass entering the body. Also, satellite shot entrance wound marks would typically reflect the shot size and would appear as round or slightly oblong defects in the skin much smaller in size than that seen in the photograph.
- Answer D is incorrect. The central defect is an entrance shotgun wound; the adjacent abrasion is unlikely to be caused by the scope of the shotgun.
- Answer E is correct. The central defect is an entrance shotgun wound demonstrating scalloping (i.e., range of fire is approximately 3 feet). The offset abrasion at 1 o'clock is consistent with a wadding mark as the wad exits the barrel and drifts from the main shot mass.

A3.32 The correct answer is A. Revolver

- Answer A is correct. The blanket shows a rounded defect surrounded by soot, consistent with the muzzle of a gun. Also, an area of soot is to the right of the photograph and was most likely caused by a cylinder gap, which is present on revolvers.
- Answer B is incorrect. The soot to the right of the blanket was likely caused by a cylinder gap, present on revolvers.
- Answer C is incorrect. The soot to the right of the blanket was likely caused by a cylinder gap, present on revolvers.
- Answer D is incorrect. The soot to the right of the blanket was likely caused by a cylinder gap, which is present on revolvers.

A3.33 The correct answer is B. Close range

- Answer A is incorrect. Although there is a small amount of either soot and/or bullet wipe around the defect created by the bullet, there are also gunpowder particles around the defect.
- Answer B is correct. The photograph demonstrates a small amount of either soot and/or bullet wipe around a defect created by a bullet. More significant is the presence of associated gunpowder particles around the defect. These particulates would likely have created stippling on skin had the shirt not been an intermediate target. In this instance, the shirt is light colored and relatively not blood stained, and thus the gunpowder particles are visible. This might not be the case in dark-colored shirts and extensively bloodied clothing items. The presence of the gunpowder particles illustrates the importance of examining the clothing of any gunshot victim. Analogous to measuring the spread of stippling on the skin, it may be important to measure the spread of the gunpowder deposition on the clothes in order to assist in narrowing the range of fire if the suspected weapon is test fired. In this regard, the photograph provided lacks a ruler. Thus, measurement information from the photographic record is hindered.
- Answer C is incorrect. Soot/bullet wipe and gunpowder particulates are present, so this is not a distant gunshot wound. Distant gunshot wounds do not characteristically have soot or stippling but would be expected to have an abrasion collar.
- Answer D is incorrect. Gunpowder particulates are present so the general range of fire is able to be determined.

A3.34 Correct answer is E. Keyhole gunshot wound

- Answer A is incorrect. This is a classic patterned injury. It is a keyhole gunshot wound.
- Answer B is incorrect. This wound has characteristics of both an entrance wound on the left and characteristics of an exit on the right.
- Answer C is incorrect. This wound has characteristics of both an entrance wound on the left and an exit on the right.
- Answer D is incorrect. A graze gunshot wound is identified by the pattern of soft tissue. Classically the skin tags point to where the bullet originated.
- Answer E is correct. Keyhole gunshot wounds have characteristics of both entrance and exit wounds. They are usually seen in the skull and occur because of the angle of the bullet in relation to the roundness of the skull. In the photograph accompanying the question, the internal beveling on the left side has the characteristics of an entrance wound, and the external beveling on the right side has the characteristics of an exit wound.

A3.35 Correct answer is B. Left to right

- Answer A is incorrect. Since the keyhole-type gunshot wound possesses both entrance and exit characteristics, these can be used to help determine the direction. If the wound as pictured was rotated 90° to the right, then choice A would be correct.
- Answer B is correct. Since the entrance portion is on the left and the exit portion is on the right, then the direction of the bullet is left to right.
- Answer C is incorrect. This is the opposite of choice B.
- Answer D is incorrect. If the bullet proceeded toward the viewer, it would be perpendicular to the skull and you would see an exit-type wound, with external beveling, not a keyhole.
- Answer E is incorrect. If the wound as pictured was rotated 90° to the left, then choice E would be correct.

A3.36 Correct answer is A. Cannot be determined

- Answer A is correct. A number of factors prohibit interpretation of the range of fire. Most importantly, the wound is skeletonized. In addition it was found in wet conditions. Since the skin is gone and it has been in a wet environment, it is hard to establish the presence of soot or stippling that may help to estimate the range of fire. Since it is not known if these existed, range of fire cannot be definitively established.
- Answer B is incorrect. A distance of less than 0.1 inches is consistent with contact or close contact wounds, which would have soot and thermal injury in the skin from the blast. These cannot be determined in this case because of the skeletonization and environmental factors.
- Answer C is incorrect. A distance between 1 and 6 inches is consistent with intermediate wounds, which would have stippling on the skin and possibly soot. These cannot be determined in this case because of the skeletonization and environmental factors.
- Answer D is incorrect. A distance of approximately 12 inches is consistent with intermediate wounds, which would have stippling on the skin but likely not soot. These cannot be determined in this case because of the skeletonization and environmental factors.
- Answer E is incorrect. A distance of approximately 30 feet is consistent with a distant-type wound, which would most likely only show abrasion of the skin. Since there is no skin, it is impossible to determine this.

A3.37 The correct answer is C. Reposition the x-ray plate to include all the chest soft tissue

- Answer A is incorrect. Exiting a natural orifice is unlikely.
- Answer B is incorrect. The photograph depicts a classic entrance gunshot wound. An ice pick may be considered once a gunshot wound is excluded.
- Answer C is correct. Positioning of x-ray plates is critical in assessing gunshot wound victims. In this case, the soft tissue of the lateral chest is not included in the view. Repositioning to include the flanks results in demonstration of the projectile (see below). This is especially important when evaluating obese individuals where it is difficult to fit entire cross sections of the body onto one film.
- Answer D is incorrect. Caseless ammunition would have no bearing on the presence of a radiopaque projectile.
- Answer E is incorrect. Reloaded ammunition would have no bearing on the presence of a radiopaque projectile.

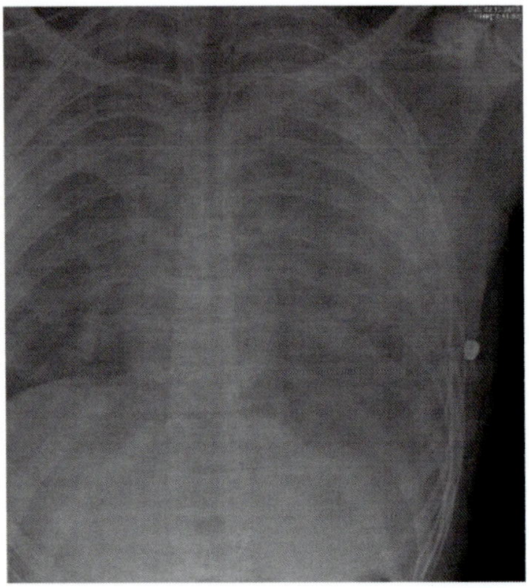

Figure 3.42

A3.38 The correct answer is D. By definition, detonation velocities of high explosives are at least 3300 feet per second.

(See International Fire Service Training Association. 2010. *IFSTA Hazardous Materials for First Responders*, 4th Edition. Oklahoma City. Oklahoma State University Fire Protection Pub.)

A3.39 The correct answer is C. Pulmonary barotrauma

- Answer A is incorrect. Cardiac arrhythmia is arguably the cause of death in everybody, but the underlying cause of death in those who initially survive an explosion is the complications associated with the blast injury, which in this case is due to barotrauma involving the lungs, also known as blast lung.
- Answer B is incorrect. Although the gastrointestinal tract is a "hollow organ" and is susceptible to blast trauma, it is not the most common cause of death for survivors of an explosion.
- Answer C is correct. The most common cause of death for people who initially survive an explosion is pulmonary barotrauma, also known as blast lung, which can manifest as contusion, intraparenchymal hemorrhage, edema, or any combination of these.
- Answer D is incorrect. Spleen rupture is not the most common cause of death in those who initially survive a blast injury.
- Answer E is incorrect. Sepsis is the most common cause of death for those who survive thermal injury such as seen in a house or automobile fire.

A3.40 The correct answer is C. Tertiary

- Answer A is incorrect. Primary blast injuries are due to the direct effects of the overpressure (shockwave) of the blast. A fractured bone could be considered primary if it was due to the direct effect of the blast wave, but in the depicted scenario, the injury is due to an impact with another object and not due to the blast wave. Thus, it is not a primary injury.
- Answer B is incorrect. Secondary blast injuries occur as a result of shrapnel that impacts the body as a result of detonation. Shrapnel may include screws, ball bearings, or other metal fragments that are packed into the explosive device. An IED is designed to be antipersonnel in nature, and wounds may look similar to distant-type gunshot wounds. In this case, the bone fracture was not sustained as the result of shrapnel and would not be classified as secondary.
- Answer C is correct. Blast injury patterns can be classified into four groups: primary, secondary, tertiary, and quaternary. Tertiary blast injuries are those that are due to nonpenetrating impact damage or as the result of a person being thrown or propelled into an object. In this case, the fracture occurred as a result of an impact of the soldier into a vehicle and would be best classified as tertiary.
- Answer D is incorrect. Quaternary blast injuries are those that are not the result of primary, secondary, or tertiary injuries. Examples include chemical burns, thermal burns, radiation burns, and toxic inhalation.

A3.41 The correct answer is B. Secondary

- Answer A is incorrect. Primary blast injuries are due to the direct effects of the overpressure (shockwave) of the blast. The hollow organs such as the lungs and gastrointestinal tract are often affected and no visible injuries may be appreciated. Internal hemorrhage, pneumothorax, and pulmonary contusion are examples of primary blast injury.
- Answer B is correct. Blast injury patterns can be classified into four groups: primary, secondary, tertiary, and quaternary. Secondary blast injuries occur as a result of shrapnel that impacts the body as a result of detonation. This may include screws, ball bearings, or other metal fragments that are packed into the explosive device. It is designed to be antipersonnel in nature, and wounds may look similar to gunshot wounds. In the depicted scenario case, the wound pattern is due to impact of shrapnel, which qualifies as a secondary blast injury.
- Answer C is incorrect. Tertiary blast injuries are those that are due to *nonpenetrating* impact damage or as the result of a person being thrown or propelled in an object. In this case, the photograph depicts a penetrating wound that would not be classified as tertiary.
- Answer D is incorrect. Quaternary blast injuries are those that are not the result of primary, secondary, or tertiary injuries. Examples include chemical burns, thermal burns, radiation burns, and toxic inhalation.

A3.42 The correct answer is A. Milliseconds

- Answer A is correct. The photograph depicts a pulmonary contusion which is due to primary blast effects. These effects are due to the overpressure generated by the blast wave and are seen within the first few milliseconds of an explosion.
- Answer B is incorrect. The order of magnitude of the injury is in the order of milliseconds and not seconds.
- Answer C is incorrect. The time frame here is too prolonged as the injuries were sustained in a few milliseconds.
- Answer D is incorrect. A person who dies after initially surviving the blast most commonly would die as a result of pulmonary barotrauma, but the injury pattern was initiated in the few milliseconds after detonation.
- Answer E is incorrect. Pulmonary congestion can be seen postmortem as a result of gravity-dependent settling of blood, but this would give a uniform blue-purple appearance and not the one depicted here.

A3.43 The correct answer is A. Differentiation between a single-edged knife and a double-edged knife cannot definitively be made

- Answer A is correct. Differentiation between a single-edged knife and a double-edged knife cannot definitively be made. The featured stab wound shows some blunting on the right. This is consistent with a single-edged knife. However, a double-edged knife may create blunted edges as well if the blade enters deep enough to reach the ricasso (a short, unsharpened portion between the blade and the handle).
- Answer B is incorrect. Although double-edged knives classically leave pointed edges on each end, blunted edges can be created if a double-edged blade enters deep enough to reach the ricasso.
- Answer C is incorrect. A single-edged knife classically creates a stab wound with one pointed edge and one blunted edge (as featured in the photograph). However, a double-edged knife may create blunted edges as well if the blade enters deep enough to reach the ricasso. Of note, a single-edged knife may also create a wound with pointed edges on each end if the sharp edge cuts the skin prior to the blade entering to a depth.
- Answer D is incorrect. Although a scale is not provided in the photograph, a flathead screwdriver would be expected to have bilateral blunt ends and marginal abrasions. A Phillips head screwdriver creates a star-/cross-shaped injury on the skin surface.
- Answer E is incorrect. A target arrow has a conical arrowhead and creates rounded cutaneous defect upon penetration.

A3.44 The correct answer is D. Phillips head screwdriver

- Answer A is incorrect. The featured injuries are most consistent with a Phillips head screwdriver. Arrows may have a similar stellate shape but are not typically this small.
- Answer B is incorrect. A double-edged knife wound would most likely have an ovoid or slit-like shape and not the stellate pattern seen here.
- Answer C is incorrect. An ice pick would likely be round or oval and not the stellate pattern observed.
- Answer D is correct. The small, stellate configuration of the facial injuries is most consistent with a Phillips head screwdriver. Note: Be careful predicting weapon type; often it is better to pick the "most consistent" weapon from a provided selection.
- Answer E is incorrect. The featured injuries are most consistent with a Phillips head screwdriver. Scissors typically leave a paired mark. These injuries are not paired.

A3.45 The correct answer is E. Self-inflicted incisions

- Answer A is incorrect. An accidental injury from broken glass would probably be more diffuse and have more varying sizes and random direction rather than the perpendicular orientation to the hand as seen in the photograph.
- Answer B is incorrect. An avulsion is a blunt force type of injury that occurs due to tearing of the tissue. When tearing of the tissue occurs, you would expect to see some tissue bridging, which is not seen in the photograph. The injury pattern depicted is from sharp force injury.
- Answer C is incorrect. Defensive injuries on the forearm are classically associated with the ulnar surface of the forearm. In addition, it would be unusual to see defensive wounds in the pattern of hesitation marks. One clue these are hesitation marks is the orientation of the wounds. Parallel wounds are more consistent with hesitation marks and not defensive injury.
- Answer D is incorrect. This injury is most likely an incision and not a stab wound as it is longer than it is deep. The location suggests it is self-inflicted, which is more consistent with suicide than homicide.
- Answer E is correct. The finding illustrated is a group of sharp force injuries (incisions) that are self-inflicted, as evidenced by the anterior location of the incisions and the presence of hesitation marks on the antecubital fossa, forearm, and wrist.

A3.46 The correct answer is C. Serrated knife

- Answer A is incorrect. The weapon used was most likely a serrated knife. A broken glass bottle would result in sharp force injuries that have smooth edges.
- Answer B is incorrect. The weapon used may have been a pair of scissors; however, the better answer would be serrated knife as scissors typically leave paired marks.
- Answer C is correct. The patterned, zigzag margin of the injury is consistent with serrations from a knife.
- Answer D is incorrect. The weapon used may have been a single-edged knife; however, the better answer would be serrated knife.
- Answer E is incorrect. The weapon used may have been a double-edged knife; however, the better answer would be serrated knife.

A3.47 The correct answer is A. Assaulted from behind with knife

- Answer A is correct. The photograph demonstrates a classic sweeping incised wound created by an individual standing behind the decedent. It should be noted, however, that a similar wound may be created from an assailant in front of the decedent if the knife is held differently. So, such conclusions are best left to the investigative team.
- Answer B is incorrect. Hanging with a large distance drop may actually result in decapitation. However, several other incised wounds are visible in the photograph, suggesting a mechanism other than hanging.
- Answer C is incorrect. An ax creates a crushing injury that may have an incised-like appearance on the skin; however, the sweeping, curvilinear nature of the incision in the photograph is most consistent with an incised wound.
- Answer D is incorrect. The injury in the photograph is an incision, not blunt trauma laceration. A laceration would have typical tissue bridging which is not observed here.
- Answer E is incorrect. Classic hyperextension injuries occur in the groin area (i.e., nearer to the site of vehicular impact).

A3.48 The correct answer is A. Defensive injuries

- Answer A is correct. Injuries along the ulnar surfaces of the forearms and the palms are consistent with defensive injuries.
- Answer B is incorrect. Although injuries along the ulnar surfaces of the forearms and the palms may be from other sources, in this scenario, they are most consistent with defensive injuries.
- Answer C is incorrect. Although injuries along the ulnar surfaces of the forearms and the palms may be self-inflicted, in this scenario, they are most consistent with defensive injuries.
- Answer D is incorrect. Incised or stab wounds to the feet and soles would raise the index of suspicion for attempted sexual assault.
- Answer E is incorrect. Sharp force injuries along the forearms are not classic for terminal fall trauma. A terminal fall from height would be expected to have a blunt force injury pattern that would manifest as lacerations, abrasions, and/or fractures, which are not described in the question.

A3.49 The correct answer is D. V = IR

- Answer A is incorrect. In its simplest form, Ohm's law is defined by the formula V = IR, where *V* stands for voltage expressed in volts, *I* stands for current expressed in amps, and *R* stands for resistance expressed in ohms.
- Answer B is incorrect. In Ohm's law, current (*I*) and resistance (*R*) are multiplied, not added together, to obtain the voltage.
- Answer C is incorrect. In Ohm's law, current (*I*) and resistance (*R*) are multiplied, not subtracted, to obtain the voltage.
- Answer D is correct. This is Ohm's law as explained above.
- Answer E is incorrect. Ohm's law does not involve the square of any term.

A3.50 The correct answer is E. Lightning strike

- Answer A is incorrect. Depending on the etiology of asphyxia, physical findings may or may not be present. However, aside from petechial and sometimes purpural hemorrhages, hemorrhage is not a hallmark of asphyxia in the absence of other blunt trauma.
- Answer B is incorrect. Although blunt head trauma may result in basilar skull fracture and resultant bleeding from the external ear canal, there is no evidence of blunt trauma in this case.
- Answer C is incorrect. Inner ear or eustachian tube infections may be viral or bacterial but do not cause bleeding from the outer ear canal. In cases where the eardrum is perforated surgically and tubes are placed, serous or purulent drainage (otorrhea) might be expected. Otherwise, no outward signs will be apparent.
- Answer D is incorrect. Invasive fungal species may lead to significant hemorrhage; however, the blood would not be expected to drain from the external ear canal, which is separated from sinus cavities anatomically.
- Answer E is correct. The effect of a lighting strike on a body is analogous to a blast injury. A common finding is rupture of the tympanic membrane that may be associated with hemorrhage from the external ear. Other common findings include singeing of hair. It is believed that the massive voltage direct current discharge accompanying a lightning strike is not universally fatal due to the extremely short duration of the incident as well as the fact that those "struck by lightning" may actually experience secondary lightning impacts or arcing injury. Examination of the clothing including the shoes may also be informative as it may demonstrate extensive tearing and possibly burning beyond that expected for the condition of the remains.

A3.51 The correct answer is E. Ventricular arrhythmia

- Answer A is incorrect. The photograph depicts a low-voltage electrical injury. Very high-voltage electrocutions as seen in lightning strikes cause severe disruption of the central nervous system.
- Answer B is incorrect. High-voltage electrocutions, defined as being greater than 1000 volts, show extensive thermal injury many times seen as full-thickness burns.
- Answer C is incorrect. Low-voltage electrocution injuries may cause some small amount of thermal effect as seen in the photograph, but this is the cause of death and not the mechanism of death.
- Answer D is incorrect. Thermal injuries can be seen in low- and high-voltage electrocutions but this small amount of thermal injury would not result in death.
- Answer E is correct. Ventricular arrhythmias are the mechanism of death in low-voltage electrocutions. More than 30 mA (0.03 amps) of alternating current (AC) or 300–500 mA (0.3–0.5 amps) of direct current (DC) can cause ventricular fibrillation.

A3.52 The correct answer is B. Electrical injury

- Answer A is incorrect. ECM is a feature of Lyme disease and is characterized by a rash with a bull's eye appearance that expands out from the tick bite.
- Answer B is correct. This injury is a classical electrocution, with a crater surrounded by a white rim, surrounded by a band of erythema. Not all electrocutions will leave such pronounced markings, if any markings at all. This injury is from contact with high-voltage power lines.
- Answer C is incorrect. Although resuscitative defibrillation often leaves markings, they are generally limited to reddened outlines of the pads and aggregates of dried/abraded skin. The location of the featured injury is not in a characteristic location for a medicinal defibrillation, either.
- Answer D is incorrect. Necrotizing fasciitis typically appears as diffuse erythema that becomes dusky as the infection progresses.
- Answer E is incorrect. This injury is a classical electrocution, not a partial or full-thickness liquid burn.

A3.53 The correct answer is C. 100 mA

- Answer A is incorrect. 1 mA (1 milliamp or .001 amp) is at the threshold for appreciation of an electrical current; thus, although one may experience a tingling, neither tissue damage nor dysrhythmia are likely.
- Answer B is incorrect. At 10 mA, most will experience a "shock" that is perceptible, but not likely to lead to tissue damage or dysrhythmia. However, in those with low skin resistance such as children and elderly or in moist or wet conditions, this current may lead to skeletal muscle tetany and potentiate local tissue damage.
- Answer C is correct. Electrical injury may lead to cardiac arrhythmia in those cases where the current passes through the chest. The ideal current to produce ventricular fibrillation is 50–100 mA (milliamperes) and possibly as low as 30 mA. Above 2A (2000 mA), asystole is more likely. Amperes are a measure of the flow of electrons or current. Ohm law states that amperage is defined by the equation $I = V/R$ (I = current or amperes, V = voltage, and R = resistance), thus the current is directly related to the voltage and inversely related to the resistance. This fact makes household electrical current particularly dangerous, which in the United States has a voltage of 110. The corresponding resistance is dependent primarily on the skin surface contacted by the electrical device. Another factor making household current potentially dangerous is that it is generally an alternating current. Alternating currents in excess of about 15 mA (lower in children and others with thinner skin or in moist conditions due to lower resistance) cause muscular tetany; thus, the individual becomes unable to extricate himself or herself from the electrical device, effectively prolonging contact with the electrical current and potentiating the injurious effects. (Also see Leibovici D, Shemer J, Shapira SC. Electrical injuries: Current concepts. *Injury* 1995, 26(9): 623–7.)
- Answer D is incorrect. 2000 mA (2 A) is more likely to lead to tissue burns and necrosis. At this current, asystole rather than ventricular fibrillation is likely to result.

A3.54 The correct answer is D. 1000. By definition all the other answers are incorrect.

A3.55 The correct answer is C. Electrical power lines

- Answer A is incorrect. The findings illustrated are similar to insect activity, particularly ant activity. However, insect activity patterns generally group irregularly or line up abutting clothing lines. This picture shows a large region of abnormality and no insects are present. In addition, the skin surface remains intact unlike in the case of insect activity, which denudes the skin (also see Campobasso CP et al. Postmortem artifacts made by ants and the effect of ant activity on decompositional rates. *Am J Forensic Med Pathol* 2009, 30[1]: 84–7).
- Answer B is incorrect. Road rash is typified by multiple linear parallel abrasions, which are not seen here.
- Answer C is correct. The photograph shows electrical arcing injury from high-voltage power lines. One typical scenario might be that of an individual driving a forklift or excavator, lifting up the bucket or forks and striking lines.
- Answer D is incorrect. Mushroom toxicity generally results in hepatic changes. However, there is a dermatitis (flagellate mushroom dermatitis or flagellate erythema) caused by the ingestion of edible shiitake mushrooms (*Lentinula edodes*), which has an appearance of linear erythematous streaks or papules on the skin and thought secondary to a toxic reaction to a mushroom polysaccharide (also see Girard C, Bessis D. Flagellate dermatitis. Shiitake dermatitis [toxicoderma]. *Arch Dermatol* 2010, 146[11]: 1301–6); serious complications are uncommon.
- Answer E is incorrect. Superheated water may lead to a scald, which may generate an irregular pattern on the skin or may show a line of demarcation depending on the extent of the burn and how the water came into skin contact. The pattern in the photograph, however, would be difficult to produce with a scald-type injury and is not the best answer.

Chapter 4

ENVIRONMENTAL AND EXPOSURE-RELATED DEATHS

QUESTIONS

Q4.1 What is the most useful marker of acute anaphylaxis?

A. C-reactive protein
B. Diphenhydramine
C. Epinephrine
D. Procalcitonin
E. Tryptase

Q4.2 A 45-year-old male complained of shortness of breath during a meal, collapsed, and could not be resuscitated. The neck organs were removed during autopsy and are pictured. What is the most likely cause of death?

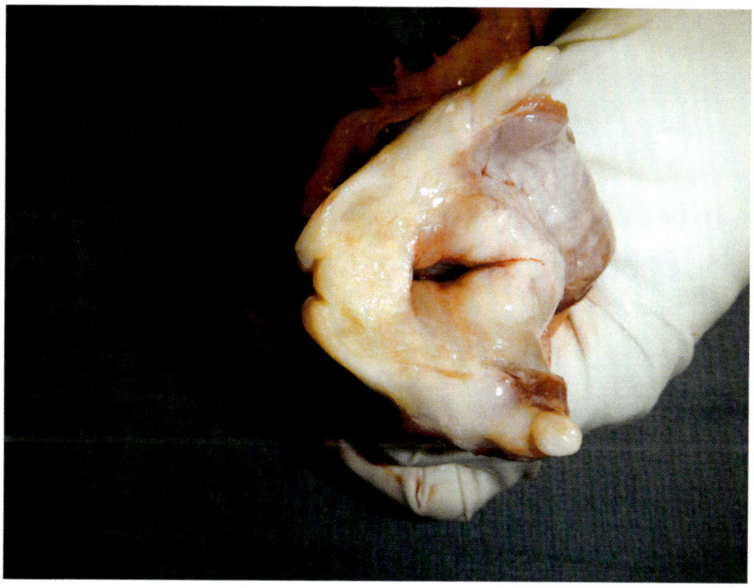

Figure 4.1 Photograph courtesy of Forensic Medical Management Services of Texas, P.A., Beaumont, TX.

A. Anaphylactic shock
B. Choking
C. Congestive heart failure
D. Strangulation
E. Systemic mastocytosis

Q4.3 A 20-year-old man with no known medical problems or drug abuse history dies inside an industrial tank while performing maintenance and cleaning. Prior to the maintenance, the tank was completely flushed with nitrogen gas. He was found at the bottom of the exit ladder. Rescue personnel noted that the oxygen measurement was 0%. The autopsy findings including toxicology were negative. What is the most likely cause of asphyxial death in this case?

A. Choking
B. Chemical
C. Mechanical
D. Suffocation
E. Strangulation

Q4.4 What is indicated by the findings in this brain section?

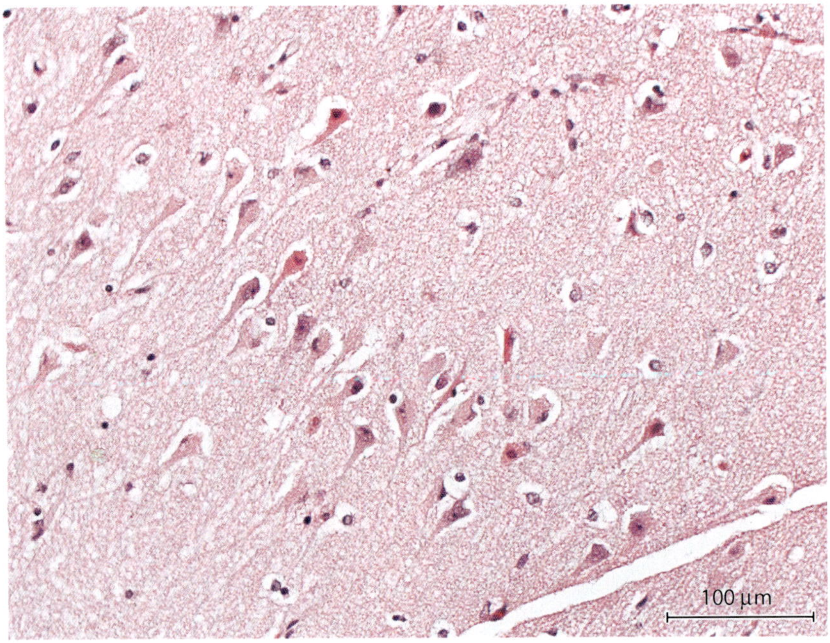

Figure 4.2

A. Acute carbon monoxide toxicity
B. Cytomegalovirus infection
C. Ethanol toxicity
D. Hypoxic neuronal injury
E. Toxoplasmosis

Q4.5 A 38-year-old man suddenly collapses while participating in a triathlon in the middle of July in Charleston, South Carolina. His core body temperature is 43.3°C (110°F). He has no past medical history. Which of the following is a likely finding?

A. Cessation of sweating
B. High levels of endotoxin in circulation
C. Mutation of RYR1
D. Normal thermoregulatory mechanisms
E. Peripheral vasoconstriction

Q4.6 What is a likely cause of this gastric mucosal finding?

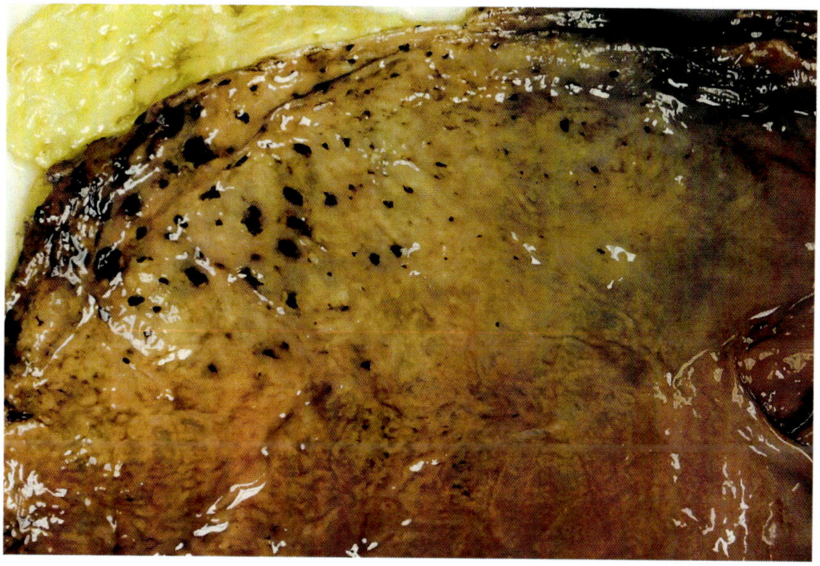

Figure 4.3

A. Decomposition artifact
B. *Helicobacter pylori* infection
C. Hemangioma
D. Hypothermias
E. Nonsteroidal anti-inflammatory medication

Q4.7 Hypothermia is defined by a core body temperature of less than ______ °C?

A. 20
B. 25
C. 30
D. 35
E. 40

Q4.8 Hyperthermia is defined by a core body temperature of greater than or equal to ______ °C?

A. 35
B. 37.5
C. 38
D. 39.5
E. 41

Q4.9 What is the leading cause of death in burn victims?

A. Burn infection with sepsis
B. Carbon monoxide toxicity
C. Chemical lung injury
D. Electrolyte imbalance
E. Pulmonary thromboembolism

Q4.10 What is the most likely source of the linear, criss-crossed injuries depicted in this photograph?

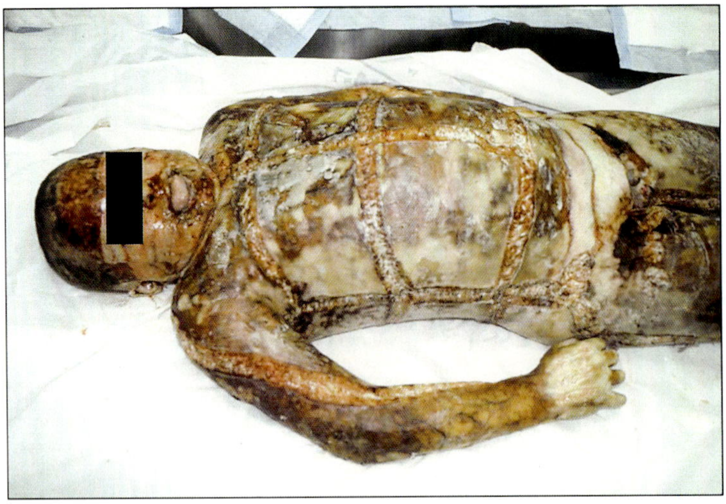

Figure 4.4

A. Electricity
B. Fire
C. Medical intervention
D. Postmortem artifact
E. Religious ritual

Q4.11 What is the most likely explanation for the lesions seen on the anterior and anteromedial left thigh of this decedent who was recovered from a house fire?

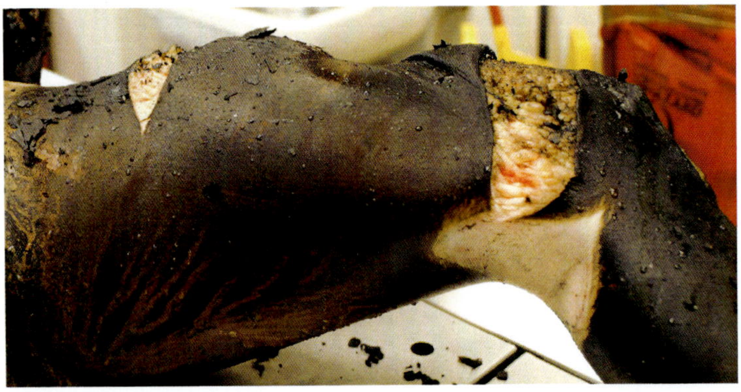

Figure 4.5

A. Antemortem skin ulcerations
B. Autopsy incisions
C. Blunt trauma lacerations
D. Postmortem thermal artifacts
E. Sharp force injuries

Q4.12 What is the best conclusion regarding this individual's cause of death?

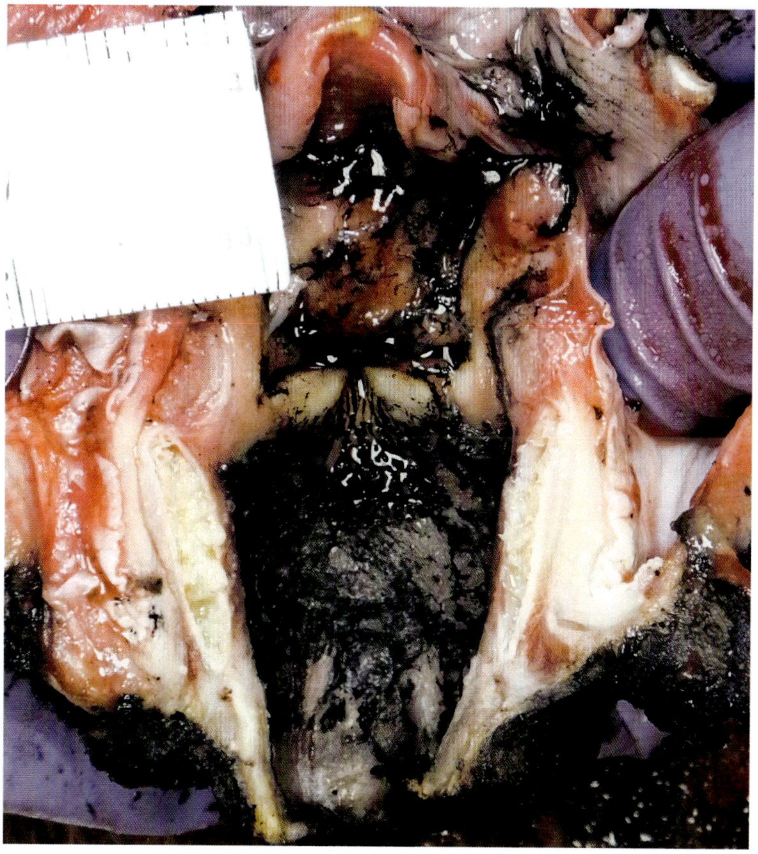

Figure 4.6

A. Aspiration
B. Melanoma
C. Minocycline overdose
D. Smoke inhalation
E. Thermal or steam injury

Q4.13 A 25-year-old man is involved in a motor vehicle collision and a car fire ensues. The man is entrapped and subsequently recovered from the vehicle deceased, with extensive thermal changes including widespread charring. Which of the following cannot be assessed during autopsy?

A. Antemortem bone fractures
B. Internal organ trauma
C. Rigor mortis
D. Toxicological analysis of blood
E. Vitreous analytes

Q4.14 What is the type of ionizing radiation that penetrates biological tissue the deepest?

A. Alpha particles
B. Beta particles
C. Electrons
D. Gamma rays
E. Ions

Q4.15 The remains of an adult man are recovered from a house fire. Extensive charring of the body is present. The depicted finding is observed inside the calvarial skull cap. What is the most likely underlying diagnosis?

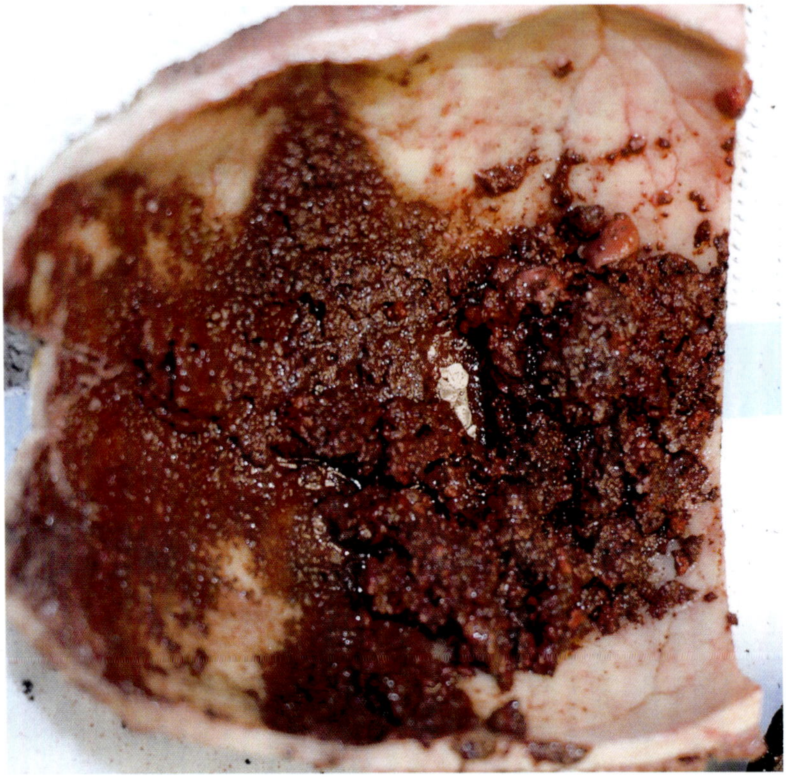

Figure 4.7

A. Accidental temporoparietal skull fracture
B. Heat artifact
C. Hemorrhagic bacterial meningitis
D. Inflicted blunt head trauma
E. Ruptured arteriovenous malformation

Q4.16 What is the unit defined as the absorption of 1 joule of ionizing radiation energy per 1 kilogram?

A. Ampere
B. Gray
C. Ohm
D. Rad
E. Volt

Q4.17 What is the pathognomonic finding at autopsy indicative of drowning?

A. Fluid in the sphenoid sinuses
B. Pruning of the hands and feet
C. Pulmonary edema
D. Water in the stomach
E. There are no pathognomonic findings

Q4.18 Featured below is the parietal surface of the right pleural cavity. What was this person most likely exposed to during life?

Figure 4.8

A. Aflatoxin
B. Asbestos
C. Cigarette smoke
D. Crack cocaine
E. Silica

Q4.19 A scuba diver is found dead at the bottom of a coral reef. His instrumentation indicates his maximum depth was 132 feet. What is the pressure (in atmospheres) that he was subjected to at that depth?

A. 2
B. 3
C. 4
D. 5
E. 6

Q4.20 One atmosphere in pressure is added for approximately every _____ feet in depth in water.

A. 33
B. 37
C. 42
D. 45
E. 67

Q4.21 Based on the cross section of liver below, to which of the following substances was this patient most likely exposed during life?

Figure 4.9

A. Asbestos
B. Ethanol
C. Ethylene glycol
D. Cigarette smoke
E. Illicit intravenous drugs

Q4.22 What is a likely scenario regarding the death of this 22 year old decedent (nose, mouth area featured)?

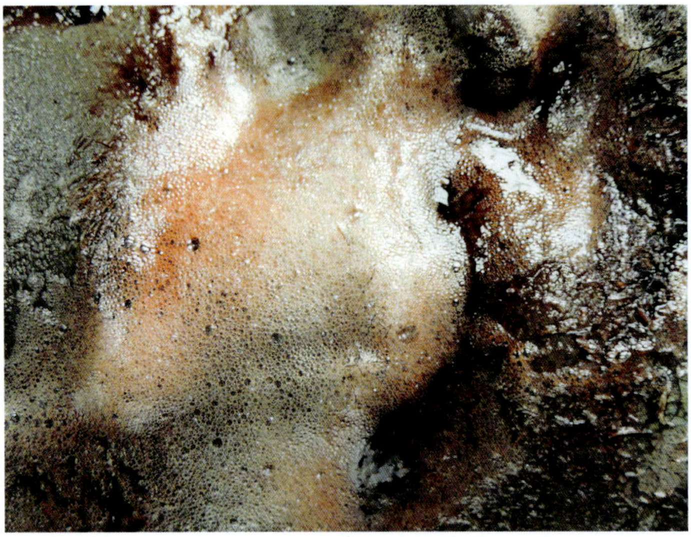

Figure 4.10

A. Collapsed while playing basketball
B. Driver involved in a motor vehicle crash
C. Extensive resuscitative efforts were employed
D. History of tibia fracture 2 weeks prior to death
E. Recovered from pool

ANSWERS: CHAPTER 4

A4.1 The correct answer is E. Tryptase

- Answer A is incorrect. C-reactive protein is a marker of acute inflammation and not of anaphylaxis.
- Answer B is incorrect. Diphenhydramine is a drug that can be used to treat anaphylaxis and is not diagnostic of anaphylaxis.
- Answer C is incorrect. Epinephrine is a drug that can be used to treat anaphylaxis and is not diagnostic of anaphylaxis.
- Answer D is incorrect. Procalcitonin is a marker that can be used in the diagnosis of sepsis and response of sepsis to antibiotic therapy. It is more specific than other inflammatory markers such as lactate in the setting of sepsis.
- Answer E is correct. Tryptase levels are elevated in acute anaphylaxis and can be elevated in systemic mastocytosis. Mast cells release tryptase and histamine, which can be measured in serum. Both of these are metabolized quickly. Tryptase has a longer half-life than histamine and is more useful. Elevated tryptase levels can be detected for up to 6 hours, and elevated histamine levels can be seen up to 60 minutes after an event. Although elevated tryptase levels support the diagnosis of anaphylaxis, normal levels do not exclude the diagnosis.

A4.2 The correct answer is A. Anaphylactic shock

- Answer A is correct. The photograph shows a trachea that is nearly occluded from massive edema. In conjunction with the history, this is highly suggestive of anaphylaxis due to exposure to an allergen such as peanuts.
- Answer B is incorrect. This does not represent choking, as no object that may cause internal airway occlusion is noted in the image. Since the decedent was eating, choking is a reasonable consideration in the formulation of a differential diagnosis. However, at autopsy a source of complete occlusion such as food is not seen in the larynx or trachea. Notably, in many instances of choking, responding medical personnel may remove oropharyngeal foreign objects when attempting to secure airway access (and thus removing signs of a potential cause of death).
- Answer C is incorrect. Congestive heart failure does cause edema, but it is more likely seen in the lungs and extremities and not necessarily in the neck tissue.
- Answer D is incorrect. Strangulation is not likely as there is no visible hemorrhage or fracture.
- Answer E is incorrect. Systemic mastocytosis is a rare disorder characterized by increased mast cells seen mainly in the skin but also in other areas such as the bone marrow and spleen. The most common subtype is indolent mastocytosis. Mastocytosis is possible but is not as likely as anaphylaxis due to food allergen consumption.

A4.3 The correct answer is D. Suffocation

- Answer A is incorrect. Choking is a form of asphyxial death in which the internal airway, usually the trachea, is blocked so there is no gas exchange. In the case scenario, the autopsy was negative so it may be concluded that nothing blocked the airway.
- Answer B is incorrect. Chemical asphyxia occurs when a compound prevents utilization of oxygen by interfering with its uptake of oxygen such as seen in carbon monoxide poisoning when carbon monoxide binds so tightly to the heme molecule that oxygen cannot be carried to tissue. Another example is when hydrogen sulfide converts hemoglobin in the blood from oxyhemoglobin to methemoglobin, rendering the hemoglobin unable to transport oxygen. The scenario is described a nitrogen gas flush. Nitrogen gas is inert and does not alter the body's ability to transport oxygen.
- Answer C is incorrect. Mechanical asphyxia is when an outside force or trauma prevents respiration from occurring, usually by preventing the act of respiration. For example, a person working on a car placed on jacks and becomes wedged beneath the car when the jacks collapse the weight of the car prevents respiration.
- Answer D is correct. Suffocation is the failure of oxygen to reach the blood and is a subtype of asphyxia. Two broad types of asphyxia are defined based on the amount of deprivation: anoxia, total deprivation of oxygen; and hypoxia, partial deprivation of oxygen. Normally, oxygen is present in the atmosphere in concentrations between 20% and 21%. Impairment in judgement occurs when the oxygen concentration is 10%–15%. Loss of consciousness occurs at 8%–10%, and death occurs in cases where oxygen content is less than 8%. In this scenario, the decedent was found on the floor of the tank that had no oxygen available for breathing. Thus, suffocation is the reason for the death.
- Answer E is incorrect. Strangulation is a type of asphyxia death in which the vessels of the neck and/or the airway are closed off to prevent oxygen delivery.

A4.4 The correct answer is D. Hypoxic neuronal injury

- Answer A is incorrect. Grossly, acute carbon monoxide toxicity may manifest as bright cherry-red visceral and blood discoloration. Microscopically, there is no pathognomonic finding associated with acute carbon monoxide toxicity. Chronic carbon monoxide exposure may result in degenerative changes in the central nervous system (i.e., basal ganglia necrosis).
- Answer B is incorrect. Cytomegalovirus nuclear inclusions classically demonstrate an "owl's eye" appearance, which is not seen here.
- Answer C is incorrect. Ethanol toxicity does not generally lead to ischemic brain damage in the absence of other factors. In fact, neuronal changes aside from chronic injury such as cerebellar vermal atrophy and Purkinje cell dropout are unlikely to be evidenced in ethanol toxicity.
- Answer D is correct. The photomicrograph depicts an area with large neurons (in this case, the hippocampus) that has been affected by significant hypoxia or ischemia. It demonstrates an admixture of normal-appearing neurons in which the nuclei and nucleoli are distinct, and the cell bodies are purple-blue. However, several red neurons have condensation of the nuclear material indicative of neuronal cell death. These changes take several hours to develop.
- Answer E is incorrect. Toxoplasmosis is not likely as no organisms or signs of inflammation are present in the photomicrograph.

A4.5 The correct answer is A. Cessation of sweating

- Answer A is correct. This is a case of heat stroke, which classically occurs in warm, humid temperatures during prolonged physical exertion. The elderly are also susceptible. Thermoregulatory mechanisms fail and individuals paradoxically cease sweating. Mortality is over 50% when rectal temperatures reach 106°F.
- Answer B is incorrect. Endotoxin is associated with gram-negative sepsis, not suspected in this scenario.
- Answer C is incorrect. RYR1 is a receptor that regulates calcium release in skeletal muscle. Mutations in this receptor are associated with malignant hyperthermia where muscle contractions and markedly elevated core body temperatures follow exposure to common anesthetics. There is some evidence that those with mutations of *RYR1* may be predisposed to the development of exertional heat stroke.
- Answer D is incorrect. In heat stroke, normal thermoregulatory mechanisms fail.
- Answer E is incorrect. In heat stroke, there is notable peripheral vasodilation.

A4.6 The correct answer is D. Hypothermia

- Answer A is incorrect. It is thought that this depicted epiphenomenon occurs in the agonal stages and not postmortem; thus, decomposition artifact is less likely.
- Answer B is incorrect. *Helicobacter pylori* infection may be subclinical or may lead to mucosal erosions, which are not present here.
- Answer C is incorrect. Hemangiomas are generally of a more solitary nature, so again, the diagnosis is less likely and, if suspected, could be confirmed by histologic examination of lesion(s).
- Answer D is correct. The photograph demonstrates gastric mucosa that is exposed as the stomach has been opened along the greater curvature. There is attenuation of the rugal folds. Also present are numerous dark round regions of discoloration. These are most compatible "Wischnewsky" spots. One hypothesis regarding the etiology of this finding, since gross hemorrhage and ulceration are not generally identified, is hematinized hemoglobin from exposure of hemorrhagic glands to gastric acid.
- Answer E is incorrect. Nonsteroidal anti-inflammatory drugs (NSAIDs) may also lead to gastric mucosal injury, but these changes, which may range from normal appearance to mucosal erosion, are characteristically at the gastroduodenal region, while these pictured lesions appear to affect the gastric body. In addition, if this was suspected, histological examination in this case would exclude ulceration and reactive gastropathy secondary to NSAID use.

A4.7 The correct answer is D. 35°C. Hypothermia is defined as a core body temperature of less than 35°C (95°F). All of the other temperatures are incorrect.

A4.8 The correct answer is B. 37.5°C. Hyperthermia is defined as an elevated body temperature of at least 37.5°C due to failed thermoregulation. The thermal set point of the body remains unchanged in contrast to fever in which the body has an elevated temperature and an increased temperature set point. All of the other temperatures are incorrect.

A4.9 The correct answer is A. Burn infection with sepsis

- Answer A is correct. Skin is the primary defense against infection and when compromised significantly by burn injury, the skin flora and hospital-acquired organisms have a direct route to the systemic circulation. In addition, multi-antibiotic-resistant organisms are becoming a significant cause of death following severe burns (also see Williams FN et al. The leading causes of death after burn injury in a single pediatric burn center. *Critical Care* 2009, 13: R183, doi: 10.1186/cc8170). Note that some sources indicate multisystem organ failure frequently with systemic inflammatory response syndrome (SIRS) as the most frequent cause of death (also see Bloemsma GC et al. Mortality and causes of death in a burn centre. *Burns* 2008, 34[8]: 1103–7, doi: 10.1016/j.burns.2008.02.010).
- Answer B is incorrect. Carbon monoxide toxicity frequently co-exists with thermal heat damage to the body; however, one may experience one without the other. If a patient survives the initial thermal event, however, carbon monoxide toxicity becomes an uncommon cause of death in these patients as they are provided with supplemental oxygen and other support to reverse the immediate effects.
- Answer C is incorrect. Depending on the type of fire, chemical lung injury is certainly a possible sequelae of a thermal/fire event. However, deaths due to chemical lung injury are less frequent than those due to complications of infection.
- Answer D is incorrect. The loss of skin integrity leads to many complications including electrolyte imbalance commonly including hyponatremia and hyperkalemia. However, with modern methods of electrolyte monitoring and replacement as well as diuresis and dialysis, this cause of death is less frequent than infection.
- Answer E is incorrect. Deep venous thrombosis and pulmonary thromboembolism are common complications in severe burn injury due to stasis from immobility as well as hypercoagulability. However, sepsis is the more common cause of death.

A4.10 The correct answer is C. Medical intervention

- Answer A is incorrect. The linear, criss-crossed injuries are not due to electricity.
- Answer B is incorrect. The linear, criss-crossed injuries are not due to fire injury.
- Answer C is correct. The decedent pictured demonstrates incisions characteristic of fasciotomy, and the skin surfaces appear affected by thermal injury. Fasciotomy is performed when compartment syndrome occurs, in this case from exposure to a brush fire fueled by gasoline, in order to improve tissue perfusion and avoid tissue necrosis from compression of vasculature.
- Answer D is incorrect. The linear, criss-crossed injuries are characteristic of fasciotomies for compartment syndrome and not a postmortem artifact.
- Answer E is incorrect. The linear, criss-crossed injuries are characteristic of fasciotomies for compartment syndrome.

A4.11 The correct answer is D. Postmortem thermal artifacts

- Answer A is incorrect. The featured lesions are skin splits resulting from the heat generated by the fire. They are postmortem in nature, as evidenced by the lack of vital reaction such as hemorrhage in the tissue.
- Answer B is incorrect. Although autopsy incisions are postmortem injuries, the location of the featured lesions in the area of thermal damage coupled with the notable skin contraction and history of a house fire are more consistent with postmortem thermal skin splits.
- Answer C is incorrect. Lacerations are characterized by tissue bridging and possibly marginal abrasions. The featured lesions appear sharp, and there is no associated hemorrhage that might indicate antemortem trauma.
- Answer D is correct. The depicted lesions are skin splits that result from heat causing the skin to shrink and split, revealing the underlying subcutaneous tissue. These skin splits are postmortem changes as evidenced by the lack of associated hemorrhage. Heat from fires may also induce shrinkage of the skeletal muscle to such a degree that bony fractures may result.
- Answer E is incorrect. Although the featured lesions appear sharp, there is no associated hemorrhage that might indicate antemortem trauma.

A4.12 The correct answer is D. Smoke inhalation

- Answer A is incorrect. Aspiration suggests the inhalation of solid material into the airways. In this case, smoke is not considered a solid but a gaseous agent, so aspiration would not be a correct response. Aspiration also suggests a mass effect such as that found when gastric contents enter the airways.
- Answer B is incorrect. Melanoma lesions may demonstrate extensive black to brown pigmentation. Such lesions are thought to arise from melanocytic cells of the skin, retina, and elsewhere. This is not a characteristic appearance of a primary or metastatic melanoma, which would likely form a mass lesion and not appear to coat a mucosal surface. Case history will also be informative.
- Answer C is incorrect. Minocycline is an antibiotic in the tetracycline class used to treat various infections of the lungs, genitourinary tract, and skin. If used during development, it may lead to yellow-gray-brown discoloration of the teeth and discoloration of mucus membranes and the thyroid (so-called "black thyroid").
- Answer D is correct. The gross photograph depicts soot within the oropharynx and larynx that extends below the level of the vocal cords. The soot forms a thin coating over the mucosal surfaces but does not demonstrate a mass effect. These findings are compatible with smoke inhalation in one who was alive and breathing during a fire. Soot may be found in the oropharynx as an artifact of the fire, but if below the level of the vocal cords indicates active inhalation.
- Answer E is incorrect. Thermal or steam injury would appear similar to any burn injury. If the thermal damage was received in a fire, charring of the body parts may be observed, which would involve full-thickness damage to the area affected. Erythema and vital reaction including significant tissue swelling and tissue and pulmonary edema may result if the steam is inhaled.

A4.13 The correct answer is C. Rigor mortis

- Answer A is incorrect. Postmortem bone fractures may be produced with significant heat exposure by substantial contraction of skeletal muscles and via direct thermal injury of exposed bones. Antemortem fractures can usually be assessed by their location and associated vital reaction/hemorrhage. However, in the cases of severe thermal injury with exposed charred bone, differentiation may not be possible.
- Answer B is incorrect. Despite significant external thermal changes that may be present in house fire victims, internal organ preservation is often remarkably good, thus allowing assessment of antemortem trauma.
- Answer C is correct. Rigor mortis, a common metric used to assist in postmortem interval estimation, cannot be assessed when significant thermal injury is present due to the heat contraction of the skeletal muscles, often "fixing" limbs in place.
- Answer D is incorrect. Despite significant external thermal changes that may be present in house fire victims, blood specimens are typically obtainable.
- Answer E is incorrect. Despite significant external thermal changes that may be present in house fire victims, vitreous is often obtainable.

A4.14 The correct answer is D. Gamma rays

- Answer A is incorrect. Alpha particles are essentially helium nuclei and consist of two neutrons and two protons. Since the particle has an overall positive charge, it interacts with other particles in tissue more readily by virtue of its charge and does not travel very far. Many times alpha particles are stopped by the skin.
- Answer B is incorrect. Beta particles are electrons. Since they have a negative charge they interact readily and do not penetrate too deeply.
- Answer C is incorrect. An electron is the same as a beta particle.
- Answer D is correct. Gamma rays are neutral and as such will only "react" when they actually collide with another particle. This is distance dependent and mathematically is expressed logarithmically. Thus, they can go farther and penetrate deeper.
- Answer E is incorrect. Ions are charged particles usually in a solution and do not travel far.

A4.15 The correct answer is B. Heat artifact

- Answer A is incorrect. The photograph demonstrates epidural red-brown, granular appearing material, which is characteristic of a heat-induced artifact. Fractures are not visible.
- Answer B is correct. The photograph demonstrates an epidural hematoma. The characteristic red-brown granular appearance of the material is consistent with an artifact induced by extreme heat that leads to extrusion of blood and bone marrow into the epidural space. Antemortem epidural hematomas are often associated with temporal bone fracture with disruption of the middle meningeal artery; these appear less granular.
- Answer C is incorrect. Bacterial meningitis would be most evident involving the leptomeninges.
- Answer D is incorrect. The photograph demonstrates calvarial epidural blood with a red-brown, granular appearance characteristic of a heat-induced artifact. Antemortem epidural hematomas are often associated with temporal bone fracture and disruption of the middle meningeal artery.
- Answer E is incorrect. A ruptured cerebral arteriovenous malformation would likely result in intracerebral, subarachnoid, or subdural blood. The photograph demonstrates epidural blood with a red-brown, granular appearance characteristic of a heat-induced artifact.

A4.16 The correct answer is B. Gray

- Answer A is incorrect. The ampere is the SI unit for current in electricity. It is defined as the flow of 1 Coulomb per second of electric charge across a surface.
- Answer B is correct. The gray, symbol Gy, is the International System of Units (SI) for ionizing radiation. It is defined as the absorption of 1 joule of energy per kilogram of matter: 1 Gy = 1 J/Kg.
- Answer C is incorrect. The ohm is the SI unit for electrical resistance.
- Answer D is incorrect. The rad is a unit of absorbed radiation dose that was previously used: 1 rad = 0.01 Gy or 100 rad = 1 Gy.
- Answer E is incorrect. A volt is the SI unit of potential difference used in electricity.

A4.17 The correct answer is E. There are no pathognomonic findings.

- Answer A is incorrect. Although the pathologist may attempt to draw fluid from the sphenoid sinuses to support a diagnosis of drowning, such fluid may also be present with postmortem immersion.
- Answer B is incorrect. Pruning of the hands and feet indicates prolonged exposure to liquid but does not indicate whether the exposure was ante- or postmortem.
- Answer C is incorrect. Pulmonary edema may be seen in numerous scenarios, including heart failure, drug overdose, resuscitative efforts, and drowning.
- Answer D is incorrect. The presence of water in the stomach is nonspecific.
- Answer E is correct. There is not one single autopsy finding that is absolutely definitive for drowning. All of the incorrect choices can be found in drowning but none occur 100% of the time.

A4.18 The correct answer is B. Asbestos

- Answer A is incorrect. Aflatoxin is a naturally occurring mycotoxin produced by *Aspergillus* species. These toxins are carcinogenic and generally associated with hepatocellular carcinoma upon chronic exposure (particularly with aflatoxin B1) and with hepatic necrosis with significant acute exposure.
- Answer B is correct. The gross photograph of the pleural parietal surface demonstrates plaque formation that is distinctive to asbestos exposure. Such plaques are commonly found on the parietal surface of the diaphragm as well, and appropriate histologic sampling may be desirable in order to exclude another asbestos-associated finding, mesothelioma.
- Answer C is incorrect. Cigarette smoke and crack cocaine usage would be expected to affect the lung parenchyma with demonstration of a degree of respiratory bronchiolitis and carbon pigment deposition (anthracosis). Cigarette smoking does not increase the risk of mesothelioma.
- Answer D is incorrect. Cigarette smoke and crack cocaine usage would be expected to affect the lung parenchyma with demonstration of a degree of respiratory bronchiolitis and carbon pigment deposition (anthracosis).
- Answer E is incorrect. Silica is more likely to cause a nodular interstitial lung disease which would most likely manifest as discrete hyalinized nodules in the lungs instead of a lesion on the pleura as seen in the photograph. Polarization of silica nodules typically demonstrates birefringent silica particulates.

A4.19 The correct answer is D. 5 atmospheres (atm).

One atmosphere (atm) of pressure is 14.7 pounds per square inch (psi). For every foot in depth in water, add an additional 0.445 psi. To add 1 atmosphere of pressure add 14.7 psi × (1 foot/0.445 psi) = 33 feet of depth. Since the decedent was 132 feet below the surface that is the equivalent to 132/33 = 4 atmospheres of added pressure. Do not forget he started with 1 atm of pressure at the surface for a total of 4 + 1 = 5 atmospheres.

Another way to remember this is every 33 feet is 1 atm of pressure, beginning with 1 atm at the surface.

All of the other answers are incorrect.

A4.20 The correct answer is A. Once below the surface, underwater pressure increases at the rate of 1 additional atmosphere (14.7 pounds per square inch) for every additional 33 feet in depth. The relationship is linear in nature (e.g., if you dive to 3300 feet you will have added 100 atmospheres in pressure as a result of the depth). All of the other choices are incorrect since they do not describe the correct relationship of change in pressure with change in depth.

A4.21 The correct answer is D. Cigarette smoke

- Answer A is incorrect. Asbestos exposure is linked to malignant pleural mesothelioma, which most commonly displays progressive locoregional invasion with extensive parietal and pleural plaque formation. An autopsy study demonstrated that more than half of advanced cases result in metastatic disease. However, the extent of this metastatic disease to the liver is characteristic of small cell carcinoma of the lung, associated with cigarette smoking.
- Answer B is incorrect. Chronic ethanol exposure may lead to hepatitis, steatosis, and cirrhosis, none of which are highlighted.
- Answer C is incorrect. Ethylene glycol may be identified in the kidney by histopathology. Calcium oxalate crystals may be seen in the renal tubules when polarized light is used. Gross findings would not be expected.
- Answer D is correct. This extent of metastatic disease shown in the photograph is characteristic of small cell carcinoma of the lung. This tumor type is heavily linked to cigarette smoking. Histopathological correlation is required to form the appropriate diagnosis.
- Answer E is incorrect. Illicit intravenous drug use may introduce various drugs, toxins, carrier substances, solvent agents, and infectious agents to the bloodstream. Acute assaults of the pulmonary vasculature would be expected with prominence of foreign material such as talc and granuloma formation when subacute or remote. There are numerous metastatic lesions of the liver pictured. Hepatitis B and C may increase the risk for development of cirrhosis and hepatocellular carcinoma (HCC); however, a prominent primary nodule would be more compatible with HCC.

A4.22 The correct answer is E. Recovered from pool

- Answer A is incorrect. A sudden collapse in a young athlete suggests a cardiac arrhythmia, not profound pulmonary edema as evidenced by the foam cap in the photograph.
- Answer B is incorrect. A decedent involved in a motor vehicle crash may exhibit pulmonary edema, in particular when ethanol or other respiratory depressant drugs are involved, but this is not the best answer.
- Answer C is incorrect. Pulmonary edema may be evident in those receiving extensive resuscitative efforts and may be more prominent in those receiving abundant intravascular fluids, but that does not usually manifest as a foam cap.
- Answer D is incorrect. A history of lower extremity trauma raises the possibility of deep venous thromboses with pulmonary thromboembolism, but a foam cap is not a feature associated with this scenario.
- Answer E is correct. The photograph demonstrates the foam cap, a frothy translucent fluid that is sometimes tinged pink, and results from significant pulmonary edema. In drownings, this finding supports respiratory effort and with profound pulmonary edema during/after immersion, but may not be present (i.e., "dry drowning" or in prolonged postmortem intervals). Other scenarios in which such profound pulmonary edema may be present include drug overdoses, in particular opioid toxicities.

CHAPTER 5

ANALYSIS AND INTERPRETATION

QUESTIONS

Q5.1 All of the following scientific methods may be used to confirm identity except which one of the following?

A. DNA analysis
B. Dental records/films
C. Fingerprints
D. Surgical prosthesis
E. Social Security card

Q5.2 What is the method of choice for measuring selenium in biological fluids?

A. Gas chromatography
B. Enzyme-linked immunosorbent assay
C. Flame photometry
D. Ion selective electrode
E. Inductively coupled plasma-mass spectrometry

Q5.3 What is the best colored top tube to use to collect blood for quantitation of selenium?

A. Green
B. Gray
C. Lavender
D. Red
E. Royal blue

Q5.4 What is the method employed for the detection of gunshot residue?

A. Atomic absorption spectroscopy
B. Flame photometry
C. Gas chromatography
D. Mass spectrometry
E. Scanning electron microscopy/energy dispersive x-ray spectrometry

Q5.5 Which collection tube additive should be used for postmortem blood specimens for toxicological analysis?

A. Clot activator and gel
B. Ethylene diamine tetra-acetic acid
C. No additive ("blank")
D. Sodium fluoride
E. Sodium heparin

Q5.6 The Combined DNA Index System (CODIS) utilizes what unique identification feature?

A. Fingerprint
B. Single nucleotide polymorphism
C. Short tandem repeat
D. Restriction-length polymorphism
E. Whole exome sequence

Q5.7 What is the proper method for removing the tape featured in the photograph below?

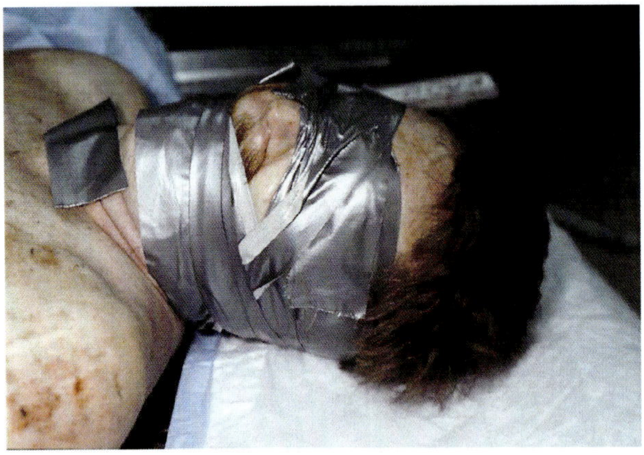

Figure 5.1

A. Cut the tape along the left side of the head
B. Cut the tape away from the end pieces
C. Pull tape over head
D. Unravel the tape starting at one end

Questions 5.8 through 5.10 refer to Table 5.1.

Table 5.1 DNA Analysis Results

System	Child	Alleged Father	Paternity Index
D8S1179	12, 14	13, 14	1.17
D21S11	30, 31.2	29, 31.2	2.64
D7S820	7, 10	9, 10	0.92
CSF1PO	11, 12	10, 11	0.79
D3S1358	16, 16	15, 16	2.19
TH01	9.3, 9.3	9, 9.3	1.72
D13S317	10, 12	10, 10	11.26
D16S539	9, 11	10, 11	0.78
D2S1338	23, 24	20, 24	2.13
D19S433	12, 13	12, 14	3.23
vWA	15, 16	15, 16	3.28
Tpox	9, 11	8, 11	0.96
D18S51	12, 15	12, 21	1.80
AMEL	X, X	X, Y	
D5S818	12, 12	11, 12	1.42
FGA	20, 22	20, 24	1.80

Q5.8 What is the combined paternity index?

A. .9999
B. 36.09
C. 1000
D. 5648
E. 7402

Q5.9 What is the probability of paternity expressed as a percentage?

A. 9.9
B. 59.9
C. 79.90
D. 90.00
E. 99.99

Q5.10 What conclusion can be drawn regarding the child and alleged father?

A. The child is an exact genetic match
B. The child is not related
C. Inconclusive
D. That paternity cannot be excluded
E. That paternity is excluded

Q5.11 What is the best characterization of the findings featured on the hand in the photograph below?

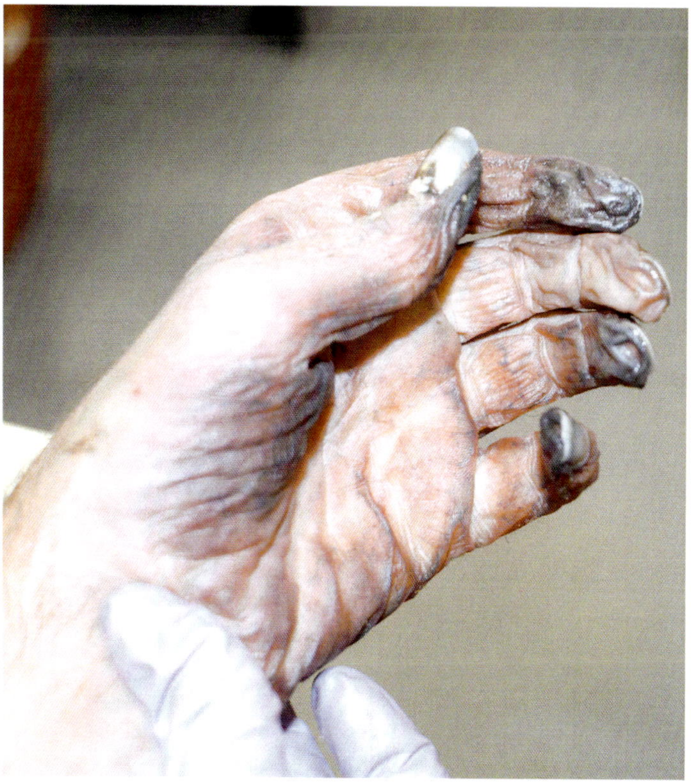

Figure 5.2

A. Immersion change
B. Postmortem animal artifact
C. Postmortem environmental artifact
D. Spray paint debris
E. Thermal injury

Q5.12 These granular white patches are seen on the surface of the liver in a decomposing adult man. What is the most appropriate next step?

Figure 5.3

A. No steps are needed as this is a finding of decomposition
B. Obtain blood cultures
C. Review the death scene for a possible source of electrocution
D. Sample the white patches for histology to diagnose metastatic disease
E. Swab the white patches and culture

Q5.13 A bloody deposit is recovered from the bottom of a vehicle suspected in a hit-and-run and stained with hematoxylin and eosin (H&E). What conclusion can be made regarding the deposit?

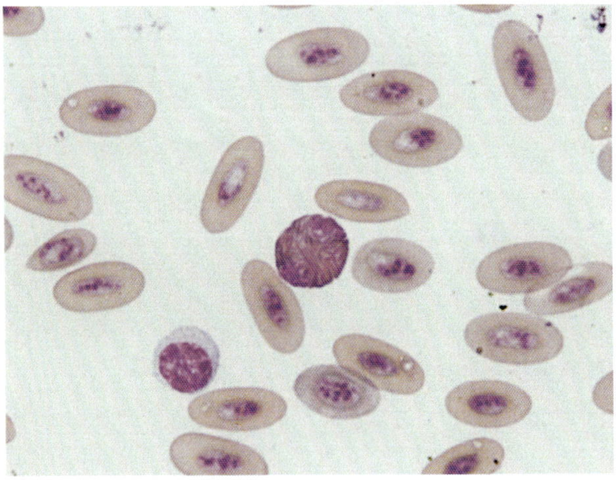

Figure 5.4

A. Contamination of the sample is likely
B. PCR analysis should be performed
C. The hit-and-run victim was pregnant
D. The hit-and-run victim was severely anemic
E. The sample is avian blood

Q5.14 What is the most likely cause of the arm injury featured in a man found on the road with gunshot wounds to the chest?

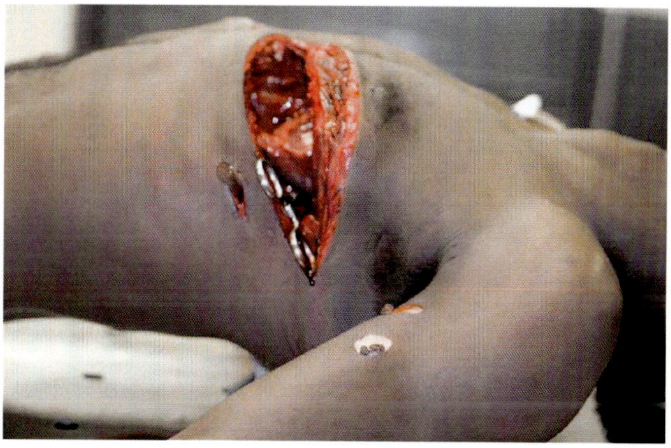

Figure 5.5

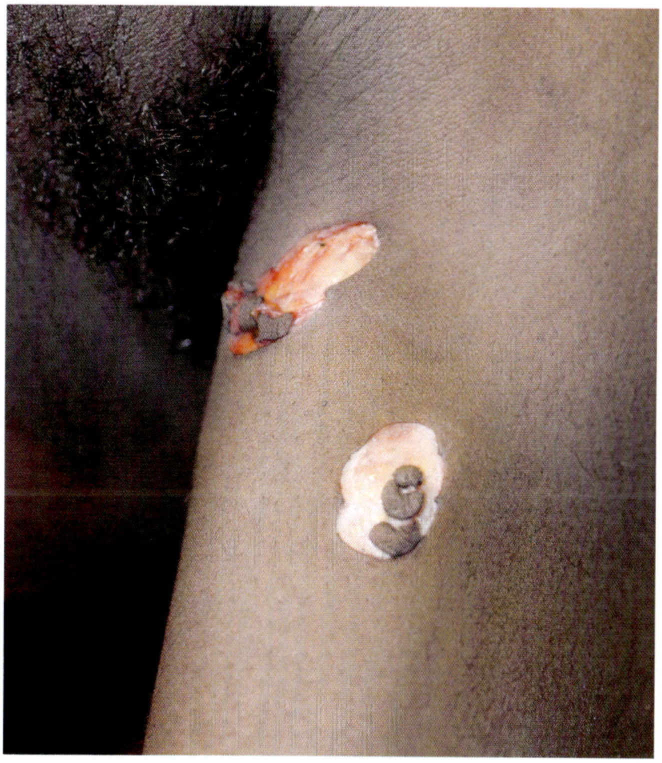

Figure 5.6

A. Graze gunshot wound
B. Iatrogenic intervention
C. Incised wound with serrated knife
D. Incised wound with wine bottle opener
E. Tire avulsion injury

Q5.15 What is the injury depicted on the shoulder in the photograph of this individual consistent with?

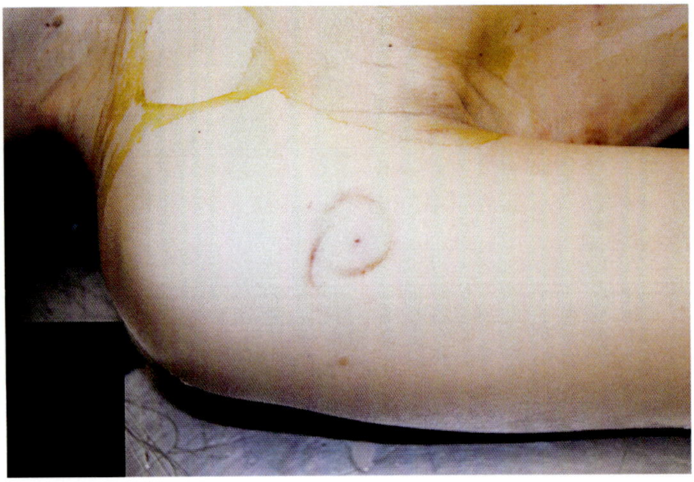

Figure 5.7

A. Cupping stigmata
B. Illicit drug use
C. Intraosseous port site
D. Lyme disease
E. Stinging insect mark

Q5.16 A 48-year-old obese man was standing in the back of a pickup truck when it was allegedly struck by another vehicle. He was taken to the hospital with head and pelvic trauma but died from his injuries 30 minutes later despite medical intervention. Autopsy showed bilateral cutaneous defects of the right and left lateral hips (Figures 5.8 and 5.9, right hip pictured below). An antemortem pelvic x-ray was reviewed (Figure 5.10). What is the likely cause of the bilateral cutaneous hip defects?

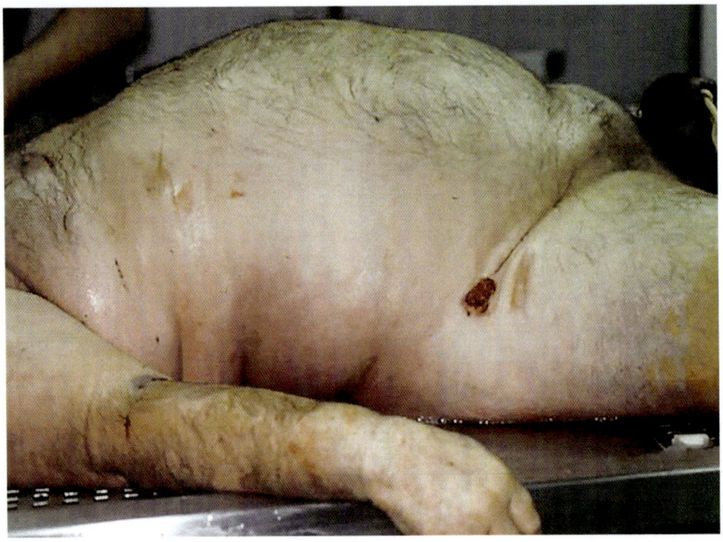

Figure 5.8

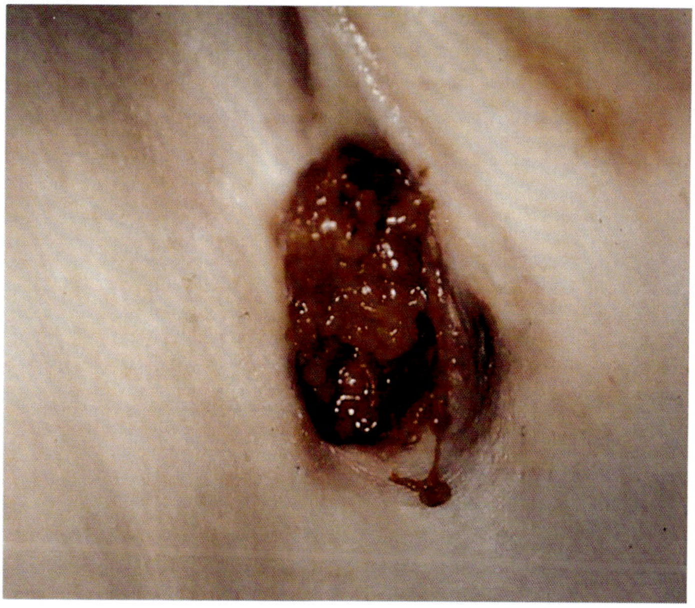

Figure 5.9

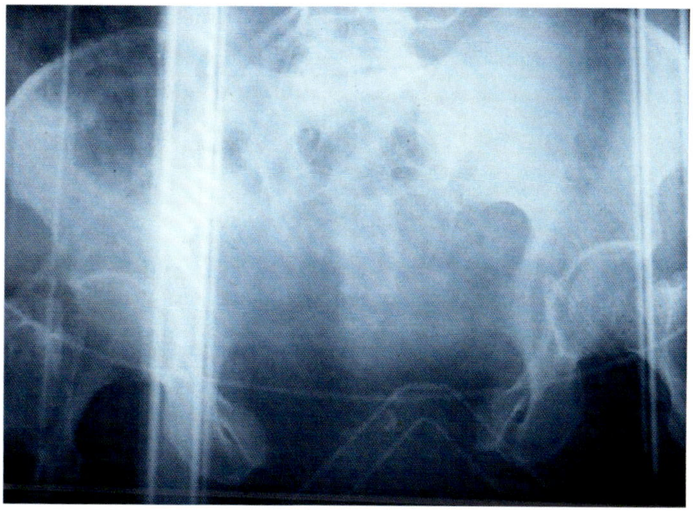

Figure 5.10

A. Attempted intravascular catheter access
B. Blunt trauma from the motor vehicle crash
C. Pelvic stabilizer
D. Perforating gunshot wound
E. Pre-existing decubitus ulcers

Q5.17 What is the minimum probability of paternity expressed as a percentage?

A. 90
B. 95
C. 99
D. 99.9
E. 99.99

Q5.18 A 9-year-old boy with a history of asthma complained of difficulty breathing. He was later found by a playmate unresponsive in the garage. Emergency medical services personnel responded. Despite aggressive resuscitative efforts, he was pronounced dead. Autopsy showed the pictured laryngeal finding. No strap muscle hemorrhage was present. The hyoid bone was intact. What is the most likely conclusion?

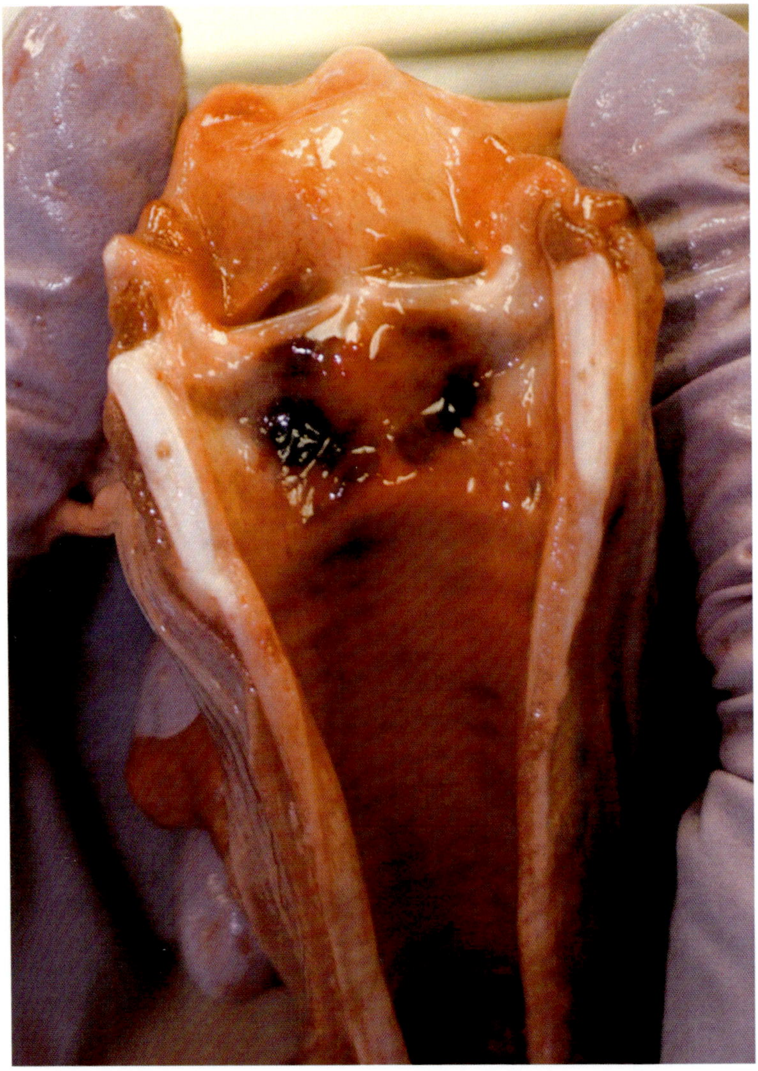

Figure 5.11

A. Direct trauma due to the choking game
B. Epiglottitis
C. Resuscitative trauma
D. Postmortem artifact due to prone positioning
E. Strangulation

Q5.19 An adult man is found decomposing at home. Medical history included hypertension and recent complaints of abdominal pain. At autopsy, the bladder is opened to reveal the finding depicted below. What is the best interpretation of this finding?

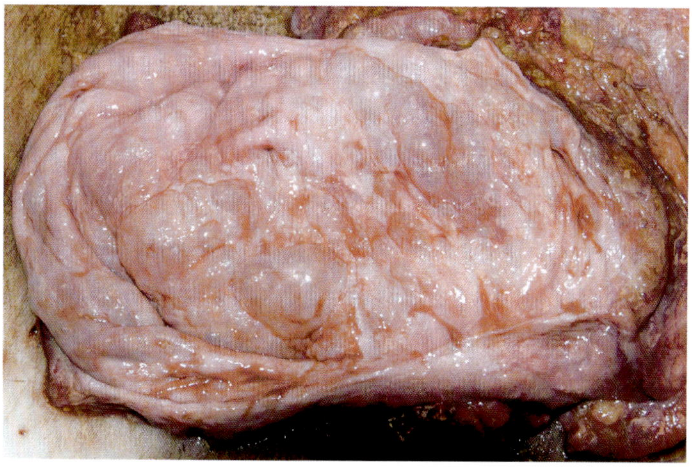

Figure 5.12

A. Acute necrotizing cystitis
B. Benign prostatic hyperplasia
C. Eosinophilic cystitis
D. Congenital malformation
E. Postmortem gaseous distention

Q5.20 The pictured lesion is observed at autopsy on a homeless man found dead in an alleyway. What is the most likely diagnosis?

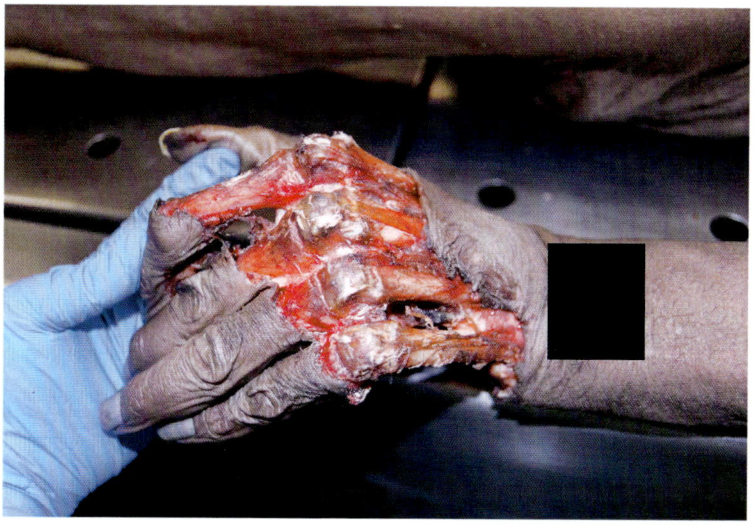

Figure 5.13

A. Chemical burn
B. Necrotizing fasciitis
C. Postmortem anthropophagy
D. Self-mutilation injury
E. Thermal injury

Q5.21 A man is found deceased in his yard after a night of drinking. Injuries are seen around his waist and his arms, as featured below. What is the best interpretation of these injuries?

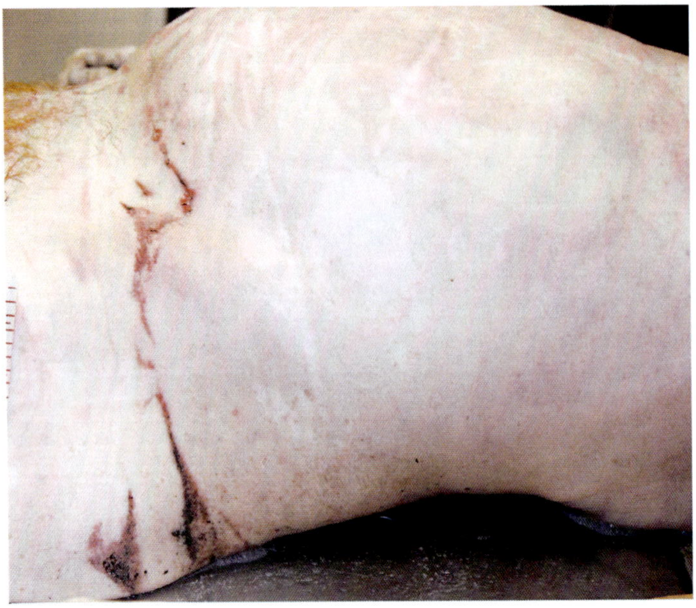

Figure 5.14

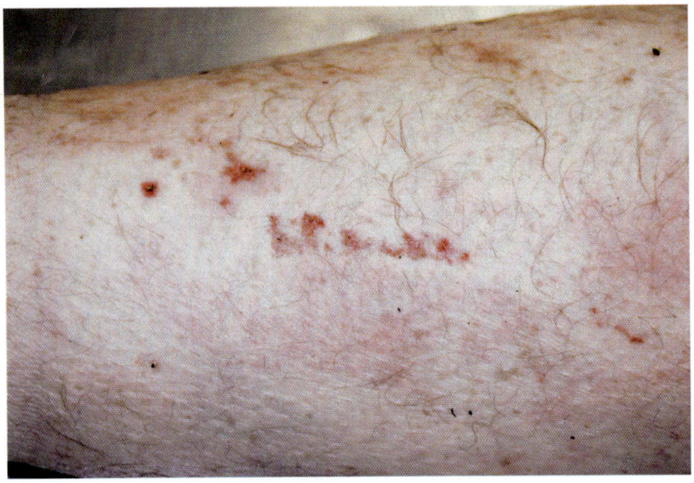

Figure 5.15

A. Allergic reaction
B. Eczematous dermatitis with scratching
C. Hidradenitis suppurativa
D. Postmortem ant bites
E. Whip marks

Q5.22 Unidentified adult skeletal remains are recovered from a wooded area. A skull defect of the posterior right parietal bone is found. What is the best interpretation of this defect?

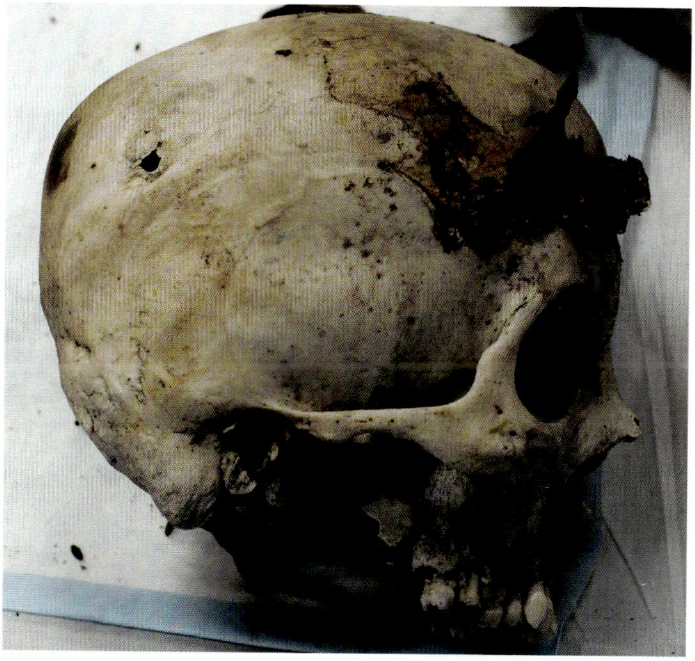

Figure 5.16

Figure 5.17

A. Entrance gunshot wound
B. Exit gunshot wound
C. Medical intervention
D. Penetrating ice pick injury
E. Postmortem animal activity

Q5.23 A 52-year-old obese man is seen to collapse suddenly while mowing the lawn. Pathology residents assist in the postmortem autopsy and perform an external exam that same day. Prior to beginning the internal exam, the pathologist examines the body and visualizes the depicted eye finding. Which of the following is the most likely interpretation of this finding?

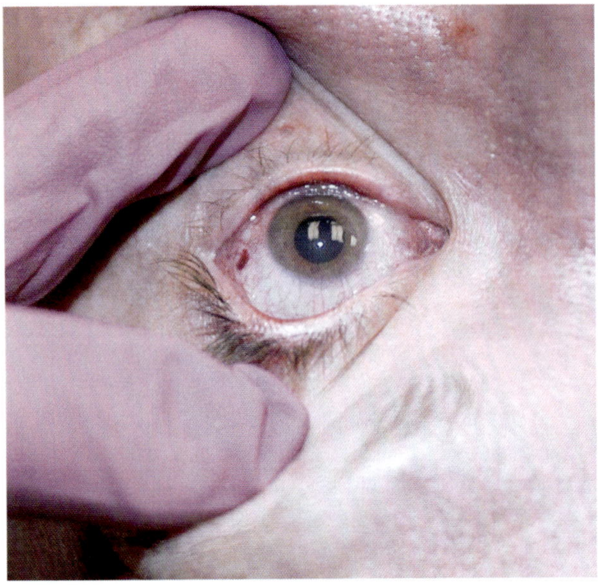

Figure 5.18

A. Blunt trauma to the eye
B. Keratoconjunctivitis
C. Tache noire
D. Tardieu spot
E. Vitreous removal artifact

Q5.24 A 42-year-old woman is found deceased on her screened back porch at home. What do the irregular purple-red lines on the left thigh indicate?

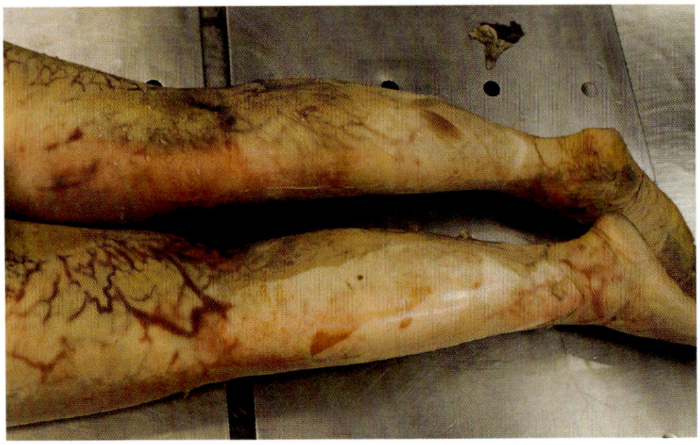

Figure 5.19

A. Lightning injury
B. Low-voltage electrical injury
C. Postmortem spread of bacteria
D. Sepsis
E. Varices

Q5.25 A 50-year-old man with a history of hyperlipidemia collapsed unexpectedly outside his hotel room while vacationing in Florida. Emergency medical personnel responded and initiated resuscitative efforts, which lasted over 1 hour without success. What is the underlying etiology of the findings on the right chest wall (with postmortem incision)?

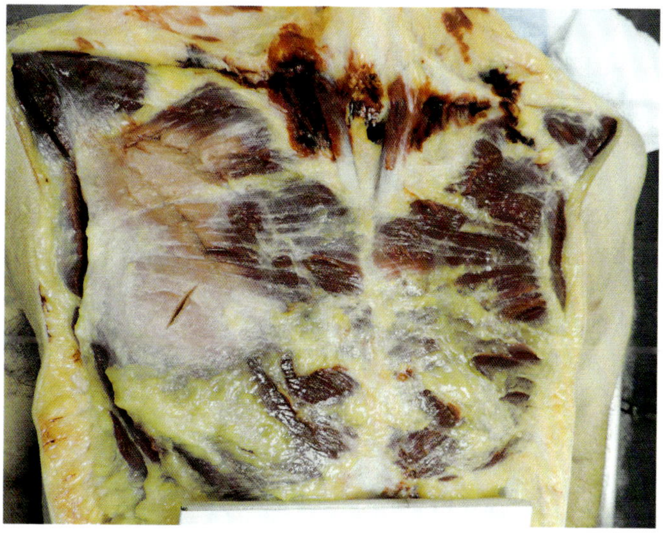

Figure 5.20

A. Electroporation due to defibrillation
B. Heat stroke with rhabdomyolysis
C. Lightning artifact
D. Myositis with skeletal muscle edema

Q5.26 Which of the following does this eye finding most likely represent?

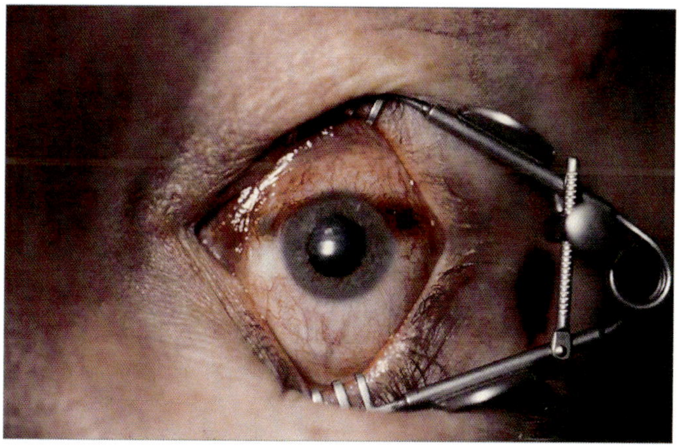

Figure 5.21

A. Choking
B. Direct eye trauma
C. Hanging
D. Hepatic disease
E. Postmortem change

Q5.27 A man is found deceased in a hotel room after not checking out at his scheduled time. He had a history of hypertension and drug use and had complained of shortness of breath and fatigue earlier in the day. He had been in a motor vehicle crash 2 weeks prior, sustaining only superficial abrasions and contusions. At autopsy, the following mass was recovered from the main pulmonary artery. What is the best interpretation of this mass?

Figure 5.22

A. Hyperviscosity syndrome
B. Mural thrombosis
C. Postmortem blood clot
D. Pulmonary thromboembolus
E. Septic embolus

Q5.28 Which of the following is a risk factor for the depicted finding in this lung?

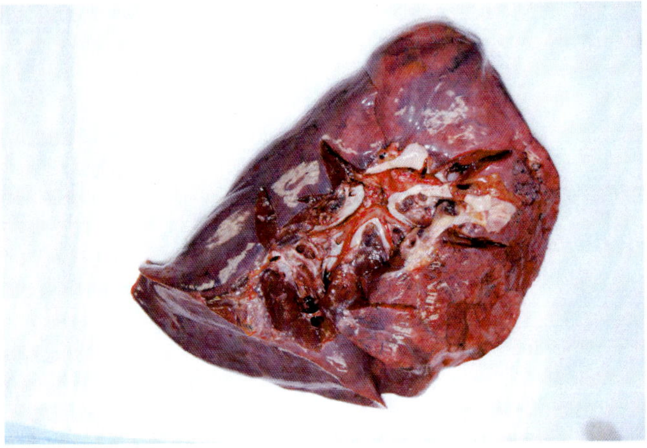

Figure 5.23

A. Disseminated intravascular coagulation
B. Factor V Leiden
C. Hyperlipidemia
D. Systemic lupus erythematosus
E. None of the above

Q5.29 A coronal section of formalin fixed brain is examined 2 weeks after the autopsy of a 50-year-old man is found dead in bed at home. The man had a history of hypertension and hypercholesterolemia. What is the most likely interpretation of the cavitary lesions featured below?

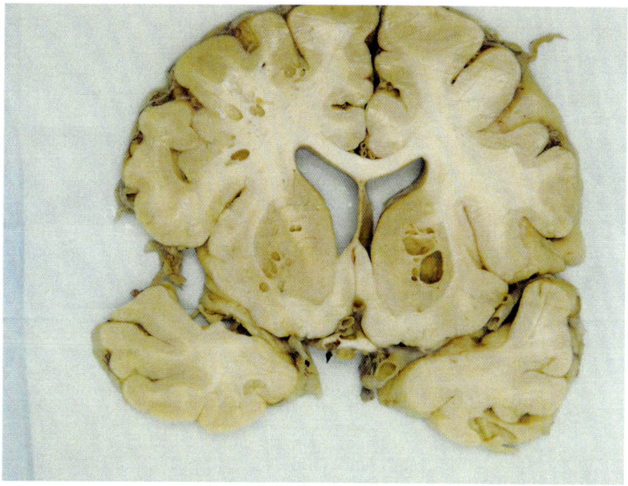

Figure 5.24

A. Chronic carbon monoxide toxicity
B. Congenital malformation
C. Creutzfeldt–Jakob encephalopathy
D. Postmortem bacterial gas production
E. Remote hypertensive strokes

Q5.30 The following decedent was recovered from the woods in a temperate location. The aggregates featured below were also at the nares and lips. Excluding unusual circumstances, which of the following postmortem intervals is most likely?

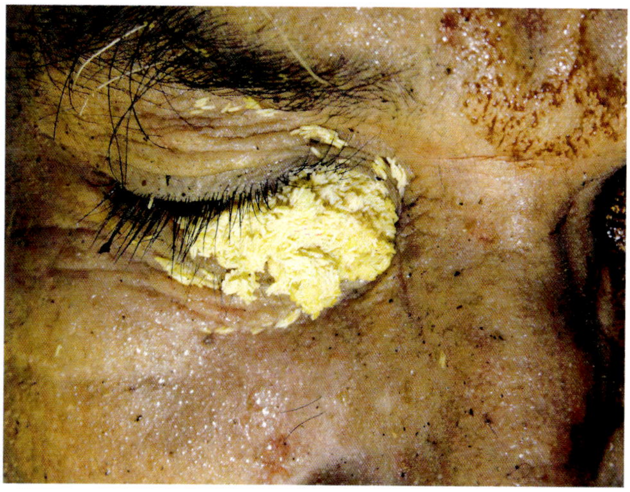

Figure 5.25

A. 1–2 days
B. 1 week
C. 2 weeks
D. 3 weeks
E. 1 month

Q5.31 A 35-year-old man is found deceased on the floor in his home. The front door is unlocked. He had no significant past medical history and expressed no complaints. Autopsy showed the findings depicted below. Which of the following ancillary autopsy procedures should be utilized in this case?

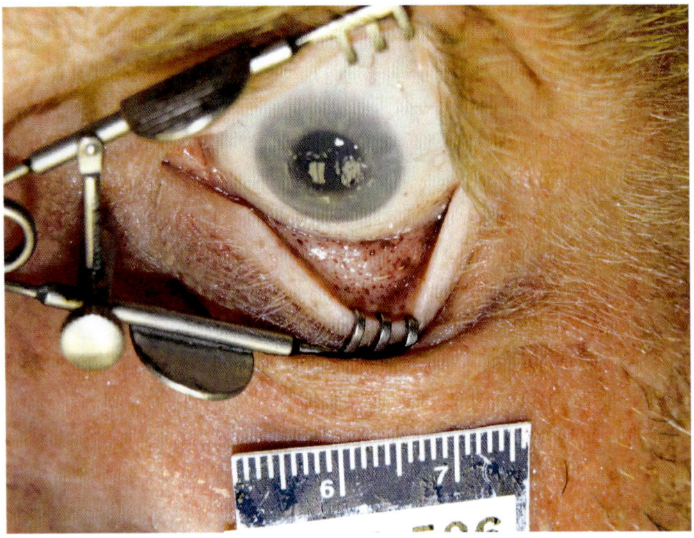

Figure 5.26

A. Anterior neck dissection
B. Cerebrospinal fluid culture
C. Head and neck x-rays
D. Middle ear removal
E. Vitreous analytes

Q5.32 A 35-year-old woman is recovered from the bank of a swamp in the southeastern United States and exhibits the defects featured below. What is the likely etiology of the defects along the chest and right arm?

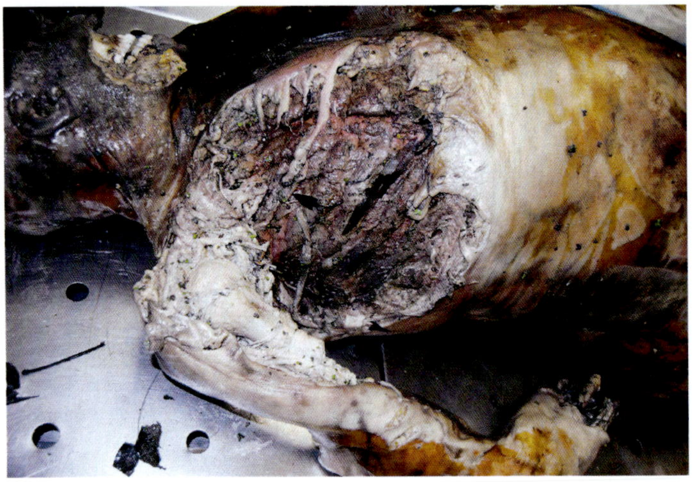

Figure 5.27

A. Alligator anthropophagy
B. Antemortem sharp force injury
C. Chemical injury
D. Maggot activity
E. Postmortem degradation via autolysis and bacterial overgrowth

Q5.33 From which of the following scenarios was the decedent whose hand is featured in the photograph most likely recovered?

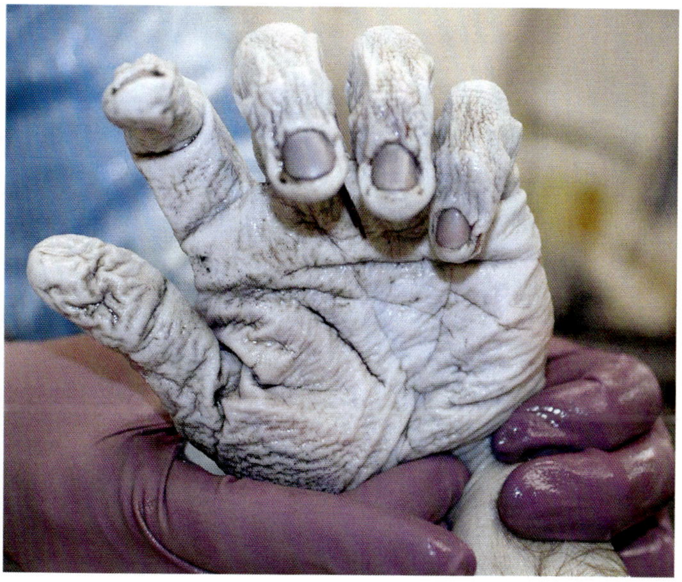

Figure 5.28

A. Hospital cardiac intensive care unit (ICU)
B. House fire
C. Refrigerator
D. River
E. Shallow grave

Q5.34 A 35-year-old man is found deceased in bed. He had a history of asthma and opioid dependency but no other significant medical conditions. He recently complained of upper respiratory tract symptoms. What is the most likely conclusion of the lung histopathology?

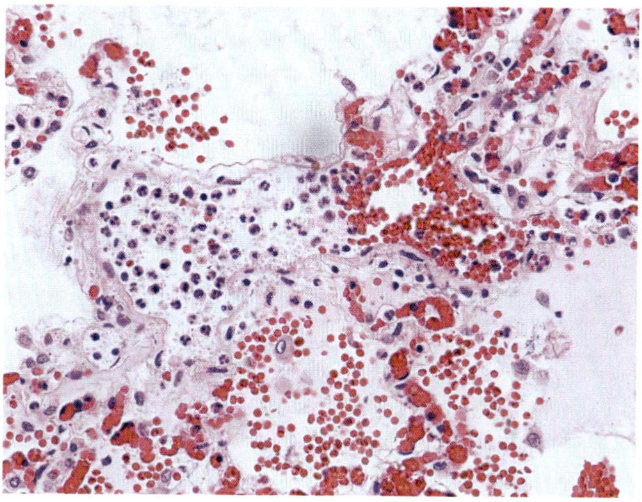

Figure 5.29

A. Acute leukemia
B. Bronchopneumonia
C. Iron deficiency anemia
D. Postmortem artifact
E. Sepsis

Q5.35 This decedent is found in a car and the identity is not known. The mouth is edentulous and some hair is noted in the body bag. Fingerprints cannot be obtained and you are asked about another reliable method of identification. What is the most reliable means of identification?

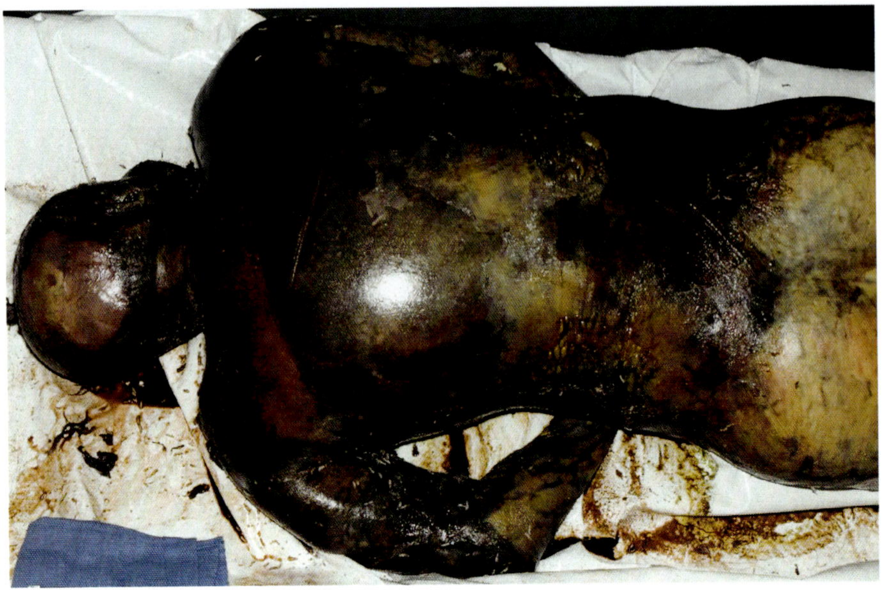

Figure 5.30

A. Blood
B. Car registration
C. Femur bone marrow
D. Hair
E. Wallet

ANSWERS: CHAPTER 5

A5.1 The correct answer is E. Social Security card

- Answer A is incorrect. DNA analysis can be used to identify people based on short tandem repeats as used in the Combined DNA Index System (CODIS) database.
- Answer B is incorrect. Dental records are an acceptable scientific method of identification.
- Answer C is incorrect. Fingerprints are an acceptable scientific method of identification.
- Answer D is incorrect. A surgical prosthesis is an acceptable scientific method of identification because much of the orthopedic hardware, breast implants, and pacemakers have serial numbers that can be cross-referenced for identification verification.
- Answer E is correct. A Social Security card should not be used since it does not have a photograph and no comparison can be made. It is possible the person was carrying somebody else's card for any number of reasons.

A5.2 The correct answer is E. Inductively coupled plasma-mass spectrometry

- Answer A is incorrect. Gas chromatography has many uses in forensics but is primarily used in the determination of low molecular weight volatiles such as ethanol. It is not useful for determining trace elements such as selenium. Gas chromatography uses a mobile phase and a stationary phase. The mobile phase or gas phase consists of an inert carrier gas such as nitrogen. The stationary phase consists of a solid support material coated by a waxy substance. The test substance is injected into the instrument where it separates into its components and interacts with the stationary phase. The components then elute or come off of the stationary phase at different times and a plot is made of the times. The retention time is used to identify the compounds in question.
- Answer B is incorrect. Enzyme-linked immunosorbent assay (ELISA) is a method for detecting antibodies or antigens in blood or serum. A common application is in the detection of antibodies to the human immunodeficiency virus (HIV). The basic principle is that the antigen to the antibody is attached to a solid matrix such as a bead or well plate. This matrix is incubated with the serum in question and a color developer such as horseradish peroxidase. If an antibody is present in the patient's fluid, it will attach to the antigen and cause a color reaction to develop that is then measured. If no antibody is present, a color change does not occur.
- Answer C is incorrect. Flame photometry is based on the principle that certain elements such as sodium, potassium, and lithium emit energy after they are excited by heat and return to their ground state. The emission spectrum is measured and quantified. Flame photometry has been replaced in the current measurement of sodium and potassium as these are usually measured with some type of ion-selective electrode. Lithium can be measured with colorimetric methods.
- Answer D is incorrect. Ion-selective electrode measurement is based on the principle that a specific ion in solution has a measureable electrical potential. The electrical potential varies with the concentration of the ion measured, and the potential is measured by a voltmeter.
- Answer E is correct. Inductively coupled plasma-mass spectrometry is a method for measuring trace elements and can measure concentrations as low as one part in 10^{15} (part per quadrillion, ppq). It starts by creating energized plasma that is energized by inductively heating the mixture, usually with an electromagnetic coil. Once the energized plasma is created, the sample to be measured is introduced and the ions created are introduced into the mass spectrometer. The ions are then extracted through a series of cones usually called a quadrupole. After this the ions are further separated based on their mass to charge (m/z) ratio, and a detector receives a signal in proportion to the concentration.

A5.3 The correct answer is E. Royal blue top tube

- Answer A is incorrect. Manufacturers of test tubes for analysis of blood, serum, and plasma use color coding to identify the type of anticoagulant or lack thereof contained within the tube. A green top tube designates that the tube contains some type of heparin such as lithium heparin or sodium heparin as the anticoagulant. Generally, the powder or liquid heparin in the tube does not present a problem in routine analysis. However, the heparin has not been manufactured to remove contaminating salts such as chromium or selenium. These salts pose no problem in routine testing such as glucose, electrolytes, protein, and enzyme analysis. However, when measuring micronutrients or heavy metals such as chromium or selenium which may only be present in microgram or picogram quantities, the contamination cannot be allowed as it would falsely elevate the results.
- Answer B is incorrect. The gray top tubes designate potassium oxalate or sodium fluoride as the anticoagulant. Sodium fluoride is also a great preservative and is useful in the prevention of in vitro hydrolysis of cocaine in postmortem assays. It is not useful for trace analysis for the reason cited above.
- Answer C is incorrect. The lavender top tube designates either sodium or potassium EDTA (ethylenediaminetetraacetic acid) as the anticoagulant and is used in the measurement of hemoglobin A1C and in the measurement of hematologic testing such as complete blood counts and erythrocyte sedimentation rate (ESR). This is also subject to contamination as described above and as such is not useful for trace element analysis.
- Answer D is incorrect. A red top tube or "plain red" designates that no anticoagulant is used. It is the specimen type to collect for analysis that requires serum instead of plasma. This can be used for testing in transfusion medicine, general chemistry, and many serological applications. Although no anticoagulant is present, the glass can still introduce false-positive results and should not be used in the collection of samples for trace element analysis.
- Answer E is correct. The royal blue top tube designates a tube that is specifically designed with heavy metal or trace element testing in mind. It comes with or without anticoagulant depending on the specific test you need to order. The tubes and anticoagulant are prepared so that there is no contamination by trace elements or heavy metals. The plain tube is used for serum and has no anticoagulant in it. The tubes with anticoagulant contain either heparin or EDTA depending on the manufacturer.

A5.4 The correct answer is E. Scanning electron microscopy/energy dispersive x-ray spectrometry

- Answer A is incorrect. Atomic absorption spectroscopy is used to detect trace elements and rare earth elements. It has application in fluids for measurement of such elements as zinc and selenium.
- Answer B is incorrect. Flame photometry is used in the evaluation of class I and class II metal ions such as lithium, potassium, and sodium. It does not measure any of the three principal components of gunpowder (lead, antimony, and barium).
- Answer C is incorrect. Gas chromatography is a method of volatile measurement in biological fluids. One of the most common applications is in measuring various alcohols such as ethanol. It does not detect or measure any of the three principal components of gunpowder.
- Answer D is incorrect. Mass spectrometry is a laboratory method that can be used in toxicology by measuring mass to charge (m/z) ratios and comparing the pattern seen to known compounds. It has no real-world application in gunshot residue measurement.
- Answer E is correct. Scanning electron microscopy/energy dispersive x-ray spectrometry (SEM-EDX) is the method used to detect gunshot residue on clothing and skin. This method uses particle composition, morphology, and size looking for a pattern of lead, antimony, and barium. Lead, antimony, and barium are found in the primers of bullets and have a characteristic appearance using SEM-EDX.

A5.5 The correct answer is D. Sodium fluoride

- Answer A is incorrect. A clot activator with gel tube is a serum separator in which the sample should be allowed to clot for several minutes and then centrifuged to separate serum, which can then be removed and used for serum assays or frozen for future use. Note that depending on environmental conditions, blood may begin to clot in the vessels (in situ) within about an hour of death. In addition, hemolysis is common in postmortem samples, which may hinder analysis of serum in an assay-dependent fashion.
- Answer B is incorrect. Ethylenediamine tetra-acetic acid (EDTA) and sodium heparin are anticoagulants; however, their ability to prevent metabolic degradation of substances within the blood is limited and is not as good as sodium fluoride. EDTA is a preferred additive for eventual DNA extraction.
- Answer C is incorrect. A preservative should be utilized to prevent degradation of possible toxicological compounds contained within a specimen.
- Answer D is correct. Since some substances important for forensic pathology case work continue to degrade in the blood after death (e.g., cocaine), it is vital to preserve the blood as quickly as practical for toxicological analysis. In this question, sodium fluoride is the only preservative agent listed and is one of the most commonly used. Of note, sodium fluoride is also a weak anticoagulant.
- Answer E is incorrect. Ethylene diamine tetra-acetic acid (EDTA) and sodium heparin are anticoagulants; however, their ability to prevent degradation is limited and is not as good as sodium fluoride. EDTA is a preferred additive for eventual DNA extraction, while sodium heparin may inhibit some molecular assays.

A5.6 The correct answer is C. Short tandem repeat

- Answer A is incorrect. Fingerprints are the basis of the Integrated Automated Fingerprint Identification System (IAFIS) in the United States; INTERPOL (International Criminal Police Organization) maintains an international database of fingerprints (automatic fingerprint identification system or AFIS).
- Answer B is incorrect. Single nucleotide polymorphisms (SNPs) are not currently employed for widespread identification purposes.
- Answer C is correct. The current methodology for the CODIS database is short tandem repeat (STR) analysis. An STR consists of 2–13 nucleotides repeated a number of times in a row on the DNA strand. Using relatively few STR regions, one can obtain sufficient information for human identification with great specificity. CODIS also provides analysis tools for Y-STR and mitochondrial DNA analysis.
- Answer D is incorrect. Prior to STR analysis, which became practical with the advent of polymerase chain reaction (PCR) technology, restriction fragment length polymorphism (RFLP) analysis was employed for identity testing. This assay was abandoned with adoption of STR analysis since STR analysis requires less sample size, is more sensitive, and is less time intensive.
- Answer E is incorrect. Whole exome sequencing (WES) is currently an expensive and time-consuming process that requires a large bioinformatics and interpretive infrastructure. A common use of WES is interrogation of genes for mutations involved in inherited disease. An example of this is identification of the mutation responsible for Freeman–Sheldon syndrome (FSS), a rare autosomal dominant disorder known to be caused by a mutation in the gene *MYH3*.

A5.7 The correct answer is B. Cut the tape away from the end pieces

- Answer A is incorrect. One of the cut/torn ends of the duct tape is visible on the left side of the face. This end may be "fracture-matched" to the roll of duct tape from which it was removed and therefore should be left intact.
- Answer B is correct. Any cut or torn ends may be "fracture-matched" to the roll of duct tape from which they were removed and therefore should be left intact. Once removed, the duct tape should be placed in a rigid container such as a cardboard box to prevent the tape from sticking together.
- Answer C is incorrect. The duct tape in the photograph appears tightly adherent to the decedent's face. Removing the tape by pulling it over the head would likely distort the tape and certainly obscure the application pattern.
- Answer D is incorrect. Unwrapping the tape from the head would likely result in the loss of the tape application pattern, especially if multiple segments of tape have been used.

A5.8 The correct answer is E. 7402. The combined paternity index, also known as genetic odds in favor of paternity, is calculated by determining which genetic marker each person has in common. This is done by looking at each "system" and seeing if a common locus exists. For example, the D8S1179 system has a shared allele (in this case, 14) between the child and alleged father, so it is used in the calculation. Once it is determined which systems are matched then the paternity index is multiplied by each other. The paternity index is a calculated value generated for a single genetic marker or locus (chromosomal location or site of DNA sequence of interest). In our example, all of the systems had one shared allele and are multiplied together yielding 7402.38 as the product that rounds to 7402. Of note the AMEL system does not have a number since it is used to define sex of the individual and is assumed to be 1. Another way of saying this is that the odds are 7402 to 1 that the alleged father is *not* the father. All of the other answers are incorrect as they do not yield the correct calculation. Choice A is the probability of paternity, not the combined paternity index. Choice B is the indices added instead of multiplied.

A5.9 The correct answer is E. 99.99%—The probability of paternity is calculated as follows:

[1–(1/probability of paternity)] * 100%

In our example this yields [1–(1/7402)]*100% = [1–0.001350]*100% = 0.999864*100% = 99.99%. Generally, 99% is the cutoff for paternity except in cases of immigration and then the cutoff used rises to 99.5%.

Answers A to D are incorrect.

A5.10 The correct answer is D. Paternity cannot be excluded

- Answer A is incorrect. In genetic testing for identification or paternity you will not see "an exact match" in the terminology.
- Answer B is incorrect. In our particular case the child is related.
- Answer C is incorrect. A conclusion can be made so this is incorrect.
- Answer D is correct. "Paternity cannot be excluded" is the phrase used for a positive match. Paternity and identity testing are based on probability algorithms and therefore can never be absolutely definitive. However, when you reach a combined paternity index of 100 or a probability of paternity of 99%, then you have met the legal threshold for establishing identification.
- Answer E is incorrect. This phrase would be used if the combined paternity index of 100 or probability of paternity of 99% was not reached.

A5.11 The correct answer is C. Postmortem environmental artifact

- Answer A is incorrect. Immersion changes would demonstrate a pruning of the skin without the appearance of dehydration or discoloration (prior to decomposition), resulting in "washerwoman hands."
- Answer B is incorrect. Postmortem animal artifact generally includes a measure of tissue loss, which is not seen here.
- Answer C is correct. The photograph demonstrates drying or mummification of the fingertips and palm of the hand, particularly the thenar eminence. The discoloration along with the wrinkling and apparent dehydration of the skin suggest postmortem exposure to a dry climate, but may also be seen in more humid climates on body parts with a small surface area.
- Answer D is incorrect. Spray paint debris could account for the discoloration of the fingertips; however, the tissue dehydration and location of discoloration are more consistent with mummification changes.
- Answer E is incorrect. Thermal injury may result in soot deposition, red discoloration, or tissue loss, none of which are apparent. The pattern of discoloration is also not indicative of thermal injury.

A5.12 The correct answer is A. No steps are needed as this is a finding of decomposition

- Answer A is correct. These patches, referred to as milia, occur in the setting of decomposition.
- Answer B is incorrect. This finding of decomposition does not exclude antemortem microbial disease; however, cultures of blood are unreliable especially after approximately 24 hours postmortem due to overgrowth of commensal and colonizing organisms.
- Answer C is incorrect. Electrocution injuries are generally identified on the skin surface rather than the viscera and may demonstrate a central ulcerated region with raised edges.
- Answer D is incorrect. Although numerous metastatic diseases affect the liver, these plaques appear grossly superficial and adherent to the capsule rather than a result of metastasis. One could see if the plaques could be scraped off in order to feel confident regarding this differential diagnosis and if still uncertain, histologic sections could assist.
- Answer E is incorrect. The depicted finding is encountered with decomposition; cultures would not be helpful in assessing antemortem disease.

A5.13 The correct answer is E. The sample is avian blood

- Answer A is incorrect. The sample appears to be from a single source, so contamination is not the best answer.
- Answer B is incorrect. If the sample was human and comparative samples were available, PCR analysis for short tandem repeats would assist with identification of the sample. The sample, however, is not human. Thus, PCR analysis of this sample would not assist in a hit-and-run case, assuming the victim was human.
- Answer C is incorrect. Technically, birds lay eggs; they do not "get pregnant." In addition, there is no indication from this sample one way or the other.
- Answer D is incorrect. This sample demonstrates all nucleated red blood cells. While nucleated red blood cells can be seen in severe anemia in humans, not *all* of the red blood cells in a field will be nucleated as seen here.
- Answer E is correct. The shape of the red blood cells in combination with the presence of uniformly nucleated red blood cells is indicative of an avian source.

A5.14 The correct answer is B. Iatrogenic intervention

- Answer A is incorrect. The arm lesions show curlicues, not a typical feature of gunshot wounds, and appear to lack significant hemorrhage, suggesting a peri- to postmortem injury.
- Answer B is correct. The photograph shows a thoracotomy incision and a chest tube incision (with a part of the chest tube protruding from the incision). The cutaneous defects on the left arm are secondary to the skin being caught in the winding mechanism of a thoracotomy rib spreader.
- Answer C is incorrect. The arm lesions show curlicues, not a typical feature of an incised wound created by a knife. When viewed in context with the thoracotomy incision and chest tube, it is more likely this pattern is not from a serrated knife.
- Answer D is incorrect. Although one might expect a curlicue configuration to an injury created by a wine bottle opener, these arm lesions are superficial and appear to lack significant hemorrhage, suggesting a peri- to postmortem injury. When viewed in context with the thoracotomy incision and chest tube, it is more likely this pattern is not from a wine bottle opener.
- Answer E is incorrect. The arm lesions may have been created by a vehicle; however, the arm lesions are superficial and do not show avulsion. Avulsion describes a body structure forcibly detached from its point of origin with multiple layers of skin torn away exposing underlying structures such as deep soft tissue, muscle, or bone, which is not seen here.

A5.15 The correct answer is C. Intraosseous port site

- Answer A is incorrect. Cupping is a form of alternative therapy that involves drawing skin (usually of the back) into a round container using heat or vacuum. Generally, there are multiple near-identical lesions, and characteristically, erythema is the primary apparent skin change although petechiae and abrasion may also be present.
- Answer B is incorrect. Illicit drug use would also involve a puncture; however, one would expect the puncture site to overlay a vein and would not expect the associated abrasion.
- Answer C is correct. The photograph depicts the right shoulder and upper arm of a person and shows a rounded abrasion with a central red spot, compatible with a puncture. This is a typical appearance of an intraosseous port site or attempt at the humerus region.
- Answer D is incorrect. Lyme disease (*Borelli burgdorferi* infection) may be present with a targetoid lesion of the skin. However, the characteristic lesion demonstrates significant erythema, which is lacking here. As the targetoid lesion expands, the center may clear.
- Answer E is incorrect. A stinging insect mark would be expected to cause vital reaction in the surrounding tissue with swelling and erythema; in addition, the abrasion would not be usual for an insect injury.

A5.16 The correct answer is C. Pelvic stabilizer

- Answer A is incorrect. The defect on the anterolateral hip is not in a location normally used for vascular access. This would normally be seen in the femoral triangle.
- Answer B is incorrect. Blunt trauma from the motor vehicle crash is a possibility, but in light of the symmetrical nature of the hip defects, it is more likely the result of a pelvic stabilizer.
- Answer C is correct. The defects are the result of use of a pelvic stabilizer (clamp), which is used in order to decrease the pelvic volume in rim fractures where the pelvic ring is opened. The x-ray demonstrates a wide separation of the pubic symphysis.
- Answer D is incorrect. There was no history of a gunshot wound or any findings at autopsy to suggest such.
- Answer E is incorrect. The decedent had no risk factors for decubitus ulcers, and the anterolateral locations of the acute hip lesions are not consistent with decubitus ulcers.

A5.17 The correct answer is C. 99%—For the majority of cases the minimum probability of paternity is 99%. One notable exception is immigration cases that involve the State Department where the minimum is 99.5%.

A5.18 The correct answer is C. Resuscitative trauma (intubation artifact)

- Answer A is incorrect. The choking game, also known as "5 minutes in heaven" or "blackout" is a game played by children in which oxygen supply is deliberately reduced by compression of the neck vasculature in order to get a euphoric rush. It may or may not leave neck trauma but would not be expected to produce laryngeal mucosal hemorrhage.
- Answer B is incorrect. The epiglottis in the photograph appears to be normal in size, without swelling, which argues against epiglottitis.
- Answer C is correct. The location of the focal mucosal hemorrhages coupled with the scenario support a conclusion of intubation trauma.
- Answer D is incorrect. Postmortem red cell leakage is known to occur, especially in dependent areas and with decomposition. However, with the scenario presented, the finding is likely intubation trauma.
- Answer E is incorrect. The absence of any neck trauma and no description of facial petechiae, coupled with the provided scenario, support intubation trauma as the cause of the laryngeal mucosal hemorrhage.

A5.19 The correct answer is E. Postmortem gaseous distention

- Answer A is incorrect. Acute necrotizing cystitis would be expected to have pus and areas of visible necrosis and some loss of tissue. This is not demonstrated in the photograph.
- Answer B is incorrect. The prostate gland, on the right side of the photograph, does not appear to be enlarged.
- Answer C is incorrect. Eosinophilic cystitis would most likely have scattered punctate hemorrhage in the bladder mucosa, which is not seen here.
- Answer D is incorrect. A congenital malformation would probably have been diagnosed by adulthood.
- Answer E is correct. This is an incidental decomposition finding, not reflective of antemortem pathology.

A5.20 The correct answer is C. Postmortem anthropophagy

- Answer A is incorrect. The base of the wound has a dark orange-yellow coloration, consistent with this being postmortem in nature. The scalloped margins are suggestive of small animal activity. A chemical burn would be less likely to result in this degree of focal tissue loss.
- Answer B is incorrect. The base of the wound has a dark orange-yellow coloration, consistent with a postmortem defect. The scalloped margins are suggestive of small animal activity. In necrotizing fasciitis, the tissue damage is largely limited to the fascial planes, which are beneath the skin surface. In fact, minimal or no evidence of skin disruption may be identifiable.
- Answer C is correct. The featured postmortem anthropophagy was secondary to rats. Close examination of the wound margins demonstrates scalloped "chew marks" characteristic of rodents. The base of the wound has a dark orange-yellow coloration, consistent with a postmortem event.
- Answer D is incorrect. The base of the wound has a dark orange-yellow coloration, consistent with this being postmortem in nature. The scalloped margins are suggestive of small animal activity. No indication of vital tissue reaction such as hemorrhage is noted.
- Answer E is incorrect. The base of the wound has a dark orange-yellow coloration, consistent with this being postmortem in nature. The scalloped margins are suggestive of small animal activity. No changes suggestive of thermal injury are apparent (i.e., soot, gloving, charring, etc.).

A5.21 The correct answer is D. Postmortem ant bites

- Answer A is incorrect. Skin manifestations of an allergic reaction include wheals or fluid-filled blisters that may have blanching.
- Answer B is incorrect. The weeping blisters and crusted plaques of eczema would likely demonstrate a more generalized distribution than pictured.
- Answer C is incorrect. Hidradenitis suppurativa, also known as acne inversa, is characterized by clusters of abscesses usually found in apocrine sweat gland areas such as the axilla, inner thighs, groin, and buttocks, which are not pictured.
- Answer D is correct. The grouped appearance (i.e., along waistband) and the red-orange base of the lesions are consistent with postmortem ant bites.
- Answer E is incorrect. The red-orange base and loss of epidermis reflect postmortem insect activity.

A5.22 The correct answer is C. Medical intervention

- Answer A is incorrect. The hole in the skull does not have the sharp edges typically associated with an entrance gunshot wound of a flat bone.
- Answer B is incorrect. The hole in the skull does not have the beveled edges typically associated with an exit gunshot wound of a flat bone.
- Answer C is correct. The hole featured in the skull is a burr hole. This is deducible because of the location and the signs of bony healing with no sharp or beveled edges associated with gunshot wounds to flat bones. This finding may assist narrowing the search for identification if medical records are available. In this case, the burr hole was used to treat congenital hydrocephalus.
- Answer D is incorrect. The hole appears larger than an ice pick defect and also appears remote, with evidence of bony healing.
- Answer E is incorrect. This is not a typical area of isolated bony anthropophagy, and also shows antemortem healing.

A5.23 The correct answer is E. Vitreous removal artifact

- Answer A is incorrect. Blunt trauma to the eye may result in scleral hemorrhage, but the purpuric hemorrhage featured in the photograph appears focal and is unlikely to have resulted from blunt trauma.
- Answer B is incorrect. Inflammation of the conjunctiva and cornea may produce red coloration of the eye, but the isolated purpuric hemorrhage is more consistent with vitreous removal artifact.
- Answer C is incorrect. Tache noire appears as a red-brown discoloration transversely along exposed sclera (i.e., when the eyelids are not closed).
- Answer D is incorrect. Tardieu spots develop in areas of lividity when gravity causes blood contained within small vessels to rupture through, creating postmortem petechiae/purpura.
- Answer E is correct. The photograph shows an isolated scleral hemorrhage at the lateral aspect of the eye as well as vascular congestion. Although Tardieu formation is a consideration in the presence of anterior lividity, the timeline in the given example is not ample enough for its development. The finding is most consistent with postmortem vitreous removal and illustrates why an external examination should be completed prior to removal of body fluids.

A5.24 The correct answer is C. Postmortem spread of bacteria

- Answer A is incorrect. Lightning strikes may produce a temporary cutaneous coloration termed "ferning," which has similar appearance, but the broad, arborizing purple coloration in conjunction with other signs of decomposition are most consistent with marbling.
- Answer B is incorrect. Electrocution may produce varying degrees of cutaneous injury, from no markings at all, to an area of erythema, to the classic crater surrounded by a white rim, surrounded by a band of erythema. It does not produce the pattern featured in the photograph.
- Answer C is correct. The irregular dark purple-red lines on the legs is termed *marbling*, a finding created by the postmortem spread of bacteria within the vasculature and caused by the bacterial production of hydrogen sulfide interacting with hemoglobin produced by postmortem red cell hemolysis.
- Answer D is incorrect. Although marbling/decomposition may occur more rapidly with sepsis, marbling itself does not indicate antemortem spread of bacteria.
- Answer E is incorrect. Varices are dilated veins. The broad, branching purple coloration of the leg vasculature in conjunction with other signs of decomposition is most consistent with marbling.

A5.25 The correct answer is A. Electroporation due to defibrillation

- Answer A is correct. The pale patch of skeletal muscle on the right chest wall (left side of the photograph) shows no underlying hemorrhage at the site of incision and is consistent in appearance and location with defibrillation attempts.
- Answer B is incorrect. This localized area of muscular discoloration is unlikely to be the result of generalized heatstroke with rhabdomyolysis. In addition, in a case of rhabdomyolysis, the history might include muscle pain or weakness.
- Answer C is incorrect. Ferning (also termed *Lichtenberg figures*) is the finding seen on the skin associated with a lightning strike.
- Answer D is incorrect. Although the light coloration of the right chest musculature may be caused by edema, with the decedent's history and the location of the finding, the cause is more likely attributable to defibrillation attempts.

A5.26 The correct answer is E. Postmortem change

- Answer A is incorrect. Choking may lead to rupture of the delicate venules of the skin and eye structures with resultant petechial and even florid hemorrhage, which is not seen here.
- Answer B is incorrect. Direct eye trauma is likely to leave blunt traumatic injury such as hemorrhage, which is not pictured.
- Answer C is incorrect. If hanging involves significant weight suspension, it often constricts both the veins and arteries of the neck. Often there are no eye findings. However, the photograph shown could be present in a hanging victim.
- Answer D is incorrect. In significant hepatic disease, one may find yellow discoloration of the sclerae or icterus, which is not shown.
- Answer E is correct. The prominent finding in the provided photograph is a line across the scleral surface. This line (also referred to as tache noire) represents a postmortem change, specifically drying artifact, and its location recapitulates the extent of eyelid closure. Also demonstrated in the photograph is vascular congestion; hemorrhages are not noted.

A5.27 The correct answer is C. Postmortem blood clot

- Answer A is incorrect. There are no historical findings to suggest hyperviscosity syndrome. Hyperviscosity syndrome findings may include bleeding from mucous membranes, visual disturbances, headache, seizure, and coma. Hyperviscosity occurs when there is alteration of the proteins in the blood and may be seen in plasma cell myeloma, Waldenström macroglobulinemia, sickle cell anemia, and sepsis. The photograph shows a postmortem blood clot.
- Answer B is incorrect. A mural thrombosis would be adherent to the endothelial wall and demonstrate some reactivity/organization.
- Answer C is correct. The photograph demonstrates a classic postmortem blood clot, with distinct areas of "chicken fat" formed by white cells and fibrin, and "currant jelly" formed by red cells. There are no intertwining lines of Zahn to support formation of this clot during life. The postmortem clot takes on the cast of the main pulmonary arteries at its bifurcation (versus being composed of casts of deep leg veins in the case of thromboemboli).
- Answer D is incorrect. The featured blood clot shows no lines of Zahn, instead being composed of distinct "chicken fat" and "currant jelly" regions, making this a postmortem blood clot.
- Answer E is incorrect. With the history provided, septic embolus is a possibility, but the photograph depicts a postmortem blood clot.

A5.28 The correct answer is E. None of the above

- Answer A is incorrect. Disseminated intravascular coagulation (DIC) is a consumptive coagulopathy that results in a bleeding diathesis, which is not pictured here. System-wide coagulation occurs with nonspecific deposition of fibrin and consequent inappropriate clotting, usage of available coagulation factors, and eventual depletion of coagulation factors. DIC may occur following massive trauma or in cases of sepsis or other procoagulant release and/or systemic inflammatory response mechanisms.
- Answer B is incorrect. Factor V Leiden (fVL) is an abnormal coagulation factor due to an autosomal dominant genetic abnormality, most commonly replacement of the critical arginine amino acid with a glutamine at protein position 506. Heterozygously affected individuals have an approximately four to eight times greater likelihood of developing venous thrombosis, while the risk of homozygously affected individuals is as high as 80-fold. The abnormal factor V leads to activated protein C resistance. APC cannot cleave fVL and leads to continued presence of an active clotting factor and to insufficient production of the anticoagulant factor Vac, which is a cofactor in APC-mediated cleavage of another procoagulant, factor VIIIa (also see Van Cott EM, Khor B, Zehnder JL. Factor V Leiden. *Am J Hematol* 2016, 91[1]: 46–9).
- Answer C is incorrect. Shown in the vascular lumens of the lung are postmortem clots that have a fatty appearance, hence the description of a postmortem clot (chicken fat and currant jelly). This appearance is due to the separation of the red blood cells from the other blood elements and is not indicative of lipemia.
- Answer D is incorrect. Pulmonary complications of systemic lupus erythematosus include pulmonary hypertension, diffuse alveolar hemorrhage, interstitial lung disease/lupus pneumonitis, restrictive lung disease, and pleuritis. In the presence of anticardiolipin antibodies, intravascular thrombosis is associated (also see Swigris JJ et al. Pulmonary and thrombotic manifestations of systemic lupus erythematosus. *Chest* 2008, 133[1]: 271–80). None of these entities is highlighted in the photograph.
- Answer E is correct. The entity shown is a postmortem blood clot. The pulmonary arteries are dissected to reveal "chicken fat" blood clot. Postmortem clots may be difficult to differentiate from pathological thromboembolic disease. The chicken fat and currant jelly appearance, the propensity of the postmortem clot to mimic the shape of the vascular lumen where it is discovered, the absence of adhesion to the vessel intima, and absence of lines of Zahn histologically can assist in this differential diagnosis.

A5.29 The correct answer is D. Postmortem bacterial gas production

- Answer A is incorrect. Chronic carbon monoxide exposure may result in neurological deficits, with basal ganglia necrosis being a classic finding. The cavitary defects in the photograph are spread throughout the parenchyma.
- Answer B is incorrect. No congenital malformation is apparent.
- Answer C is incorrect. The classic finding in Creutzfeldt–Jakob disease is microscopic (spongiform encephalopathy) and not gross (no to minimal changes). The photograph depicts obvious gross defects throughout the parenchyma.
- Answer D is correct. In the photograph, cavitary defects in the parenchymal tissue are spread sporadically throughout the specimen, to include gray matter, white matter, and the gray-white matter junction. The sharp edges and lack of vital response (acute or chronic) are consistent with postmortem microbial gas production. The overall appearance has also been described as "Swiss cheese."
- Answer E is incorrect. The sporadic arrangement of the cavitary defects and the lack of vital reaction (i.e., no yellow-orange coloration from hemosiderin deposition) are more consistent with postmortem gas production than remote hypertensive stroke.

A5.30 The correct answer is A. 1–2 days

- Answer A is correct. In order to answer this question with confidence, one must consider the life cycle of the fly. Shown in the photograph are numerous fly eggs, which have been compared to rice grains in appearance. Although different species demonstrate differences in life cycle and species should be considered, it has been shown that flies will lay eggs on a body within minutes of death during daylight hours. Fly eggs generally hatch in about 24 hours. At this point, they are called larvae or maggots and are no longer stationary. Thus, the best answer is 1–2 days.
- Answers B, C, D, and E are incorrect. If the body is in the open, fly eggs will hatch in about 24 hours.

A5.31 The correct answer is A. Anterior neck dissection

- Answer A is correct. Since the scene is not secure (front door unlocked), the pathologist must include the possibility of strangulation or other neck vessel compression in the differential diagnosis. A layer-by-layer neck dissection may identify soft tissue trauma compatible with applied force and will provide the pathologist ample opportunity to examine the hyoid bone and thyroid cartilage for fractures, which could assist the investigation. This finding is nonspecific, however, and other possibilities include increased intrathoracic pressure such as during coughing and vomiting, mechanical asphyxia preventing venous return, heart disease, seizure activity, or even dependent changes associated with loss of vascular integrity during decomposition. It is preferable to perform the neck dissection after removal of the brain to decrease the possibility of iatrogenic soft tissue changes (e.g., red blood cell extravasation).
- Answer B is incorrect. A cerebrospinal fluid culture might be important if petechial hemorrhages were widespread, indicative of coagulopathy, which could be secondary to sepsis. However, the photograph demonstrates focal petechial hemorrhages of the sclera and conjunctiva, which is more typical of a combination of venous stasis and arterial flow.
- Answer C is incorrect. An anterior neck dissection is a higher yield procedure in the detection of neck trauma than is a radiograph. However, a radiograph may provide additional evidence of blunt trauma in strangulation, such as hyoid bone fracture.
- Answer D is incorrect. Middle ear removal would be indicated if sepsis was suspected to have arisen from bacterial infection at that site. This history and photograph do not provide information to suggest this.
- Answer E is incorrect. Vitreous analytes (e.g., sodium, chloride, potassium, urea nitrogen, creatinine, glucose) may assist the pathologist in a rough estimation of the time of death and provide information regarding processes such as diabetes mellitus, hydration status, and renal function. However, it will not help to exclude strangulation.

A5.32 The correct answer is A. Alligator anthropophagy

- Answer A is correct. Although antemortem injury cannot be excluded since blood tends to leach from wounds when a body is immersed in water (which may be the case when a body is recovered next to water), the presence of gnaw marks on the amputated forearm bones and long strands of tissue consistent with large teeth marks, means the most likely answer is alligator anthropophagy. Of note, American alligators (*Alligator mississipiensis*) can be found in the southeast United States as far north as Oklahoma, as far south as Florida, as far west as Texas, and as far east as the coastal region of the Carolinas.
- Answer B is incorrect. Although antemortem sharp force injury cannot be excluded, the presence of gnaw marks and apparent tissue bridging on the amputated forearm bones and long strands of tissue consistent with large teeth marks suggest animal activity.
- Answer C is incorrect. Although chemical injury may show skin manifestations that may be confused with thermal injury, no specific findings on the decedent appear consistent with chemical injury.
- Answer D is incorrect. Although maggot activity would not be unexpected on an exposed individual in this state who was not submerged, the most prominent findings, including the amputated forearm bones and long strands of tissue, are suggestive of large teeth marks.
- Answer E is incorrect. The discrete soft tissue defects with tissue stranding and the evident extremity amputation are consistent with animal consumption and not autolysis and bacterial overgrowth.

A5.33 The correct answer is D. River

- Answer A is incorrect. Although ICU patients may develop edematous extremities, the featured hand shows extensive wrinkling, more consistent with immersion changes.
- Answer B is incorrect. Thermal injury may result in "gloving," as can decomposition, but the extensive wrinkling of the hand is characteristic of immersion in a liquid.
- Answer C is incorrect. Cooling the body does not produce immersion changes.
- Answer D is correct. The hand demonstrates extensive wrinkling, consistent with immersion in a liquid, also referred to as "washerwoman hands." Immersion changes are not indicative of drowning and only indicate prolonged submersion of the body part in a liquid.
- Answer E is incorrect. Although some minor immersion changes may develop if a shallow grave is damp, river is a better answer.

A5.34 The correct answer is D. Postmortem artifact

- Answer A is incorrect. The lung demonstrates aggregates of polymorphonuclear leukocytes in a vessel; these are mature granulocytes and do not represent an acute leukemia.
- Answer B is incorrect. The featured neutrophils are in a vessel, not an alveolar space, and thus do not represent pneumonia.
- Answer C is incorrect. There is no evidence of iron deficiency anemia in the photograph.
- Answer D is correct. The lung demonstrates aggregates of polymorphonuclear leukocytes in a vessel, most likely a reflection of postmortem stasis.
- Answer E is incorrect. The lung demonstrates aggregates of polymorphonuclear leukocytes in a vessel, which may be expected in septic patients. However, the decedent had no symptoms to suggest a septic state and postmortem examination of vessel contents for the purpose of cell counts is inadvisable due to stasis changes.

A5.35 The correct answer is C. Femur

- Answer A is incorrect. The photograph shows a body in putrefactive decomposition. Ordinarily, blood can be used as a source of DNA to confirm or exclude identity. Based on the changes seen in the photograph, viable blood is not likely to be found at autopsy.
- Answer B is incorrect. Car registration should never be used to confirm identity. Just because someone is found in a car, does not imply that he or she is the owner found on the car registration.
- Answer C is correct. Given the degree of decomposition, a protected sequestered source of DNA should be sought. DNA can still be found in sufficient quantities in the marrow of the femur for use in identification. Another source of DNA in decomposed bodies is the dental pulp in a tooth. In this case, the decedent had no teeth that could be used for analysis.
- Answer D is incorrect. The roots or hair follicles contain DNA that can be used for analysis. Hair cannot be used in this case as the body is so decomposed that the hair has slipped off as can be seen in the body bag. When hair has slipped off due to decomposition, the roots are not intact. All that remains is the hair shaft that contains no DNA for analysis. Another point to recognize is that the hair in the body bag should not be used for DNA even if it had intact roots because it cannot be assured that the hair came from the decedent.
- Answer E is incorrect. Although a wallet may contain forms of photographic identification, the amount of decomposition precludes a visual identification.

CHAPTER 6

DEATHS OF THE YOUNG AND ELDERLY

QUESTIONS

Q6.1 A 3-month-old male infant presents to the autopsy service with a history significant for bed sharing with two adults. A complete radiological skeletal survey is performed, and one of the films is depicted here. What is the best interpretation of this lower extremity film?

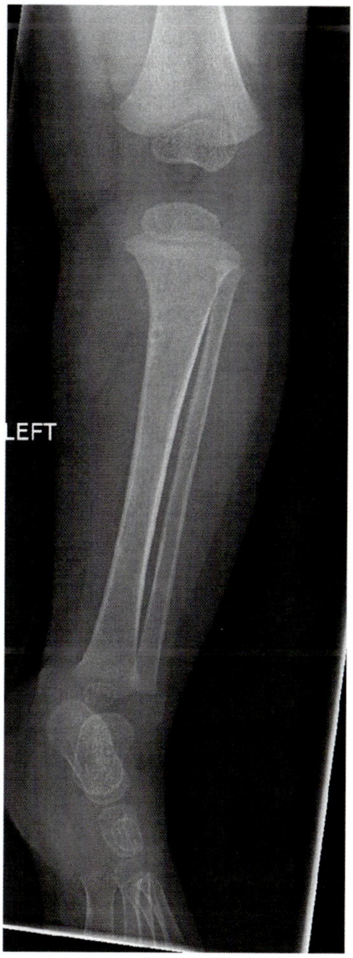

Figure 6.1

A. Birth injury
B. Iatrogenic injury
C. Inflicted trauma
D. Multiple myeloma
E. Normal variant

Q6.2 A 22-month-old child was removed dead from a pond. He arrives at the morgue Friday evening and the autopsy is performed the following afternoon. What is the best interpretation for the neck finding?

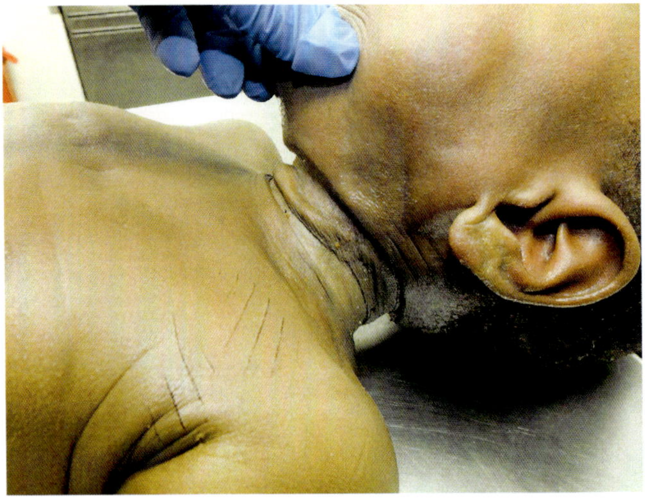

Figure 6.2

A. Animal (marine) activity
B. Ligature furrow
C. Manual strangulation
D. Refrigeration artifact

Q6.3 A 14-month-old child born at 24 weeks gestational age has chronic respiratory disease due to prematurity and is found dead in her playpen in a supine position at home by her grandmother. She was last fed 10 hours prior by her mother when she placed her in the playpen to sleep. How should the finding on the back, sacrum, and buttocks be further evaluated?

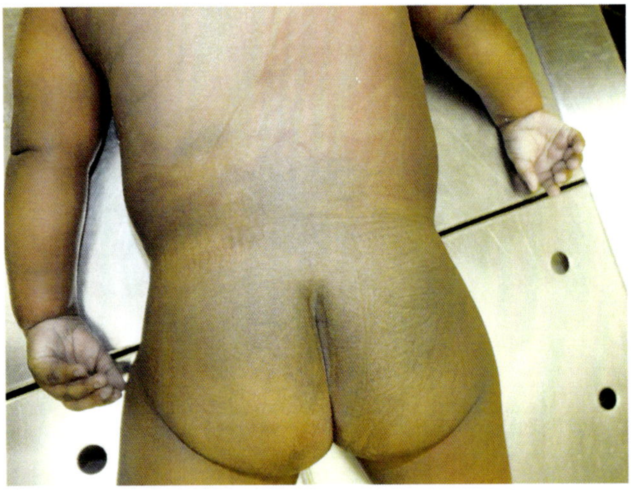

Figure 6.3

A. External examination only
B. Factor V Leiden assay
C. Microbiological cultures
D. Radiological exam
E. Skin cut down

Q6.4 A 1.5-month-old infant was found deceased by her mother in a prone position in her bassinet at ~10:30 a.m. She was reportedly placed to sleep on her side against the bassinet side at ~3:00 a.m. Medical history was significant for recent immunizations with resolved low-grade fever and history of fluconazole treatment for thrush. Birth history included shoulder dystocia with vacuum-assisted delivery at full-term gestation. A complete radiological skeletal survey is performed, and one of the films is depicted here. What is the best interpretation of this film?

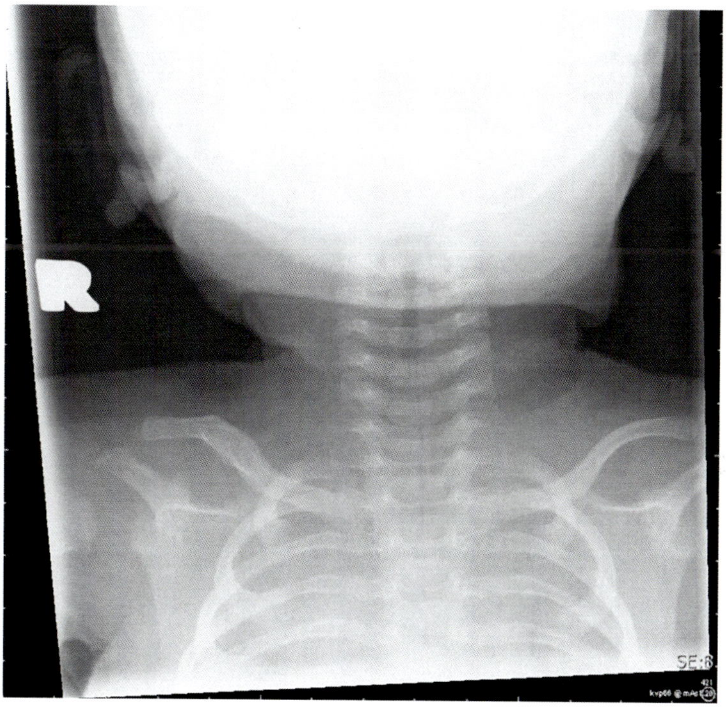

Figure 6.4

A. Benign tumor
B. Birth injury
C. Infection
D. Inflicted injury
E. Normal x-ray

Q6.5 A 9-month-old male infant is found deceased in a crib. A bottle is propped up nearby. External examination reveals weight at less than 5% expected for length, and there is muscular atrophy and minimal subcutaneous fat. No trauma is present. However, internal examination demonstrates an absent thymus and mild aortic coarctation. What do you suspect?

A. Cri-du-chat syndrome
B. DiGeorge syndrome
C. Miller–Dieker syndrome
D. Prader–Willi syndrome
E. Turner syndrome

Q6.6 What is the most reliable way to diagnose smothering in an infant?

A. Confession by the perpetrator
B. Fractured hyoid bone
C. Oral injuries of the lips and frenula
D. Scleral and conjunctival petechiae
E. Strap muscle hemorrhages in the neck

Q6.7 A 2-year-old boy was found deceased in bed. Investigation of the scene and circumstances surrounding the death was not suspicious. The decedent's parents reported an untreated febrile illness with associated rash ~1 month prior to his death. Autopsy showed coronary artery aneurysms, with thrombosis of the right coronary artery. What is the likely underlying cause of death?

A. Coxsackie viral infection
B. Histiocytoid cardiomyopathy
C. Homozygous familial hypercholesterolemia
D. Kawasaki disease
E. Takayasu disease

Q6.8 What does this hepatic finding in a neonate indicate?

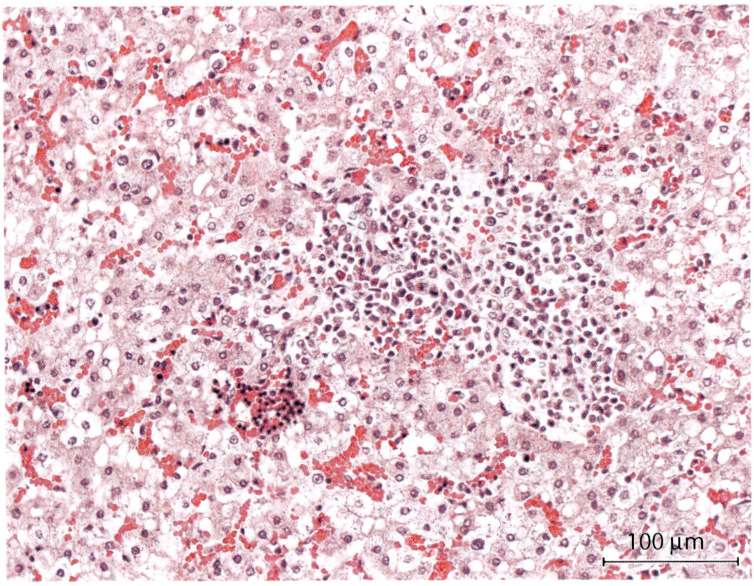

Figure 6.5

A. Acute myelogenous leukemia
B. Chronic myelogenous leukemia
C. Erythroblastosis fetalis
D. Neonatal hepatitis
E. Normal finding

Q6.9 A 6-week-old term gestation infant with no birth complications and a normal prenatal course is found deceased face down in a full-sized bed while bed sharing with two obese parents. During scene reconstruction, the parents convey that they were on the edges of the bed. Autopsy shows anterior and posterior lividity. A respiratory viral panel is positive for rhinovirus, and histology shows a mild chronic bronchiolitis. How should the manner of death be classified?

A. Accident
B. Homicide
C. Natural
D. Suicide
E. Undetermined

Q6.10 Which of the following infant death scenarios is expected to show diagnostic findings at autopsy?

A. Bed sharing
B. Co-sleeping
C. Physical neglect
D. Sudden Infant Death Syndrome (SIDS)
E. Sudden Unexpected Death in Infancy (SUDI)

Q6.11 A 22-month-old child is brought to the hospital in distress. Despite medical intervention, she dies. What is the best conclusion regarding the finding at autopsy depicted below?

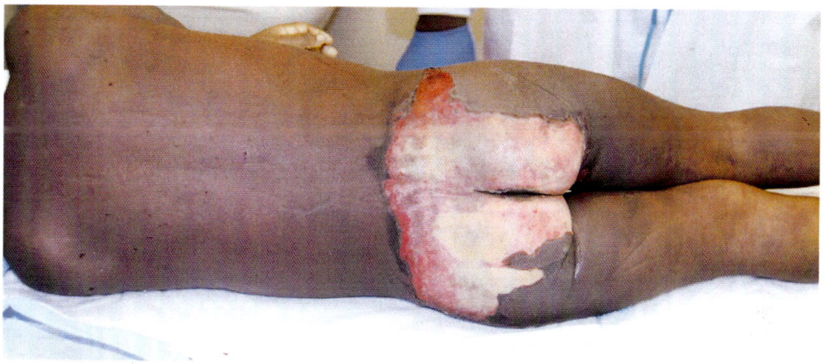

Figure 6.6

A. Accidental thermal injury
B. Decomposition artifact with skin sloughing
C. Inflicted immersion burn
D. *Staphylococcus aureus* infection
E. Stevens–Johnson syndrome

Q6.12 What is the most likely diagnosis in this heart from a 9-year-old child?

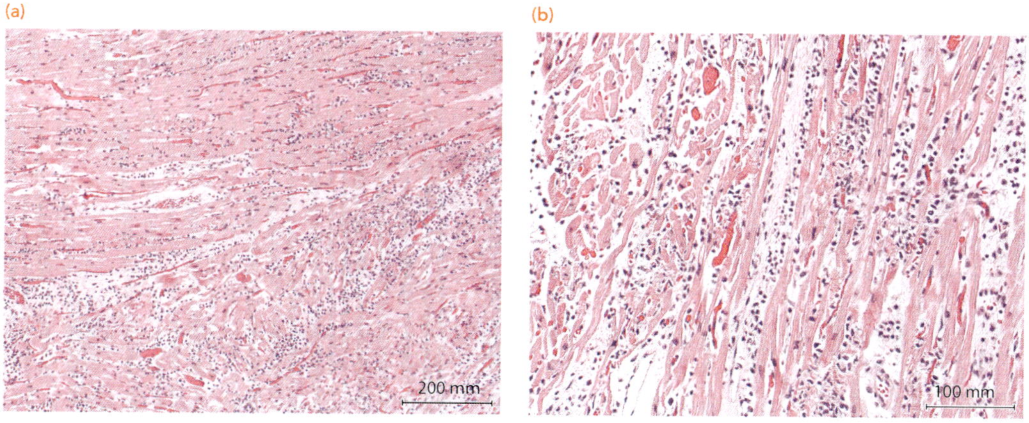

Figure 6.7

A. Viral myocarditis
B. Acute myocardial infarction
C. Churg–Strauss
D. Sarcoidosis
E. *Trypanosoma cruzi* infection

Q6.13 A 2-month-old boy is found deceased in his crib. The mom reports that the baby often strained while trying to pass urine or feces. There is no additional medical history and the baby's birth was vaginal and at term with no complications. Autopsy shows hydronephrosis and hydroureter, exudative material in the renal pelves, trabeculated bladder mucosa, and 15 mL of yellow urine in the bladder. What should the forensic pathologist be suspicious for?

A. Congenital infection
B. Dehydration
C. Hirschsprung disease
D. Posterior urethral valve
E. Potter syndrome

Q6.14 What process is featured in the sampled lungs of this 27-week gestational age live-born fetus?

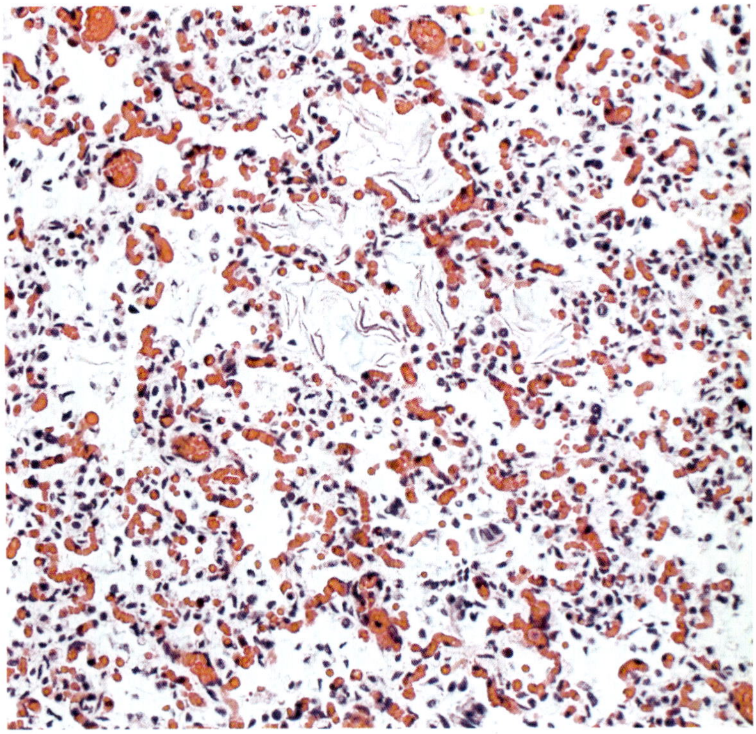

Figure 6.8

A. Amniotic fluid emboli
B. Congenital pneumonia
C. Hyaline membrane disease
D. Normal amniotic fluid squamous cells
E. Viral pneumonia

Q6.15 A 3-month-old infant is found dead on the couch. Autopsy shows a nondisplaced linear fracture of the lateral left parietal skull with associated non-space-occupying hemorrhage limited to the fracture. The remainder of the autopsy is unremarkable. Upon questioning, the parents report the infant rolled off the changing table 2 days earlier. What is the best interpretation of the underlying mechanism of the parietal skull fracture?

A. Accidental injury
B. Inflicted blunt head trauma
C. Probable cesarean birth injury
D. Probable vaginal birth injury
E. Shaken baby syndrome (SBS)

Q6.16 A 2-month-old infant is found deceased in her crib. There was no significant medical history. External exam is unremarkable. A postmortem x-ray is featured below. What is the proper interpretation of the featured abnormality?

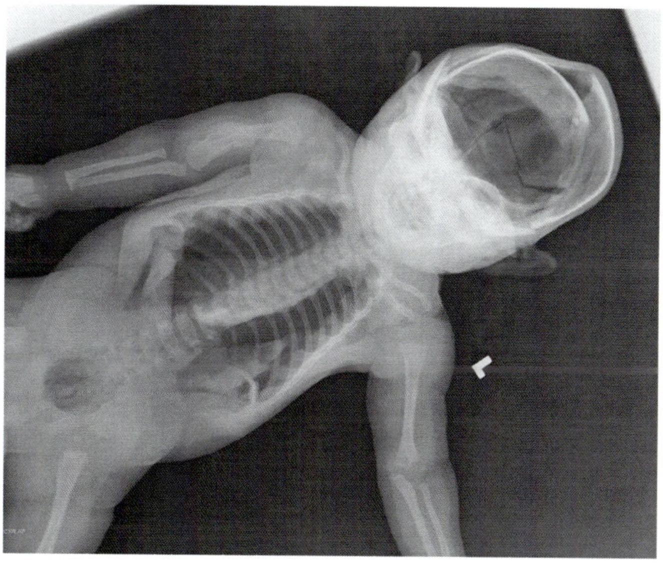

Figure 6.9

A. Accidental injury
B. Birth injury
C. Inflicted trauma
D. Osteogenesis imperfecta
E. Rickets

Q6.17 What is the best interpretation of the injuries featured below on a 4-year-old child?

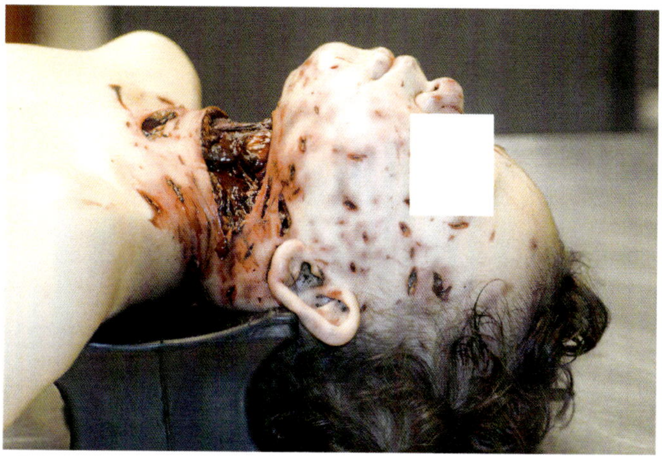

Figure 6.10

A. Assault with a sharp weapon
B. Boat propeller injury in water
C. Dog mauling
D. Motor vehicle crash
E. Postmortem animal activity

Q6.18 What is the most likely underlying cause of the finding on the left aspect of the abdomen in this 6-year-old child?

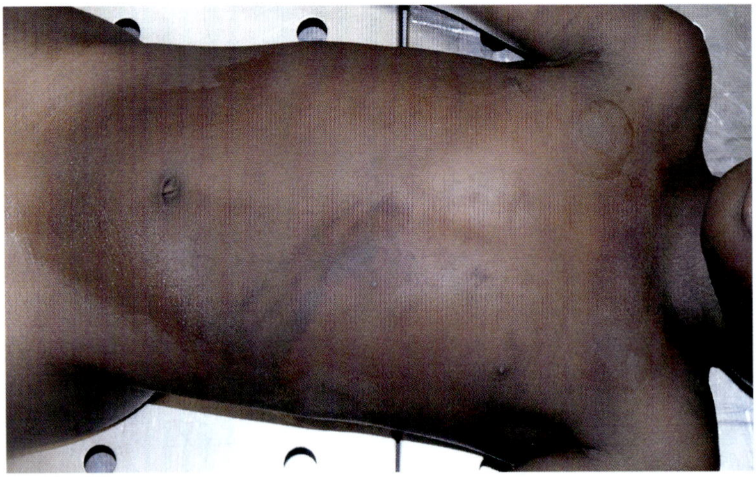

Figure 6.11

A. Belt
B. Neuroblastoma
C. Pancreatitis
D. Thrombocytopenia
E. Waterhouse–Friderichsen syndrome

Q6.19 A 34-year-old woman with no prenatal care delivers a stillborn infant. Autopsy shows the findings below. What is the most likely diagnosis?

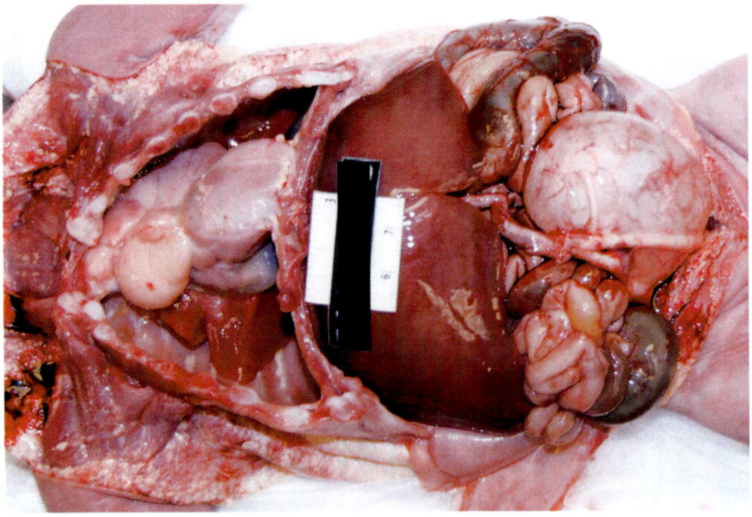

Figure 6.12

A. Dextrocardia
B. Gastroschisis
C. Posterior urethral valve
D. Renal aplasia
E. Ureteropelvic junction obstruction, bilateral

Q6.20 A term infant is born at home to a 16-year-old girl who had concealed her pregnancy. She reported delivering the infant into a toilet and that he was not breathing. The infant's grandmother called 911 as soon as she found the infant in the bathroom with the 16-year-old. Postmortem external exam showed the findings featured below. What is the most likely conclusion?

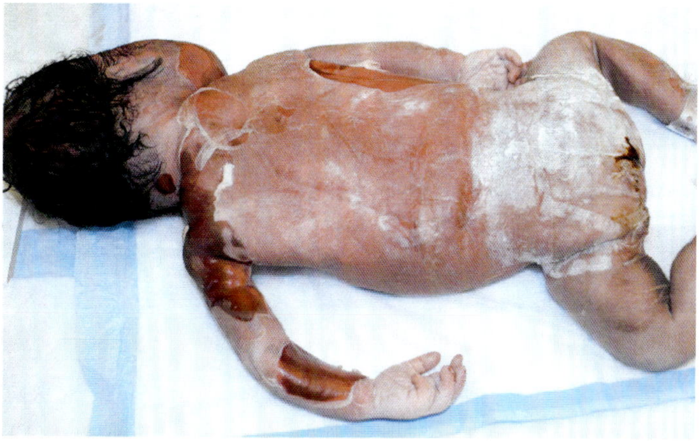

Figure 6.13

A. Drowning
B. Intrauterine fetal demise
C. Necrotizing fasciitis
D. Scalding injury
E. *Streptococcal* infection

Q6.21 A 6-month-old male infant was found deceased in adult bedding in which two adults were bed sharing. External exam at autopsy documented this finding on the hand, present bilaterally, but was otherwise unremarkable. With which of the following is the hand finding most likely associated?

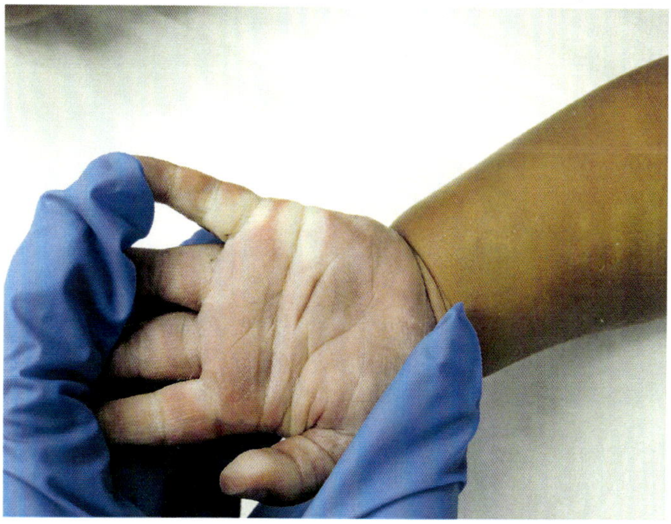

Figure 6.14

A. Congenital syphilis
B. Down syndrome
C. No clinical significance
D. Rubella syndrome
E. Scarlet fever

Q6.22 A 2-month-old infant is found deceased in her crib. Postmortem external exam shows the following finding on her right hand. Her left hand and feet show similar abnormalities. What is the most likely etiology of her hand and feet findings?

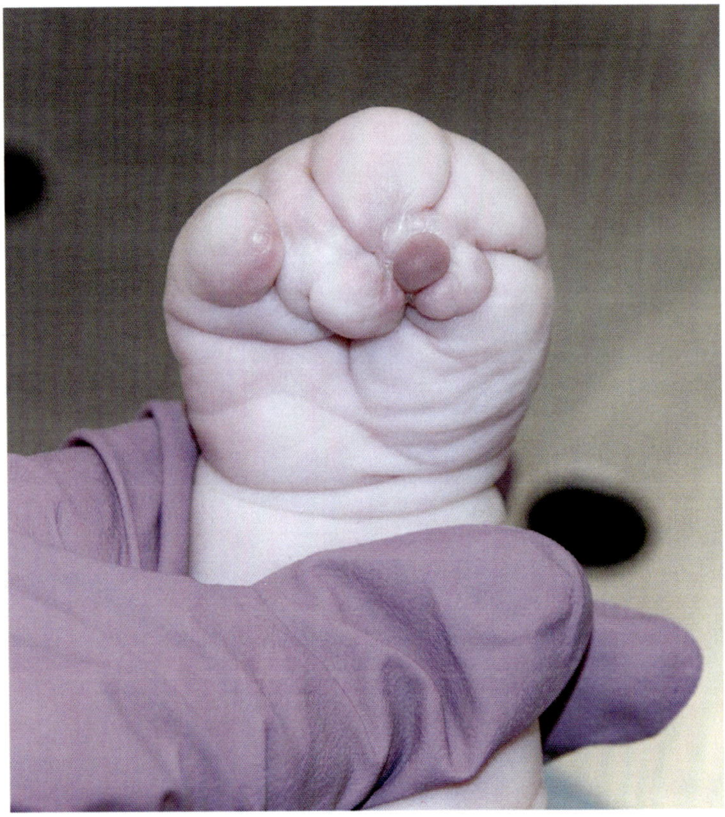

Figure 6.15

A. Genetic mutation
B. Intrauterine amniotic bands
C. Maternal cocaine use
D. TORCH infection
E. Toxic shock syndrome

Q6.23 Which of the following is a reliable indicator of a live birth?

A. Food in the stomach
B. Hydrostatic float test
C. Meconium at the anus
D. Microscopic aeration of lungs
E. Subgaleal hemorrhage

Q6.24 How many U.S. states have laws that require residential care facilities to notify the coroner or medical examiner of the death of a resident of that facility?

A. Two
B. Three
C. Four
D. Five
E. Six

Q6.25 A 4-month-old infant is found unresponsive in adult bedding. Parents call 911, and he is transported to the hospital where he is resuscitated and on life support for 2 days prior to being pronounced brain dead. At autopsy, the findings depicted below are seen on the scalp. What is the most likely cause of the scalp findings?

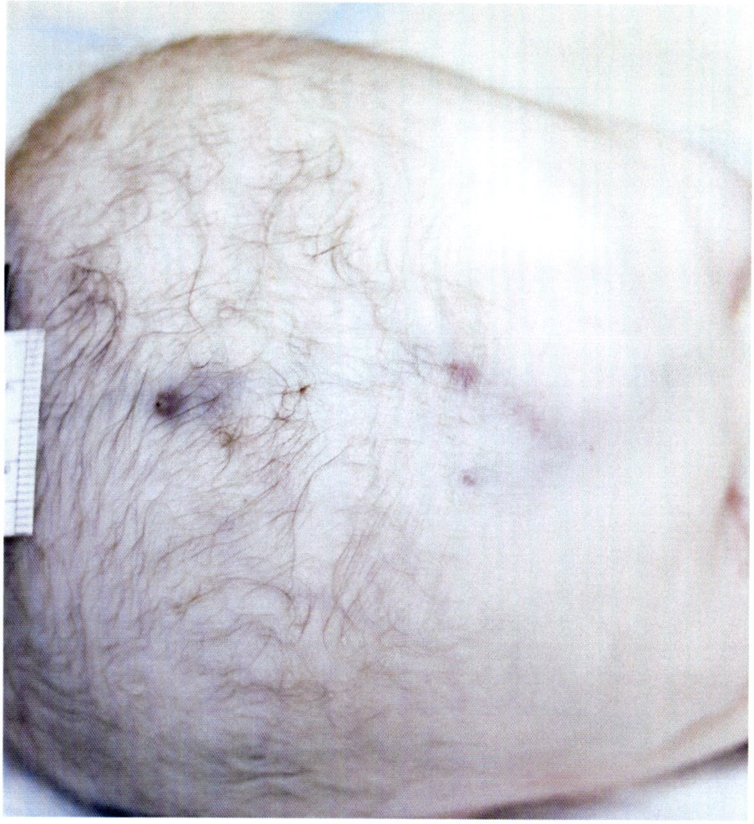

Figure 6.16

A. Cellulitis
B. Inflicted blunt head trauma
C. Iatrogenic injury
D. Post-resuscitative coagulopathy
E. *Staphylococcal* infection

Q6.26 An 83-year-old man with paraplegia called 911 and requested transport to the hospital due to his concern for his expanding decubitus ulcer. He explained his caretaker said she was worried about it the preceding week, but he ignored her because it was not painful. At the hospital, his ulcer was seen to extend over the mid-back, sacrum, buttocks, and proximal thighs and involve the underlying skeletal musculature with focal exposure of sacral bone. During his hospital course, he developed sepsis and died. What is the best classification of manner of death in this scenario?

A. Accident
B. Homicide
C. Natural
D. Suicide
E. Undetermined

Q6.27 A 3-year-old child is brought to the hospital by his mother's boyfriend claiming that the child became unresponsive after he tripped on a toy on the floor and fell on top of it. Resuscitative efforts were unsuccessful. Autopsy documented a ruptured spleen and a reverse Y incision across the back/buttocks showed the following findings. What is the manner of death?

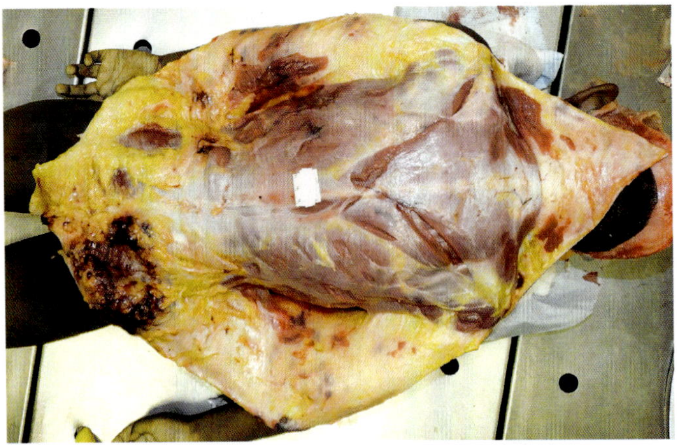

Figure 6.17

A. Accident
B. Homicide
C. Natural
D. Suicide
E. Undetermined

Q6.28 What conclusion can be drawn regarding the infant female genitalia featured below?

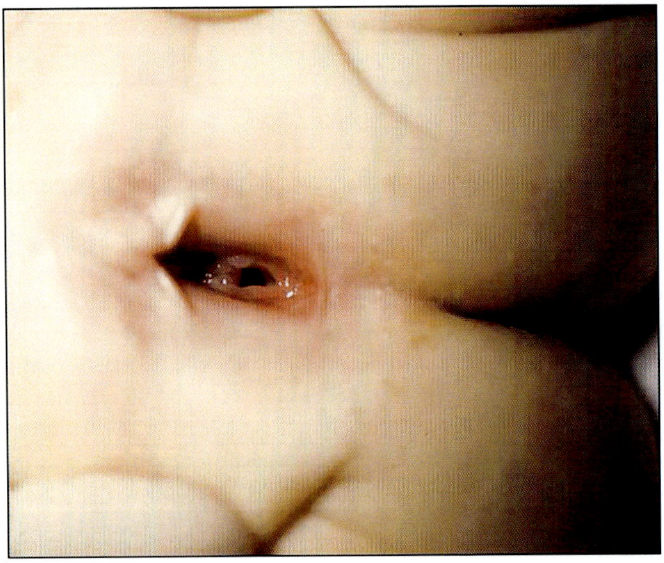

Figure 6.18

A. Candidal yeast infection
B. Digital penetration with erythematous hymen
C. Herpes simplex virus infection
D. Normal with intact hymen
E. Probable sexual assault with perforated hymen

Q6.29 A 1-week-old neonate born via an uncomplicated vaginal delivery with vacuum extraction at term develops a yellow hue and has decreased oral intake. The mother brings him to the hospital where he is admitted for fluids and observation. The neonate subsequently develops respiratory distress and later disseminated intravascular coagulation. Medical intervention is unsuccessful, and he is pronounced dead. Autopsy documented the following liver findings. What is the diagnosis?

(a)

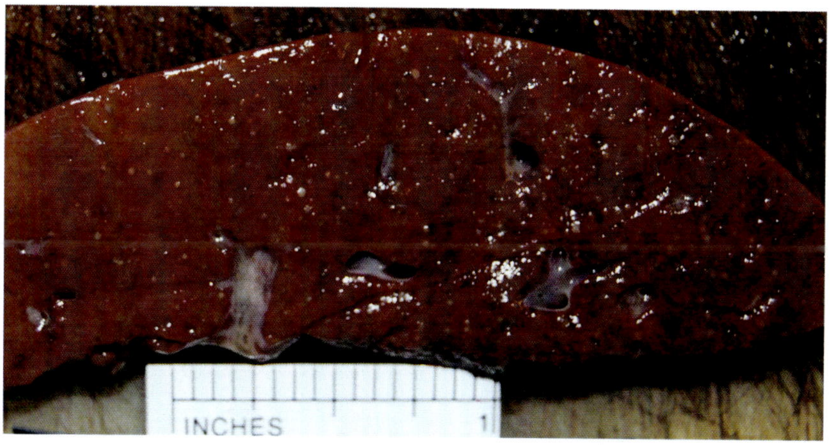

(b)

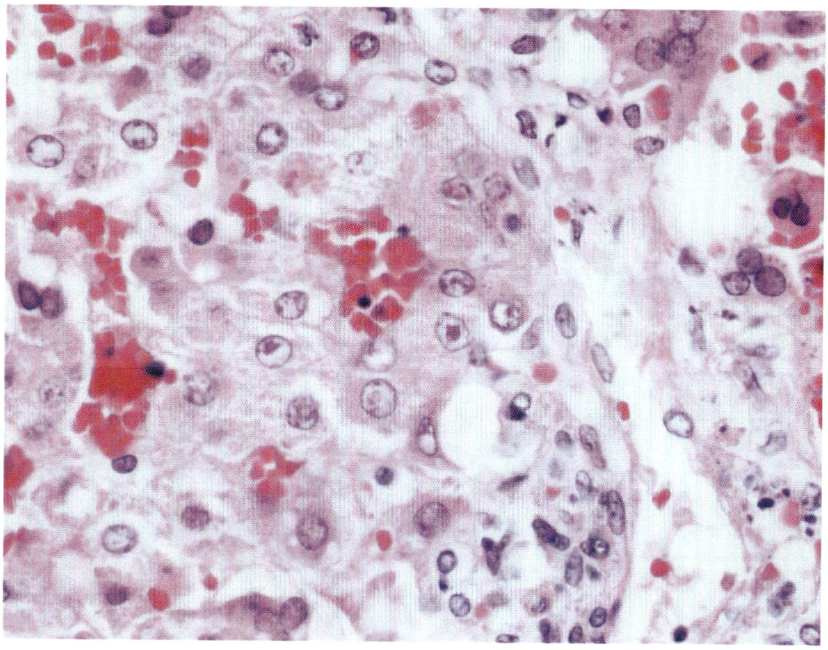

Figure 6.19

A. Acetaminophen toxicity
B. Hepatitis C viral infection
C. Herpes simplex virus infection
D. Neonatal biliary atresia
E. Reyes syndrome

Q6.30 What is the approximate percentage of people over age 65 and 80 years, respectively, that will experience a fall within a year?

A. 10, 20
B. 20, 30
C. 30, 50
D. 50, 50
E. 75, 95

Q6.31 The following infant eye was removed at autopsy and bisected coronally (posterior portion featured). What is the best interpretation of the retinal findings?

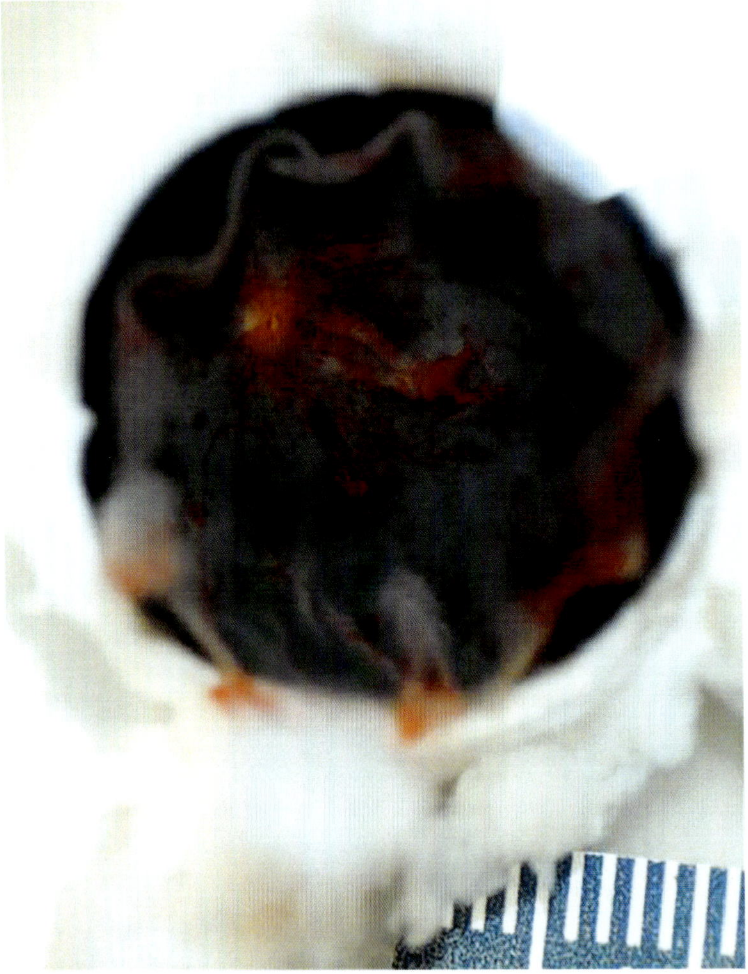

Figure 6.20

A. Increased intracranial pressure
B. Inflicted head trauma
C. Normal retinal
D. Postmortem artifact
E. Antemortem retinal detachment

Q6.32 What is the most common form of elder maltreatment?

A. Physical abuse
B. Psychological abuse
C. Sexual abuse
D. Neglect
E. Restraints

Q6.33 What is the stage of the pictured decubitus ulcer?

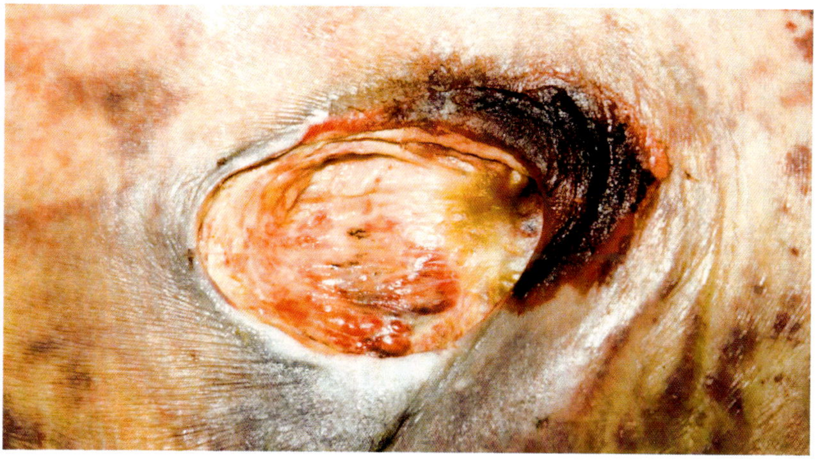

Figure 6.21

A. 1
B. 2
C. 3
D. 4
E. 5

ANSWERS: CHAPTER 6

A6.1 The correct answer is B. Iatrogenic injury

- Answer A is incorrect. Although humeral and femoral injuries may be seen after a difficult birth, that is very uncommon and not the featured finding in this x-ray.
- Answer B is correct. The small round lucent defect of the tibial bone is compatible with intraosseous line placement.
- Answer C is incorrect. There is no indication of acute or healing fractures in this x-ray.
- Answer D is incorrect. A round lucency such as this may be seen with myeloma; however, this patient is an infant making this diagnosis unlikely.
- Answer E is incorrect. There is a small round lucent defect of the tibial bone, which is not a variant of normal.

A6.2 The correct answer is D. Refrigeration artifact

- Answer A is incorrect. There is no sign of animal activity. Two aggregates of parallel linear abrasions over the left chest are present but not characteristic of marine activity typically encountered in a pond.
- Answer B is incorrect. This is a postmortem artifact that can be definitively differentiated from inflicted trauma by the absence of any underlying hemorrhage.
- Answer C is incorrect. This is a postmortem artifact that can be definitively differentiated from inflicted trauma by absence of any underlying hemorrhage.
- Answer D is correct. During refrigeration, the brown fat characteristic of infancy tends to congeal, and the resultant crease pattern is accentuated over that seen with adults and older children. This artifact can be definitively differentiated from inflicted trauma by the absence of any underlying hemorrhage.

A6.3 The correct answer is E. Skin cut down

- Answer A is incorrect. Although the discoloration of the buttocks appears most compatible with benign "Mongolian" spots, cut-down of the regions of discoloration should be undertaken to assure that significant soft tissue hemorrhage is not present. External examination is not adequate under most circumstances.
- Answer B is incorrect. Factor V Leiden assay may be valuable if bleeding is apparent in the absence of trauma or hepatic disease; however, the featured finding is characteristic of benign "Mongolian" spots.
- Answer C is incorrect. This finding is not indicative of infectious disease and does not define a reason for radiology, although microbiological cultures and radiological examination are frequently routine in infant autopsy.
- Answer D is incorrect. This finding is not indicative of infectious disease and does not define a reason for radiology, although microbiological cultures and radiological examination are frequently routine in infant autopsy.
- Answer E is correct. Although the discoloration of the buttocks appears most compatible with benign "Mongolian" spots, cut-down of the regions of discoloration should be undertaken to assure that significant soft tissue hemorrhage is not present. External examination is not sufficient under most circumstances.

A6.4 The correct answer is B. Birth injury

- Answer A is incorrect. The radiograph evidences no signs of infection or tumor.
- Answer B is correct. The radiograph demonstrates a bony callus at the right clavicle. Clavicular fracture is a known complication of vaginal delivery. Assisted delivery could lead to iatrogenic clavicular fracture, but other injuries (e.g., head and neck trauma) are more classic.
- Answer C is incorrect. The radiograph evidences no signs of infection or tumor.
- Answer D is incorrect. The callus of the right clavicle is indicative of a healing fracture, and since clavicular fracture is a known complication of birth injury, inflicted injury is less likely and would have had to occur around the time of birth (1.5 months prior) for this degree of healing.
- Answer E is incorrect. With the exception of the bony callus at the right clavicle, the x-ray is normal.

A6.5 The correct answer is B. DiGeorge syndrome

- Answer A is incorrect. Infants born with 5p- or cri-du-chat syndrome have a characteristic high-pitched cry that sounds like a cat. Low birth weight and developmental delay, abnormal facies, and microcephaly are also common. Heart defects have been described, but thymic aplasia does not appear to be a feature of the disease.
- Answer B is correct. DiGeorge syndrome, also known as velocardiofacial syndrome or 22q11.2 deletion syndrome, demonstrates a constellation of features that often includes thymic hypoplasia or aplasia and cardiac defects that range in severity from asymptomatic (small aortic coarctation) to emergent (tetralogy of Fallot). The neonate may present with hypocalcemia as the parathyroid glands may also be abnormal. Other midline abnormalities such as cleft palate may result in feeding difficulties. DiGeorge syndrome may be detected by chromosomal microarray studies and usually also by FISH analysis with deletion of one 22q11.2 probe signal; however, a normal FISH analysis does not exclude DiGeorge syndrome, which is a compendium of clinical findings. Since many individuals with DiGeorge syndrome can be sufficiently managed medically and surgically, the case described is also worrisome for neglect, which should be investigated along with studies to demonstrate the suspected genetic abnormality. Note also that an ectopic thymus gland may be present, but not found by autopsy, so additional evidence for the syndrome should be present before making this diagnosis (such as genetic evidence).
- Answer C is incorrect. Miller–Dieker syndrome is similar to DiGeorge syndrome in that it involves a microdeletion, this time on chromosome 17p13.3. This syndrome may result in numerous congenital anomalies involving multiple organ systems and with dysmorphic faces, sometimes cleft palate, developmental delay, and lissencephaly. Thymic aplasia is not described in this syndrome.
- Answer D is incorrect. Prader–Willi syndrome is due to abnormality at 15q11.2-15q13.1 when inherited from the paternal allele (if the maternally inherited allele is affected, it is Angelman syndrome). This disease is associated with failure to thrive and developmental delay and later in childhood with overeating and skin picking behavior.
- Answer E is incorrect. Turner syndrome is due to the presence of a single sex chromosome: 45,X. This syndrome is characterized by a female who may be phenotypically normal or may demonstrate variable abnormalities including short stature, ovarian failure, neck webbing, congenital cardiac defects (often aortic coarctation), and other anomalies. Thymic aplasia is not a usual feature. The great variation is thought to be due to likely mosaicism with 46,XX.

A6.6 The correct answer is A. Confession by the perpetrator

- Answer A is correct. Smothering is a diagnosis of exclusion and, without perpetrator confession, may leave no signs on the infant's body. However, in cases of infant death, careful inspection of the oral cavity for abrasions or lacerations (more common if teeth are present) or frenulum tears and inspection of the facial skin, sclerae, and conjunctivae for petechial hemorrhage may assist in the differential diagnosis. Absent these, however, smothering remains a possibility.
- Answer B is incorrect. Fracture of the hyoid bone in an infant would be uncommon as the bone is poorly mineralized during the first several decades of life. In addition, hyoid fracture, if present, along with neck strap muscle hemorrhage would more likely implicate strangulation than smothering, which is likely to leave no signs on the body.
- Answer C is incorrect. Smothering in an infant would be less likely to result in oral injuries. This is especially true for ages less than 6 months as deciduous (primary) teeth have not erupted. These signs would be concerning, but their absence would not exclude smothering.
- Answer D is incorrect. Scleral and conjunctival petechiae may or may not be present in an infant upon strangulation but are not expected in smothering, which does not affect blood flow dynamics.
- Answer E is incorrect. Strap muscle hemorrhages in the neck would be more concerning for strangulation, not smothering, which may be expected to leave no physical signs.

A6.7 The correct answer is D. Kawasaki disease

- Answer A is incorrect. Coxsackie viral infection may be associated with a prodromal febrile illness but would more likely result in viral myocarditis.
- Answer B is incorrect. Histiocytoid cardiomyopathy results in primarily subendocardial accumulation of histiocytoid cells in the heart and may lead to conduction abnormalities and sudden death.
- Answer C is incorrect. Homozygous familial hypercholesterolemia would result in atherosclerotic, not aneurysmal, coronary artery disease.
- Answer D is correct. Kawasaki disease is an acute febrile vasculitis of young children that affects small- to medium-sized vessels. The etiology is not known; an RNA virus is postulated and genetic vulnerability suspected. A rash is frequently seen and described as generalized and erythematous. Cervical lymphadenopathy is common, and strawberry tongue, lip fissures, and mucocutaneous rashes are seen. The presenting symptoms are nonspecific and may include vomiting, diarrhea, irritability, and weakness or pain. Histologically, there will be loss of medial elastic fibers with first a neutrophilic infiltrate and later a mononuclear cell infiltrate with fibroblast response. Chronically, arterial remodeling or occlusion may be present. Aneurysm is a rare complication of treated Kawasaki disease, but echocardiology is recommended at intervals to identify cardiac vascular pathology due to the high risk of morbidity and mortality associated with the lesions. Thrombosis may occur as well. The most frequently affected are the proximal portions of the right and left anterior descending coronary arteries, although lesions have been described throughout the cardiac circulation.
- Answer E is incorrect. Takayasu arteritis may have a similar presentation as Kawasaki disease, but it is more common in persons in their teens or 20s. The inflammation is granulomatous and affects the large vessels, particularly the aorta and its branches.

A6.8 The correct answer is E. Normal finding

- Answer A is incorrect. With acute myelogenous leukemia, it would be less likely to find a group of malignant cells in the liver than in the peripheral blood or bone marrow. In addition, the cells would be expected to be monotonous, not multilineage as seen here. That being said, if this individual was older, extramedullary hematopoiesis may be potentiated by bone marrow failure, which could be due to hematological malignancy with replacement of the bone marrow by malignant cells.
- Answer B is incorrect. Chronic myelogenous leukemia is another hematological malignancy where findings would be more commonly seen in the bone marrow and blood than in the solid organs. Depending on the phase, one may see primarily mature granulocytes in the peripheral blood (which could be apparent in the liver sinusoids) or myeloblasts (in the accelerated or blast crisis phases). Small, hypolobated "dwarf" megakaryocytes would be expected which are not observed here.
- Answer C is incorrect. In erythroblastosis fetalis (also called hydrops fetalis), the liver and spleen are frequently enlarged and extramedullary hematopoiesis (EMH) as seen in the photomicrograph would be present. However, EMH is a normal finding in a neonate and does not indicate a diagnosis of erythroblastosis fetalis, which is a hemolytic disease due to maternal sensitization to Rh antigen when the infant is Rh– (and other fetal–maternal incompatibilities such as in the ABO groups). It has been shown that the increased liver weight is due more to hepatic congestion from high-output heart failure than to increased EMH (Taweevisit M; Thorner PS. The contribution of extramedullary hematopoiesis to hepatomegaly in anemic hydrops fetalis: A study in alpha-thalassemia hydrops fetalis. *Pediatr Dev Pathol.* 2012; 15(3):206–12 (ISSN: 1093-5266)).
- Answer D is incorrect. Neonatal hepatitis has many causes and may also demonstrate extramedullary hematopoiesis, but the photomicrograph shows no sign of hepatitis, which could include periportal inflammation, ballooning hepatocytes, and other changes.
- Answer E is correct. The photomicrograph shows a collection of cells that mimics the population you would expect to see in bone marrow such as nucleated red blood cells and immature white blood cells. This is most compatible with extramedullary hematopoiesis. This finding is normal in the neonate but may persist in cases where there is bone marrow failure for any reason.

A6.9 The correct answer is E. Undetermined

- Answer A is incorrect. If there was evidence that the baby had been underneath one of the parents, the manner could be classified as accident. In this case, however, the parents do not endorse overlaying, and no definitive evidence is apparent. If there was adequate evidence of airway obstruction by bedding, that could also be considered accident.
- Answer B is incorrect. Although homicide cannot be excluded, there are no overt signs of injury to this infant; thus, intentional harm cannot be concluded with the available evidence.
- Answer C is incorrect. Although the infant's pulmonary histopathology is not normal, it is also not definitive for a cause of death. Many infants demonstrate such histologic findings and in the absence of significant symptoms, such as respiratory distress, the pulmonary findings may be incidental.
- Answer D is incorrect. Suicide implies intent to harm oneself and does not apply to infants without the apparent physical or mental capacity for significant intentional self-harm.
- Answer E is correct. Since the differential diagnosis includes overlay, unsafe bedding, prone position, and possibly natural disease (cardiac conduction anomalies, for example), and because homicide by smothering cannot be excluded as it may leave no physical marks, the best manner of death classification in this case is undetermined.

A6.10 The correct answer is C. Physical neglect

- Answer A is incorrect. Bed sharing indicates that two or more individuals were sleeping in the same place such as a bed, couch, or other area. There may be no physical signs of bed sharing, which may only be disclosed upon scene reenactment or through interview.
- Answer B is incorrect. Co-sleeping includes bed sharing but also includes sharing the same environment, such as the same room, and does not necessarily indicate immediate physical proximity of the individuals involved. Again, no physical signs would be expected, and interview with scene reenactment would be the most reasonable way to obtain this history.
- Answer C is correct. In the case of physical neglect, signs are likely to be apparent at autopsy. Depending on the age of the child, there may be an appearance of dehydration such as skin tenting or sunken fontanels, apparent lack of reasonable cleanliness and bodily maintenance, and lack of foodstuffs within the gastrointestinal tract with loss of fat reserves in the subcutis if the neglect is longstanding.
- Answer D is incorrect. Sudden Infant Death Syndrome (SIDS) is determined by the lack of findings upon complete autopsy including ancillary studies and scene examination including scene reconstruction and appropriate witness interviews. Thus, no physical findings would be present.
- Answer E is incorrect. Similar to SIDS, sudden unexpected death in infancy is predicated upon a lack of physical findings at autopsy or only minimal findings, such as increased lymphocytes in lung sections in the absence of history of signs or symptoms of illness.

A6.11 The correct answer is C. Inflicted immersion burn

- Answer A is incorrect. Although accidental injury is possible, the burn pattern would have to be explained by scene investigation. The pattern confined to the buttocks is more compatible with an inflicted injury.
- Answer B is incorrect. Skin sloughing is seen in decomposition; however, the pattern is not compatible with decompositional skin sloughing. In addition, associated findings such as bulla formation and marbling are not apparent making this interpretation highly unlikely.
- Answer C is correct. In cases of inflicted burn injury in children, the pattern of the injury is paramount to diagnosis. The location of the injury is suggestive of heat applied to the buttocks such as inappropriate response to soiling of the diaper or clothing. Accidental burns generally display less focal, more diffuse, and variable severity and patterns such as from spilling or splashing of a hot substance (e.g., boiling water on the stovetop). In this case, hot water was poured purposefully into the child's underpants.
- Answer D is incorrect. The photograph does not show any indication of infection; there is no swelling or pus that one might find with an infection of the skin. A boil or carbuncle would be more characteristic of such an infection.
- Answer E is incorrect. Stevens–Johnson syndrome (SJS) is a form of toxic epidermal necrolysis (TEN) due to immunoreactivity to medications or infections. In the absence of a history of exposure to sulfa antibiotics or other commonly indicated medications or to recent infection, SJS is less likely. In addition, SJS results in diffuse epidermal cell death and would not present with the focal findings shown here but with mucus membrane lesions (mouth, lips, anogenital region, and conjunctiva). It may then appear more as a generalized red rash.

A6.12 The correct answer is A. Viral myocarditis

- Answer A is correct. This is a lymphocytic myocarditis, most likely viral in etiology (e.g., Coxsackie B).
- Answer B is incorrect. An acute myocardial infarction would feature varying grades of coagulation necrosis, such as contraction bands, neutrophilic inflammation, and ghost myocytes, which are not pictured.
- Answer C is incorrect. Churg–Strauss syndrome is a vasculitis of small- to medium-sized arteries associated with eosinophilia.
- Answer D is incorrect. Noncaseating granulomas are expected in sarcoidosis.
- Answer E is incorrect. Also known as Chagas disease, with *Trypanosoma cruzi* infection one would expect protozoa (amastigotes) in degenerating myocytes.

A6.13 The correct answer is D. Posterior urethral valve

- Answer A is incorrect. Although the infant likely had an infection, it is likely associated with a congenital anomaly.
- Answer B is incorrect. There was no description of signs or symptoms of dehydration.
- Answer C is incorrect. Hirschsprung disease would manifest as difficulty passing stool, not in urination, and often presents with a distended abdomen.
- Answer D is correct. This is a classic description of posterior urethral valves, a congenital defect that makes it difficult to initiate and maintain micturition, thus leading to hydroureter and consequent hydronephrosis. Such valves are often difficult to appreciate grossly.
- Answer E is incorrect. Potter syndrome results from decreased intrauterine amniotic fluid and may be precipitated by urinary anomalies, but there are no findings described reflecting the components of this syndrome. Most of those affected with Potter syndrome die in utero, and those that are live-born only live 1–2 days due to pulmonary insufficiency. The scenario depicts a 2-month-old boy, which is beyond the age of survivability for Potter syndrome.

A6.14 The correct answer is D. Normal amniotic fluid squamous cells

- Answer A is incorrect. Emboli are not evident although special staining may be necessary to delineate such.
- Answer B is incorrect. There is no evidence of congenital pneumonia.
- Answer C is incorrect. No hyaline membranes are discernible in the featured histology.
- Answer D is correct. Normal amniotic fluid squamous cells are present in alveolar spaces, an expected finding as the fetus "breathes" amniotic fluid while in utero.
- Answer E is incorrect. No viral inclusions are evident in the featured histology.

A6.15 The correct answer is A. Accidental injury

- Answer A is correct. A linear, nondisplaced parietal skull fracture is a classic and usually nonfatal accidental injury in infants, where explanation exists to explain such (i.e., does not exclude inflicted trauma in isolation).
- Answer B is incorrect. Although the described injury may be inflicted, it is a classic accidental injury explained by the circumstances.
- Answer C is incorrect. It is unlikely any birth injuries would remain unresolved at 3 months.
- Answer D is incorrect. It is unlikely any birth injuries would remain unresolved at 3 months.
- Answer E is incorrect. The described injury does not fit the increasingly controversial term *shaken baby syndrome*.

A6.16 The correct answer is C. Inflicted trauma

- Answer A is incorrect. The location and healing nature of the right humeral fracture suggests abusive trauma.
- Answer B is incorrect. Although humeral fracture may result from a difficult birth, it would likely be resolved after 2 months.
- Answer C is correct. The depicted, healing fracture of the mid humerus is highly suspicious for abusive trauma, not only due to its location in a nonmobile infant, but because the callus indicates previous trauma.
- Answer D is incorrect. Osteogenesis imperfecta, depending on type, would likely involve fractures of multiple bones—many more than depicted in this x-ray.
- Answer E is incorrect. Vitamin D deficiency in infants would typically manifest as "rosary beads" or "rachitic rosary" on chest x-ray (prominences/widening at the costochondral junctions).

A6.17 The correct answer is C. Dog mauling

- Answer A is incorrect. The constellation of punctures with associated contusions and large gaping defects in concert with the predominant location of the injuries suggests a dog-mauling incident.
- Answer B is incorrect. Boat propellor trauma typically results in parallel, curvilinear, chop-type injuries.
- Answer C is correct. The numerous punctures with associated contusions and large gaping defects in concert with the predominant location of the injuries suggest a dog-mauling incident.
- Answer D is incorrect. The constellation of punctures with associated contusions and large gaping defects in concert with the predominant location of the injuries suggests a dog-mauling incident.
- Answer E is incorrect. The associated bruising/hemorrhages is consistent with antemortem trauma.

A6.18 The correct answer is A. Belt

- Answer A is correct. This injury depicted on the abdomen is a classic whip-type injury, with parallel linear marks separated by a blanched area. In this case, the injury was made with a belt.
- Answer B is incorrect. Abdominal ecchymoses may be a feature of neuroblastoma, but in the photograph, the bruising is patterned.
- Answer C is incorrect. Abdominal ecchymoses may be a feature of pancreatitis, but in the photograph, the bruising is patterned.
- Answer D is incorrect. Cutaneous petechiae are a feature of thrombocytopenia, but in the photograph, the bruising is patterned.
- Answer E is incorrect. Cutaneous petechiae and purpura may be a feature of sepsis, but in the photograph, the bruising is patterned.

A6.19 The correct answer is C. Posterior urethral valve

- Answer A is incorrect. Organs are in their proper location.
- Answer B is incorrect. The photograph does not illustrate gastroschisis; organs appear to be in their correct location and not protruding through an abdominal wall defect.
- Answer C is correct. The photograph depicts hypoplastic lungs and a distended bladder (megacystis), thus supporting the diagnosis of obstructive posterior urethral valves and resultant Potter syndrome with hypoplastic lungs. Oligohydramnios is likely to have been documented and is the cause of pulmonary hypoplasia if it arises in early pregnancy and is persistent (also see McHugo J, Whittle M. Enlarged fetal bladders: Aetiology, management and outcome. *Prenat Diagn* 2001, 21: 958–63).
- Answer D is incorrect. The bladder is distended (with urine); thus, renal aplasia is not likely.
- Answer E is incorrect. The bladder is distended (with urine); thus, bilateral uteropelvic junction obstruction (UPO) is not likely. Frequently, UPO is unilateral (also see Chevalier RL. Congenital urinary tract obstruction: The long view. *Adv Chronic Kidney Dis* 2015, 22[4]: 312–9 http://dx.doi.org/10.1053/j.ackd.2015.01.012 accessed 7/18/16).

A6.20 The correct answer is B. Intrauterine fetal demise (IUFD)

- Answer A is incorrect. Skin slippage may indicate prolonged submersion in water, but the finding in this case is consistent with an intrauterine fetal demise.
- Answer B is correct. The signs of maceration, including skin slippage and dusky red coloration, indicate intrauterine fetal demise.
- Answer C is incorrect. Maceration indicates intrauterine fetal demise.
- Answer D is incorrect. Maceration indicates intrauterine fetal demise.
- Answer E is incorrect. Although infection may have resulted in fetal death, the conclusion from the photograph is limited to IUFD.

A6.21 The correct answer is C. No clinical significance

- Answer A is incorrect. None of the features of congenital syphilis such as saddle nose deformity, Hutchinson teeth, or corneal clouding were described in this scenario.
- Answer B is incorrect. Down syndrome (trisomy 21) is associated with a single palmar crease, but the rest of the external exam in this case was negative, thus making trisomy 21 highly unlikely.
- Answer C is correct. Approximately 10% of the normal population have a single palmar crease on one hand; 5% have it on both.
- Answer D is incorrect. None of the complications of congenital rubella infection such as cataracts or cardiac defects was described in this scenario.
- Answer E is incorrect. Scarlet fever is manifested by a sandpaper rash associated with group A streptococcal infection and is not associated with a single palmar crease.

A6.22 The correct answer is B. Intrauterine amniotic bands

- Answer A is incorrect. As there is only partial amputation of the fingers, this suggests a cause other than a genetic mutation. If this were a malformation, it is more likely the entire finger or the entire hand would not be developed. Since partial fingers are seen, this argues against a genetic basis.
- Answer B is correct. The photograph illustrates the result of intrauterine amniotic bands. The bands are fibrous amniotic tissue, which constricts fetal tissue causing amputation of fetal parts such as the fingers seen in the photograph. The entrapment can be severe enough to cause intrauterine fetal demise (IUFD).
- Answer C is incorrect. The photograph illustrates the result of intrauterine amniotic bands.
- Answer D is incorrect. TORCH is an acronym that stands for Toxoplasmosis, Other agents, Rubella, Cytomegalovirus, and Herpes. Loss of fingers as depicted in the photograph is not associated with any of the TORCH infections.
- Answer E is incorrect. Toxic shock syndrome is classically associated with *Staphylococcus aureus* infection and TSST-1 toxin from the use of tampons. Toxic shock is a complication of sepsis and would be expected to manifest clinically as hypotension, fever or tachycardia without the immediate loss of any of the extremities.

A6.23 The correct answer is A. Food in the stomach

- Answer A is correct. Food in the stomach is a reliable indicator of life after birth. However, it is often absent in cases of neonatacide due to the short survival period. Similarly, umbilical cord changes may be helpful in cases with 1+ day survival.
- Answer B is incorrect. The hydrostatic float test assumes a live birth will result in lung inflation due to breathing and thus flotation when portions of lung are placed in formalin (versus sinking of uninflated lungs and compared to flotation of liver from the same decedent to assess for decomposition gases). However, this classic procedure is of limited value in assessing live birth for a variety of reasons. Decomposition may produce gas and induce floating of tissue in a stillborn. Live birth with subsequent drowning and inhalation of water may result in lungs sinking. Lung sections are also well known to sink in cases of diffuse alveolar damage.
- Answer C is incorrect. Meconium may be released in utero during fetal stress.
- Answer D is incorrect. Microscopic assessment of pulmonary tissue for aeration is unreliable.
- Answer E is incorrect. Subgaleal hemorrhage can be consistent with birth trauma but not necessarily extrauterine life.

A6.24 The correct answer is A. Two

- Answer A is correct. Missouri and Arkansas are the only two states that have laws requiring notification to the coroner or medical examiner by residential care facilities for deaths of a resident in the facility.
- Answers B to E are incorrect.

A6.25 The correct answer is C. Iatrogenic injury

- Answer A is incorrect. The photograph demonstrates hemorrhage rather than cellulitis.
- Answer B is incorrect. The ecchymoses are reflective of red cell leakage from vessel disruption due to catheter insertion, not blunt trauma.
- Answer C is correct. The punctures over scalp veins and associated ecchymoses are consistent with intravascular access attempts, an iatrogenic injury. The ecchymoses are reflective of red cell leakage from vessel disruption, not blunt trauma.
- Answer D is incorrect. The hemorrhage is confined to a single area, which is not supportive of coagulopathy.
- Answer E is incorrect. The photograph demonstrates hemorrhage rather than an infectious process.

A6.26 The correct answer is E. Undetermined

- Answer A is incorrect. In this case, the cause of paraplegia would dictate the manner of death. Since that is not elucidated, the best answer is "Undetermined."
- Answer B is incorrect. Decubitus ulcers in someone solely dependent on others for care are sometimes considered a basis for a manner of death of homicide from neglect. In this case, however, the individual chose to ignore the advancing lesions, so a caretaker is not at fault.
- Answer C is incorrect. In this case, the cause of paraplegia would dictate the manner of death. Since that is not elucidated, the best answer is "Undetermined."
- Answer D is incorrect. There is no indication that the individual understood that reticence to seek care would lead to his death, and it is unlikely (although not impossible) that his paraplegia was due to a suicide attempt. Thus, suicide is not the best answer.
- Answer E is correct. In this case, the manner of death would align with the original cause of the patient's paraplegia. Until that is known, a manner of "Undetermined" would be appropriate.

A6.27 The correct answer is B. Homicide

- Answer A is incorrect. The multiple bruises across the back and buttocks and the splenic laceration are not adequately explained by the account given by the caregiver and are more suspicious for inflicted injury.
- Answer B is correct. The multiple bruises across the back and buttocks and the splenic laceration are not adequately explained by the account given by the caregiver and are most consistent with inflicted injury (i.e., beating), not a simple fall.
- Answer C is incorrect. Regardless of any natural condition predisposing to hemorrhage, the multiple bruises across the back and buttocks and the splenic laceration were the result of trauma, thus not suggestive of a natural death.
- Answer D is incorrect. The depicted injuries are not in a characteristic location for self-inflicted injury.
- Answer E is incorrect. The multiple bruises across the back and buttocks and the splenic laceration are consistent with inflicted trauma, thus not an undetermined manner of death.

A6.28 The correct answer is D. Normal with intact hymen

- Answer A is incorrect. Vaginal yeast infection can be characterized by watery to thick and white odorless discharge, erythema of the vagina and vulva, which is not seen in the photograph.
- Answer B is incorrect. This is a normal intact hymen that lacks erythematous change.
- Answer C is incorrect. Herpes simplex virus infection in this anatomic location would most likely present as vesicles or papules with erythema of the genitalia resembling cold sores. Also, the most common subtype of herpes associated with genital infection is HSV2; however, HSV1 can cause herpes genitalis with the same clinical presentation and additional testing would be needed to classify the subtype.
- Answer D is correct. This is a normal intact hymen. Normal anatomic variants include cribriform and septate hymen.
- Answer E is incorrect. This is a normal intact hymen and as such this choice can be excluded.

A6.29 The correct answer is C. Herpes simplex virus infection

- Answer A is incorrect. Although acetaminophen toxicity could precipitate hepatic necrosis, the histopathology demonstrates the pink-purple intranuclear inclusions characteristic of herpes simplex virus.
- Answer B is incorrect. The histiologic appearance of the intranuclear inclusions in the photograph is characteristic of herpes infection. Active hepatitis C infection characteristically expands portal triaditis and induces an interface hepatitis.
- Answer C is correct. This is the classic gross and histologic appearance of herpetic hepatic infection, likely acquired from the vaginal tract during delivery (fatal neonatal herpes). A minute white-tan nodularity is throughout the hepatic parenchyma grossly and pink-purple intranuclear inclusions characteristic of herpes simplex virus are present on histology (around the edges of the photograph).
- Answer D is incorrect. Neither the white-tan nodularity of the liver nor the histological features are associated with biliary atresia.
- Answer E is incorrect. Reyes syndrome is associated with microvesicular steatosis, which is not featured in the provided photomicrograph.

A6.30 The correct answer is C. 30, 50.

- Answer C is correct. All of the other answers are incorrect as they do not have the correct percentage.

A6.31 The correct answer is A. Increased intracranial pressure

- Answer A is correct. Retinal hemorrhages as featured here are likely the result of increased intracranial pressure, whether the underlying etiology of the increase in pressure is traumatic or organic.
- Answer B is incorrect. Retinal hemorrhages can result from increased intracranial pressure, which may be the result of an inflicted injury, accidental trauma, or organic disease.
- Answer C is incorrect. Numerous retinal hemorrhages are present.
- Answer D is incorrect. The bisected eye is submersed in water. The retina appears wavy, and this is an effect of sectioning. However, the acute red hemorrhages are not.
- Answer E is incorrect. The apparent retinal detachment is due to postmortem sectioning and cannot be ascribed to antemortem events.

A6.32 The correct answer is D. Neglect

- Answer A is incorrect. Physical abuse is defined as the use of physical force that may result in bodily injury, physical pain, or impairment.
- Answer B is incorrect. Psychological or emotional abuse is defined as the infliction of anguish, pain, or distress through verbal or nonverbal acts. Examples include verbal assaults, insults, threats, intimidation, humiliation, and harassment.
- Answer C is incorrect. Sexual abuse is defined as sexual contact of any kind without consent. Sexual contact with a person who is incapable of providing consent is considered sexual abuse as well.
- Answer D is correct. Neglect is defined as the failure to provide basic goods or services to ensure physical/psychological needs. It is the most common form of elder maltreatment.
- Answer E is incorrect. Restraints may be needed to help a patient from self-harm. While their use may be increased with the elderly, it is generally regarded as treatment albeit as a last resort with proper documentation.

A6.33 The correct answer is C. Stage 3

- Answer A is incorrect. Stage 1 decubitus ulcers are defined as nonblanchable erythema without a break in the skin. Since this is deeper than the skin, this is beyond stage 1.
- Answer B is incorrect. Stage 2 decubitus ulcers are defined by partial thickness loss of epidermis and dermis without visible subcutaneous tissue. The photograph depicts full-thickness loss of epidermis and dermis, and there is visible subcutaneous tissue so this ulcer is beyond stage 2.
- Answer C is correct. Decubitus ulcers are classified into four stages. A stage 3 ulcer is full thickness with visible subcutaneous tissue. Based on the photograph, these criteria are met and the ulcer is best classified as stage 3.
- Answer D is incorrect. Stage 4 ulcers, in addition to visible subcutaneous tissue, also have visible bone, tendon, and/or muscle, which is not seen in the photograph.
- Answer E is incorrect. Decubitus ulcers are only classified using four stages.

CHAPTER 7

TOXICOLOGY

QUESTIONS

Q7.1 A person is suspected of overdosing on an unknown white powder. A syringe and spoon with residue are found at the scene. What is the most likely location of the parent drug?

A. Heart blood

B. Peripheral blood

C. Spoon or syringe

D. Urine

E. Vitreous fluid

Q7.2 This mass was recovered from the gastric lumen of a 29-year-old woman who was found dead at home in bed. What is the probable manner of death?

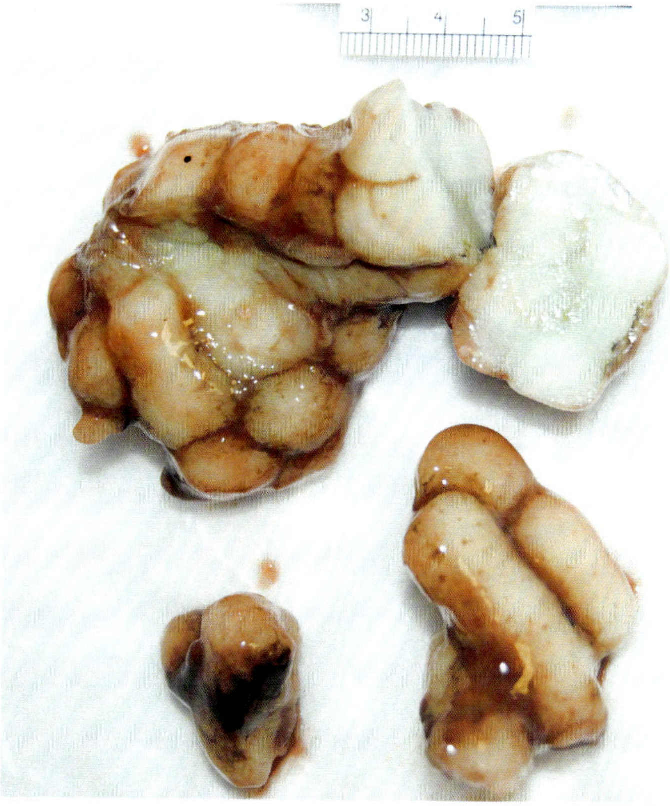

Figure 7.1

A. Accident

B. Homicide

C. Natural

D. Suicide

E. Undetermined

Q7.3 What is the principle substance used to screen for cocaine use?

A. Anhydroecgonidine
B. Benzoylecgonine
C. Cocaine
D. Ester methyl ecgonine
E. Norcocaine

Q7.4 A 25-year-old male was admitted to the hospital with a blood urea nitrogen (BUN) of 100 mg/dL and a creatinine of 8.7 mg/dL. He also had tachycardia and was restless. He admitted to smoking a green brown leafy substance he bought at a smoke shop. What drug is most likely responsible for these symptoms?

A. Cocaine
B. Dronabinol
C. Heroin
D. Tetrahydrocannabinol
E. XLR-11

Q7.5 What is the most prevalent ketone in alcoholic ketoacidosis?

A. Acetone
B. Acetic acid
C. Acetoacetic acid
D. β-hydroxybutyric acid
E. Diacetic acid

Q7.6 What is the receptor associated with 3,4-methylenedioxy-methamphetamine?

A. CB1
B. CB2
C. 5-HT2A
D. μ
E. Norepinephrine

Q7.7 Which receptor is directly activated by opioids?

A. CB1
B. CB2
C. 5-HT2A
D. μ
E. Norepinephrine

Q7.8 A 25-year-old man with a history of drug use is found dead in bed with various drug paraphernalia items nearby. Autopsy shows heavy wet lungs with pulmonary edema. Comprehensive toxicology analysis on peripheral blood reveals morphine and benzoylecgonine. What additional toxicological studies should be pursued?

A. Blood cocaine
B. Blood codeine
C. Blood morphine-3-glucoronide
D. Urine 6-monoacetylmorphine
E. Urine morphine-3-glucoronide

Q7.9 What drug or metabolite is most likely to be detected in the blood of this person's pictured lung tissue?

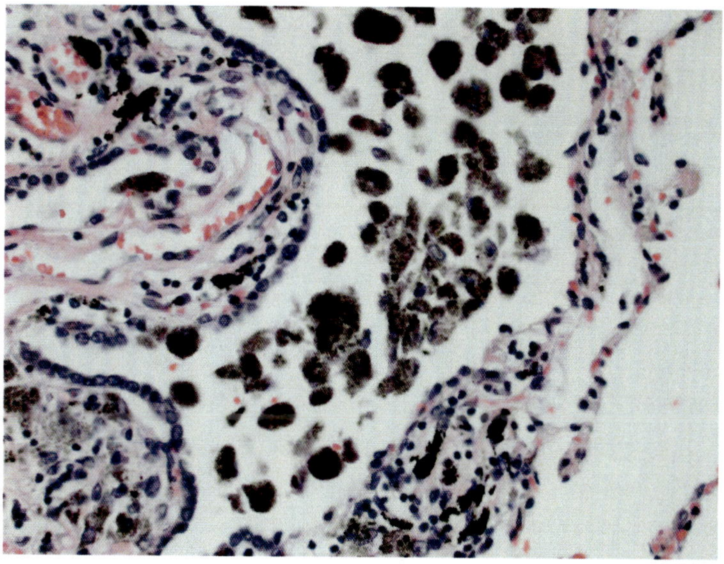

Figure 7.2

A. Caffeine
B. Cocaine
C. Cotinine
D. Heroin
E. THC

Q7.10 A 21-year-old man is found dead in bed. History reveals recent complaints of general malaise and excessive thirst and urination. No other medical history is known. Autopsy was unremarkable grossly. In addition to toxicology, what ancillary postmortem studies should most likely be pursued?

	Insulin	C-Peptide	Hemoglobin A1C	Glucose	Ketones
A. Blood	X	X			
B. Blood			X	X	
C. Urine				X	X
D. Vitreous		X	X		
E. Vitreous				X	X

Q7.11 A 24-year-old woman with a history of depression is brought to the emergency department by her mother with intractable nausea and vomiting that developed several days after ingesting numerous acetaminophen tablets. What is the underlying mechanism explaining her symptoms?

A. Acetylation of platelet cyclooxygenase
B. Depletion of glutathione (GSH)
C. Interference with aminolevulinic acid dehydratase
D. Production of acetic acid
E. Production of a metabolic alkalosis

Q7.12 What is acetyl fentanyl?

A. Active metabolite of medicinal fentanyl

B. Illicit synthetic opioid with more potency than heroin

C. Medicinal μ-receptor agonist used in surgical anesthesia

D. Medicinal μ-receptor antagonist used to counter the effects of opioid overdose

Q7.13 A 25-year-old man is found deceased on a couch at home. External examination shows cutaneous ulcerations on the arms. The decedent is emaciated. Autopsy shows profound pulmonary edema and foreign body granulomas in the lungs. Which of the following is the most likely drug used by the decedent?

A. Acetone

B. Acetyl fentanyl

C. Cocaine

D. Ethanol

E. Isopropanol

Q7.14 Two teenagers taken into police custody are put in the backseat of a police cruiser. Video shows one of the teenagers consuming a substance contained in a plastic baggie. He subsequently becomes delirious then exhibits seizures. A body temperature of 110°F is recorded at the hospital prior to his demise. What did the decedent likely consume?

A. Cocaine

B. Fentanyl

C. Heroin

D. Marijuana

E. Oxycodone

Q7.15 A 23-week-old gestational age fetus dies in utero. What is the implication of detecting benzoylecgonine in fetal meconium?

A. Additional toxicological analysis is required to determine significance

B. Fetus was alive at the time of maternal cocaine use

C. Fetus was deceased at the time of maternal cocaine use

D. No conclusion can be definitely made

Q7.16 A 50-year-old man is found deceased unexpectedly in bed. Autopsy shows an undiagnosed 8 cm facial squamous cell carcinoma and a perforated gastric ulcer. What is likely to be elevated on toxicology?

A. Acetylsalicylic acid

B. Fentanyl

C. Oxycodone

D. Marijuana

E. Methamphetamine

Q7.17 A 16-year-old previously healthy girl is found deceased in her bedroom lying on her bed. There is no sign of an altercation or disturbance. The gross autopsy is negative. Of the following, what scene investigation finding would most likely be significant in determining the cause of death?

A. Half-empty carton of cigarettes under her bed
B. Marijuana paraphernalia and residue in her bedside table
C. Receipt for three bottles of aerosol hairspray dated the day of death
D. Recent pregnancy test in her trash can
E. Text messages describing a recent sexual encounter on her phone

Q7.18 A 58-year-old man with a history of chronic ethanolism is found in the garage of an abandoned house. Insect activity is minimal, but decomposition is advanced, with collapse of the organs. Excluding near liquefaction of the brain tissue, no obvious gross abnormalities are appreciated. Histology on which of the following organs would likely be helpful in the complete investigation of this death?

A. Brain
B. Heart
C. Kidney
D. Liver
E. Lungs

Q7.19 Polarization of sampled kidneys in a decomposing 54-year-old alcoholic shows numerous calcium oxalate crystals. What toxicological analysis should be specifically requested?

A. Hydrocarbons
B. Ethanol
C. Ethylene glycol
D. Methanol
E. Propanol

Q7.20 A 25-year-old man entering a manhole collapses and dies within moments. First responders report a strong rotten egg odor. Autopsy shows cyanosis and pulmonary edema. What chemical should be suspected?

A. Ammonia
B. Carbon monoxide
C. Cyanide
D. Hydrogen sulfide
E. None, death was likely due to oxygen exclusion

Q7.21 A 2-year-old child who lives in a historic district downtown presents with altered mental status. Subsequent hospital workup documents a microcytic, hypochromic anemia. A skeletal survey reveals radiopaque densities at multiple metaphyseal plates. What underlying disease process should be suspected?

A. Lead toxicity
B. Folate deficiency
C. Fracture with callus formation
D. Vitamin B_{12} deficiency
E. Vitamin D deficiency

Q7.22 A 26-year-old man with previous suicidal ideation is found deceased in a car by passersby. Handwritten signs on the car windows indicate that no one should approach the vehicle and that there is poisonous danger in the car. Inside the car, several household cleaners are recovered. Autopsy shows pulmonary edema but no other significant findings. What should the laboratory analyzing the postmortem toxicology samples be advised to analyze specimens for?

A. Acetylcholinesterase inhibitors
B. Carbon monoxide
C. Ethanol
D. Methane
E. Thiosulfate

Q7.23 During the autopsy of a 32-year-old man found deceased at home, the pathologist makes a notation of a cherry-red coloration to the decedent's lividity. Upon opening the body, the autopsy technician remarks on the odor of almonds. What is the mechanism of action that most likely explains these findings?

A. Decreased reuptake of neurotransmitters
B. Induction of cytochrome P450 system
C. Inhibition of the mitochondrial electron transport chain
D. Refrigeration artifact of lividity
E. Shifting of the oxyhemoglobin dissociation curve to the left

Q7.24 A 35-year-old man presents to the hospital with multiple pulmonary abscesses. Autopsy shows the heart valve featured below. What is the most likely cause of the decedent's illness?

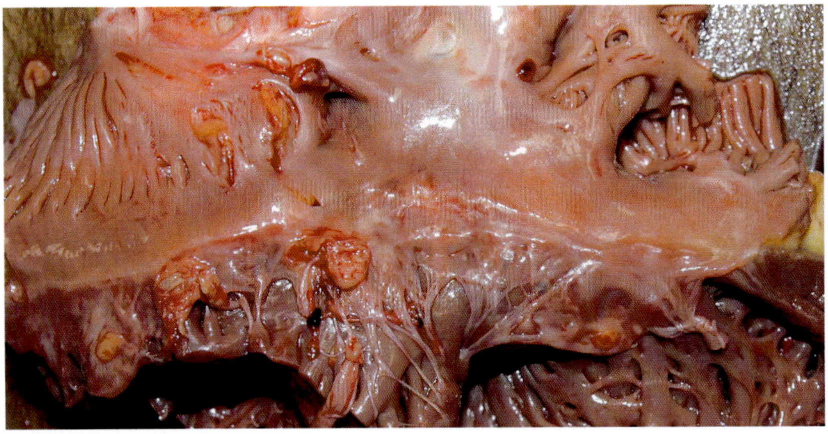

Figure 7.3

A. Congenital valvular anomaly
B. Human immunodeficiency virus infection
C. Intravenous drug use
D. Marantic endocarditis
E. Marfan syndrome

Q7.25 Toxicological analysis of cardiac blood in a decomposing man reveals an ethanol concentration of 60 mg/dL. What is the correct interpretation of this finding?

A. Cannot differentiate antemortem ingestion versus postmortem production of ethanol
B. Conclude a combination of antemortem ingestion and postmortem production of ethanol
C. Conclude acute ethanol toxicity
D. Conclude postmortem production of ethanol
E. Toxicological analysis of vitreous fluid will differentiate antemortem ingestion from postmortem production of ethanol

Q7.26 A 39-year-old woman is struck by a car. Based on the internal findings depicted below, what drug did she most likely abuse?

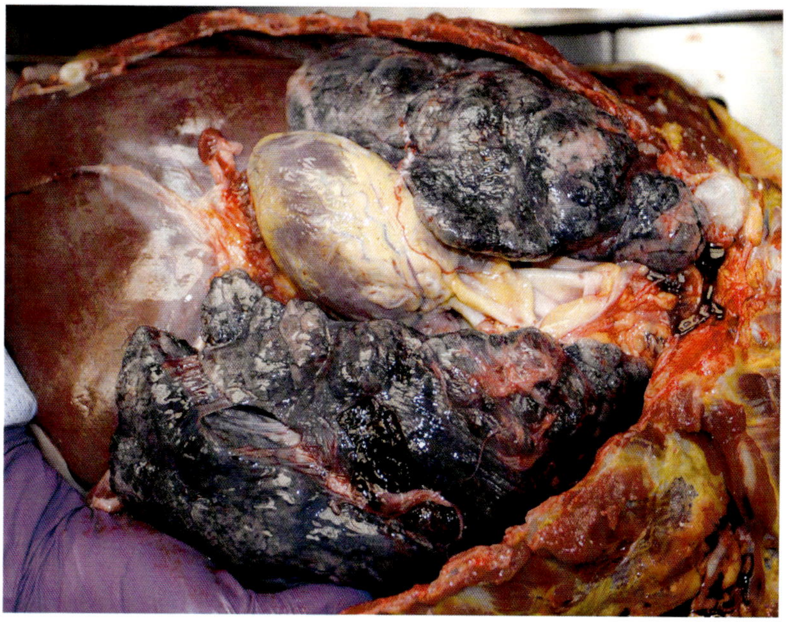

Figure 7.4

A. Cocaine
B. Marijuana
C. Methamphetamine
D. Nicotine (cigarettes)
E. Opioids

Q7.27 A 55-year-old inebriated man with a history of chronic ethanolism was jailed for nonpayment of child support. He endorsed no medical history and was not on medications. Within 3 days, he began demonstrating odd behavior and described visual hallucinations. He subsequently experienced seizure-like activity and then became unresponsive. He could not be resuscitated. What is the likely underlying cause of his death?

A. Delirium tremens
B. Diabetic ketoacidosis
C. Hypertensive crisis
D. Ingestion of baggie with cocaine at time of incarceration
E. Ruptured arteriovenous malformation

Q7.28 A 22-year-old woman was found deceased in bed by her mother. Other than a possible psychiatric history, there were no significant past or recent illnesses. At autopsy, the gastric contents were strained, revealing the following.

What is the mechanism of death?

Figure 7.5

A. Inhibition of norepinephrine and dopamine reuptake
B. Inhibition of monoamine oxidase enzymes
C. Inhibition of serotonin reuptake
D. Stimulation of serotonin release
E. Stimulation of presynaptic release of norepinephrine

Q7.29 A 38-year-old woman was found deceased at home on her bedroom floor with early decomposition changes. Autopsy showed mild coronary artery atherosclerosis. There were no signs of trauma. Toxicology was negative. Vitreous chemistry was as follows: sodium 120 mmol/L, potassium 25 mmol/L, and glucose 10 mg/dL.

Which of the following should be pursued?

A. Blood carboxyhemoglobin
B. Serum cortisol
C. Serum tryptase
D. Vitreous β-hydroxybutyrate
E. Vitreous 6-monoacetyl morphine

Q7.30 A 28-year-old man is found in the woods with a gunshot wound to the head and a moderate degree of decomposition, including skin slippage, diffuse green-brown coloration, and gaseous bloating. Focal maggot aggregates are present. Toxicology shows a blood ethanol concentration of 100 mg/dL (0.100%). What is the best conclusion regarding the source of ethanol?

A. Conclusion cannot be reached regarding ethanol source
B. Combination of antemortem ingestion and postmortem production
C. Solely antemortem ethanol consumption
D. Solely postmortem ethanol production

Q7.31 Blood ethanol at autopsy was 120 mg/dL in a 25-year-old man involved in a fatal motor vehicle crash. His friends reported he quit drinking 2 hours prior to the crash. What is the best approximation of the decedent's blood ethanol at the time he quit drinking?

A. 90 mg/dL
B. 100 mg/dL
C. 120 mg/dL
D. 140 mg/dL
E. 150 mg/dL

Q7.32 These items are recovered from the pants' pockets of a man involved in a motor vehicle crash. Which of the following drugs would most likely be positive on toxicology screening?

Figure 7.6

A. 6-Monoacetylmorphine
B. 3,4-Methylenedioxymethamphetamine
C. Benzodiazepine
D. Cocaine
E. Fentanyl

Q7.33 A 35-year-old man with a known history of drug abuse is witnessed to be acting "crazy," including doing somersaults in the nude and talking unintelligibly. He collapses 1 hour later and cannot be resuscitated. The family reports no known medical conditions. Autopsy shows no obvious injuries or disease processes. Standard comprehensive toxicological analysis is negative. What additional testing should be requested?

A. Directed analysis for synthetic cannabinoids
B. Heavy metal panel
C. Serum tryptase
D. Toxicological screening of gastric contents
E. Vitreous glucose and ketones

Q7.34 A 3-month-old infant was found unresponsive in adult bedding in a supine position. Cardiopulmonary resuscitation was attempted by first responders who reported significant rigor and posterior fixed lividity. The infant had been bed sharing with an adult and a sibling. The mother stated the infant had a cold over the last few days. The infant's birth was at term with no reported complications. Autopsy showed an appropriately developed female infant with no gross injuries or disease processes. Toxicological analysis of blood and liver documented an ethanol concentration of 0 and 211 mg/100 g, respectively.

Which of the following additional chemicals were likely present in the liver?

A. Acetaldehyde and acetone
B. Acetone and beta hydroxybutyrate
C. Formaldehyde and methanol
D. Isopropanol and methanol

Q7.35 In the scenario described in Q7.34, the microscopic examination showed some pulmonary edema and minimal peribronchiolar lymphocytic aggregates.

Ancillary studies included the following:

- Vitreous analytes: within expected ranges
- Metabolic screen: negative
- Respiratory viral panel of nasopharyngeal swab: positive rhinovirus
- Blood cultures: negative
- Skeletal survey: negative
- Cardiac blood toxicology: chlorpheniramine, dextromethorphan, acetaminophen at concentrations reported to be therapeutic in adults

How should the cause of death be reported?

A. Chlorpheniramine, dextromethorphan, and acetaminophen toxicity
B. Sudden Infant Death Syndrome (SIDS)
C. Sudden Unexpected Infant Death (SUID)
D. Overlay
E. Undetermined

Q7.36 A 65-year-old man falls at home and strikes his head. He is transported to the hospital where a subdural hematoma is documented. He remains obtunded during hospitalization and dies 1 week after presentation. Hospital blood drawn around the time of admission has all been disposed. What is the best postmortem source to send for toxicology in this scenario?

A. Liver tissue
B. Peripheral blood
C. Subdural blood
D. Urine
E. Vitreous fluid

Q7.37 The following cutaneous lesions are seen on a 39-year-old man at autopsy. What is the most likely diagnosis?

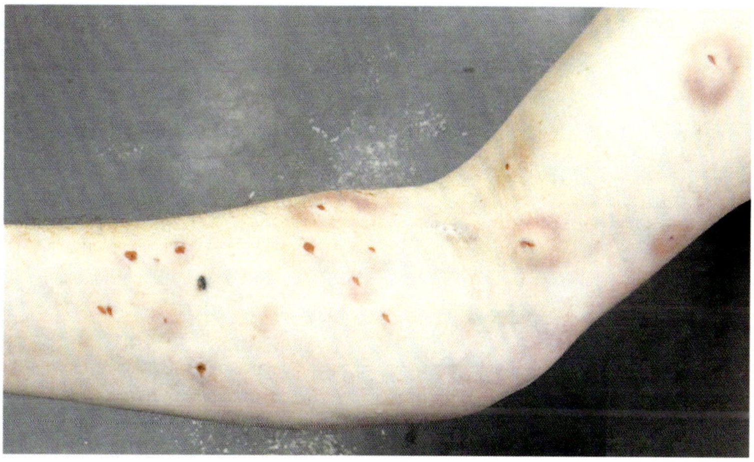

Figure 7.7

A. Acne vulgaris
B. Cigarette burns
C. Acute envenomations
D. Skin popping
E. Syphilis

Q7.38 Peripheral blood is sent for comprehensive toxicological analysis in this decedent. Which of the following is most likely present?

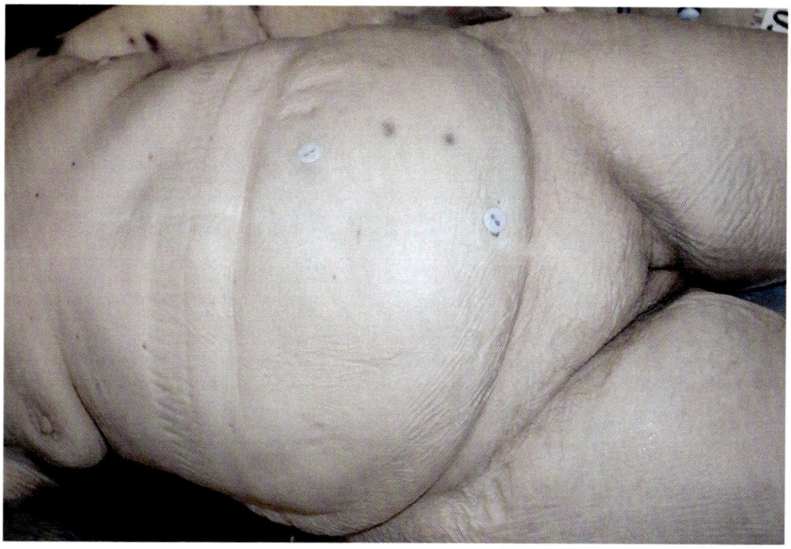

Figure 7.8

A. Ethanol
B. Ethylene glycol
C. Gasoline
D. Isopropanol
E. Methanol

Q7.39 A man was found unresponsive at home after a suspected overdose. Emergency medical personnel initiated resuscitative efforts, including intubation, but were unsuccessful. At autopsy, the finding pictured was apparent. What drug did the decedent likely consume?

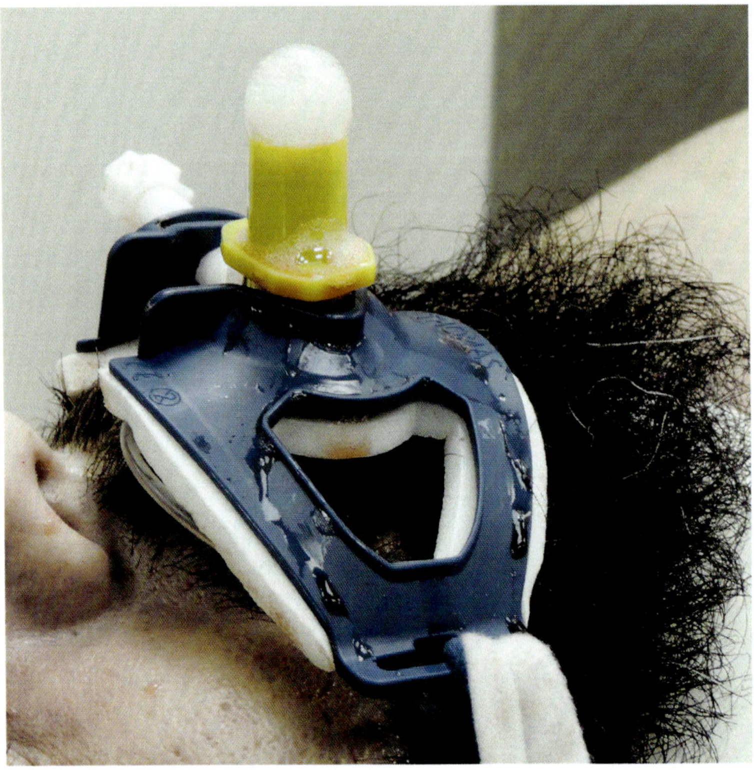

Figure 7.9

A. Cocaine
B. Caffeine
C. Marijuana
D. Methamphetamine
E. Opiate

Q7.40 Vitreous and blood ethanol concentrations at autopsy were 0 and 50 mg/dL, respectively, in a 25-year-old man involved in a fatal motor vehicle crash. What is the best interpretation of this data?

A. Death was likely prolonged
B. The decedent quit drinking several hours prior to the crash
C. The decedent was drinking for about an hour directly before the crash and continued to drink while driving
D. There was likely postmortem production of ethanol

ANSWERS: CHAPTER 7

A7.1 The correct answer is C. Spoon or syringe

- Answer A is incorrect. This scenario suggests the possibility of a heroin overdose. Heroin is almost immediately metabolized to 6-monoacetylmorphine and then to morphine after injection. Thus, heroin (diacetylmorphine) is not readily detected in body fluids such as urine, vitreous, blood, or bile.
- Answer B is incorrect. See explanation given in choice A.
- Answer C is correct. The only likely place that the heroin is to be found is in the spoon or syringe since it has not been metabolized by the body.
- Answer D is incorrect. See explanation given in choice A.
- Answer E is incorrect. See explanation given in choice A.

A7.2 The correct answer is D. Suicide

- Answer A is incorrect. The photograph demonstrates a bezoar that is composed of a mass of medication capsules. Ingestion of this number of pills at once is frequently associated with suicidal intent and accident would be less likely.
- Answer B is incorrect. Homicide is not as likely a manner of death as there is no evidence presented to support force-feeding of the drug.
- Answer C is incorrect. The photograph demonstrates a bezoar that is composed of a mass of medication capsules. Since the cause of death would be related to the toxicity of the drug(s) ingested, it would not be considered a natural death.
- Answer D is correct. The photograph demonstrates a bezoar that is composed of a mass of medication capsules. Ingestion of this number of pills at once is frequently associated with suicidal intent.
- Answer E is incorrect. The photograph demonstrates a bezoar that is composed of a mass of medication capsules. Although it is possible that somebody could accidentally ingest this number of capsules, it is unlikely that a person would do so without immediately seeking assistance. Ingestion of this number of pills at once is frequently associated with suicidal intent, and choice D reflects the *most probable* manner of death.

A7.3 The correct answer is B. Benzoylecgonine

- Answer A is incorrect. Anhydroecgonidine is a specific metabolite of crack cocaine but has little use in screening for the use of cocaine.
- Answer B is correct. Benzoylecgonine is the main metabolite of cocaine used to detect previous use. It has a longer half-life than cocaine, and most, if not all, of the urine drug screens use benzoylecgonine as the basis of previous cocaine use.
- Answer C is incorrect. Cocaine is not directly tested in urine screens because of its short half-life and low yield.
- Answer D is incorrect. Ester methyl ecgonine is another metabolite of cocaine that is not used for screening.
- Answer E is incorrect. Norcocaine is a metabolite of cocaine not used for screening.

A7.4 The correct answer is E. XLR-11

- Answer A is incorrect. Cocaine can cause restlessness and is usually in the form of a white powder or off-white crystalline form known as crack.
- Answer B is incorrect. Dronabinol is the generic name for Marinol which is a synthetic cannabinoid used to stimulate appetite in patients who are severely malnourished. Its active ingredient is synthetic delta-9-tetrahydrocannabinol. It has similar side effects to the tetrahydrocannabinol derived from the marijuana plant.
- Answer C is incorrect. Heroin causes respiratory depression and acute use is not associated with renal failure.
- Answer D is incorrect. Naturally occurring tetrahydrocannabinol (THC) is the main psychoactive ingredient in marijuana. THC may induce tachycardia but is not associated with renal failure.
- Answer E is correct. XLR-11 is a synthetic cannabinoid that has been implicated in acute renal failure, tachycardia, restlessness, and bizarre behavior. Synthetic cannabinoids have their basis in the THC molecule but have been altered by adding different alkyl, phenol, or other groups to make it legal. A drug is illegal based on its chemical nomenclature, so an illegal drug that has a different active group added is technically not illegal. Although the effects may be similar, the effects can be deadly.

A7.5 The correct answer is D. β-Hydroxybutyric acid

- Answer A is incorrect. The body makes three primary ketones when glucose is low. They are acetone, acetoacetic acid, also known as diacetic acid, and β-hydroxybutyric acid. The most prevalent of these in alcoholic ketoacidosis is β-hydroxybutyric acid.
- Answer B is incorrect. Acetic acid is not a ketone. It is a carboxylic acid that at around a concentration of 5% is used to enhance many peoples' salads as vinegar.
- Answer C is incorrect. Acetoacetic acid is not the most prevalent ketone in alcoholic ketoacidosis.
- Answer D is correct. β-Hydroxybutyric acid is the most prevalent ketone in alcoholic ketoacidosis. Alcohol causes depletion of NAD+ and creation of NADH. This results in a decreased ratio of NAD+ to NADH and causes a shift in the equilibrium of ketone production toward β-hydroxybutyric acid. In this scenario acetone and acetoacetic acid are virtually nonexistent. This is in contrast to diabetic ketoacidosis (DKA) in which there is the presence of all three ketones, though beta hydroxybutyrate is the most abundant ketone in DKA, as well.
- Answer E is incorrect. This is another name for acetoacetic acid.

A7.6 The correct answer is C. 5-HT2A

- Answer A is incorrect. The cannabinoid receptors CB1 and CB2 are associated with the active ingredient in marijuana, THC, and other synthetic cannabinoids such as XLR-11.
- Answer B is incorrect. The cannabinoid receptors CB1 and CB2 are associated with the active ingredient in marijuana, THC, and other synthetic cannabinoids such as XLR-11.
- Answer C is correct. 5-HT2A is a serotonergic receptor of which 3,4-methylenedioxymethamphetamine (MDMA) or Ecstasy is an agonist.
- Answer D is incorrect. The μ-receptor is associated with opiates and opioids.
- Answer E is incorrect. Norepinephrine receptor effects are associated with drugs such as cocaine.

A7.7 The correct answer is D. μ

- Answer A is incorrect. The cannabinoid receptors CB1 and CB2 are associated with the active ingredient in marijuana, THC, and other synthetic cannabinoids such as XLR-11.
- Answer B is incorrect. The cannabinoid receptors CB1 and CB2 are associated with the active ingredient in marijuana, THC, and other synthetic cannabinoids such as XLR-11.
- Answer C is incorrect. 5-HT2A is a serotonergic receptor of which MDMA or Ecstasy is an agonist.
- Answer D is correct. The μ-receptor is associated with opiates and opioids.
- Answer E is incorrect. Norepinephrine receptor effects are associated with drugs such as cocaine.

A7.8 The correct answer is D. Urine 6-monoacetylmorphine (6-MAM)

- Answer A is incorrect. Cocaine may be found in conjunction with heroin (i.e., speedball), but both cocaine and benzoylecgonine would have been detected in the blood during routine toxicological analysis.
- Answer B is incorrect. Morphine may be a metabolite from codeine, but codeine would have been detected in the blood during routine toxicological analysis.
- Answer C is incorrect. Morphine-3-glucoronide is a metabolite of morphine and would not help differentiate heroin from morphine use.
- Answer D is correct. Morphine may be a metabolite from heroin. While heroin's half-life is 2–3 minutes, its metabolites have a longer half-life. For example, morphine's half-life is 2–3 hours and 6-MAM is usually excreted within 6–8 hours but may be excreted for up to 24 hours into the urine. Since 6-MAM is specific for the parent compound heroin, it is an excellent surrogate marker. Depending on the demographics of the population served and the medical history of the decedent, it may be advantageous to determine the parent compound. Heroin (diacetylmorphine) is more potent and more readily crosses the blood–brain barrier when injected than many other opiates including morphine. It may cause physical addiction with resultant tolerance due to upregulation of opioid receptors. In the absence of urine, vitreous may also be analyzed for 6-MAM.
- Answer E is incorrect. Morphine-3-glucoronide is a metabolite of morphine and would not help differentiate heroin from morphine use.

A7.9 The correct answer is C. Cotinine

- Answer A is incorrect. The predominant finding in the lung photograph is the abundant pigmented macrophages. There is no association between pulmonary macrophages and caffeine.
- Answer B is incorrect. Pulmonary macrophages can be associated with smoking crack cocaine, but cocaine use is not as common as is cigarette smoking.
- Answer C is correct. Cotinine is a metabolite of nicotine, arguably the most abused drug in the world, and as such would be the most likely metabolite to be found.
- Answer D is incorrect. Intravenous abuse of heroin can produce granulomas in the lung that may have giant cells with polarizable refractile material. Pulmonary macrophages can be associated with smoking heroin, but its use is not as common as cigarette smoking.
- Answer E is incorrect. The main active ingredient in marijuana is THC, tetrahydrocannabinol. Chronic marijuana smoking may cause the finding seen in the photograph, but cigarette smoking is the most common cause of the pigmented alveolar macrophage as seen in the photograph.

A7.10 The correct answer is E. Vitreous glucose and ketones

- Answer A is incorrect. Blood insulin concentrations in diabetic patients are widely variable and dependent on the individual patient's response to administration. C-Peptide concentrations would differentiate endogenous versus exogenous insulin usage. These studies may be considered in suspect cases of insulin overdose but would not contribute useful information in this scenario.
- Answer B is incorrect. Postmortem blood glucose is unreliable. Postmortem hemoglobin A1C is relatively stable but reflects long-term glucose control and would not contribute useful information in this scenario.
- Answer C is incorrect. Urine glucose and ketones would likely be positive in cases of diabetic ketoacidosis, but values are better interpreted in vitreous.
- Answer D is incorrect. Vitreous hemoglobin A1C and C-peptide concentrations would not contribute the most useful information in this scenario.
- Answer E is correct. An initial screen for vitreous glucose and ketones (such as β-hydroxybutyrate, the most prominent ketone produced in diabetic ketoacidosis) is likely to provide ample evidence of diabetes mellitus. Generally, vitreous glucose levels greater than 200 mg/dL are indicative of diabetes mellitus. In combination with significant glucose elevation, the presence of ketones will assist in differentiation of ketoacidosis versus non-ketotic hyperglycemic coma.

A7.11 The correct answer is B. Depletion of glutathione (GSH)

- Answer A is incorrect. Acetylation of platelet cyclooxygenase is associated with aspirin usage.
- Answer B is correct. In an environment of excess acetaminophen, the usual hepatic conjugation to glucuronide and the sulfate moiety of acetaminophen are overwhelmed, and a hepatotoxic metabolite, *N*-acetyl-*p*-benzo-quinone imine (NAPQI), is produced via the cytochrome P450 (including 2E1) enzymatic pathway. Glutathione may conjugate with NAPQI to form nontoxic metabolites, but in the presence of overwhelming NAPQI, glutathione reserves are depleted and the toxic metabolite concentration increases. An antidote, *N*-acetylcysteine (NAC), is a prodrug to L-cysteine, which is converted to glutathione.
- Answer C is incorrect. Interference with aminolevulinic acid dehydratase is associated with lead toxicity.
- Answer D is incorrect. Production of acetic acid is not the underlying mechanism of her symptomatology.
- Answer E is incorrect. Metabolic alkalosis is not the underlying mechanism of her symptomatology.

A7.12 The correct answer is B. Illicit synthetic opioid with more potency than heroin

- Answer A is incorrect. Acetyl fentanyl is not a metabolite of fentanyl, but another synthetic opioid that is an analog of fentanyl. Norfentanyl is a major metabolite of fentanyl created by piperidine *N*-dealkylation by the liver.
- Answer B is correct. Acetyl fentanyl is an analog of fentanyl that is significantly more potent (approximately five times) than heroin. It has been the focus of recent forensic pathology reviews since it has now been implicated in overdose cases. Due to its potency, emergency personnel must use much more naloxone to counteract the opioid effects. If an ELISA test used for screening is positive for fentanyl, confirmatory testing should be pursued to determine whether fentanyl or an analog (such as acetyl fentanyl) is present.
- Answer C is incorrect. Acetyl fentanyl has not been licensed for medical use and is considered an illicit substance.
- Answer D is incorrect. Naloxone is a μ-opioid receptor competitive antagonist that is used to treat opiate/opioid toxicity. It demonstrates both blockade and antagonist activities.

A7.13 The correct answer is B. Acetyl fentanyl

- Answer A is incorrect. The depicted scenario describes the stigmata of intravenous drug use and respiratory depression, typically seen with opioids.
- Answer B is correct. Acetyl fentanyl use is becoming increasingly common, typically detected in combination with or as a substitute for heroin. Like heroin, acetyl fentanyl is often used intravenously, with the resultant stigmata of intravascular drug abuse (cutaneous ulcerations, pulmonary foreign body granulomas). Like heroin, acetyl fentanyl, which is more potent, induces prominent pulmonary edema and profound respiratory depression.
- Answer C is incorrect. The depicted scenario describes the stigmata of intravenous drug use and respiratory depression, typically seen with opioids.
- Answer D is incorrect. Although ethanol can cause pulmonary edema and respiratory depression, the scenario also depicts the stigmata of intravenous drug abuse, classically seen with opioids such as acetyl fentanyl.
- Answer E is incorrect. Isopropanol is typically abused as an alternative to ethanol or is ingested accidentally. Isopropanol consumption is typically oral.

A7.14 The correct answer is A. Cocaine

- Answer A is correct. Stimulant drugs are more likely to be associated with increased body temperature, and cocaine and amphetamines are notoriously associated with hyperthermia and elevated postmortem body temperatures. However, hyperthermic response may occur after use (generally excess use) of many different drugs through various mechanisms such as serotonin excess, dopamine blockade, and muscle damage. Genetic predisposition and other factors such as environmental temperature and exercise may play a role in some cases.
- Answer B is incorrect. Although hyperthermia is possible with fentanyl overdose, opiates do not commonly cause hyperthermia, and cocaine is a better answer. A more likely observation with a fentanyl overdose would be respiratory depression and possible foam cone from pulmonary edema.
- Answer C is incorrect. Although hyperthermia is possible with heroin overdose, cocaine is a better answer. A more likely observation with a heroin overdose would be respiratory depression and possible foam cone from pulmonary edema.
- Answer D is incorrect. Hyperthermia may rarely present with isolated marijuana use in combination with other factors, but cocaine is a better answer. Interestingly, medical marijuana has been suggested as a possible treatment for seizures.
- Answer E is incorrect. Although hyperthermia is possible with oxycodone overdose, hypothermia is more frequently reported. As in other opiate/opioid overdoses, respiratory depression is much more likely to be observed.

A7.15 The correct answer is B. Fetus was alive at the time of maternal cocaine use

- Answer A is incorrect. No additional testing is needed to ascertain the significance of the finding.
- Answer B is correct. Benzoylecgonine is an inactive metabolite of cocaine. However, it does not readily cross the placenta while the parent compound, cocaine, does. Thus, the finding of benzoylecgonine in a fetal sample indicates that the fetus was alive and able to metabolize cocaine at the time the mother was exposed. It should be noted, however, that the placenta may also metabolize cocaine, so direct effects may be on the placenta or the fetus and such metabolism may serve to protect the fetus to some extent as well.
- Answer C is incorrect. Benzoylecgonine does not cross the placenta, so this answer is incorrect.
- Answer D is incorrect. Since cocaine crosses the placenta and benzoylecgonine does not, the conclusion that the fetus was exposed to cocaine while alive can be made.

A7.16 The correct answer is A. Acetylsalicylic acid

- Answer A is correct. Acetylsalicylic acid is aspirin, which is associated with peptic ulcer disease, primarily by inhibition of mucosal cyclooxygenase. Gastric ulcer perforation is not associated with the remainder of drugs listed (see http://www.uptodate.com/contents/nsaids-including-aspirin-pathogenesis-of-gastroduodenal-toxicity).
- Answer B is incorrect. Fentanyl is not associated with peptic ulcer disease.
- Answer C is incorrect. Oxycodone is not associated with peptic ulcer disease.
- Answer D is incorrect. Marijuana is not associated with peptic ulcer disease.
- Answer E is incorrect. Methamphetamine is not directly associated with peptic ulcer disease.

A7.17 The correct answer is C. Receipt for three bottles of aerosol hairspray dated the day of death

- Answer A is incorrect. A half-empty carton of cigarettes is not likely to be significant in the cause of death investigation.
- Answer B is incorrect. Although marijuana usage is not typically fatal, marijuana is considered a gateway drug. Should drug screening prove negative in this scenario, one should consider synthetic cannabinoid usage, which has been associated with odd destructive behavior and increasing numbers of fatalities.
- Answer C is correct. A receipt for three bottles of aerosol hairspray dated the day of death would raise the suspicion for a huffing death. Not only is the purchase recent, but the number of hairspray bottles purchased is larger than would be expected. Directed toxicological analysis for volatiles should be requested.
- D is incorrect. A pregnancy test in her trash can is not likely to be significant to the cause of death.
- E is incorrect. Text messages of a recent sexual encounter are not likely to be significant in elucidating the cause of death.

A7.18 The correct answer is C. Kidney

- Answer A is incorrect. Tissue sampling for histopathology on liquified brain would likely be unhelpful.
- Answer B is incorrect. Due to the degree of decomposition, histopathology of the myocardium would be markedly obscured. In cases where decomposition is not as severe, larger areas of scarring may be discernible (highlighted by a Masson trichrome stain).
- Answer C is correct. Histologic sampling of the kidney would normally be low yield in advanced decomposition; however, in cases of chronic ethanolism, the possibility of ethylene glycol (antifreeze) consumption should be considered. Ethylene glycol toxicity would result in calcium oxalate crystal formation in the kidney. Despite decomposition of the soft tissues, these crystals remain readily visible under the microscope and are highlighted via polarized light. Ethylene glycol is not typically screened for in routine toxicological analysis and thus would be missed without microscopic evaluation of the kidney.
- Answer D is incorrect. Tissue sampling of decomposing liver is likely to be unhelpful. Histological examination may confirm cirrhosis, but this would be seen grossly. Changes such as steatosis are often obscured by gaseous distortion.
- Answer E is incorrect. Signs of intravascular drug abuse (IVDA) (i.e., polarizable crystals) would be visible in histologic sections of decomposing lung. In this case, an IVDA history was not given, thus making kidney a better choice.

A7.19 The correct answer is C. Ethylene glycol

- Answer A is incorrect. Hydrocarbons are not known to cause calcium oxalate crystals. There is a controversial association between hydrocarbon exposure and chronic glomerulonephritis (also see Mutti A et al. Exposure to hydrocarbons and renal disease: An experimental animal model. *Ren Fail* 1999, 21[3–4]: 369–85; Jacob S et al. Effect of organic solvent exposure on chronic kidney disease progression: The GN-PROGRESS cohort study. *J Am Soc Nephrol* 2007, 18[1]: 274–81, Epub 2006 Nov 29).
- Answer B is incorrect. Ethanol use may increase the incidence of nephrolithiasis due to purine exposure and chronic dehydration, but this is not a hallmark of acute intoxication.
- Answer C is correct. Ethylene glycol toxicity may be identified at the autopsy by polarization of the kidney on routine hematoxylin and eosin stained sections. Calcium oxalate crystals appear in the proximal tubular lumina as birefringent under polarized light, where they lead to inflammatory mediated cell necrosis (also see Schepers MS et al. Crystals cause acute necrotic cell death in renal proximal tubule cells, but not in collecting tubule cells. *Kidney Int* 2005, 68[4]: 1543–53). A common source of ethylene glycol is antifreeze. The clinical course includes increased anion gap metabolic acidosis followed by acute renal failure (also see Latus J et al. Ethylene glycol poisoning: A rare but life-threatening cause of metabolic acidosis—A single-centre experience. *Clin Kidney J* 2012, 5[2]: 120–3). Metabolism of ethylene glycol results in accumulation of glycoaldehyde and then glycolic acid, which support increased production of pyruvate. Glycolic acid is further converted to glyoxylic acid, which can be converted to oxalic acid and deposited in the kidney in the form of calcium oxalate crystals (also see Scalley RD et al. Treatment of ethylene glycol poisoning. *Am Fam Physician* 2002, 66[5]: 807–12).
- Answer D is incorrect. Although it also leads to increased anion gap metabolic acidosis, the effects of methanol toxicity on the kidney are primarily from metabolites. Alcohol dehydrogenase leads to formation of formaldehyde from methanol in the liver, which is transformed to formic acid via aldehyde dehydrogenase. Primary effects are on the optic system and basal ganglia (also see http://emedicine.medscape.com/article/1174890-overview?src=refgatesrc1, accessed 7/14/16). It should be mentioned that methanol is often also present in antifreeze, so a mixed toxicity may be considered.
- Answer E is incorrect. 1-Propanol and 2-propanol (isopropanol) may be found in products containing solvents such as cleaning products and hand sanitizer. Ingestion of 1-propanol may lead to an ionic gap metabolic acidosis (metabolized by alcohol dehydrogenase to aldehyde and then propionic acid with eventual formation of lactic acid). 2-Propanol is rapidly metabolized to acetone and results in consequent ketosis without metabolic acidosis (also see Vujasinovic M et al. Poisoning with 1-propanol and 2-propanol. *Hum Exp Toxicol* 2007, 26[12]: 975–8, http://www.inchem.org/documents/ehc/ehc/ehc102.htm accessed 7/14/16, http://www.inchem.org/documents/pims/chemical/pim290.htm accessed 7/14/16). Lethal propanol toxicity is not common, and the primary acute effects are to the central nervous system and gastrointestinal system; acute kidney injury is also common, but deposition of crystals is not.

A7.20 The correct answer is D. Hydrogen sulfide

- Answer A is incorrect. Ammonia gas has a caustic smell and can cause death through chemical burns to the respiratory system and direct neurogenic effects. Hydrogen sulfide is associated with the rotten egg odor.
- Answer B is incorrect. Carbon monoxide is an odorless gas produced by the imperfect oxidation of carbon. Unless there is a nearby running engine (i.e., generator), carbon monoxide poisoning is unlikely. Carbon dioxide may be elevated due to the presence of decomposing matter.
- Answer C is incorrect. Cyanide toxicity typically results in cherry red lividity and, to those genetically inclined, a "bitter almond" smell.
- Answer D is correct. Hydrogen sulfide is a toxic compound produced when bacteria degrade organic wastes with sulfur. This gas can accumulate in enclosed spaces and be rapidly neurotoxic. Autopsy findings may be nonspecific and may include pulmonary edema; green coloration of the brain is described in the literature. Of note, at very high concentrations, the classic rotten egg odor may not be apparent to the victim due to the overwhelming central nervous system effect.
- Answer E is incorrect. It would likely take longer than "moments" to succumb to a reduced environmental oxygen concentration. Also, no abnormal smell would be associated with the lack of oxygen.

A7.21 The correct answer is A. Lead toxicity

- Answer A is correct. The described scenario is classic for lead toxicity. Children are susceptible to developing lead toxicity due to their increased gastrointestinal absorption of ingested lead and more permeable blood–brain barrier. Lead interferes with multiple enzymes including those involved in the synthesis of heme and in the sodium potassium pump, thus leading to a microcytic hypochromic and hemolytic anemia, respectively. Lead also interferes with metaphyseal-epiphyseal remodeling in children, with the development of dense radiopaque lines at the metaphyseal plate.
- Answer B is incorrect. Folic acid deficiency presents as a macrocytic anemia; mental status changes are less common than other signs of anemia such as lethargy.
- Answer C is incorrect. Callus formation would occur around a healing bone fracture. Isolated fractures are not associated with mental status changes and anemia.
- Answer D is incorrect. Vitamin B_{12} (cobalamin) deficiency presents as a macrocytic anemia; mental status changes are less common than other signs of anemia such as lethargy.
- Answer E is incorrect. Radiographic findings in vitamin D deficiency in children (rickets) include bowing of the weight-bearing long bones (genu varum or genu valgum), decreased bony opacity with decreased growth plate mineralization, epiphyseal widening, and metaphyseal fraying and cupping. Abnormalities of the other long bones, ribs, pelvis, and spine may also be seen.

A7.22 The correct answer is E. Thiosulfate

- Answer A is incorrect. Acetylcholinesterase inhibitors or anti-cholinesterases are frequently encountered in scenarios involving pesticides (organophosphates) and are the basis for some chemical warfare agents ("nerve gas"). These agents target both muscarinic (urinary incontinence, salivation, defecation, miosis, and diaphoresis) and nicotinic receptors (respiratory paralysis), which are treated with atropine and pralidoxime (2-PAM). This scenario depicts a potential suicide by hydrogen sulfide, which is not created from pesticides but by mixing detergents containing sulfur and hydrochloric acid.
- Answer B is incorrect. Although carbon monoxide should be considered in an individual found deceased in a vehicle, the scenario depicts a potential suicide by hydrogen sulfide by mixing detergents containing sulfur and hydrochloric acid. Carbon monoxide toxicity is classically associated with cherry-red livor which is not described in this case.
- Answer C is incorrect. Ethanol itself is not a hazard to people who come in contact with the environment in which it has been used.
- Answer D is incorrect. Methane is an organic compound produced when bacteria ferment decomposing materials. The scenario depicts generation of hydrogen sulfide and not methane.
- Answer E is correct. The scenario depicts a potential suicide by hydrogen sulfide by mixing detergents containing sulfur and hydrochloric acid. Hydrogen sulfide is quickly metabolized into thiosulfate and may be quantitated. Autopsy findings may be nonspecific and may include pulmonary edema; green coloration of the brain is described in the literature. Of note, first responders are at risk of chemical exposure in enclosed environments such as described in the scenario.

A7.23 The correct answer is C. Inhibition of the mitochondrial electron transport chain

- Answer A is incorrect. Many drugs decrease the reuptake of neurotransmitters including cocaine and the selective serotonin reuptake and/or norepinephrine reuptake inhibitor antidepressants (SSRIs, SNRIs). However, this scenario describes cyanide toxicity, which is caused by inhibition of the mitochondrial electron transport chain.
- Answer B is incorrect. Many drugs and alcohol result in the induction of the cytochrome P450 system, but this scenario describes cyanide toxicity that is caused by inhibition of the mitochondrial electron transport chain.
- Answer C is correct. This scenario described cyanide toxicity with the cherry-red coloration and the smell of "bitter almonds." Not everyone has the genetic make-up to appreciate the smell. Cyanide acts as an asphyxiant by inhibiting the mitochondrial electron transport chain.
- Answer D is incorrect. Refrigeration can cause a cherry-red coloration to lividity but is not associated with an almond smell.
- Answer E is incorrect. Carbon monoxide causes cherry-red lividity and shifts the oxyhemoglobin dissociation curve to the left but is not associated with an almond smell.

A7.24 The correct answer is C. Intravenous drug use/abuse (IVDA)

- Answer A is incorrect. The depicted pathology does not illustrate a congenital valvular anomaly.
- Answer B is incorrect. Although bacterial endocarditis may occur in HIV infection, it is not common and almost always associated with IVDA.
- Answer C is correct. The photograph demonstrates tricuspid valve vegetations (endocarditis), which, in light of the normally formed valve, are likely a complication of illicit intravenous drug use. Tricuspid vegetations embolized to the lungs (septic emboli) resulting in pulmonary abscesses.
- Answer D is incorrect. Marantic endocarditis is abacterial endocarditis, often associated with malignancy or lupus.
- Answer E is incorrect. Marfan syndrome may result in a number of cardiovascular abnormalities including mitral valve prolapse, which may predispose to endocarditis, but the scenario and depicted pathology support IVDA.

A7.25 The correct answer is A. Cannot differentiate antemortem ingestion versus postmortem production of ethanol

- Answer A is correct. Postmortem ethanol production can produce blood ethanol concentrations up to 100 mg/dL (0.1%) with some reports up to 0.2%. Postmortem production cannot be differentiated from antemortem ingestion.
- Answers B, C, D, and E are incorrect. Postmortem production of ethanol cannot be differentiated from antemortem ingestion. Vitreous fluid is also less likely to be present with advancing decomposition.

A7.26 The correct answer is A. Cocaine

- Answer A is correct. Although smoking any sort of material may result in anthracosis, in the authors' experience, smoking crack cocaine is associated with a remarkable accumulation of carbon pigment (anthracosis).
- Answers B, C, D, and E are incorrect. Although smoking any sort of material may result in anthracosis, in the authors' experience, smoking crack cocaine is associated with a remarkable accumulation of carbon pigment.

A7.27 The correct answer is A. Delirium tremens

- Answer A is correct. The decedent's history of chronic ethanol abuse coupled with his clinical presentation of odd behavior, hallucination, and seizures occurring within several days of ethanol abstinence support a diagnosis of delirium tremens, a severe form of ethanol withdrawal. A complete autopsy would be necessary to exclude other disease processes or toxicological exposures.
- Answer B is incorrect. The described scenario could possibly result from ketoacidosis in a diabetic; however, such history is not given and the timeline in light of the chronic ethanol history suggests delirium tremens.
- Answer C is incorrect. The decedent's history of chronic ethanol use and his presentation coupled with the timeline of events suggests delirium tremens.
- Answer D is incorrect. Signs of extreme cocaine intoxication including marked agitation and hyperthermia are not described. In addition, acute intoxication is less likely in a setting of incarceration.
- Answer E is incorrect. Although the decedent may have experienced a ruptured arteriovenous malformation, his chronic ethanol history and clinical presentation coupled with the timeline of events suggests delirium tremens due to alcohol withdrawal.

A7.28 The correct answer is A. Inhibition of norepinephrine and dopamine reuptake

- Answer A is correct. The pills are clearly labeled "Wellbutrin" for which the generic name is bupropion. The mechanism of action is inhibition of norepinephrine and dopamine reuptake.
- Answer B is incorrect. The pills are clearly labeled "Wellbutrin." The monoamine oxidase inhibitors (MAOIs) are typically last-line antidepressants due to their potential for hypertensive crisis.
- Answer C is incorrect. The pills are clearly labeled "Wellbutrin." Selective serotonin reuptake inhibitors (SSRIs) are another class of antidepressants and have been associated with serotonin syndrome.
- Answer D is incorrect. The pills are clearly labeled "Wellbutrin." MDMA (Ecstasy) is an example of a drug causing stimulation of serotonin release.
- Answer E is incorrect. The pills are clearly labeled "Wellbutrin." Cocaine is an example of a drug causing stimulation of presynaptic release of norepinephrine.

A7.29 The correct answer is D. Vitreous β-hydroxybutyrate

- Answer A is incorrect. There is no indication of exposure to a carbon source.
- Answer B is incorrect. There is no indication of deranged cortisol metabolism.
- Answer C is incorrect. There is no indication of an anaphylactic-like exposure.
- Answer D is correct. The vitreous glucose concentration is 10 mg/dL, despite the obvious prolonged postmortem interval, as evidenced by a low sodium and markedly elevated potassium. One would expect the glucose to be nondetectable, and its presence raises the distinct possibility of diabetic ketoacidosis. Therefore, the ketone β-hydroxybutyrate or a surrogate ketone should be quantified.
- Answer E is incorrect. There is no described indication of possible heroin use.

A7.30 The correct answer is A. Conclusion cannot be reached regarding ethanol source

- Answer A is correct. Antemortem ingestion of ethanol cannot be differentiated from the postmortem bacterial production of ethanol, where blood ethanol concentrations up to 0.1% have been reported. Bacterial production may even occur in non-decomposing decedents when the procured specimen is en route to the toxicology laboratory; therefore, blood specimens should be collected in tubes containing the appropriate preservative that inhibits bacterial proliferation (i.e., gray top tubes with sodium fluoride).
- Answers B, C, and D are incorrect. Antemortem ingestion of ethanol cannot be distinguished from the postmortem bacterial production of ethanol.

A7.31 The correct answer is E. 150 mg/dL

- Answers A, B, C, and D are incorrect. Ethanol is metabolized at approximately 15 mg/dL per hour (0.015%).
- Answer E is correct. In an average adult man with an average weight, ethanol is metabolized at approximately 15 mg/dL per hour (0.015%). Therefore, assuming no confounding variables such as chronic ethanolism or other intoxications, his blood concentration at the time he quit drinking (2 hours prior to the fatal crash) would have been approximately 150 mg/dL (0.15%).

A7.32 The correct answer is D. Cocaine

- Answer A is incorrect. 6-Monoacetylmorphine is a heroin metabolite; although smoking heroin with a crack pipe cannot be excluded, heroin is more commonly injected.
- Answer B is incorrect. Although smoking 3,4-methylenedioxymethamphetamine (also referred to as MDMA and Ecstasy) with a crack pipe cannot be excluded, it is usually ingested orally.
- Answer C is incorrect. Benzodiazepines are normally ingested orally.
- Answer D is correct. The middle object is a classic example of a homemade crack pipe, with a tubular pipe and metal mesh material plugging one end. The object on the lower portion of the picture is a remnant of a cigar wrapper, which may have also been used to smoke a variety of drugs.
- Answer E is incorrect. Although smoking fentanyl with a crack pipe cannot be excluded, it is more often applied transdermally.

A7.33 The correct answer is A. Directed analysis for synthetic cannabinoids

- Answer A is correct. The described scenario suggests illicit drug consumption, possibly by a designer drug. As designer drugs emerge, toxicology laboratories must develop new assays to identify these compounds that are not detectable by current methods. Synthetic cannabinoids are one such group of illicit drugs gaining in popularity (also see Wessinger WD et al. Synthetic cannabinoid effects on behavior and motivation. In: Campolongo P, Fattore L, eds. *Cannabinoid Modulation of Emotion, Memory, and Motivation*. New York, NY: Springer; 2016, 205–24).
- Answer B is incorrect. Heavy metal toxicity is rare, and presentation depends on the acuteness of the exposure as well as the specific heavy metal. Unless there is additional history or distinct symptomatology (often neurological) to suggest a heavy metal, a heavy metal panel is unlikely to be fruitful in the presented case.
- Answer C is incorrect. The described clinical scenario is not suggestive of an anaphylactoid reaction, which would present similarly to an anaphylactic reaction.
- Answer D is incorrect. It is unlikely that analyzing the gastric contents with the same methods as used for the blood would yield useful information.
- Answer E is incorrect. Vitreous glucose and ketones should be considered, but without a history of type I diabetes mellitus, an acute presentation of diabetic ketoacidosis is unlikely at this age. In addition, the behavior is not typical for DKA. DKA may rather present with fatigue, nausea, and vomiting along with polydipsia and polyuria.

A7.34 The correct answer is A. Acetaldehyde and acetone

- Answer A is correct. In light of the negative blood ethanol, it is likely the liver ethanol was produced by postmortem microbial growth and fermentation. Acetaldehyde is a metabolite of ethanol and acetone is a metabolite of isopropanol, all of which may be present with decomposition.
- Answer B is incorrect. In light of the negative blood ethanol, it is likely the liver ethanol was produced by postmortem microbial growth and fermentation. Although acetone is a metabolite of isopropanol and may be present as a decomposition product, β-hydroxybutyrate is typically not. The presence of β-hydroxybutyrate would suggest (diabetic) ketoacidosis, an unlikely diagnosis in this scenario.
- Answer C is incorrect. In light of the negative blood ethanol, it is likely the liver ethanol was produced by postmortem microbial growth and fermentation. Methanol and one of its metabolites, formaldehyde, are usual constituents of embalming fluid and not related to decomposition.
- Answer D is incorrect. In light of the negative blood ethanol, it is likely the liver ethanol was produced by postmortem microbial growth and fermentation. Isopropanol may be present as a product of decomposition but not methanol.

A7.35 The correct answer is E. Undetermined

- Answer A is incorrect. Interpretation of drug concentrations in the pediatric population is difficult as studies documenting such are sparse, and safe concentrations are not necessarily equivalent to adult therapeutic concentrations. In this case, the history also supported an unsafe sleeping environment, making overlay a possibility.
- Answer B is incorrect. This described scenario excludes SIDS as the history and scene investigation revealed an unsafe sleeping environment.
- Answer C is incorrect. Some forensic pathologists may classify this death as SUID, while others would advocate using the more accurate designation of Undetermined in light of the confounding variables. Of note, the U.S. Centers for Disease Control and Prevention characterizes SUID deaths as the combination of accidental suffocation and strangulation in bed, SIDS, and Unknown cause deaths (also see https://www.cdc.gov/sids/data.htm, accessed 2/2/2017).
- Answer D is incorrect. It is not unlikely that this death resulted from an overlay; however, with the limited postmortem findings, a natural cause such as a cardiac conduction defect cannot be excluded.
- Answer E is correct. There are multiple confounding variables in this scenario. A differential includes possible natural causes (i.e., cardiac conduction defect), drug-related death (adult therapeutic cold medications present), and asphyxia, whether intentional smothering or unintentional overlay. Thus, "undetermined" is the most accurate "cause" of death.

A7.36 The correct answer is C. Subdural blood

- Answer A is incorrect. Due to the 1-week lapse between injury and death, any drugs or alcohol present at the time of injury would no longer be present in liver tissue.
- Answer B is incorrect. Due to the 1-week lapse between injury and death, any drugs or alcohol present at the time of injury would no longer be present in peripheral blood.
- Answer C is correct. Subdural blood would purportedly reflect blood drug and ethanol concentrations present at the time of the fall. However, data suggest that subdural blood drug/ethanol concentrations are not consistently or reliably reflective of concentrations present at the time of injury. Nevertheless, by convention, this subdural specimen is usually chosen as others would not be expected to have any remnants of toxicological agents present from the time of the original incident.
- Answer D is incorrect. Due to the 1-week lapse between injury and death, any drugs or alcohol present at the time of injury would no longer be present in urine.
- Answer E is incorrect. Due to the 1-week lapse between injury and death, any drugs or alcohol present at the time of injury would no longer be present in vitreous.

A7.37 The correct answer is D. Skin popping

- Answer A is incorrect. The cutaneous lesions do not have the appearance of comedones; the distribution of acne vulgaris is typically the face and trunk.
- Answer B is incorrect. Although some of the rounded ulcerations resemble cigarette burns, several ulcerations are elongate and most have an ecchymotic rim, which is not usual for cigarette burns.
- Answer C is incorrect. Unless circumstances are suggestive, the lack of edema and/or necrosis and the signs of healing do not support acute envenomation.
- Answer D is correct. The rounded ecchymotic lesions with central ulcerations are the result of skin popping, where traumatic, vasoconstrictive, and/or infective manifestations of injected medications can be seen cutaneously. Track marks with associated punctures are also visible in the antecubital fossa.
- Answer E is incorrect. The rash of stage 2 syphilis usually appears on the trunk and proximal extremities, and later classically involves the palms and soles; the rash appears as red-brown macules and/or papules.

A7.38 The correct answer is E. Methanol

- Answer A is incorrect. Although ethanol may be present, in light of the trochar buttons, the better answer is embalming fluid.
- Answer B is incorrect. Ethylene glycol is the toxic ingredient of antifreeze.
- Answer C is incorrect. There is no evidence in the photograph to suggest gasoline would be in the decedent's blood.
- Answer D is incorrect. Isopropanol is the ingredient of rubbing alcohol.
- Answer E is correct. Due to the presence of the trochar buttons on the decedent's abdomen, it is likely that she was embalmed. Embalming fluid is typically a mixture of methanol and formaldehyde.

A7.39 The correct answer is E. Opiate

- Answer A is incorrect. Cocaine is less likely to present with pulmonary edema in overdose; arrhythmia with sudden death may be encountered. However, if resuscitation was prolonged and iatrogenic fluids provided, pulmonary edema may be evidenced at autopsy.
- Answer B is incorrect. Caffeine toxicity may lead to dysrhythmia or seizures due to release of catecholamines; at very high concentrations, caffeine inhibits phosphodiesterase, theoretically increasing cAMP and cGMP levels. Pulmonary edema is not a significant factor in most cases.
- Answer C is incorrect. Although marijuana contains hundreds of known active compounds, delta-9-tetrahydrocannabinol is the most commonly associated with symptoms. Respiratory effects may include bronchodilation, but pulmonary edema is not common in the absence of comorbid conditions.
- Answer D is incorrect. The primary effect of amphetamines including methamphetamine is central nervous system stimulation. Pulmonary edema is not a significant factor in toxicity in the absence of other comorbid conditions.
- Answer E is correct. If noncardiogenic, opioids are a common cause of pulmonary edema in overdose. Pulmonary edema is considered to be one of the major mechanisms of death in such overdoses (e.g., heroin; also see Dettmeyer R et al. Pulmonary edema in fatal heroin overdose: Immunohistological investigations with IgE, collagen IV and laminin—No increase of defects of alveolar-capillary membranes. *Forensic Sci* 2000, 110[2]: 87–96).

A7.40 The correct answer is D. There was likely postmortem production of ethanol

- Answer A is incorrect. If the death had been prolonged and ethanol had been consumed, ethanol would be expected to be in the vitreous.
- Answer B is incorrect. If the decedent consumed ethanol then stopped several hours prior to the crash, ethanol would be expected to be in the vitreous.
- Answer C is incorrect. With continued drinking, ethanol would be expected to be present in both blood and vitreous.
- Answer D is correct. Unless ethanol consumption and death were very rapid, it is likely the blood ethanol was produced postmortem. Postmortem production has been shown to result in significant ethanol concentrations (also see Kugelberg FC, Jones AW. Interpreting results of ethanol analysis in postmortem specimens: A review of the literature. *Forensic Sci Int* 2007, 165[1]: 10–29).

CHAPTER 8

PREGNANCY AND SEX-RELATED DEATHS

QUESTIONS

Q8.1 A 32-year-old woman had a prolonged, complicated period of labor with associated excessive bleeding prior to death. Her pituitary gland is featured below. What is the most likely diagnosis?

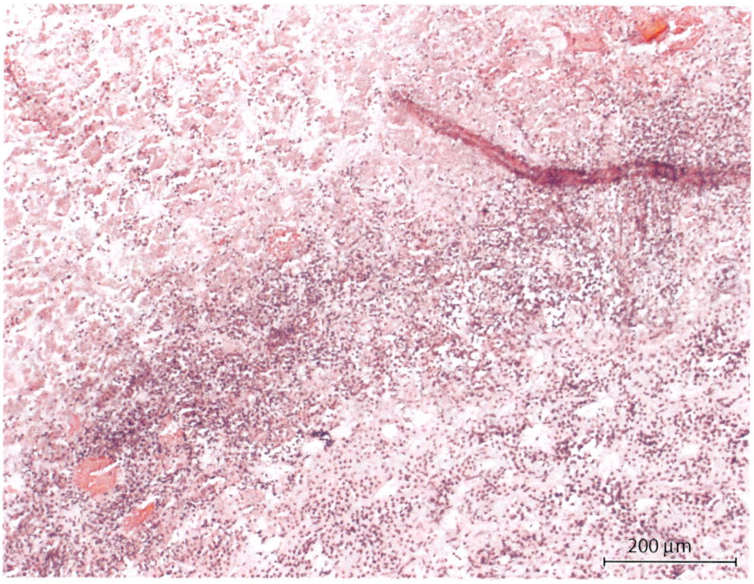

Figure 8.1

A. Chiari malformation
B. Empty sella syndrome
C. Hydrocephalus ex vacuo
D. Meningitis
E. Sheehan syndrome

Q8.2 A 30-year-old gravid female at 36 weeks gestation is suspected of dying from acute fatty liver of pregnancy. What is the most effective postmortem testing to confirm this diagnosis?

A. Cytogenetics
B. Platelet count
C. Prothrombin time measurement
D. Staining frozen liver tissue with Sudan Black
E. Serum triglyceride measurement

Q8.3 A 28-year-old pregnant woman with five healthy children dies suddenly after difficult, prolonged labor and delivery of a term infant despite aggressive resuscitative efforts. Prior to death, she experienced severe shortness of breath followed by respiratory failure and then cardiac collapse. Her prenatal course had been unremarkable. Which of the following is the likely cause of death?

A. Amniotic fluid embolus
B. Eclampsia
C. Fat embolus syndrome
D. Hyaline membrane disease
E. Iatrogenic pulmonary edema

Q8.4 A pregnant woman complains of shortness of breath at delivery and suddenly dies. You suspect amniotic fluid embolism. What is the most useful test to use to confirm this diagnosis?

A. Cytogenetics
B. CD34 immunostain
C. Pancytokeratin immunostain
D. p57 immunostain
E. S100 immunostain

Q8.5 Which of the following scenarios most likely accounts for the histological findings depicted in this liver?

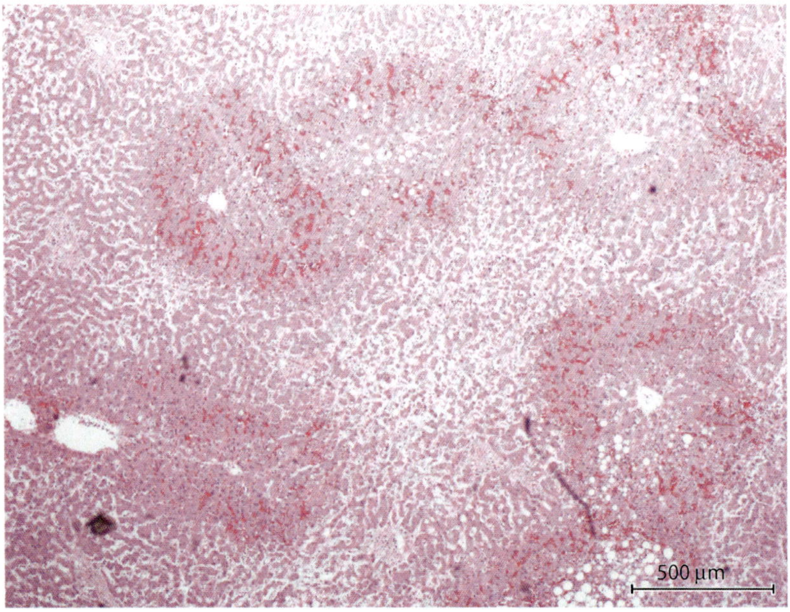

Figure 8.2

A. Alpha-1-antitrypsin deficiency with pulmonary emphysema
B. Fatal acute ethanol toxicity
C. Gunshot wound to head with brainstem disruption
D. Motor vehicle crash with atlanto-occipital separation and leg fractures
E. Placental abruption with disseminated intravascular coagulation

Q8.6 A term infant is recovered from a trash can at a high school campus. The suspected teenaged mother who concealed her pregnancy relays that the infant was born unexpectedly into the toilet with no signs of life; foamy fluid was noted in the toilet upon investigation. External exam documented froth at the nares. Assuming no additional findings at autopsy, what probable conclusion can be made regarding the infant's death?

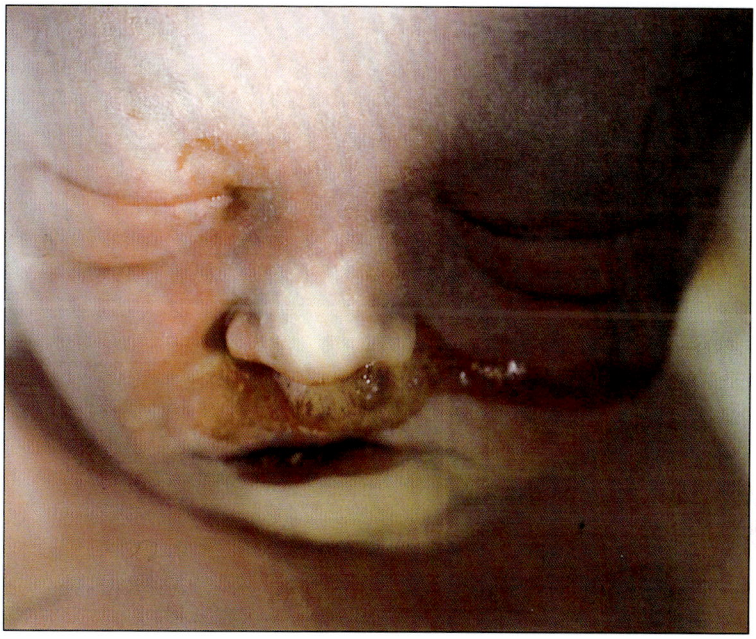

Figure 8.3

A. Drowning
B. Exposure with hypothermia
C. Intrauterine fetal demise
D. Smothering
E. Undetermined

Q8.7 From the above scenario, what probable conclusion can be made regarding the most likely manner of death?

A. Accident
B. Homicide
C. Natural
D. Undetermined

Questions 8.8 and 8.9 refer to the photograph below.

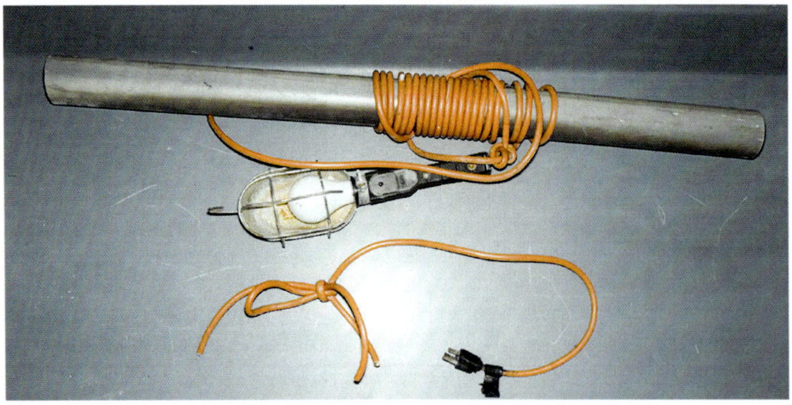

Figure 8.4

Q8.8 A man was found suspended from the beam pictured. Scattered pornography was found at the scene including Internet pornography. What is the underlying cause of death?

A. Autoerotic asphyxiation
B. Choking
C. Hanging
D. Smothering
E. Trauma to the cervical spine

Q8.9 From the scenario above, what is the manner of death?

A. Accident
B. Homicide
C. Natural
D. Suicide
E. Undetermined

Q8.10 A 25-year-old female is found with multiple stab wounds to the torso. She is found with her bra pushed up exposing her breasts and her pants below her knees exposing her genitalia. Before performing the autopsy, photographs are obtained. What is the next most appropriate step?

A. Collect fingerprints to establish identity
B. Initiate sexual assault kit collection
C. No additional testing is necessary
D. Perform x-rays looking for retained knife tip(s)
E. Place evidence in a large plastic bag

Q8.11 In general, in female victims of sexual assault with vaginal ejaculation, sperm remain motile for how long?

A. 3 hours
B. 12 hours
C. 1 day
D. 3 days
E. 5 days

Q8.12 A 34-year-old man found unresponsive on the lawn outside his home was transported to the hospital where, despite medical intervention, he was pronounced dead. His larynx at autopsy is depicted. What is the most likely cause of this injury?

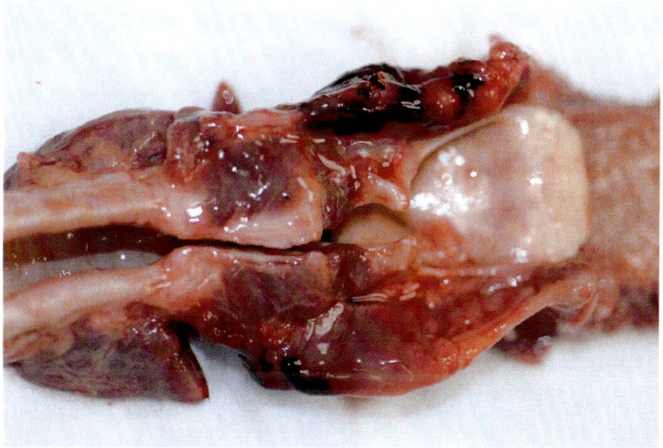

Figure 8.5

A. Intubation attempts
B. Judicial-style hanging
C. Postmortem neck organ removal trauma
D. Resuscitative intravascular catheter insertion
E. Strangulation

Q8.13 A 28-year-old man is found deceased, hanged at home, dressed as depicted, and wearing female panties. Red candle wax was on his chest and abdomen. The ligature around his neck, wrist, and ankles was suspended from a ceiling beam. What is the most important information to consider when investigating the scene?

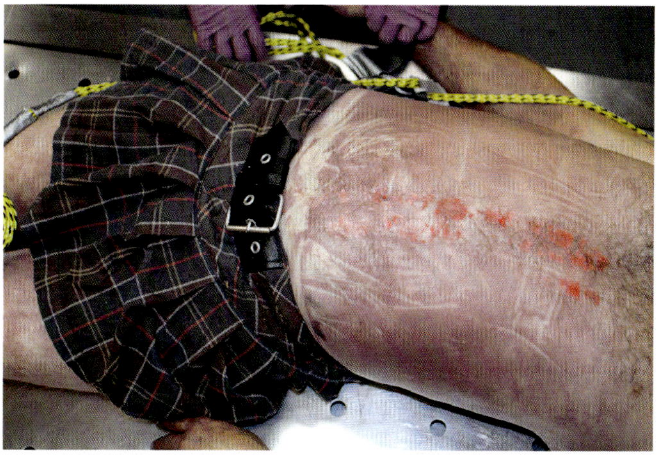

Figure 8.6

A. History of depression
B. Homosexual history
C. Release mechanism of ligature
D. Security of home
E. Transgender sexuality

ANSWERS: CHAPTER 8

A8.1 The correct answer is E. Sheehan syndrome

- Answer A is incorrect. Chiari malformation is often due to a congenital structural cerebellar-spinal cord defect. Rarely, Chiari malformation results from trauma, toxin exposure, or infection. Arnold–Chiari malformation is also called type II Chiari malformation and is often associated with spina bifida.
- Answer B is incorrect. Empty sella syndrome describes a radiological finding in which the sella turcica appears to be empty or the pituitary appears significantly diminutive. Although pituitary necrosis as seen in the photomicrograph could be a feature due to external compression or other secondary damage to the gland, histological findings will vary depending on the cause.
- Answer C is incorrect. Hydrocephalus ex vacuo is also a radiologic description of the brain that indicates shrinking secondary to injury or vascular accident of the brain and consequent compensatory increase in cerebrospinal fluid. Hydrocephalus ex vacuo is a pressure-neutral condition by definition.
- Answer D is incorrect. The photomicrograph is of a pituitary, and no overlying meninges are present. Thus, this photograph would not lead to a diagnosis of meningitis. The crowded blue cells in the middle of the image are inflammatory cells and are a response to the pituitary necrosis rather than infection.
- Answer E is correct. Sheehan syndrome is defined as pituitary necrosis with a degree of failure occurring in the setting of pregnancy and is more common when significant blood loss occurs around the time of delivery. The pituitary gland is at risk of necrosis from abrupt decrease in blood pressure more so in association with pregnancy since it is enlarged. Such necrosis may be an incidental finding at autopsy depending on the extent of necrosis or may be the cause of death from acute panhypopituitarism.

A8.2 The correct answer is D. Staining frozen liver tissue with Sudan Black

- Answer A is incorrect. Cytogenetics is most useful in detecting chromosomal abnormalities, especially in fetal deaths that occur in the first trimester. Although it may be helpful for fetal demise, it would not be useful in evaluating maternal death.
- Answer B is incorrect. In this scenario, thrombocytopenia would most likely characterize HELLP syndrome (Hemolysis, Elevated Liver enzymes, Low Platelets). HELLP syndrome is thought to be a severe form of preeclampsia that has liver manifestations. However, these are manifest as elevated liver enzymes and not acute fatty liver. It should be noted that many laboratory tests such as platelet count cannot be reliably performed on postmortem samples.
- Answer C is incorrect. Prothrombin time is prolonged in cases of disseminated intravascular coagulation, which may be a serious complication seen in pregnancy. The prothrombin time is usually in the normal range in cases of fatty liver whether due to alcohol, pregnancy, or diabetes. It should be noted that many laboratory tests such as coagulation studies cannot be reliably performed on postmortem samples.
- Answer D is correct. Since lipids are lost in the traditional histologic processing of tissue, using fresh frozen tissue and a lipophilic staining technique with Sudan Black or oil red O is the best way to confirm fat within the liver.
- Answer E is incorrect. Serum triglycerides can be elevated for a variety of reasons and have no direct correlation with hepatic steatosis. Triglycerides greater than 1000 mg/dL may cause some people to be more susceptible to acute pancreatitis. It should be noted that many laboratory tests such as triglyceride levels cannot be reliably performed on postmortem samples.

A8.3 The correct answer is A. Amniotic fluid embolus

- Answer A is correct. Other symptoms may include seizure, bleeding with disseminated intravascular coagulopathy, or altered mental status. The clinician must have a high index of suspicion since none of the presenting signs or symptoms are pathognomonic, and they often develop very quickly. The etiology appears to be entrance of amniotic fluid components into the maternal circulation, and the mechanism appears to be immune mediated and is alternatively termed *anaphylactoid syndrome of pregnancy*. At autopsy, the pathologist may identify components of amniotic fluid in the pulmonary circulation including fetal squames, mucin, and other foreign material. Special stains such as Movat, which incorporates Alcian Blue for mucopolysaccharides or Attwood with Alcian Green, may be used to accentuate these findings. Polarized light may assist in the identification of lanugo hair, which is refractile.
- Answer B is incorrect. Eclampsia is a condition wherein the mother demonstrates seizures or loss of consciousness in the setting of preeclampsia, and this was not described in the patient history.
- Answer C is incorrect. Although fat embolism syndrome (FES) may lead to similar symptoms as amniotic fluid embolism, there is no increased risk for FES in pregnancy and no reason to suspect recent soft tissue trauma in this patient.
- Answer D is incorrect. Hyaline membrane disease or neonatal respiratory distress syndrome is a disease secondary to lack of surfactant in infants. Adult respiratory distress syndrome (RDS) shows similar histopathology to neonatal RDS and is an infrequent consequence of intubation, which is not apparent in this case. Both conditions prevent gas exchange in the lungs.
- Answer E is incorrect. Significant fluid overload may occur iatrogenically by intravenous fluid infusion unequaled by urinary output. However, no mention of this factor is made in the case.

A8.4 The correct answer is C. Pancytokeratin

- Answer A is incorrect. Cytogenetics is most useful in detecting genetic anomalies in first-trimester abortions.
- Answer B is incorrect. CD34 stains normal endothelium of blood vessels and blood progenitor cells. It is useful in evaluating different malignancies but currently has no usefulness in the evaluation of amniotic fluid embolism.
- Answer C is correct. Pancytokeratin (AE1/AE3) is useful for the detection of fetal squamous cells within the pulmonary vasculature following death due to amniotic fluid embolism.
- Answer D is incorrect. $P57^{kip2}$, also called CDKN1C, is a strongly paternally imprinted gene on 11p15.5 in which maternal expression predominates. It is useful for differentiating complete hydatidiform mole (p57 negative) from partial hydatidiform mole or spontaneous abortion (p57 positive).
- Answer E is incorrect. S100 is commonly used for distinguishing melanoma and neural lesions. It is not useful for confirming amniotic fluid embolism.

A8.5 The correct answer is E. Placental abruption with disseminated intravascular coagulation

- Answer A is incorrect. The liver diseases most associated with alpha-1-antitrypsin deficiency are hepatitis and cirrhosis. A Periodic Acid Schiff (PAS) stain would highlight retained alpha-1-antitrypsin globules in hepatocytes.
- Answer B is incorrect. The hepatotoxic effects of alcohol are many and include hepatitis and cirrhosis. In addition, steatosis is a common feature of both acute and chronic ethanol use. Focal steatosis is seen here; however, steatosis is quite common.
- Answer C is incorrect. A gunshot wound to the head can be presumed to be quickly fatal; no significant vascular changes would be expected.
- Answer D is incorrect. A motor vehicle collision resulting in atlanto-occipital separation and leg fractures would lead to imminent death and be unlikely to demonstrate the pictured changes.
- Answer E is correct. Since the oxygenation to zone 3 of the liver is suboptimal, shock (systemic hypotension) can be seen in the liver as centrilobular congestion and necrosis or "shock liver." One hallmark of diffuse intravascular coagulopathy that may be identified at autopsy is shock liver (also referred to as ischemic hepatitis).

A8.6 The correct answer is A. Drowning

- Answer A is correct. Although drowning is a diagnosis of exclusion, the froth emanating from the decedent's nares in combination with the investigative finding of froth or foamy material in the toilet water is consistent with extrauterine survival and, with the provided scenario, likely occurred while breathing toilet water.
- Answer B is incorrect. The froth emanating from the nares is not associated with hypothermia.
- Answer C is incorrect. Air admixed with fluid forms the froth seen at the nares. This finding is suggestive of active breathing. Additionally, there is no sign or description of maceration to indicate intrauterine fetal demise. Investigation and witness interrogation may assist this determination.
- Answer D is incorrect. Smothering is a diagnosis of exclusion and cannot be completely excluded. However, the scenario coupled with the froth suggests drowning. The blanching about the nose and chin may have occurred postmortem.
- Answer E is incorrect. The froth emanating from the decedent's nares in combination with the investigative finding of froth or foamy material in the toilet water is consistent with extrauterine survival and, with the provided scenario, likely occurred while breathing toilet water.

A8.7 The correct answer is B. Homicide

- Answer A is incorrect. Since the death resulted from the actions of the mother (neonatacide by drowning), this is best classified as a homicide.
- Answer B is correct. The manner of death is homicide (neonatacide by drowning).
- Answer C is incorrect. The manner of death is homicide. Neonatacide by drowning is not considered a natural death.
- Answer D is incorrect. The manner of death is homicide. Since the manner can be determined, this choice is incorrect.

A8.8 The correct answer is C. Hanging

- Answer A is incorrect. Although the pornography at the scene suggests this is more than just a hanging death and should be classified to reflect this. Autoerotic asphyxiation is a technique used by some people to enhance a feeling of sexual euphoria by deliberately compressing the neck vasculature in the belief that the asphyxia heightens pleasure. However, this choice is incorrect in that autoerotic asphyxia is the immediate cause of death due to the underlying or proximate cause, which is hanging. Many times this involves the act of hanging, but the common feature regardless of the techniques used is asphyxia. The people doing this have no intent to die.
- Answer B is incorrect. Choking is a specific type of asphyxia defined as occlusion of the proximal airway. It is not caused by compression of the neck.
- Answer C is correct. Hanging is the underlying cause of death even though the asphyxia may have been autoerotic in nature as suggested by the scene findings. The death certificate in the case might reflect this by indicating autoerotic asphyxia due to hanging.
- Answer D is incorrect. Smothering is asphyxia that is caused when the external airways become occluded.
- Answer E is incorrect. Trauma to the cervical spine would be the cause of death seen in a judicial execution in which the method would be hanging.

A8.9 The correct answer is A. Accident

- Answer A is correct. In autoerotic asphyxiation, the person does not have the intent to die. The person accidentally dies when the escape mechanism he or she has in place, such as a release lever of the ligature, fails and the person cannot release himself or herself before losing consciousness.
- Answer B is incorrect. Since the death is not caused by another person, it is not a homicide.
- Answer C is incorrect. This is not a natural death.
- Answer D is incorrect. Most but not all hangings are suicides. In our case, lack of a note, lack of intent to do self-harm, and pornography on the scene are consistent with an accidental death.
- Answer E is incorrect. The manner of death can be determined in this case.

A8.10 The correct answer is B. Initiate sexual assault kit collection

- Answer A is incorrect. Collecting fingerprints is a part of many forensic autopsies, but other vital evidence from the sexual assault may be destroyed or lost if a sexual assault kit is not performed first.
- Answer B is correct. The scene findings are highly suggestive of a sexual assault occurring in conjunction with the stabbing. One very important aspect of forensics is to obtain possible evidence before it is destroyed by the autopsy. The sexual assault kit should be obtained as soon as practical before the start of the autopsy. This may include vaginal swabs and smears, oral swabs and smears, breast swabs, anal/rectal swabs and smears, pulled head hair, pulled pubic hair, fingernail scrapings and/or clippings, combings of pubic hair, and combing of the body for foreign debris. Many kits also include a set of diagrams to complete and request specific photographs be obtained.
- Answer C is incorrect. Additional testing is required because of the circumstances.
- Answer D is incorrect. Imaging studies should be performed taking care to observe the presence of any retained parts of the stabbing weapon. However, the first priority should be to obtain physical evidence first before assessing the stab wounds.
- Answer E is incorrect. Items for evidence should not be placed into plastic bags as moisture can condense, promoting microbial growth, and ruin evidentiary value. Evidence should be placed in paper envelopes or packaging that will allow drying and preservation without contamination (until the items can be removed and properly dried).

A8.11 The correct answer is A. 3 hours

- Answer A is correct. In general, sperm normally maintain their motility for up to 3 or 4 hours, although there have been reports of detecting motile sperm at 60 hours.
- Answers B, C, D, and E are incorrect. In general, sperm maintain their motility for up to 3 or 4 hours; however, one report describes intact but nonmotile vaginal sperm present in deceased women for an average of 23 hours. (See Collins KA, Bennett AT. Persistence of spermatozoa and prostatic acid phosphatase in specimens from deceased individuals during varied postmortem intervals. *Am J Forensic Med Pathol* 2001, 22(3): 228–32.)

A8.12 The correct answer is E. Strangulation

- Answer A is incorrect. Intubation attempts may easily produce perilaryngeal soft tissue hemorrhages but are rarely associated with thyroid cartilage fractures.
- Answer B is incorrect. The classic judicial-style hanging injury is a cervical vertebral fracture at C2 ("hangman's fracture"). Hangings do not typically fracture the hyoid or thyroid cartilage as the noose is situated above these structures.
- Answer C is incorrect. The hyoid bone and thyroid cartilage cornu may easily be fractured during removal of the neck organs at autopsy, but these "injuries" would not be associated with hemorrhage.
- Answer D is incorrect. Catheter insertion may cause perivascular soft tissue hemorrhage at sites of insertion and vascular perforation but would not cause thyroid cartilage fractures.
- Answer E is correct. The photograph shows a fractured thyroid cartilage cornu with associated soft tissue hemorrhage. In conjunction with other possible autopsy findings, such as scleral and conjunctival and possibly facial petechiae/hemorrhages, this is suspicious for strangulation.

A8.13 The correct answer is C. Release mechanism of ligature

- Answer A is incorrect. This death has features of an autoerotic asphyxiation. Although it would be important to review and consider medical history in the death investigative process, it would be essential to search for the presence of a self-release mechanism while at the scene.
- Answer B is incorrect. Homosexuality is not a feature of autoerotic asphyxiation.
- Answer C is correct. This death has features of an autoerotic asphyxiation. A self-release mechanism is an essential component of the purported scenario. Scene investigation should include a search for such a mechanism.
- Answer D is incorrect. This death has features of an autoerotic asphyxiation. Although it would be important to document the security of the home, it would be essential to search for the presence of a self-release mechanism while at the scene.
- Answer E is incorrect. Transgenderism is not a specific feature of autoerotic asphyxiation.

Chapter 9

MISCELLANEOUS TOPICS

QUESTIONS

Q9.1 What organism causes plague?

A. *Bacillus anthracis*
B. *Chlamydophila psittaci*
C. *Clostridium botulinum*
D. *Variola major*
E. *Yersinia pestis*

Q9.2 What is the biosafety level of the pictured organism?

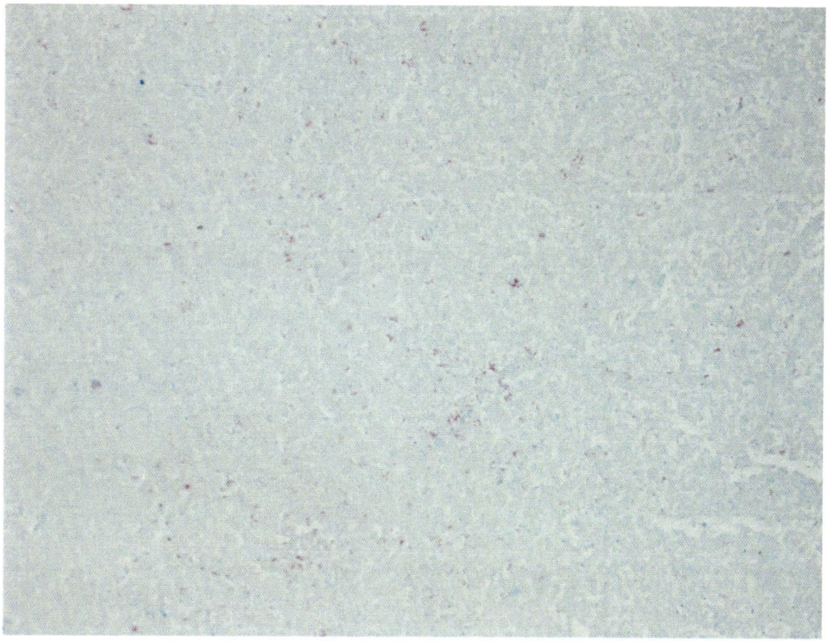

Figure 9.1

A. 1
B. 2
C. 3
D. 4
E. 5

Q9.3 Which of the following infectious diseases are considered notifiable to the Centers for Disease Control and Prevention (CDC)?

	Human Immunodeficiency Virus	Legionnaires' Disease	Mycobacterium Avium Complex Infection	Norwalk Virus	Syphilis	Tuberculosis	Vibriosis
A	X	X		X	X	X	
B	X		X	X		X	
C		X	X	X			X
D	X	X			X	X	X
E	X		X		X		X

Q9.4 A 6-year-old child dies after tonsillectomy. Pharmacogenomics testing demonstrated *CYP2D6* allele duplication. Of the following, what is the likely cause of death?

A. Heparin toxicity
B. Morphine toxicity
C. Oral midazolam toxicity
D. Sevoflurane adverse effect
E. Penicillin

Q9.5 Remains are recovered from an island off the southeastern coast of the United States. They consist of a portion of hair-bearing skin and subcutaneous tissue. The skeletal muscle anatomy, hair pattern, and complexion are compatible with a male Caucasian abdominal wall. Short tandem repeat (STR) analysis is performed on DNA extracted from the hair bulbs. The coroner identifies possible parents by reviewing a missing person database and collects DNA samples for comparison.

The following STR profiles are generated:

Sample	TPOX	D3S1358	FGA	D5S818	CSF1PO	D7S820	TH01	VWA	D8S1179	D13S317	D16S539	D18S851	D21S11
Decedent	11	14,17	24,26	8,12	10,12	8,10	7,9	14,19	11,14	14,15	10,11	12,15	29,30.2
Father A	8,11	14,18	24	12,13	10	9,10	6,9	19,20	10,11	8,14	10	15,18	28,30.2
Father B	11	16,17	22,26	10,12	11	8	6,10	14,20	13,14	12,13	11,13	10,12	29,30
Mother A	10,11	14,16	23,25	9,13	11,12	8,11	10,11	19	10,13	11,15	8,10	12,13	28,30
Mother B	8,11	17,18	22,26	8,13	12,13	8,9	6,7	14,16	11,14	10,15	9,11	12,18	29,30

What is the best conclusion?

A. His parents are Mother A and Father A
B. His parents are Mother B and Father A
C. His parent are Mother A and Father B
D. Mother A may be his, but his father is not represented in this cohort
E. Mother B may be his, but his father is not represented in this cohort

Q9.6 What statement is true regarding mitochondrial DNA (mtDNA)?

A. Does not evolve as quickly as nuclear DNA
B. Each cell has multiple copies
C. Is analyzed by STR analysis
D. Is commonly analyzed from whole blood samples
E. Is paternally inherited

Q9.7 What gene is the most likely to be mutated in this tumor that was removed from the stomach?

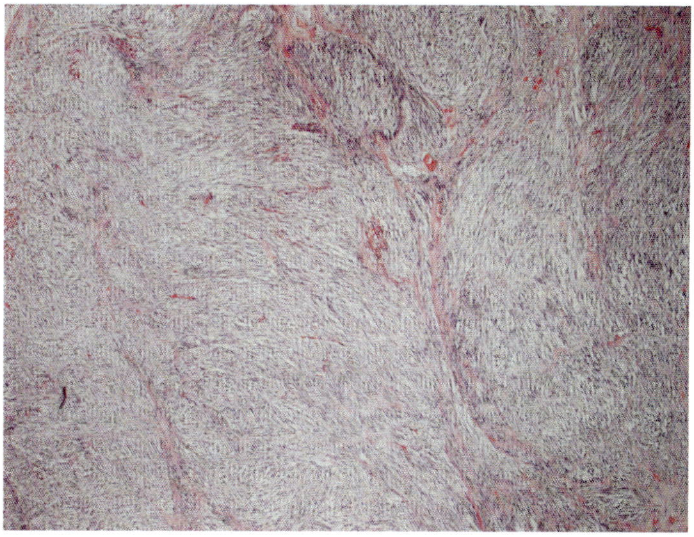

Figure 9.2

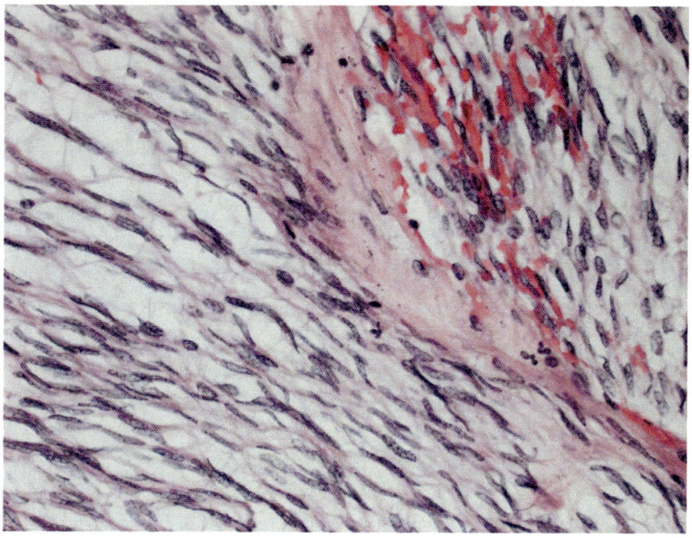

Figure 9.3

A. *ALK*
B. *KIT*
C. *EGFR*
D. *JAK2*
E. *KRAS*

Q9.8 What is the enzyme used in the polymerase chain reaction?

A. Reverse transcriptase
B. RNAse
C. Taq polymerase
D. Telomerase
E. Terminal deoxynucleotidyl transferase

Q9.9 What is the federal agency tasked with investigating every civil aviation crash as well as significant crashes in other modes of transportation?

A. Centers for Disease Control and Prevention
B. Civil Air Patrol
C. National Highway Traffic Safety Administration
D. National Transportation Safety Board
E. Occupational Safety and Health Administration

Q9.10 What is the leading cause of occupation-related deaths?

A. Asphyxiation
B. Electrocution
C. Fall from a height
D. Highway transportation collisions
E. Thermal injuries

Q9.11 An adult man is found deceased in temperate weather conditions. The external exam shows the following findings. What is the best approximation of the decedent's postmortem interval in hours?

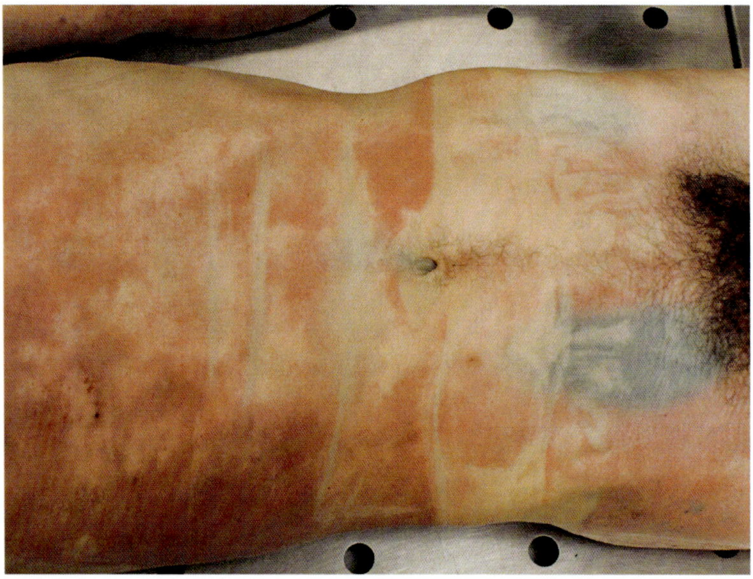

Figure 9.4

A. 2
B. 12
C. 36
D. 60
E. 72

Q9.12 Assuming temperate conditions, which of the following postmortem intervals best fits with the livor mortis pattern on the adult back featured below?

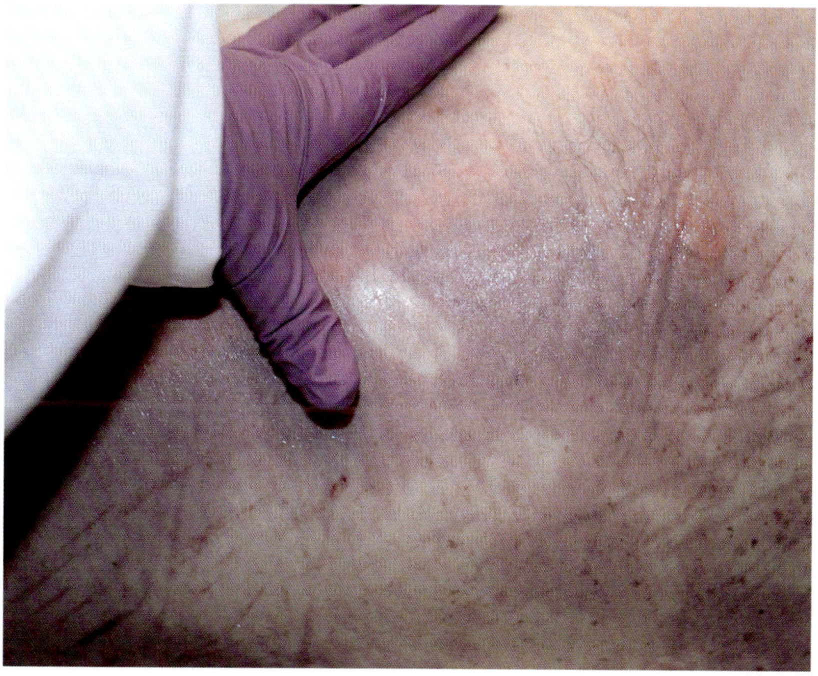

Figure 9.5

A. 15 minutes
B. 6 hours
C. 2 days
D. 1 week
E. 2 weeks

ANSWERS: CHAPTER 9

A9.1 The correct answer is E. *Yersinia pestis*

- Answer A is incorrect. *Bacillus anthracis* causes anthrax.
- Answer B is incorrect. *Chlamydophila psittaci*, formerly known as *Chlamydia psittaci*, causes psittacosis, a lung disease spread by birds.
- Answer C is incorrect. *Clostridium botulinum* is the bacterium responsible for botulism.
- Answer D is incorrect. *Variola major* is the virus responsible for smallpox.
- Answer E is correct. *Yersinia pestis* is the agent responsible for the black death, or plague.

A9.2 The correct answer is C. Biosafety level 3

- Answer A is incorrect. Biosafety levels are classified on a progressive scale of 1–4 with 1 being the least harmful and 4 being the most harmful. *Escherichia coli*, K-12, is an innocuous strain of *E coli* that typically does not cause disease in healthy subjects. It is classified as level 1.
- Answer B is incorrect. Biosafety level 2 organisms can cause disease in otherwise healthy people. An example of this is infection by *Staphylococcus aureus*.
- Answer C is correct. The photograph depicts a microscopic field of red acid fast bacilli in a blue background of lung tissue. This is a typical picture of *Mycobacterium tuberculosis* that is considered a biosafety level 3 organism. Biosafety level 3 agents cause disease in otherwise healthy people, and they have the additional characteristic of having airborne transmissibility.
- Answer D is incorrect. Level 4 organisms are classified as such because of their exceptionally high mortality rate. An example of this is Ebola virus.
- Answer E is incorrect. Currently, there is no biosafety level 5.

A9.3 The correct answer is D. Human immunodeficiency virus (HIV), Legionnaires' disease, Syphilis, Tuberculosis (TB), Vibriosis

Other notifiable infectious disease processes include the viral hemorrhagic fevers (e.g., Hantavirus, Ebola); acute hepatitis A, B, and C; shiga toxin-producing *E coli*; and many others. In addition, the CDC lists notifiable outbreaks (e.g., foodborne disease) and noninfectious conditions (e.g., carbon monoxide poisoning). While the notifiable diseases represent voluntary notification, local and state governments generally create yearly mandatory reportable disease lists. In many cases in the United States, the state health agency notifies the CDC.

- Answer A is incorrect. All of those diseases checked except Norwalk virus are notifiable as is vibriosis.
- Answer B is incorrect. *Mycobacterium avium-intracellulare* (MAI) complex infection is not currently a notifiable disease. This is likely due to the fact that the organisms do not affect the immunocompetent host and are ubiquitous in the environment. In addition, Legionnaires' disease is notifiable.
- Answer C is incorrect. HIV, Syphilis, and TB (mycobacterium tuberculosis) are also notifiable, while MAI and Norwalk virus are not.
- Answer D is correct. All of those infectious diseases checked are considered notifiable diseases by the CDC for the 2016 year. Each year, the CDC creates a list of infectious agents that they consider notifiable in order to perform public health surveillance. The list is available online at the CDC website: http://www.cdc.gov/nndss/conditions/notifiable/2016/infectious-diseases/.
- Answer E is incorrect. In addition to those checked, Legionnaires' disease and TB are also notifiable. *Mycobacterium avium-intracellulare* (MAI) complex infection is not currently a notifiable disease.

A9.4 The correct answer is B. Morphine toxicity

- Answer A is incorrect. At doses of 10 international units (IU) heparin is a common agent used for maintenance of intravenous lines. In doses above 1000 IU/mL it is used for anticoagulation. Practitioners must be vigilant when administering heparin in order to avoid iatrogenic bleeding. Heparinases degrade heparin and are produced by the liver and hematopoietic system and do not involve the cytochrome P450 enzymes.
- Answer B is correct. Allelic duplication at *CYP2D6* (a cytochrome P450 gene) leads to an ultrametabolic state for codeine and increased metabolism of codeine to morphine. Thus, ultrametabolizers are significantly more likely to suffer from toxic side effects of increased morphine when prescribed codeine.
- Answer C is incorrect. Oral midazolam is a common medication given to children prior to surgery. Midazolam is a short-acting benzodiazepine; the major cytochrome P450 enzymes responsible for metabolism are within the 3A group.
- Answer D is incorrect. Sevoflurane is a common anesthesia agent used during surgery. Sevoflurane is a volatile that is eliminated primarily via the lungs while the cytochrome P450 enzymes are produced in the liver.
- Answer E is incorrect. Penicillin is cleared renally and does not involve cytochrome P450 enzymes.

(See also U.S. Food and Drug Administration. FDA Drug Safety Communication: Codeine use in certain children after tonsillectomy and/or adenoidectomy may lead to rare, but life-threatening adverse events or death. www.fda.gov/drugs/drugsafety/ucm313631.htm.)

A9.5 The correct answer is B. His parents are Mother B and Father A

- Answer A is incorrect. Mother A cannot be a natural parent. For example, her FGA loci demonstrate 22 and 26 repeats. Neither of these is seen in the child (decedent). No discrepancies are noted for Father A, however.
- Answer B is correct. In order to determine likely parentage using short tandem repeat (STR) analysis, one compares the number of repeats on the alleles of the purported child to that of his or her parents to determine whether the parents could have collectively donated the allele demonstrated by the child. In this case, Mother B in combination with Father A could provide the alleles shown by the decedent (child). For example, looking at the row comparing the TPOX STRs, the decedent has an 11 (presumed to be 11,11), Father A or B and Mother A or B may have donated 11; thus, this marker does not distinguish parentage. Each of the other STR loci demonstrate distinguishing STRs that in total support parentage as Mother B and Father A. Practically, one might cross off any parent who will not support the STRs demonstrated by the child until only those that will remain.
- Answer C is incorrect. Discrepancies are between both Mother A and Father B with the child; thus, neither is a parent. For example, at the CSF1P0 loci, Father B demonstrates 11 repeats, while the child demonstrates 10 and 12 repeats (10 on one allele and 12 on the other). Thus, Father B is not the child's natural parent.
- Answer D is incorrect. Father A is likely the child's parent by this analysis. Discrepancies show that Mother A is not the child's parent (see explanation for answer A).
- Answer E is incorrect. Father A is likely the child's parent by this analysis. No discrepancies are between Mother B and the child, supportive of parentage.

A9.6 The correct answer is B. Each cell has multiple copies

- Answer A is incorrect. Mitochondrial DNA mutates at a much higher rate than nuclear DNA. However, it remains a useful technique to follow maternal lineage over time and is used in population genetics for this purpose.
- Answer B is correct. Although each nucleated cell has two copies of nuclear DNA (one copy from each parent), each cell cytoplasm contains hundreds to thousands of copies of mtDNA depending on the cell type with each mitochondrion holding several copies.
- Answer C is incorrect. Currently, nuclear DNA is analyzed by STR analysis (using PCR technology), while mtDNA variance is detected by sequence analysis using HVR1 and HVR2 areas (hypervariable region 1 and 2, also see Melton T, Holland C, Holland M. Forensic mitochondrial DNA analysis: Current practice and future potential. *Forensic Sci Rev* 2012, 24[2]: 101–22).
- Answer D is incorrect. When whole blood samples are utilized, nuclear DNA is much more frequently used as it can better delineate between individuals and is not reliant on a female relative for comparison.
- Answer E is incorrect. In most organisms, including humans, the mitochondrial DNA is maternally inherited. Although a few mitochondria are within the sperm, these are thought to be lost with loss of the tail or marked by ubiquitin for destruction. Also, the egg contains many thousands of copies of mtDNA, which confers an advantage by dilution.

A9.7 The correct answer is B. *KIT*

- Answer A is incorrect. *ALK*, anaplastic lymphoma kinase, mutations are associated with neuroblastomas, anaplastic large cell lymphoma, and adenocarcinoma of the lung but not gastrointestinal stromal tumors (GISTs).
- Answer B is correct. The photographs show a gastrointestinal stromal tumor. *KIT* mutations are associated with gastrointestinal stromal tumors.
- Answer C is incorrect. *EGFR*, epidermal growth factor receptor, mutations are associated with some lung and colon cancers.
- Answer D is incorrect. *JAK2* is associated with myeloproliferative neoplasms such as essential thrombocythemia, polycythemia vera, and primary myelofibrosis.
- Answer E is incorrect. *KRAS*, Kirsten RAt Sarcoma viral oncogene homolog, is associated with lung and colorectal cancers.

A9.8 The correct answer is C. Taq polymerase

- Answer A is incorrect. Reverse transcriptase is an enzyme used by retroviruses such as HIV to make a complementary copy of the viral RNA that allows incorporation into the host DNA. Reverse transcriptase is also used to convert RNA to cDNA in laboratory assays for fusion and other analyses.
- Answer B is incorrect. RNAse, also called ribonuclease, is a type of nuclease that catalyzes the degradation of RNA into smaller components.
- Answer C is correct. Taq polymerase is a heat-stable polymerase named after the thermophilic bacterium *Thermus aquaticus* from which it was originally isolated. It is used in the polymerase chain reaction because it can withstand temperatures in excess of 90°C.
- Answer D is incorrect. Telomerase is the enzyme that adds the nucleotide sequence "TTAGGG" to the 3′ end of telomeres, which are found at the ends of eukaryotic chromosomes.
- Answer E is incorrect. Terminal deoxynucleotidyl transferase (TDT) is the enzyme that allows diversity of the heavy chains of antibodies in the immune system.

A9.9 The correct answer is D. National Transportation Safety Board

- Answer A is incorrect. The Centers for Disease Control and Prevention (CDC) is responsible for monitoring and preventing disease and is not related to aircraft crashes or mishaps.
- Answer B is incorrect. The Civil Air Patrol is a federally supported nonprofit that serves as the official civilian auxiliary of the U.S. Air Force (USAF). It is not tasked with investigating aircraft accidents or mishaps.
- Answer C is incorrect. The National Highway Traffic Safety Administration (NHTSA) advises on such matters as general safety regarding highways but does not directly investigate individual highway collisions nor does it investigate aircraft crashes.
- Answer D is correct. The National Transportation Safety Board (NTSB) is the investigative agency that investigates civil aviation (general and commercial) mishaps and recommends any changes. Although it is a part of the Federal Aviation Administration (FAA), the NTSB has no direct enforcement authority as the FAA does. The FAA does oversee crashes and perform enforcement actions such as fines, but the investigative arm is the NTSB.
- Answer E is incorrect. The Occupational Safety and Health Administration (OSHA) investigates and enforces safety as it relates to on-the-job work exposure. It is not directly involved in the workup of aircraft crashes.

A9.10 The correct answer is D. Highway transportation collisions

- Answer A is incorrect. Asphyxiation is roughly the fifth leading cause of death on the job.
- Answer B is incorrect. Electrocution is the third leading cause of death on the job.
- Answer C is incorrect. Falls including those from a height comprise the second leading cause of death on the job.
- Answer D is correct. The leading cause of death on the job is highway transportation collisions. This includes professional drivers such as truck drivers and delivery drivers. The most common subtype of crash is a collision involving two different vehicles.
- Answer E is incorrect. Thermal injuries are the fourth leading cause of death on the job.

(Note that work-related death statistics may vary depending upon the occupation queried. Also see the website of the Occupational Safety and Health Administration for details: https://www.osha.gov/oshstats/commonstats.html.)

A9.11 The correct answer is C. 36

- Answers A, B, D, and E are incorrect. The green coloration of the lower abdomen typically occurs within 24–36 hours in temperate conditions.
- Answer C is correct. The photograph depicts the lower torso of a decedent with anterior lividity and green coloration of the lower abdominal and periumbilical areas. In temperate conditions, the green coloration appears within 24–36 hours due to the presence of the bacteria in the colon. However, in nontemperate conditions, this finding may be accelerated or delayed.

A9.12 The correct answer is B. 6 hours

- Answer A is incorrect. Lividity typically appears after approximately 30 minutes to 2 hours.
- Answer B is correct. The photograph shows unfixed livor, as evidenced by blanching of the skin by pressure from a thumb in an area of dependent livor. Lividity typically appears within 2 hours after death and becomes fixed after 8–12 hours. Therefore, with the available choices presented, the postmortem interval would be most consistent with 6 hours.
- Answer C is incorrect. In temperate conditions, lividity would be expected to be fixed (nonblanchable) after 2 days.
- Answer D is incorrect. In temperate conditions, lividity would be expected to be fixed (nonblanchable) after 1 week and changes of decomposition may be evident.
- Answer E is incorrect. In temperate conditions, lividity would be expected to be fixed (nonblanchable) after 2 weeks, and changes of decomposition may be evident.

INDEX

B

C

F

G

H

I

N

O

P

Q

R

S

T